An Economic History of Cambodia in the Twentieth Century

An Economic History of Cambodia in the Twentieth Century

Margaret Slocomb

NUS PRESS
SINGAPORE

Published with support from the Nicholas Tarling Fund.

© 2010 Margaret Slocomb

NUS Press
National University of Singapore
AS3-01-02, 3 Arts Link
Singapore 117569

Fax: (65) 6774-0652
E-mail: nusbooks@nus.edu.sg
Website: http://www.nus.edu.sg/nuspress

ISBN 978-9971-69-499-9 (Paper)

All rights reserved. This book, or parts thereof, may not be reproduced in any form or by any means, electronic or mechanical, including photocopying, recording or any information storage and retrieval system now known or to be invented, without written permission from the Publisher.

National Library Board Singapore Cataloguing in Publication Data

Slocomb, Margaret.
    An economic history of Cambodia in the twentieth century / Margaret Slocomb.
– Singapore: NUS Press, c2010.
    p. cm.
    Includes bibliographical references and index.
    ISBN-13: 978-9971-69-499-9 (pbk.)

    1. Cambodia – Economic conditions – 20th century. 2. Cambodia – Economic policy – 20th century. I. Title.

HC442
330.959604 — dc22   OCN545012232

Typeset by : Scientifik Graphics
Printed by : Mainland Press Pte Ltd

Contents

List of Tables, Figures and Illustrations   vii

Preface   xiii

Acknowledgements   xvii

List of Abbreviations   xix

Introduction   1

Chapter 1   The Colonial Economy, 1863–1953   30

Chapter 2   Post-Independence Economic Change, 1953–69   75

Chapter 3   The Wartime Economy, 1970–75   131

Chapter 4   The Revolutionary Economy, 1975–89   175

Chapter 5   Rehabilitation and Reconstruction, 1990–c. 2000   230

Conclusion   Economic Outlook for the Twenty-first Century   288

Notes   299

Selected Bibliography   330

Index   339

List of Tables, Figures and Illustrations

Tables

0.1	Main economic indicators	15
0.2	GDP by sector at constant 1993 prices	16
0.3	Percentage of households and proportion of agricultural landholdings	21
1.1	Number of functionaries of the civil services in the main provinces of Cambodia, 1914 and 1931	44
1.2	Population of Cambodia, 1900–55	46
1.3	Education in Cambodia, 1931–50	50
1.4	Land area under concessions, 1926–28	54
1.5	Concessions held by large companies, 1927–28	55
1.6	Landownership classification, 1927–30 – Ricefields	55
1.7	Main agricultural products and exports, 1922	58
1.8	Paddy cultivation, 1900–50	59
1.9	Area harvested and production of paddy in Cambodia, 1952–54	60
1.10	Areas cultivated and production of main crops of Cambodia, 1953	60
1.11	Dried fish from freshwater product, 1940–53	61
1.12	Forestry production, 1952–54 with annual averages, 1944–53	63
1.13	Main industries in Cambodia, 1951–52	64
1.14	Movement of paddy, rice and derivatives from Cambodia, 1951–53	67

2.1	Gross domestic product at 1966 prices	88
2.2	Consumer price index by class, 1964 and 1967	89
2.3	Education indicators, 1955 and 1968	91
2.4	Industrial origin of GDP at 1966 prices	92
2.5	Number and distribution of agricultural landholdings, 1962	98
2.6	Principal crops grown in Cambodia	99
2.7	Irrigated paddy area	100
2.8	Exports of agricultural products: December 1967 and December 1968	101
2.9	Revenue from principal forest products (supervised production)	104
2.10	Area covered by different types of forest	104
2.11	Share of sectors in industrial activity, 1964	108
2.12	Percentage value of rice and rubber to total Cambodian exports, 1955–57	110
2.13	Balance of trade, 1955–57	110
2.14	Source of aid and contribution to first Five-Year Plan	114
2.15	Government current revenues, 1967–69	117
2.16	National budget expenditures, 1968 and 1969	118
3.1	Estimates of the Cambodian population, selected years, 1921–74	141
3.2	Death in Kampuchean War	142
3.3	Planned exports for 1971	149
3.4	U.S. civil aid to Cambodia for the 1974 fiscal year	155
3.5	Disbursement schedule, U.S. military assistance programme, Khmer Republic	156
3.6	U.S. economic and military assistance to the Khmer Republic	156
4.1	Population by broad age group and sex, as counted at the end of 1980	193
4.2	Estimates of the Cambodian population, selected years, 1974–89	194

4.3	International migration assumptions, 1970–89	196
4.4	Paddy production, 1980–89	209
4.5	External debt, 1982–86	220
5.1	Population of Cambodia by gender	246
5.2	Regional population distribution	247
5.3	Migrants from rural areas, 1996 and 1998	249
5.4	Average monthly household expenditure by stratum, Cambodia, 1993–99	251
5.5	GDP by industrial origin, 1989–93	259
5.6	Value of timber exports and revenue of the Government	264
5.7	Garment and textile manufacturing industries, 1995–2004	269
5.8	GDP growth rates by sector and total	271
5.9	Monthly wages by sector, 1994–99	272
5.10	International trade in goods and services	273
5.11	Exports by commodity, 1993–99	274
5.12	Distribution of capital investment by sector, 1995–2001	279

Figures

0.1	Map of the Kingdom of Cambodia, 2000	3
4.1	Administrative divisions of Democratic Kampuchea	183
5.1	Paddy production and area harvested, 1980–99	259

Illustrations

Currency

Five hundred riel note of the Sangkum period, in circulation 1953 to 1974	73
One riel note of the Sangkum depicting shipping	74
Fifty riel note of the Sangkum depicting fishermen	74
One hundred riel note of the Khmer Republic depicting weaver	127
Five hundred riel note of the Khmer Republic	128

One thousand riel note of the Khmer Republic depicting education	129
One hundred riel note of the Khmer Republic	130
Smallest unit of currency prepared for Democratic Kampuchea but never issued	165
Smallest unit of currency prepared for the People's Republic of Kampuchea, circulated in 1980	166
One riel note prepared for Democratic Kampuchea depicting workers digging an irrigation channel	167
Five riel note prepared for Democratic Kampuchea, 1975, depicting Angkor Wat	168
Ten riel note prepared for Democratic Kampuchea, depicting soldier working with peasants	169
Fifty riel note prepared for Democratic Kampuchea, depicting peasants transplanting rice	170
One hundred riel note prepared for Democratic Kampuchea depicting industry	171
Note worth half of one riel, the People's Republic of Kampuchea	172
Ten riel note of the People's Republic of Kampuchea depicting pepper farming	173
Fifty riel note of the People's Republic of Kampuchea	174
One hundred riel note of the Second Kingdom of Cambodia, depicting emphasis on education	226
Five hundred riel note of the Second Kingdom of Cambodia, depicting Angkor Wat	227
One thousand riel note of the Second Kingdom of Cambodia	228
Five thousand riel note of the Second Kingdom of Cambodia, depicting King Norodom Sihanouk	229

Economy

Riparian market gardens in Kandal Province, c. 1995	5
A view of the Cambodian floodplain from Oudong Mountain, about forty kilometres from Phnom Penh	6

The flooded plain during a typical wet season	7
Urban Poverty. A slum in Phnom Penh, c. 2000	13
Fishers along the Mekong prepare prahok for the market	18
Idyllic impressions of Cambodia at the time of naturalist Henri Mouhot's visit in 1860	34
A colonial era rubber warehouse at Tonle Bet, Kompong Cham province	34
Poster for the 1906 Colonial Exhibition in Marseille depicts an iconic Khmer royal dancer	56
The road from Kompong Cham to Angkor Wat constructed with corvée and coolie labour during the French Protectorate	85
Tapping rubber on a plantation in Kompong Cham province	85
A salt farm in Kampot province	87
A ricefarmer uses the traditional light plough to turn his field	87
The small Cambodian ox is used for transport in central rural parts of Cambodia	94
A rice harvest in the Cambodian countryside	94
Hand-weaving of cotton and silk fabrics makes an important contribution to household incomes throughout the countryside	95
A silversmith at work in a village in Kandal Province	95
Teams of buffalo plough a paddy field in Kompong Thom	96
Metal-workers in the rural provinces provide essential services to farmers	97
Vietnamese troops parade before dignitaries and officials at the final withdrawal ceremony in September 1989	186
The young foreign minister, Hun Sen, casts his ballot in the 1981 elections for the National Assembly	186
Returning home from the catastrophe of the Democratic Regime, 1979 (Agence Khmère de Presse archive)	191
An irrigation system in Takeo province, reconstructed with foreign assistance after 1979	191

The tally of ballots cast in the 1993 UN-supervised elections on public display in Phnom Penh	233
Rural poverty, Battambang province, c. 2003	233
Poster for the 1998 general election showing CPP leaders Chea Sim, Hun Sen and Heng Samrin	237
Cambodian NGOs raise awareness of official corruption	240
Logs felled by foreign companies in Sandan district, Kompong Thom province, c. 2003	265
Logs line the road beside land newly planted with rubber in Tumring, Kompong Thom province, c. 2003	265
A women's micro-credit meeting in Siem Reap province, c. 2007	266

Preface

The histories of Cambodia that are available to readers of English are, for the most part, political histories and given the dramatic upheavals that such histories record, the primacy of politics should not be surprising. In the final year or two of the twentieth century, however, Cambodia entered a period of peace. For the first time in 30 consecutive years, Cambodians were not at war with one another or with their neighbours; more optimistically, there seemed to be no reason or likelihood that Cambodia would again be seriously threatened externally or dissolve into civil conflict. By the turn of the century, Cambodia was an autonomous, sovereign state with a democratically elected government, sharing membership of groupings of like-minded states such as the United Nations Organization and the Association of Southeast Asian Nations. In 2004, Cambodia fulfilled all the requirements for entry to the World Trade Organization. It is timely, therefore, to look beyond politics and to study the economic history of Cambodia in order to examine the trends in the country's economic evolution that might give insights into its further development.

This is not a groundbreaking endeavour. There are already valuable analyses that serve as important reference points for the history of the modern Cambodian economy. The earliest of these, for my purposes, is by Charles Robequain. His monograph, *The Economic Development of French Indo-China* was published in its first French edition in 1939, its aim as stated in the author's preface being "to show the changes effected in the economy of Indo-China as a result of the French occupation."[1] There is little in the text, unfortunately, which refers specifically to the then Protectorate of Cambodia and its own economy within the union of the five states comprising French Indo-China. It was the seminal work of Jean Delvert, *Le Paysan Cambodgien*, researched and documented during the ten years after 1949, which formed the basis of further studies on the Cambodian economy.[2] The collection of maps and figures, details of soil types and weather patterns, observations of the agrarian calendar, and so on, concerning almost five hundred communes throughout the country is still the most valuable baseline study for current research on the rural economy. The third is *L'Économie du Cambodge* by Rémy Prud'homme, a French academic who taught at the Faculty of Law and Economics of the Royal University of Cambodia during 1965 and 1966. He called his work "a tool for understanding the Cambodian economy, nothing more."[3] It describes a modernising, post-independence economy at its peak, but by the time he completed his analysis, in October 1967, he had already noted a stubborn tendency to stagnation in the economy of the *Sangkum Reastr Niyum*, the Popular Socialist Community, which was directed by the Cambodian monarch turned executive chief, Prince Norodom Sihanouk. Until the arrival of fact-finding missions of the United Nations, the World Bank and bilateral agencies in the late 1980s, Rémy Prud'homme's analysis was the last of its kind.

Delvert and Prud'homme (and no doubt Robequain before them) lamented the lack of bibliographical resources, not to mention reliable statistics for their studies of the Cambodian economy. "Little has been written about the geography of Cambodia," Delvert noted, "and almost everything that has been published is old (prior to 1910) ... [M]onographs and archival documents disappeared in great number between 1945 and 1954, particularly at the time of the Japanese *coup de force* (9 March 1945)."[4] Prud'homme complained that there were hardly any precise analyses of regions or sectors and continued, "The statistical sources, without which these studies are not possible, are insufficient in both quantity and quality."[5] Delvert found the *Bulletin Economique de l'Indochine* invaluable, and Prud'homme was able to make good use of the results of the 1962 official population census that were published in 1966. A curious omission from Prud'homme's bibliography is the 1959 doctoral thesis of Khieu Samphan entitled *The Economy of Cambodia and its Problems with Industrialisation* which must surely have been accessible to researchers in the 1960s. Khieu Samphan was awarded his doctorate from the prestigious University of Paris and it is unlikely that Prud'homme would have been unaware of the dissertation. After all, Khieu Samphan was not only an elected deputy of the National Assembly in 1962 but was also a secretary of state for trade. He was a controversial character on the Phnom Penh political scene as were his leftist allies in the Assembly, Hou Yuon and Hu Nim, who had also produced doctoral theses on economic issues that stressed the plight of the peasantry, with particular emphasis on their diminishing access to land and exploitation by local merchants.[6] Perhaps Prud'homme thought it wiser to be circumspect and avoid charges of political bias especially since, in 1967, these three Cambodian economists had fled Phnom Penh and joined the guerrillas in the *maquis*. Inexplicably, Prud'homme made no bibliographical reference to the French language twice-weekly publication of the Cambodian Chamber of Commerce.[7] Between 1942 and the end of March 1974, this economic journal reproduced laws and other official notices, provided information about exchange rates, shipping manifests and international markets, and offered statistical analyses of the Cambodian economy. Given the prestige of the Chamber of Commerce and its proximity to government, the bulletin's sources were practically guaranteed. In view of these omissions, therefore, Prud'homme's "tool" had limitations.

The present situation is very different in terms of sources. For an analysis of the Cambodian economy in the year 2005, taken as a convenient cut-off point, there is an abundance of statistics, reports, analyses, prognoses and so on of the Cambodian economy. A reliable general population census was conducted in 1998, and in addition to this essential resource, the National Institute of Statistics conducted regular socio-economic surveys, produced statistical yearbooks and, in 2003, published the results of a survey of industrial establishments in the country. In addition to these official sources, there are the publications of respected in-country research organisations such as the Cambodia Development Resource Institute and the Economic Institute of Cambodia, as well as reports of international financial institutions (The World Bank and Asian Development Bank) and those of Cambodia-based international and local non-government agencies.

The important point to be made about all the sources discussed above is that they are more or less static portrayals of the Cambodian economy. Robequain and Delvert do depict economies that are in the process of dynamic evolution and to this extent they are economic histories. Nevertheless, their period of study is set within rather short timeframes. Current studies of the Cambodian economy, almost without exception, lack historical hindsight. Weaknesses in economic structures and institutions are commonly attributed to general destruction caused by three decades of conflict, and historical analysis rarely goes beyond this simple reference. War and revolution most certainly did severely damage the Cambodian economy, but to what extent did these historical events change the underlying structures and relations of production, the patterns of the economy? What role did economic factors play in instigating war and revolution? An economic history should offer probable explanations, if not definitive answers, to questions like these.

The aim of this monograph, therefore, is to study the patterns and structures that persist in various aspects of the economy as well as in policy and planning approaches so that Westerners who engage with the Cambodian economy whether for investment, development or for academic purposes, or to deliver humanitarian assistance, might better understand the point in time at which they are intervening and appreciate the Cambodian people's experience and past efforts to modernise their country's economy. This is a general history of the Cambodian economy, not a technical economic treatise. It focuses on a series of deliberate efforts over the course of the twentieth century to shape Cambodia's economy into a preferred mode or according to a preferred ideology.

Cambodia, of course, was not unique in making these attempts, although the circumstances it faced and measures it adopted to overcome them were typically extreme. Other countries in the region, Indonesia under Sukarno, for example, pursued policies not dissimilar to those adopted by King Sihanouk in the post-colonial phase. With less rigour than Democratic Kampuchea, after 1975 the other states of former Indochina, Vietnam and Laos, also applied Marxist economic principles to revive their economies from near-total collapse caused by war. Since the early 1990s, and especially since the 1997 Asian financial crisis, Cambodia, along with most of the member states of ASEAN, has been required to comply with the neo-liberal reform measures dictated by The World Bank/IMF. Cambodia's economic development, therefore, has taken place within the broader context of regional economic change and development. It is hoped that this study will make a contribution to the existing scholarship on the economic history of Southeast Asia and thereby assist Cambodian scholars to make critical comparisons and draw conclusions that will deepen our understanding of the way the economy functions and how it inter-relates with other regional economies.

While conscious of the pitfalls that the various approaches to the recording of such an economic history entail, I have chosen to adopt a purely temporal approach. Following an introduction that describes the fundamental features of physical and human geography, levels of human development and benchmarks of economic activity in Cambodia around the year 2000, the history of Cambodia's modern economy is traced from the latter half of the French Protectorate, to the post-independence (first) Kingdom of Cambodia, through the Khmer Republic, the revolutionary regimes of Democratic Kampuchea and the People's Republic of Kampuchea, to around the midpoint of the third legislature of the Second Kingdom of Cambodia, that is, approximately the year 2005. Generally speaking, therefore, the time span of modern economic development in Cambodia coincides with the twentieth century. Within each of those already defined political eras, the economy is regarded from the viewpoint of the same socio-economic categories, including administration and governance, population, human development, economic activity, foreign trade, aid, investment and debt, as well as public finance, banking and credit. The concluding chapter considers some of the challenges facing the Cambodian economy in the twenty-first century.

Acknowledgements

In large part, this economic history represents a compilation and distillation of the work of those who have been observing Cambodia's political and economic progress for the past 150 years. My thanks, therefore, are due to them and their academic efforts and also to the current scholarship, especially that of the new generation of Cambodian economic researchers, that is contributing significantly to our general understanding of the major changes taking place in their country's economy at the turn of the twenty-first century. As always, I owe particular gratitude to the director and her staff at the State Archives in Phnom Penh for their professional assistance that is so graciously given to foreign researchers.

List of Abbreviations

ADB	Asian Development Bank
AFTA	ASEAN Free Trade Agreement
ARVN	Army of Republic of Vietnam
ASEAN	Association of Southeast Asian Nations
BCG	*Bulletin du Contre-Gouvernement*
BCMCAC	*Bulletin Bi-Hebdomadaire, Chambre Mixte de Commerce et d'Agriculture du Cambodge*
BKC	*la Banque Khmère pour le Commerce*
CAS	Center for Advanced Study
CDC	Council for the Development of Cambodia
CDHS	Cambodia Demographic and Health Survey
CDRI	Cambodia Development Resource Institute
CG	Consultative Group
CGDK	Coalition Government of Democratic Kampuchea
CIA	Central Intelligence Agency
CIP	Commercial Imports Programme
CMEA	Council for Mutual Economic Assistance
CPI	Consumer Price Index
CPP	Cambodian People's Party
CSES	Cambodia Socio-Economic Survey
DK	Democratic Kampuchea
DSC	Demographic Survey of Cambodia
ESAF	Enhanced Structural Adjustment Facility
FANK	*Forces Armées Nationales Khmères*
FAO	Food and Agriculture Organization
FARK	*Forces Armées Royales Khmères*
FDI	Foreign Direct Investment
Funcinpec	*Front Uni National pour un Cambodge indépendant neutre pacifique et coopératif*
FUNK	*Front Uni National du Kampuchéa*
GDP	Gross Domestic Product
GRUNK	*Gouvernement Royal d'Union Nationale du Kampuchéa*
GSP	Generalized System of Preferences

HDI	Human Development Index
HIV/AIDS	Human Immunodeficiency Virus/Acquired Immune Deficiency Syndrome
IBRD	International Bank for Reconstruction and Development
ICORC	International Committee on the Reconstruction of Cambodia
IFI	International Finance Institution
IJ	*l'Inadana Jati*
IMF	International Monetary Fund
KPNLF	Kampuchean People's National Liberation Front
KPRP	Kampuchean People's Revolutionary Party
KR	Khmer Rouge
LDC	Least Developed Country
MAFF	Ministry of Agriculture, Forestry and Fisheries
MFI	Microfinance Institution
MFN	Most Favoured Nation
MoEYS	Ministry of Education, Youth and Sports
NBC	National Bank of Cambodia
NGO	Non-Government Organization
NIS	National Institute of Statistics
OECD	Organisation for Economic Co-operation and Development
OROC	*Office Royal de Coopération*
PAVN	People's Army of Vietnam
PL-480	Public Law 480
PRK	People's Republic of Kampuchea
PRSP	Poverty Reduction Strategy Paper
RDB	Rural Development Bank
RGC	Royal Government of Cambodia
SAP	Structural Adjustment Programme
SARS	Sudden and Acute Respiratory Syndrome
SESC	Socio-Economic Survey of Cambodia
SIEC	Survey of Industrial Establishments in Cambodia
SNC	Supreme National Council
SoC	State of Cambodia
SRN	*Sangkum Reastr Niyum*
SRV	Socialist Republic of Vietnam
U.K.	United Kingdom
UN	United Nations
UNAMIC	United Nations Advance Mission in Cambodia

UNBRO	United Nations Border Relief Operation
UNDP	United Nations Development Programme
UNFPA	United Nations Population Fund
UNHCR	United Nations High Commission for Refugees
UNICEF	United Nations Children's Fund
UNTAC	United Nations Transitional Authority in Cambodia
U.S./U.S.A.	United States of America
USAID	United States Agency for International Development
USSR	Union of Soviet Socialist Republics
VAT	Value Added Tax
WHO	World Health Organization
WTO	World Trade Organization

Introduction

At the end of the twentieth century, Cambodia still bore the scars of decades of post-independence conflict. The economy had suffered greatly from mishandled experimentation according to various ideologies, experimentation that had been taken to revolutionary extremes during the brief regime of Democratic Kampuchea in the second half of the 1970s. In 1993, internationally sponsored and supervised general elections were held for a Constituent Assembly that approved a new constitution for the (Second) Kingdom of Cambodia in September that year. As a mark of confidence in the newly elected government, international financial institutions, multilateral and bilateral donors and foreign investors all offered funds urgently needed for national reconstruction and development. Hundreds of international and local non-government organisations also expressed their willingness to cooperate with the government in order to achieve sustainable growth within the parameters of the various international covenants and conventions to which Cambodia is a signatory. In addition to having regained its full status within the United Nations Organization in 1998, Cambodia became a member of the regional trading bloc Association of Southeast Asian Nations (ASEAN) in January 2000, and in 2004 it was admitted to the World Trade Organization.

Despite these commendable political gains, one decade on from the Paris Peace Agreements, which in 1991 formally ended the protracted conflict in Cambodia, the economy remained vulnerable to external shocks and to occasional internal political tremors. On the one hand, gross domestic product (GDP) had achieved modest but steady annual growth of six to seven per cent; investment in national infrastructure, particularly in roads and telecommunications, was substantial; significant structural reforms were evident in the banking and commercial sectors, and there were promises of further legal and judicial reform. Nevertheless, in most respects, Cambodia around the year 2000 was still a poor country: levels of rural poverty remained stubbornly unchanged between one national survey and the next, the vast majority of farmers still cultivated rice without the benefit of irrigation systems or fertilisers, and the provision of social services, especially publicly funded health and education systems, remained very weak, particularly in the countryside. There were also mounting concerns about the cost of development in terms of environmental degradation, disputes over land and access to natural resources, as well as popular frustration with entrenched official corruption. The future growth of the economy depended precariously on two highly volatile industries, namely garment manufacturing for the export trade and foreign tourism. Above all, in a situation where more than half of the government's annual budget was reliant on foreign assistance, genuine autonomy in economic decision-making remained elusive.

Geography

The Kingdom of Cambodia occupies a land area of 181,035 square kilometres, inclusive of inland water systems, lying between 10 and 15 degrees north latitude and 103 and 108 degrees east longitude. Its rights to 95,000 square kilometres of continental shelf in the Gulf of Thailand, which it claimed by decree in 1972, are still contested by its neighbours, Thailand and Vietnam, particularly as these waters are believed to contain valuable oil and gas reserves. About 57 per cent of Cambodia is still covered by forests of mixed quality timber, but apart from forest products and those of its inland and marine waters, Cambodia has few other exploitable natural resources.

Except for the southeast, where the downriver systems of the Mekong and the Bassac flow into Vietnam towards the vast delta at their mouth, and the area known as the Watthana Pass in the northwest which facilitates cross-border traffic with Thailand, Cambodia's land borders are defined by mountain ranges and high plateaux: the Elephant Mountains, the Kirirom Plateau and the Cardamom Chain in the west, the Dangrek Escarpment in the north, and the high cordillera in the east that ends in Cambodian territory which the French called the Haut Chhlong and Mimot plateaux.

In the lee of these ranges, Cambodia's climate is characterised by degrees of dryness. Annual rainfall during the southwest monsoon in most parts of the country is moderate. The dry season is protracted, frequently lasting from late October to May or even June, followed by an irregular wet season. Most rains fall on the eastern plateaux, around the Gulf of Siam (Sihanoukville's long-term average is 2,868.9 mm) and in the Cardamom Chain but, generally speaking, the Cambodian plain, home to the vast majority of the population and the principal rice-growing region, is in a rain shadow.

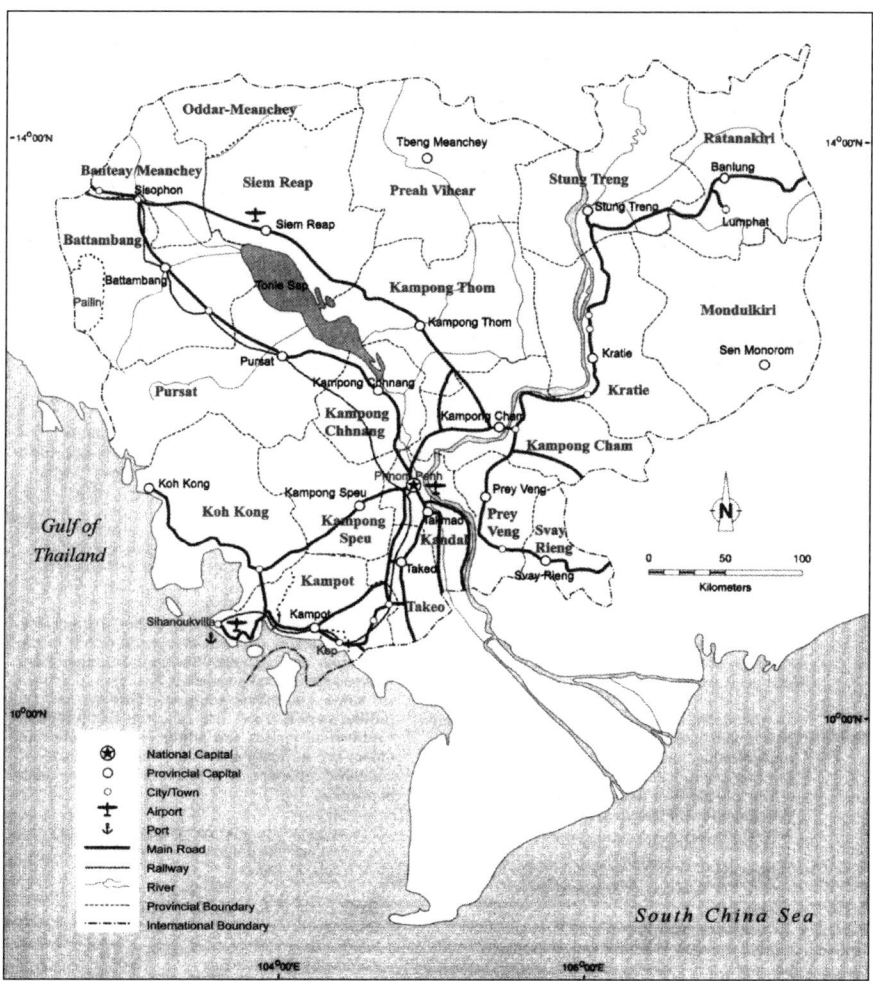

Source: MoEYS, "Report on the Assessment of the Functional Literacy Levels of the Adult Population in Cambodia," May 2000.

Figure 0.1 Map of the Kingdom of Cambodia, 2000

Despite the relatively low rainfall, more than one-third of the plain experiences annual flooding caused by ice-melt and rainwater in the higher reaches brought down by the Mekong. The volume of water at that time is so vast that at the bend between the river's upper and lower reaches, which is also the junction with the Bassac River, it is forced back up a narrow stream into the Great Lake, the Tonle Sap. The Great Lake, that has a dry season surface area of around 2,500 square kilometres, in the wet season expands to as much as 16,000 square kilometres when floodwaters inundate the peripheral wetlands.[1] Its fisheries directly support more than one million people and provide the single largest source of protein for the Cambodian population.

This annual flooding by the Mekong has always deposited rich silt on its banks which has permitted intensive polyculture there. The variety of crops and "the remarkable adaptation of plants cultivated to the very particular conditions of the soil, rainfall, the tide" fascinated Jean Delvert when he wrote about these *chamcar des berges*, the riparian market gardens, in the 1950s.[2] He estimated their area to be around 220,000 hectares, supporting half a million people or one-sixth of the peasant population of Cambodia. Crops, all introduced, included then, as now, maize, soybean, tobacco, groundnuts, tomatoes, cotton, and sesame. Delvert believed that these market gardens were originally a Chinese creation.

Away from the fertility of the riverbanks, the central plain offers the cultivator either light sandy soil or heavy clay. Delvert pronounced the soil there to be "mediocre or bad" and believed that yields in these conditions could not be other than mediocre.[3] The plain is divided into small, individually owned *srae* or paddy fields which are mostly rain-fed or hand-irrigated and which produce one wet season crop and sometimes a further crop as the waters recede. This is the most densely populated region of the country. During the dry season, cattle and water buffaloes graze the stubble and grasses of the *veal srae*, the unfenced expanse of paddy fields, and some farmers cultivate and harvest sugar palm in the traditional way, although this would now seem to be an industry in decline.

Cambodia's redlands occupy a slim arc stretching approximately 250 kilometres and no more than 50 kilometres at its widest point from the border with Vietnam to the Sandan forest of Kompong Thom province. Generally speaking, this is the area known as the Kompong Cham plateaux. The heavy basalt soil is not suitable for rice-growing, but it is ideal for the cultivation of rubber. Cambodia's rubber plantations, developed by French companies during the 1920s, once had a reputation for the finest quality product and the highest yields of latex in the world. In the past, rubber was also produced on what are known as "yellow lands" in pockets of Kandal and Kampot provinces and also near the port of Sihanoukville.

Beyond the riverbanks, the *srae* and the rubber plantations, stretch vast areas of flooded forest, savannah and clear forest, and once dense dipterocarp and leguminous forests.

Riparian market gardens in Kandal Province, c. 1995

A view of the Cambodian floodplain from Oudong Mountain, about 40 kilometres from Phnom Penh

The flooded plain during a typical wet season

Administration and Governance

Cambodia's territory is administratively divided into 20 provinces, and four *krong* or municipalities, namely Phnom Penh, the national capital; Sihanoukville, the nation's seaport; Kep, a beach resort on the south coast; and Pailin, a former rebel stronghold on the northwest border which was resumed in 1997. In the year 2000, these 24 major administrative units, each ruled over by a governor who is appointed by the Ministry of the Interior, were subdivided into 183 districts that were further divided into 1,609 communes.[4] The communes are administered by councils that are popularly elected by adult franchise. The first completed national election for commune councils was held in 2002. The communes, in turn, contain 13,406 villages.

For census purposes, Cambodia is divided into four natural regions. In order of population density, they are the plain, the Great Lake/Tonle Sap, coastal, and plateau and mountain regions. General density of population on the night the census was taken in March 1998 was 64 per square kilometre, but there are wide variations according to region.[5]

The sum of these regions constitutes the Kingdom of Cambodia which is a constitutional monarchy. According to the current constitution that was adopted by the Constituent Assembly in Phnom Penh on 21 September 1993, "Cambodia is a Kingdom with a King who shall rule according to the Constitution and to the principles of liberal democracy and pluralism. The Kingdom of Cambodia shall be independent, sovereign, peaceful, permanently neutral and non-aligned."[6] Since the national elections of May 1993, sponsored and supervised by the United Nations Transitional Authority in Cambodia (UNTAC), Cambodia has conducted multi-party elections for the National Assembly every five years. As noted previously, the first completed national elections for commune councils were conducted in 2002. Commune councils also hold five-year terms of office. Other levels of governance are appointed.

The public sector is a major employer. In 1999, the total number of civil servants was 163,592, or 1.43 per hundred of total population.[7] That number included education personnel who typically account for almost half of all the civil servants employed. Since 2002, salaries of commune councils and personnel have also been included in the national budget. In addition, the government maintains large defence and security forces (143,000 military personnel in 1998, or 1.25 per hundred of population), although large-scale demobilisation was already planned when those figures were gathered.

Civil service and security and defence personnel salaries are low. In 1998, civil servants received an average salary of US$22.9 per month, while those in the national defence force earned US$31.8, and those in public security were paid US$25.4 a month. Teachers then received only US$20.9 per month. Improvements in revenue collection allowed the government to boost public sector salaries in August 2005, but starting from such a low base, even a pay hike of 100 per cent still left public sector salaries below subsistence levels. This is generally considered to be a fundamental structural problem in Cambodia. Many low-ranking civil servants take extra jobs in the private sector, drive motorcycle taxis or engage in petty corruption to make ends meet. At higher levels, official corruption is a major inhibitor of investment and growth.

Population and Ethnicity

The 1998 national census counted a total population of 11,437,656 inhabitants of whom the overwhelming majority (9,642,081) were classified as rural. This latter figure included the populations of three *khan* or districts of Phnom Penh that have since been reclassified as urban. The urban population, in 1998, accounted for 15.7 per cent of the total population. Given an annual population growth rate of 2.49 per cent, projections based on the census estimated that the Cambodian population in 2000 would be 12.2 million (5.9 million males and 6.3 million females).[8]

Cambodia's population is young, reflecting the major reversals suffered in the latter part of the twentieth century and the subsequent recovery from severe population decline. In 1998, children accounted for 42.8 per cent of the population and the elderly for 3.5 per cent. The economically productive group, aged between 15 and 64 years, accounted for 53.7 per cent. The dependency ratio, according to these 1998 census figures was 69.1 in urban areas and 89.7 in rural areas.

Cambodia is a multi-ethnic society with a majority ethnic Khmer population. In addition to the Khmer, who account for approximately 90 per cent of the total population, other groups include the Cham, Vietnamese, Chinese, and indigenous peoples. While Cambodia is now generally free of ethnic-related strife, the issue of ethnicity remains complicated and sensitive for many Cambodians.

The Cham people, the largest Muslim minority in Cambodia who constitute roughly two per cent of the total population, live mostly in the environs of Phnom Penh and in the provinces of Kompong Chhnang, Kampot and Kompong Cham. In general, despite or perhaps because there is little genuine social interaction between the Cham and the majority Khmer population, there is almost no friction between the two groups. The Cham are free to practise their religion and to educate their children in their own schools and according to their traditions, while also participating fully in Cambodian political and economic life.

It is difficult to gauge the size of the ethnic Vietnamese community of Cambodia, in part, because any estimate is always politically contested and also because throughout the twentieth century at least, the size of the Vietnamese population in Cambodia has fluctuated significantly. Jean Delvert quoted the 1950 Statistical Yearbook of Cambodia figure of 319,000 Vietnamese, and when he wrote *Le Paysan Cambodgien* in 1957, he thought the number was around 230,000.[9] The Vietnamese in Cambodia, he wrote, had typically been a nomadic population. Vietnamese have always fished the waterways of Cambodia and especially the Great Lake, moving up and down the Mekong between one country and the other. The French Protectorate administration employed them as clerks and junior officers, while colonial rubber planters imported them to do the work that Khmers could not or would not do on the vast plantations of eastern Cambodia in the 1920s. At the outbreak of the First Indochina War in 1945, many returned voluntarily to Vietnam. There were pogroms against Vietnamese Cambodians during the Khmer Republic, and the xenophobic regime of Democratic Kampuchea expelled or executed those who remained. During the 1980s, that is, the decade of Vietnamese military occupation, the Vietnamese Cambodians returned and numbers rose again perhaps to the pre-war level. More recently, Vietnamese have been attracted to Cambodia by economic opportunity and driven by rural poverty at home. If estimates of 500,000 given by some "independent observers" around the year 2000 were correct, Vietnamese Cambodians would have accounted for four per cent of the total population of 12.2 million.

In 1996, the official estimate of ethnic Chinese in Cambodia was a little over 200,000, more than half of them residing in the capital, Phnom Penh. When Penny Edwards conducted interviews in October 1995, the Association of Chinese Nationals in Cambodia estimated the population of "pure Chinese" (that is, not Sino-Khmer) to be 300,000–340,000, including 200,000 in Phnom Penh. The Chinese Embassy at the time more or less corroborated those figures.[10] If these estimates are accurate, they suggest that ethnic Chinese account for a little more than three per cent of the total population. If we included Sino-Khmer in the mix, the figure would be much higher. Chinese and Khmer have intermarried for many centuries.

The indigenous peoples inhabit the sparsely populated areas of the far north and northeast of the country and the mountainous massif areas of the southwest. According to the 1998 census which based ethnicity on mother tongue, their total number was about 101,000 or 0.9 per cent of the total population.[11] In the northeast provinces of Ratanakiri and Mondolkiri, however, indigenous peoples constitute the majority, with 66 per cent and 71 per cent respectively of the provincial population. Most indigenous families cultivate upland rice according to the swidden method of shifting cultivation; some families also cultivate wet paddy due to contact with Khmers or government encouragement. In recent years, cultivation of fruit and other cash crops such as coffee and cashews have been trialled, introduced mainly by Khmer farmers from the plain. Since the mid-1990s, traditional lifestyles in the highland regions have been severely impacted upon by illegal logging, the forest concession system, encroachments on their land by lowlanders, and other changes wrought by tourism. These threats have led to an increase in the number of land disputes and, simultaneously, to restricted access to non-timber forest products such as resin, bamboo and rattan, wildlife, forest fruits, and vegetables that supplement the indigenous peoples' income and their diet.

Human Development

The Human Development Index (HDI) constructed annually by the United Nations Development Programme measures average achievements in basic human development in longevity, knowledge and living standards in a composite index and produces a ranking of countries. The value, ranging from zero to one, shows the distance that a country has to travel to reach the maximum possible value of one and also allows intercountry comparisons to be made. Of the 174 countries assessed in the Human Development Report for the year 2000, Cambodia ranked 136, at the low end of the medium development list, just below Pakistan but above other non-sub-Saharan countries such as Laos, Bhutan, Nepal and Bangladesh.[12]

Cambodia's index for the year 2000 was calculated according to average life expectancy of 53.5 years, an adult literacy rate of 65 per cent, a combined primary, secondary and tertiary gross enrolment ratio of 61 per cent, and GDP per capita (purchasing power parity) calculated to be US$1,257. The resulting HDI value was 0.512. The index was based on 1998 figures when the infant mortality rate (per 1,000 live births) was 104, the under-five mortality rate (per 1,000 births) was 163 and the reported maternal mortality ratio (per 100,000 live births) was 470.

Many analysts regarded those statistics as unrealistically high. Results of the 1999 Cambodia Socio-Economic Survey (CSES-99) suggested that 35.9 per cent of the Cambodian population lived below the poverty line.[13] The burden of poverty is most keenly felt in the countryside where rural households, especially those for whom agriculture remains the primary source of income, account for almost 90 per cent of all the poor.[14] The income gap between city and countryside is wide. Average monthly consumption of Phnom Penh households in 1999 amounted to the equivalent of US$263.96, compared to only US$74.56 per month for the rural sector.[15] The richest 20 per cent of Cambodians have a HDI score nearly two and one-half times higher than that of the poorest 20 per cent of Cambodians.[16] The deepest pockets of poverty persist in the northwest of the country, particularly Pailin and other areas along the border with Thailand that bore the brunt of the war after 1979. Almost the whole of Siem Reap province is poverty-stricken, with the majority of communes there indicating an incidence of poverty 75 per cent or more, and almost all the remainder with levels between 50 per cent and 75 per cent.[17]

Rural Cambodians, in general, contributed little to the steady GDP growth of the 1990s. A Cambodia Development Resource Institute (CDRI) report of January 1999 pointed out that most of that economic growth had occurred in industry and services, specifically garment manufacturing and tourism that employ a small proportion of the population. Labour productivity, on the other hand, actually fell in the same period. "In agriculture," the report noted, "labour productivity is estimated to have fallen by 16 per cent between 1992–93 and 1996."[18] Apart from unpredictable weather conditions, farmers still confront many constraints relating to rural infrastructure including irrigation systems, roads and markets, affordable credit and banking facilities, and reliable agricultural extension services. A UN report released on 28 May 2004 suggested that the plight of the rural poor, which it put at between 40 and 45 per cent of the total population, might even be worsening.[19] It noted reduced consumption, fewer public health facilities, rising infant and child mortality and growing rural under-employment. Infant mortality, it claimed,

Urban Poverty. A slum in Phnom Penh, c. 2000

rose from 66.8 per 1,000 live births in 2000 to 73.67 in 2004. In the same period, life expectancy barely changed from 57.2 to 57.4 years.

National budgets regularly allocate increased funds for health but actual expenditure on the public health system consistently falls short of estimates. Households spend more than 10 per cent of their annual income on health, but only one-fifth of that expenditure is publicly funded.[20] It should not be surprising then, that most Cambodians prefer to use the non-medical sector, including traditional healers and midwives, or self-medicate with over-the-counter drugs when they fall ill.

Education is valued highly by Cambodians and most families make great economic sacrifices to ensure that their children receive at least primary education. Generally speaking, however, educational outcomes are poor. In 1999, the Ministry of Education, Youth and Sports conducted a national literacy survey based on a scientifically designed test that was delivered to respondents randomly selected from every province in the country.[21] According to results projected onto the total population, the combined rates of complete and semi-literacy indicated that four million Cambodians over the age of 15 were, to all intents and purposes, illiterate. Two-thirds of the total illiterates were found to be in the 15 to 45 age range, with little variation by gender. Among the 37.1 per cent of literate adults, only a quarter of them were judged to be "self-learning," that is, able to study independently and read all kinds of material in order to search out new knowledge. Those provinces and towns with the highest levels of illiteracy were Mondolkiri, Kep, Ratanakiri, Pailin, Preah Vihear, and Siem Reap, that is, the highlands and other zones of social disadvantage. The report noted a high correlation between illiteracy and poverty. It concluded, "It appears that the illiterates and those living below the poverty line are the same group of the population."[22]

Economic Activity

Between 1993 and 2000, the economy suffered two severe shocks: the political *coup de force* by the major ruling party against its coalition partner in mid-1997 that shook investor confidence and deterred tourism, followed shortly after by the Asian financial crisis. The economy recovered from those shocks but, as the figures below indicate, real growth since 1993 has been modest and some trends since 2000 are disturbing. These figures are based on data from the Royal Cambodian Government, the World Bank, the International Monetary Fund, and the Asian Development Bank:[23]

Table 0.1 Main Economic Indicators

	1993	2000	2001	2002
GDP at current prices (million US$)	2,135.8	3,186.5	3,372.1	3,594.4
GDP at constant 1993 prices (million US$)	2,135.8	3,072.8	3,277.3	3,414.1
GDP per capita at constant 1993 prices (US$)	205.3	236.6	246.2	254.8
Real GDP (% increase)	7.76%	7.34%	6.66%	4.18%
Riel/US$ parity (official, year average)	2,797	3,854	3,924	3,918
Inflation in Riel (year average)	75.15%	−0.79%	0.22%	3.29%
Domestic revenue (% GDP)	4.8%	11.6%	11.6%	12.3%
Budget expenditure (% GDP)	10.1%	16.9%	19%	17.7%
Exports of goods (% GDP)	15.4%	39.6%	40.7%	40.4%
Imports of goods (% GDP)	23.9%	47.8%	47.4%	48.3%
Trade balance (% GDP)	−8.5%	−8.3%	−6.7%	−7.9%
External contribution to economy (% GDP)	13.4%	14.7%	14.6%	15.0%
Total savings (% GDP)	17.2%	21.4%	23.4%	22.2%
External debts – Recognised (% GDP)	0.2%	16.4%	18.2%	21.3%
Labour force (% population)	41.1%	41.8%	42.3%	43.5%
Unemployment (% labour force)	2%	8%	10%	11%

Source: CDRI, *Cambodia's Annual Economic Review* (2002).

This selection of figures reveals some positive outcomes of structural change. Domestic revenue has improved and inflation has been checked; total savings have grown and donors and investors have maintained a near-constant level of confidence in the economy. The trade balance is not unhealthy. Other figures, however, suggest that growth is beginning to plateau. Although real gross domestic product is increasing, the gains made may not be sufficient to account for population growth. The economy is coming under pressure from the demographic bulge that occurred in the first half of the 1980s. This generation is marrying, demanding jobs and public services, and putting pressure on the size of rural landholdings. Unemployment is showing a disturbing upward trend, although, like literacy, the term is difficult to define. Where subsistence agriculture is still the norm in the countryside, the participation rate in economic activity is very high, but this may mask actual under-employment.

A huge challenge for Cambodian leaders now and for the next decade at least is how to generate employment for a rapidly growing labour force. The annual increase in the existing labour force is approximately 140,000 people.[24] The garment factories and the burgeoning tourist industry absorbed about a quarter of this annual increase during the period 1995–2000, perhaps around 12 per cent migrated to Thailand for work and the remainder have stayed in the countryside, sharing small areas of family land.²⁵ The garment industry and tourism remain relatively buoyant but these are volatile industries and the garment factories, at least, may have already reached saturation point for employment. In order to prevent farmers from becoming poorer, the size of farmland per farming household should not decrease further because of distribution to the new labour force. Clearly, the economy must diversify in order to absorb new surplus labour in the agricultural sector while, at the same time, improving productivity within the sector.

Agriculture

Despite the high profile given to garment manufacturing and tourism, the traditional sectors of agriculture, forestry and fisheries continue to be the major contributors to GDP. The table that follows shows, however, that the overall share of the primary sector declined by around four per cent between 1993 and 2000, while growth in this sector remained at a modest but steady rate of about 2.8 per cent. The poor figures for 2001 and 2002 reveal the effects of floods and drought during both rice-growing seasons, and the political decisions to limit illegal activities by forestry and fishery concessionaires.²⁶ In longer perspective, however, the negative growth in real terms of the agricultural sector reflects insufficient investment to improve productivity on the one hand and over-exploitation of natural resources on the other.

Table 0.2 GDP by Sector at Constant 1993 Prices (million US dollars)

	1993	*2000*	*2001*	*2002*
GDP at constant 1993 prices	2,135.8	3,072.8	3,277.3	3,414.1
Agriculture, forestry & fisheries	872.0	1,136.0	1,039.0	976.0
Crops	404.9	532.0	486.1	451.5
Livestock & poultry	172.9	194.5	178.4	192.7
Fisheries	192.6	301.6	273.0	238.6
Forestry & logging	101.9	107.7	101.8	93.0

Source: CDRI, *Cambodia's Annual Economic Review* (2002).

Rice is by far the main food crop produced in Cambodia, accounting for more than 96 per cent of total food crops cultivated in 1999. The country achieved food self-sufficiency in 1995, but paddy yields remain among the lowest in Asia. In 2000, Cambodian farmers cultivated a total of 2,157,500 hectares (inclusive of 242,000 hectares for the dry season crop) and produced 4,049,900 tons of paddy, giving an average yield of 1.94 tons per hectare (1.81t/ha for wet paddy and 3.04t/ha for dry paddy).[27] The Ministry of Commerce has calculated that as little as 10 per cent of the country's farmland is irrigated.[28]

The Cambodian government is eager to develop agro-industry on the estimated 1.2 million hectares of land that is currently unused. Existing agro-industry consists of cash crops on plantations cultivating rubber, palm oil, coffee, and cashews. Cassava, coconuts, sugar cane, and horticultural crops are also designated as suitable plantation cash crops. Meanwhile, long-standing plantation cash crops, especially rubber, pepper and jute have suffered from weak and fluctuating international commodity prices, lack of investment in capital stock, and general decline. The jute factory in Battambang, dating back to the era of post-independence optimism in the 1950s and 1960s, closed down at the end of February 2000.[29] Cambodia's seven state-owned rubber plantations with a total area of approximately 50,000 hectares on the Kompong Cham plateaux were targeted for privatisation under conditions applying to the structural adjustment programme of the World Bank in the early 1990s.

Fisheries

While rice is the food staple, fish, whether fresh, dried or in the form of *prahok* or fermented fish paste, provides the main protein source in the Cambodian diet. Each Cambodian consumes about 60 kilograms of fish each year. The annual flood cycle of the Mekong triggers fish spawning cycles, and the floodplains provide rich feeding grounds for the fry that drift downstream with the current. Approximately 2 million tons of fish and other aquatic animals are caught annually in the Lower Mekong Basin, providing more than 75 per cent of animal protein intake in the diets of rural people in the river basin. When the Mekong Committee began assessing the Mekong fishery in 1994, the official estimate of the annual inland fish catch in Cambodia was 50,000–75,000 tons.[30] In 2003, this figure was revised upwards to 500,000 tons.[31] The annual value of Cambodia's freshwater fisheries catch is still in excess of US$200 million, but both the size and the value of production are declining. Among both specialists and the general population, there is deep concern that stocks of larger, commercially valuable species have dramatically decreased over the past two decades due to over-fishing and illegal fishing techniques by large-scale operators which include electrocution, the pumping dry of recession ponds and "catch-all" nets.

Fishers along the Mekong prepare prahok for the market

Forestry

In 1999, about one half of Cambodia's forested area of some ten million hectares was in the hands of private logging companies holding long-term concession contracts. For most of the decade, the rate of forest extraction had been as high as seven times the sustainable yield but national budget revenue from that level of activity was minimal.

As a result of harsh criticism of his government from all quarters for permitting concessionaires to work outside the legal framework, to avoid payment of royalties, to log unsustainably, and to infringe the rights of communities living within the concession areas, the Prime Minister ordered a crackdown on illegal logging in January 1999. A forest crime monitoring unit was established and a new forestry law was drafted, requiring the negotiation of new concession agreements.

Debate on the forestry law began in the National Assembly on 19 June 2002, but there was little confidence among civil society groups that it would be properly enforced. They claimed that concessionaires were continuing to log despite the ban by using a loophole in the way the moratorium was written. Logging was forbidden within forestry concessions, but not in land concessions which some of the same companies owned. It was widely suspected, therefore, that these companies were receiving development licences to "clear" land for plantation development and also for "stump" and firewood collection; that is, they were logging concessions by another name.[32]

The World Bank reported in December 2003 that the government had cancelled 25 "non-performing" concessions on a total of four million hectares and that it was in the process of cancelling seven more. Eight concessions remained.

Industry and Services

Industry (mining, manufacturing, electricity, gas and water, and construction) contributed 18.8 per cent of GDP in 1999.[33] Manufacturing represented more than two-thirds of the total contribution, while textiles, wearing apparel and footwear accounted for almost half of all forms of manufacturing. In fact, garment factories are driving Cambodia's economic growth; in 2003, their output represented 80 per cent of total exports and added US$1.6 billion to GDP.[34]

The garment industry was established in Cambodia in 1993 and that year, exports of garment and textile products were worth US$3.8 million.

Five years later, they were worth almost one hundred times that amount (US$378 million).³⁵ Most of these exports were destined for the United States market. In January 1999, the U.S. government introduced quotas on 12 garment products, but agreed to raise the quotas by between 6 and 14 per cent if it were shown that Cambodia had complied with requirements for improved working conditions; these requirements included the payment of legal wages and overtime, and no retaliation against union activists. For this purpose, the International Labour Organization established a special labour monitoring project in the country and the scheme worked successfully to everyone's advantage. When the quota agreement ended in January 2005, initially around 25,000 jobs were lost. Within a few months, however, the employment figures had rebounded and by the middle of that year, between 265,000 and 268,000 workers were again employed in the sector, mostly young women who migrate from the countryside to the factories in Phnom Penh and surrounding areas of Kandal province.³⁶

By 2000, the services sector contributed almost as much to GDP as agriculture did, or approximately 37 per cent. Most of the growth in the sector has been dependent on the tourism and hospitality industry. Between 1993 and 1999, the number of visitors to Cambodia doubled, and between 1999 and 2002 the number trebled. It was anticipated that more than a million tourists would visit Cambodia in 2005.³⁷ The sharp rise in the number of visitors after 1999 can be attributed largely to the open-skies policy allowing direct flights, mainly to Siem Reap province where the famous ruins of Angkor are located. These tourists, arriving on packaged tours purchased outside Cambodia, have short stays and there is little direct flow-on to the general economy. Paradoxically, while Siem Reap plays host to the vast majority of tourists to Cambodia, it remains one of the country's poorest provinces.

Land and the Environment

Recent growth in the manufacturing and service sectors notwithstanding, economic activity in Cambodia is overwhelmingly agricultural and rural-based. Most people reside in the countryside where they are self-employed in rice cultivation. Land is therefore Cambodia's most important productive asset, and the patterns of its distribution and use are intimately connected with Khmer history and culture.

Most agricultural land is divided into multiple land parcels that are used for intensive rice cultivation. The CSES-99 put the total size of agricultural land parcels at 2.88 million hectares, or 1.37 parcels per household with average parcel size of 0.90 hectares.[38] These parcels are owner-operated. Tenancy is practised in Cambodia, but its incidence has always been minimal. As elsewhere, Cambodian farmers make optimal use of the available factors of production and both lease-in and lease-out the land they use. Landlessness, however, is a growing trend.

The rate of landlessness (that is, lacking land for agricultural purposes and the means to purchase it) in rural Cambodia ranges from 11 per cent to 30 per cent depending on geographical location and gender differentiation.[39] Between September 1999 and April 2000, the international organisation, Oxfam, conducted a study of 143 villages in 15 provinces and the results showed an overall rate of landlessness of 13 per cent, or one in eight families.[40] Among families headed by single women, the rate was 20.85 per cent. Of the landless families, almost one half had previously owned land but had lost it; the major cause (44.6 per cent) was sickness and resulting debt incurred for medical treatment, but land loss may be caused by a number of factors operating simultaneously.

Other studies suggest that distribution of land up to three hectares in size is fairly uniform. The most recent studies of agricultural land size and its distribution are the CSES-99 conducted by the National Institute of Statistics, and the Follow-up-00 survey by the World Food Programme, being indeed a follow-up of its 1998 Baseline Survey. A comparison of the results are illustrated in the table below:

Table 0.3 Percentage of Households and Proportion of Agricultural Landholdings, CSES-99 (rural) and Follow-up-00

Categories of Agricultural Land Size	Percentage of Households	Proportion of Agricultural Land
CSES-99 (rural) (Gini coefficient of land concentration = 0.57)		
Landless	15.8	
>0.5ha	17.3	4.1
>0.5–1.0ha	22.6	14.2
>1.0–1.5ha	13.6	13.8
>1.5–2.0ha	13.2	18.7
>2.0–2.5ha	5.7	10.0
>2.5–3.0ha	4.4	9.5
>3.0ha	7.4	29.6

continued overleaf

Table 0.3 continued

Categories of Agricultural Land Size	Percentage of Households	Proportion of Agricultural Land
Follow-up-00 (Gini coefficient of land concentration = 0.49)		
Landless	7.4	
>0.5ha	35.6	12.7
>0.5 –1.0ha	29.4	25.2
>1.0 –1.5ha	11.3	16.1
>1.5–2.0ha	8.1	16.2
>2.0–2.5ha	2.1	5.4
>2.5–3.0ha	2.9	8.9
>3.0ha	3.2	15.6

Source: CDRI, Working Paper 19, 2001.

Both studies show that the majority of farming families own small land areas between 0.5 hectares and 1.5 hectares. Otherwise, there are obvious discrepancies in the findings. The CSES-99 results showed that 53.5 per cent of rural households fitted this median, while the Follow-up-00 study counted 76.3 per cent of households in that category. The CSES-99 data suggested that 7.4 per cent of households control between one quarter and a third of Cambodia's agricultural land. The Follow-up-00 data halve these results at the top end of the scale but suggest that the number of rural households with land but owning less than one hectare, at 65 per cent, is far higher than the 39.9 per cent reported by the CSES-99.

Tenure

For a nation emerging from a long period of war and instability, including 15 years of socialist rule when agricultural land was worked by collectives or solidarity groups, it should not be surprising that the distinction between state and public property is often blurred, that definitions of land ownership are inconsistent, and that access to common property resources is hotly contested.

Throughout the 1990s, the incidence of land grabbing, land encroachment and illegal land transactions escalated as the economy developed.[41] Results of a national survey conducted by the National Institute of Statistics in 1997 (CSES-97) and a target survey by the World Food Programme the following year (PET-98) suggested that more than 70 per cent of households had nothing to prove their possession rights for either residential or agricultural land.⁴² Traditionally, land has belonged to the tiller and most people believe that if they are occupying and productively using land that is not contested by others, then that land is legally theirs. The recognition of this right by neighbours is considered sufficient guarantee of ownership. Needless to say, in an era of fierce land speculation, arguments about traditional rights to land hold little sway.

The much-anticipated Cambodian Land Law was promulgated at the end of August 2001. Under this law, land is divided into five categories: state public, state private, private, indigenous community, and *wat* (religious) property. The law permits concessionaires, who may be foreigners, to occupy and use state land with a maximum size of 10,000 hectares for economic and social purposes for a maximum of 99 years. The economic concessions allow the beneficiaries to clear the land for industrial agricultural exploitation that must begin within 12 months of the concession being issued. By law, a social concession will allow landless citizens to apply for property for residential and subsistence farming purposes, in which case property will be allocated to approved applicants according to a sub-decree.

There is a lot of scepticism about this law, its implementation and enforcement. The matter of "common property" is of particular concern. Throughout history, Cambodian subsistence farmers and hunter-gatherers have been able to survive shrinking areas of livelihood resources as long as they have been allowed unrestricted access to common land, including forests and streams. Since 1989, when socialist rule officially ended in Cambodia, access and control over those shared communal spaces has been contested. Just one year before the Land Law was passed, CDRI economist, Sik Boreak argued:

> Although common property in Cambodia is not clearly defined by existing regulations, it has been observed to have been diverted to private ownership at an alarming rate. Considerable areas of common property resources, such as forests, rivers, lakes and agricultural land which were not redistributed in 1989 have become privately controlled. Millions of hectares of forests have been granted to private companies as concession forests. Many large plantations have been developed. Many private fishing lots have been created along the banks of major rivers and lakes; and a considerable amount of unallocated agricultural land has been illegally encroached upon and has dubiously become private property. As a result of privatisation, common property is becoming less accessible to other people, and hence, benefits to the majority have been reduced.⁴³

On a more optimistic note, by 2000, efforts were underway to conserve areas of environmental importance. The Great Lake was recognised as a biosphere reserve and in February 2001 legislation was passed to protect three core areas of the lake with a total area of 36,287 hectares, putting them off-limits to development; fishing would also be curbed in those areas through tighter regulations and increased patrols.[44] In 2002, logging was banned and two wildlife sanctuaries were established in the Cardamom Chain with a view to securing World Heritage listing for this wilderness area.

Foreign Trade, Aid, Investment and Debt

The defining characteristics of the Cambodian economy are its open trade and investment regime and its reliance on the garment manufacturing industry. These are the two drivers of current economic growth. On 1 January 2000, Cambodia was admitted to the regional economic grouping, ASEAN, and accepted guidelines of the AFTA (ASEAN Free Trade Agreement); in late 2004, the country joined the World Trade Organization. Conditions for membership in these important trade bodies have already produced significant structural alterations to the economy, but their full impact on the balance of trade, on national revenue collection and foreign investment has yet to be fully felt. There are warnings, however, that trade deregulation will undermine Cambodia's capacity to sustain customs duty collections if overall trade, and GDP in general, does not grow rapidly. Customs duties supplied 45 per cent of total tax revenues in 1999.[45]

In large measure, the recovery of the Cambodian economy since 1993 has been due to generous infusions of foreign aid, including grants and soft loans from the World Bank and the Asian Development Bank. The Consultative Group (CG) Meeting, a gathering of major donors and stakeholders, is held annually in Phnom Penh where the international community regularly pledges to provide Cambodia with aid worth approximately US$500 million. Actual disbursements usually reach about 60 per cent of the pledged amount, and loans from the major creditors represent around 20 per cent of total disbursements.[46]

The donor meetings have become more complex each year. Increasingly, they are used as forums for lobbying by civil society groups (there are around 800 local NGOs and 200 international NGOs with development and human rights agendas in Cambodia), as well as by the private sector. Multilateral organisations and bilateral donors use the occasion to pressure the Royal Government of Cambodia for structural reform and stricter monitoring of the reform process. The issues are wide-ranging and donor pledges are made in terms of conditionality. In 2001, for example, key topics of debate focused on changes to the investment law, demobilisation, funding for commune elections, and implementation of good governance reforms; other issues included progress on the Khmer Rouge tribunal, forestry reform and the land law.

The Cambodian government has largely complied with the practice of establishing benchmarks as a step towards linking aid to reform, but that compliance rankles nonetheless. In an address the Cambodian Prime Minister made on 15 September 2005 to the United Nations General Assembly, he said, "Politically driven hidden agendas and shifting ideologies to bring coercive influence on the recipients [of aid] must end. They serve only to punish the poor."[47] He also questioned the value of technical assistance, which constitutes a high proportion of foreign aid, including loans. In 1998, for example, expenditure on technical assistance exceeded the total tax revenue raised by the government.[48] Furthermore, a disproportionate amount of funding remains in the capital city for administrative purposes and its distribution among the provinces is uneven. The matter of "ownership" is also sensitive, as the selection of development projects appears to be donor-driven and susceptible to international, short-term issues and not necessarily local long-term needs. Worryingly, because development projects can afford to pay their staff salaries that are much higher than government salaries, there has been a steady drain of officials away from government institutions to the non-government sector, weakening further the capacity of the government to manage the delivery of services to the people.

Foreign direct investment is obviously preferable to foreign aid. Investment is vital to continued growth in the Cambodian economy and conditions for foreign investors have been extremely generous since the passage of the Investment Law in 1994. Its main incentives included exemption from import duties during the period of project construction and for the first year of business operations, and up to eight years' exemption from corporate profit tax. Investment in any of the designated eight "important" fields earned total exemption from export tax, while the distribution of dividends, profits or proceeds of investment, whether transferred abroad or distributed in the country, also enjoyed tax-free status.

Before the Asian financial crisis slowed the rate of foreign investment during the second half of 1997, Asian economies, particularly Malaysia, Indonesia, South Korea and Japan contributed about 80 per cent of Cambodia's foreign direct investment.[49] Garment factories and hotels represented most of total investment during the 1990s, and accumulated stocks of FDI reached approximately US$1.2 billion in 1999. Between

2000 and 2002, there was a levelling off but a boom in hotel construction in Siem Reap and Sihanoukville in 2002 led to a resumption of investment growth. More recently, the People's Republic of China has become an increasingly important source of foreign investment capital. Of the US$546 million in investment approved by the Council for the Development of Cambodia in the first half of 2005, for instance, US$402 million of that total amount was derived from Chinese business.[50] A serious challenge for the government is how to direct a fair share of all investment towards agriculture where it is urgently needed.

Cambodia's outstanding external debt is difficult to quantify. After independence in 1953, each political regime accrued foreign debt according to the political alliances it forged. Debts owed to the U.S.A., the former Soviet Union and China are either hidden or under negotiation. It is simply not known what debt Cambodia owes to Vietnam for the ten years of defence and nation-building it provided following the catastrophe of the Pol Pot era. Needless to say, the current Kingdom of Cambodia does not recognise all these outstanding debts. CDRI economists put the outstanding external debt recognised by the Cambodian government at the end of 1999 at US$350 million, while the pending debt was then estimated at $1.7 billion.[51] Their counterparts at the Economic Institute of Cambodia suggest that the outstanding debts recognised by the government amounted to around US$1,082 million at the end of 2003.[52] Whatever the actual total figure is, Cambodian economists believe that even if creditors agree to halve their claims, Cambodia's foreign debt burden will still stand at 50 per cent of GDP.[53]

In 1992, a loan from the Asian Development Bank represented Cambodia's first official borrowing from an international financial institution in more than two decades. The loan was worth US$67.7 million, repayable over 40 years, and it was undertaken to help rebuild infrastructure.[54] Interest payments of around US$1 million began in 2003; the budget that year set aside US$6.25 million for loan repayments. Since that first loan, the Cambodian government has borrowed a further US$700 million from the ADB and the World Bank/IMF.

Public Finance, Banking and Credit

In 1999, domestic revenue amounted to 1,329.957 billion riels (US$348.6 million) collected mainly from taxes, especially customs duties and consumption tax; posts and telecommunications was the main earner in the non-tax category of revenue.[55] Total expenditure that year was 1,846.225 billion riels (US$483.9 million). Civil administration and defence/security together accounted for 55.5 per cent of government spending. Foreign financing amounted to 537.957 billion riels (US$141 million), 4.363 billion riels for budget support and the remainder for project aid.

In terms of GDP, total government revenue amounted to 11.2 per cent of GDP in 1999, a sharp increase of 40 per cent over the previous year due mainly to the introduction of the consumption tax and the revenue gained from companies bidding for garment quota exports. Both of these measures were introduced in early 1999.[56] Tax revenue and the tax structure in general, however, remain very weak. Cambodians contribute less than US$30 each to the annual national budget, as opposed to about US$600 in Thailand; on the other hand, they receive only about US$5 per capita for health and education, compared to around US$150 in Thailand.[57] According to the World Bank 2000 *Country Assistance Strategy* report, donors and non-government organisations finance about 46 per cent of education expenditures, while individual households and the government finance 27 per cent each; households finance an overwhelming 82 per cent of all health expenditures.[58]

Tight budgetary policy has kept inflation in check since 1993 when it was very high. Since 1993, the value of the riel against the U.S. dollar has been relatively stable. In 1999, the riel stood at 3,815 to the U.S. dollar, 100 to the Thai baht and 365 to the Vietnamese dong.[59] There is, however, a high degree of dollarisation in the economy; the World Bank reporting that 98 per cent of bank lending was denominated in dollars and 95 per cent of total liabilities were denominated in foreign currency in 2000.[60] The riel is used mainly for small transactions and local wage and salary payments, while medium and large financial transactions are conducted in foreign currencies.[61] The high degree of dollarisation and the habit of cash transactions restricts the government's scope for running an active and effective monetary policy.

The World Bank observed that Cambodia had one of the shallowest financial systems in the world.[62] As of 31 December 1998, its report noted, the Cambodian financial system comprised 31 banks, 22 of them private banks whose ultimate owners were not always known to the National Bank of Cambodia (NBC), the central bank, and there was no public disclosure of financial information. Most of banks' assets were foreign currency loans to the private sector, while commercial bank lending to the agricultural sector accounted for less than one per cent of GDP. A law on banking and financial institutions was enacted in November 1999, granting the NBC strict and broad supervisory powers. The law divided banks and financial institutions into four categories: commercial banks, specialised banks, specialised financial institutions, and microfinance institutions. Under that law, commercial banks were required to hold minimum registered capital of 50 billion riels (around US$13 million). This relicensing requirement forced some undercapitalised banks to close or merge.

The Rural Development Bank (RDB) was created by the government in 1998 to act as a second tier bank to microfinance institutions. Its powers were strengthened by the *prakas* or regulatory law of November 1999 concerning specialised rural credit banks, and the licensing of commercial banks and microfinance institutions. Microfinance, the main form of formal credit for rural villagers and urban poor families, is dominated by the Acleda Bank and by a host of non-government development organisations. Largely because of the way these loans are disbursed, the recipients pay high interest rates (between two and five per cent each month).[63] These rates, however, are still much lower than those offered by the informal sector where the majority of rural people, those too poor to qualify for loans from other institutions, still go to borrow money. In general, these rates are between 5 and 10 per cent a month.[64]

Conclusions

According to the key indicators, the Cambodian economy started the twenty-first century seemingly confident of steady and constant growth. As long as peace endured and investor confidence remained buoyant, there was no reason to suppose that the terrible hardship of the last three decades of the previous century would be revisited.

Structural reforms throughout the 1990s have resulted in many positive changes, particularly to the urban economy. The commercial and financial sectors have been revamped, sound monetary policy has kept inflation under control, and government revenues have increased substantially. Foreign investors, especially those from the region, have found opportunities in Cambodia to be both profitable and secure.

On the other hand, significant elements of the economy remain stubbornly resistant to change. The overwhelming majority of the economically active population still consists of own account or unpaid workers cultivating paddy on small parcels of land with little assistance from technical inputs, organised credit or institutional support. While there have undoubtedly been significant increases in rice production, especially since 1995, local millers and merchants have been unable to capitalise on this growth due largely to the lack of efficient marketing and distribution networks. Entrenched rural poverty is the paramount obstacle to genuine economic development.

As the following chapters will demonstrate, agriculture, which has always been the main occupation of the people and the mainstay of the state surplus, has consistently failed to fulfil its potential as the designated catalyst for the sort of economic development that Cambodia's modernisers envisaged. It is equally true, however, that after each catastrophe that befell the nation, it was traditional agriculture that revived the national economy and salvaged the people's livelihood. Despite the rhetoric of successive governments claiming the contrary, the farmers' resilience is never repaid with the sort of capital investment required to replace traditional practices; that is, in properly managed irrigation infrastructure, accessible marketing and distribution networks, and affordable credit. Too often throughout the preceding century — as now — agricultural resources, including arable land, forests and fisheries, while touted as targets of economic reform, have instead been the objects of rent-seeking and easy personal wealth creation by rapacious officials and their cronies, or they have been held to ransom as contested arenas by political elites with conflicting ideologies.

Policy makers typically have blamed their failures on a recalcitrant, tradition-bound peasantry. The under-resourced rice farmer typically avoids risking a lower yield. From the first episode of deliberate efforts to modernise the Cambodian economy, that of the French Protectorate, policy-makers and traditional rice farmers have worked at cross purposes to each other.

CHAPTER

1

The Colonial Economy, 1863–1953

> Unhappy is the Cambodian! Hemmed in between the Siamese on the one hand, and the Annamites on the other, who together have robbed him of his richest provinces, rendered immobile by the operation of a feudal law which prevents him from acquiring lands of his own, a vigorous hand is needed to support him, and enable him to preserve his autonomy, while the ameliorating influences of European civilization are gradually brought to bear upon him.
>
> Dr Morice[1]

Long before the arrival of the French, foreigners had been taking account of Cambodia's economic potential. When the Chinese envoy, Zhou Daguan, visited the Khmer empire at the end of the thirteenth century, the power and glory of the Angkorian kings had already diminished. Zhou observed that whole villages had been laid waste. Soon Angkor itself would be besieged by the Siamese and attacks would continue for a century until the kings abandoned Angkor for a new capital at Lovek, northwest of the present capital, Phnom Penh. Despite this political decline, the lifestyle Zhou described was one of irresistible ease, as he recorded, "Chinese sailors coming to the country note with pleasure that it is not necessary to wear clothes and, since rice is easily had, women easily persuaded, houses easily run, furniture easily come by, and trade easily carried on, a great many sailors desert to take up permanent residence."[2]

At the time of Zhou's visit in 1296, Cambodia was divided into more than 90 provinces or *srok*, and every village, no matter how small, he noted, had its own local official and a *wat* or pagoda, Theravada Buddhism being the dominant religion. Zhou described an affluent, slave-owning population where "Families of wealth may own more than one hundred; those of lesser means content themselves with ten or twenty; only the very poor have none."³ The slaves, if not prisoners of war or insolvent debtors, were indigenous tribespeople, "wild men from the hills," according to Zhou. He divided these *montagnards* into two categories: those who understood the dominant language and were sold in the towns as slaves, and those who refused to submit to civilisation and who wandered about the mountains. He reported on methods of rice cultivation and on self-seeding floating rice. He also saw pepper, growing "twisted round the stems of the rattan, fastening on like a hop vine."⁴

Trade was the province of women and, Zhou observed, "For this reason, a Chinese arriving in the country loses no time in getting himself a mate, for he will find her commercial instincts a great asset."⁵ The daily markets he described differed little from local markets c. 2000, except for the currency of exchange. At the end of the thirteenth century, according to Zhou, "In small transactions barter is carried on with rice, cereals and Chinese objects; fabrics are next employed, and finally in big deals, gold or silver is used."⁶ The precious products of the country, in terms of their export potential for the Chinese market, were rare woods, kingfisher feathers, elephant tusks, rhinoceros horn, and beeswax; the more commonplace items included laka-wood, cardamoms, gamboge, lacquer and chaulmoogra oil. In return, the biggest demand was for Chinese gold and silver because, as Zhou noted, these minerals were not found in Cambodia.

Three hundred years later, Cambodia was again at war with Siam. Lovek was plundered in 1594 and the king moved his court to Srei Santhor, near today's Udong market, about 30 kilometres northwest of Phnom Penh. Spanish and Portuguese adventurers advised the Cambodian monarch to seek help from Spain. In 1604, Gabriel Quiroga de San Antonio, a Spanish Dominican friar, addressed King Philippe III urging the conquest of Cambodia for religious, as well as political and economic reasons.⁷ The Kingdom of Cambodia, he reminded his monarch, had been well known by the Portuguese for more than 108 years. He described the annual flooding of the Mekong, the abandoned city of Angkor, the royal court at Srei Santhor along with "the kingdom's councils, the audience and the chancellery through which it is governed," and the city of Churdumuco (Chatomuk, now Phnom Penh). The population there, he observed, was "very dense" and "among them there are leading citizens and common people."⁸ All acknowledged only one king and they paid the king and the high officials "a tithe of produce of the sea and soil." The many buffaloes were used for ploughing the soil "without an iron ploughshare because it is very light."[9] Potential items for trade included cotton, silk, incense, benzoin, rice and "all the lacquer which is sold across the world." He falsely reported the "renowned" mines for silver, gold, lead, copper and tin to support his argument that colonising the kingdom would increase the revenues of the Spanish king and "enrich his vassals greatly." Apart from this bounty, Cambodia, he argued, was "the necessary door which will open to the priceless wealth of the Kingdom of Laos."[10]

The Spanish king, needless to say, did not add Cambodia to his empire and the fortunes of the Khmer kingdom continued to decline at the hands of its neighbours. In 1794, the *srok* of the northwest, Battambang and Siem Reap, were transferred to the jurisdiction of Siam.[11] This was just the beginning of the paring of Cambodian territory. During the first half of the nineteenth century, Cambodia as a sovereign state almost disappeared as a result of repeated invasions, usually at the behest of princes contesting succession to the throne and seeking support from one neighbouring country or the other. In 1811, the Thai army invaded, sacked and burnt the capital, and during the retreat of 1813 carried off a large slice of the population. Cambodia was divided into two spheres of influence with the Mekong acting as the line of demarcation between the Thai sphere in the west and the Vietnamese in the east.

The 1820s and 1830s were decades of Vietnamese hegemony. Unlike the Thais who seemed intent only on territory (and the populations), the Vietnamese attempted to institutionalise their control by organising systems of tax collection and rice storage and forming a standing army, among other administrative reforms. These efforts, David Chandler notes, had little effect. He suggests that powerful *srok* officials responded to Vietnamese rule with "intentional incompetence" so that by the end of the 1830s there were still no records of landholdings or accurate population statistics, and the collection of rice for the army and the mobilisation of workers remained in the hands of the Khmer officials who, he said, "enjoyed considerable freedom of action."[12]

The administrative reforms may have had little impact on people's lives, but when Vietnamese edicts touched on Khmer daily customs, such as attire and hairstyles, the people were provoked. The anti-Vietnamese rebellion of 1840–41 occurred "because the survival of Cambodian institutions, however disorderly, … however powerless and corrupt, were thought to be at stake."[13] In 1841, the Siamese invaded again.

By the middle of the nineteenth century, Cambodia was literally at the mercy of its neighbours. The population was small and dispersed, inhabiting a territory roughly half its present size. The total population was probably less than 750,000. The chronicles from the 1840s, Chandler writes, are filled with references to famines, battles, refugees and epidemics.[14] The population was then, as now, overwhelmingly rural, and that population was concentrated in the plain to the south and east of Phnom Penh which, as Jean Delvert observed, offered poor conditions for agriculture but was safe from the routes of invasion and retreat of foreign armies. Administratively, there were 32 *srok* ruled by the *chaovay srok* who gathered taxes in rice and mobilised manpower although only irregularly, on demand. Chandler notes that in theory at least, every able-bodied male owed the king three months' service annually but, in fact, these calls for *corvée* were few.[15]

The majority Khmer population followed their traditional occupation of rice farming and fulfilled the roles for officials. Commerce, foreign trade and the riparian market gardens were the preserve of the Chinese, while the Cham fished and raised cattle. Compared to other states in the region, Cambodia was poor. Agricultural surpluses were uncommon, landholdings were small, yields were low, and irrigation systems were rare. There were few roads, so the villages were defenceless against bandits and rapacious officials.

Foreign trade was almost non-existent by 1850. Phnom Penh was effectively cut off from the outside world, and visitors required Vietnamese permission to reach it via the Mekong. Ports on the Gulf of Siam such as Kampot, Chandler records, were more integrated with Vietnamese and Thai economies than with their own.[16] Nevertheless, a few Japanese and Chinese ships still bore cargoes of ivory and pepper, cardamoms, hides, tortoise shells and aromatic woods from central Cambodia, although the quantities were small.

The French naturalist, Henri Mouhot, entered the Kingdom of Cambodia through Kampot in June 1859. His response to the Cambodian society and its ruined economy was that of a European rationalist and liberal progressive of his time. Like almost every other Western reformer since, he predicted that with good governance, investment in agriculture and proper regard for human rights, Cambodia could return to its former glory. Having seen the ruins of Angkor, he compared Cambodia unfavourably with its past:

> Now, for a country to be rich and powerful, a produce relatively great and an extended commerce must be presumed. Doubtless, Cambodia was formerly thus favoured, and would be so at the present day under

Idyllic impressions of Cambodia at the time of naturalist Henri Mouhot's visit in 1860

A colonial era rubber warehouse at Tonle Bet, Kompong Cham province

a wise government, if labour and agriculture were encouraged instead of despised, if the ruling powers exercised a less absolute despotism, and, above all, if slavery were abolished — that miserable institution which is a bar to all progress, reduces man to the level of the brute, and prevents him from cultivating more than sufficient for his own actual wants.[17]

He journeyed directly to Udong, the royal capital, which then had a population of around 12,000. From there, he went to Phnom Penh, the "great bazaar of Cambodia" with a regular population of 10,000, almost all Chinese, and a floating, and presumably transient one of more than double that figure made up of Khmers and Cochinchinese who lived on their fishing boats. He wrote, "It was the time when most of the fishermen, returning from the Great Lake, stop at Phnom Penh to sell part of their catch, and when a crowd of small merchants flock there to buy cotton which is gathered in before the rains."[18] Apart from his forays overland into Stieng territory on the Mimot Plateau, Mouhot's travels in Cambodia were largely by water or along the banks of rivers. From this perspective, he judged the soil to be generally fertile, "as fertile as Lower Cochinchina, ... which yields so abundant a return for all that is put in the ground" and blamed the poor Khmer diet on the laziness of the farmer and official incompetence.[19]

Overall, he found Cambodia's condition to be "deplorable." The population, he noted, had been seriously diminished by the incessant wars. "I do not think that the country now contains above a million of inhabitants," he estimated, "and, according to the last census, the number of free men fit to carry arms is returned at 30,000."[20] The number of Chinese was "relatively great" and there were also Malays and a floating population of Annamites, "amounting to two or three thousand." Accurate statistics on the size of the population were not available, he noted, because calculations only indicated males fit for active service.

Among the various products he listed (tobacco, pepper, ginger, sugar, gamboge, coffee, silk, and cotton), he was most interested in the cotton crop which might have supplemented French needs should the American Civil War interrupt trans-Atlantic trade. On Koh Sautin, now an island district of Kompong Cham province, he found that cotton growers rented "lots" from the Crown for one pound per lot; each lot returning an income of more than 1,200 francs. He also admired the forests and their products and reported that the mountains contained gold, lead, zinc, copper and iron, "the last two in some abundance."[21] Therefore, he wondered at the lack of exports and blamed it all on corrupt officials and the sloth of the farmer, although he had some sympathy for the latter, noting, "The taxes now weigh solely on the cultivator and producer: the more he raises, the more he has to pay: disposed, therefore, to indolence by the influence of the climate, he has little inducement to combat this vice."[22]

In 1860, during Mouhot's travels in the region, the Khmer king died. In the internecine fight for succession that ensued, Siam again found leverage and Cambodia succumbed once more to their influence. The head of the Catholic mission in Cambodia, Bishop Miche, urged French intervention to restore order. The French, however, were more persuaded by the hope of securing access to the Mekong which, if navigable to its source, would allow French penetration of southwest China. Control over Cambodia would also prevent Vietnamese opponents to their rule from finding sanctuary in Cambodia. The French authorities concluded a protectorate treaty with King Norodom I in August 1863.

The expedition of the French Commission for the Exploration of the Mekong set out from Saigon in June 1866 with the aim of finding a route to Yunnan. Arriving in Phnom Penh, Louis de Carné, a member of that expedition, noted that the city that once boasted a population of 50,000 had been reduced to about one-tenth of that size, while the total population, in his estimation, was barely one million, including 40,000 slaves and 20,000 "savages." Like Mouhot, de Carné was intrigued by the condition of Cambodian slaves: those for debt, those of the king, and the slaves of the pagoda. True slavery, he decided, "slavery simply from being basely carried off, with no deliverance but by death or escape," was only that inflicted on the "savages," that is, members of the indigenous populations of the highlands. In Phnom Penh they brought 800 francs but their value fluctuated, "like that of other things, according to the law of supply and demand."[23]

The expedition proceeded up the Tonle Sap river to Kompong Luong where the French resident lived "with his gunboat moored close to his house, near enough to the king to direct and watch him."[24] On the Great Lake, de Carné saw thousands of Vietnamese fishing boats, their loads deep with the fish they had taken. Such was the value of the catch, he wrote, that the Vietnamese sometimes gave one hundred per cent for money borrowed to buy the salt needed to preserve it. "The legal interest in Cambodia is from forty to one hundred per cent a year!" he wrote in astonishment.[25]

Like Mouhot, de Carné's impression of Cambodian agriculture was formed by what he saw from his vantage point on the Mekong. He saw large quantities of maize and cotton, and like Mouhot, singled out cotton for special mention. "The island of Koh Sautin yields, by itself, an annual revenue of 15,000 francs to the king's mother, and this represents hardly a tenth of the value of the total production," he noted.[26]

At Kratie, the expedition exchanged their steamer for canoes and regarded this as their true point of departure. This really was the Cambodian frontier. The adjoining province of Stung Treng had been lost in the eighteenth century and, as de Carné recorded, the provincial town of Stung Treng was "the first village of Laos." The navigation difficulties began almost immediately. With eloquent resignation, he admitted:

> The truth began, at last, to force itself on the most sanguine among us. Steamers can never plough the Mekong, as they do the Amazon or the Mississippi; and Saigon can never be united to the western provinces of China by this immense river-way, whose waters make it so mighty, but which seems, after all, to be a work unfinished.[27]

The French ambition of "establishing a dominion in the eastern peninsula of Asia that would go far to rival in wealth and power the empire which the British have founded in Hindustan" was dashed by the findings of the commission. Unlike the Ganges which had led the British "to wide, rich, and populous countries in the interior," the Mekong instead "conducted the weary travellers within the jaws of unsoundable gorges, overhung by Alpine precipices ... or loses itself in a labyrinth of islets, of weeds, and of trees rising from the bosom of the waters."[28] The Cambodian Protectorate was, nevertheless, a *fait accompli* and with dogged optimism, the French committed themselves to the task of amelioration:

> Cambodia is a country of magnificent natural resources, and has a noble river — the Mekong — flowing through its midst. It produces dye-woods, ebony, rice, cotton, indigo, sesame, gamboge, sugar, tobacco, iron, jasmine, and wild cattle, "all in profusion, and all useless for want of enterprise and capital." The French are anxious to supply these wants; and considering the position they hold, no doubt they will succeed in having their own way.[29]

Policies

Two over-riding principles dictated the early policy of French rule in Indochina: an unquestioning faith in progress and the moral superiority of the white race. In French colonial terms, these principles translated into *mise en valeur* and the *mission civilisatrice*. Quite literally, the new imperialism of the nineteenth century set out consciously "to modernize, develop, instruct, and civilize."[30]

No less than the British, Edward Said notes, the French were interested in profit, plantations and cheap labour, but in France's empire, he adds, "One senses little equivalent of the British 'departmental view,' and much more the personal style of being French in a great assimilationist enterprise."[31] Acclaimed historian, E.J. Hobsbawm concurs, "France believed in transforming its subjects into Frenchmen, notional descendants (as school textbooks insisted, in Timbuctoo and Martinique as in Bordeaux) of *nos ancêtres les gaulois*,' unlike the British, convinced of the essential and permanent non-Englishness of Bengalis and Yoruba."[32]

The countervailing argument to assimilation was that of association which insisted on the differences between races and cultures, their institutions and organisation. Essentially, however, the debate over assimilation versus association, Theodore Zeldin argues, was a theoretical one, "For assimilation was in practice degraded into bureaucratic uniformity rather than involving any real equality, and association, though supposed to mean indirect rule and the maintenance of indigenous cultures, was in practice difficult to distinguish from direct rule, for native chiefs were made to do what the French told them to do."[33] In short, French imperialism exported materialism more than its spiritual concerns, but French prestige was always a factor.

Cambodia was a protectorate, not a colony *per se*. Sovereignty was not officially destroyed, but as the Conventions of 1877 and 1884 proved, neither was opposition to French rule brooked. Executive decrees were the most common form of metropolitan interference, Virginia Thompson noted, even though "they violate the sacrosanct principle of the separation of powers on which French law is based."[34] Ultimately, the possession of colonies and the administration of protectorates served to ensure *la Métropole* would have access to the resources necessary for its own industrial development. France and her colonies would be a self-sufficient unit, unaffected by tariff barriers erected to protect the economies of other world powers.

Administration and Governance

In 1866, King Norodom moved the royal capital from Udong to Phnom Penh. How far did his royal power radiate? For Cambodians, the reply then and now, to a large extent, would have been given in terms of the habitation of social spaces, that is, wherever there were Khmer villages, the king reigned. Cambodia is *srok khmer*, the land of the Khmer people and the people are spiritually tied to their king, however distant the seat of his power might be. Many Cambodians still identify their territory with certain "national" and what they believe are uniquely owned symbols like the sugar palm, and they may argue that Khmer territory extends to the last sugar palm tree. Borders, marked out by stones, have long been regarded by the Khmer as Vietnamese tricks, purporting false claims on Khmer land.³⁵ The indianised Khmer state and the sinicised Vietnamese state had very little in common with each other, and neither had much meaning *vis-à-vis* the European sense of the term, least of all its bureaucratic obsession with lines, lists and scientific categories.

There were, then, no maps; more exactly, there were no maps that demarcated the Cambodian state's territory from that of others. There certainly was, however, a strong sense of social and cultural identity that was tied to occupation of that territory. When the Protectorate Treaty was concluded in 1863, actual administration by the king's officials extended in a rough inverted triangle from Pursat in the northwest across the Great Lake and Kompong Thom to Kratie in the east, and then southwest from the foothills of the Haut Chhlong to Kampot, and then back to Pursat, excluding Koh Kong which was still under Siam's jurisdiction. Territory to the east of that Haut Chhlong to Kampot line, that is, from Tay Ninh to Saigon and all land south to the sea had gradually been settled by southward Vietnamese migration. Charles Robequain noted, "At the time of the conquest the Cambodians had already been almost entirely ousted from the plains of Cochinchina where, up to the end of the seventeenth century, they had been practically the sole inhabitants."³⁶ By 1860, Robequain continued, the Khmer constituted "a few close-knit groups in the western provinces of Cochinchina" and between 1870 and 1914, these areas were officially absorbed into Vietnam. In the late 1930s, Robequain recorded 326,000 Cambodians in Cochinchina, compared with 3,979,000 Annamites. "[M]oreover," he wrote, "the Annamites are filtering gradually, and peacefully, but constantly, into Cambodia.... On the whole, Annamite southward expansion has been going on without violence ever since the European occupation."³⁷

Cambodian territory was partly compensated for the loss of Kampuchea Krom, those lands near the mouth of the Mekong, by the restitution of Stung Treng in 1904 and by the return of the *srok* from Siam: Battambang, Siem Reap, Sisophon, and Koh Kong (formerly Chantaboun and the Bay of Krat), in accordance with the 1907 Treaty of Bangkok which divided mainland Southeast Asia between the French and British colonial empires. Before the end of the Protectorate, in 1941, Cambodia would again cede this territory to Thailand, to the despair of King Monivong who died a few months after this humiliating loss.

By the terms of the Protectorate Treaty, King Norodom handed control of foreign relations to France. In return, France pledged protection and recognised the sovereignty of the king. The theory that Cambodia was a protectorate, Milton Osborne argues, was honoured to the extent that French interference stopped short of the mass of the people.[38] To all intents and purposes, however, Cambodia was a French-administered dominion that had to pay its own way.

Departures from the terms of the treaty came in two important conventions. In 1877, the French took advantage of a challenge to the king's power from his half-brother to institute fundamental administrative reforms.[39] A Council of Ministers, sitting apart from the king, was put in charge of discussing matters of state. The French resident was entitled to a consultative voice and his presence was obligatory during discussions concerning finance, laws, foreign trade, and internal disturbances. This council of ministers, alone, could institute new taxes.

The Convention of 1884 forced Norodom's compliance with the terms of the earlier convention, and added some historic terms of its own.[40] The first article stated categorically that H.M. the King would accept all administrative, judicial, financial and commercial reforms that the Government of the Republic might deem useful for facilitating the accomplishment of its Protectorate. Cambodian officials would continue, under control of the French authorities, to administer the provinces except in the matter of taxes, customs, indirect taxes, public works and "in general, services which require the management or use of engineers or European agents"(Article 3). Residents or deputy residents would in future be placed in the provincial centres, under the authority of a *résident général* who was answerable to the governor of Cochinchina. Cambodia would carry the cost of the administration of the kingdom and the protectorate (Article 6). The king and the royal family were placed on a civil list, slavery was abolished, and, most importantly from an economic viewpoint, "the land of the kingdom, so far the exclusive property of the crown, will cease to be inalienable" (Article 9).

In January 1897, Resident Superior Vernéville persuaded the Council of Ministers to agree to carry out business without consulting the king. In this way, the French representative usurped executive power and placed himself firmly in the position of chairman of the Council of Ministers. "In one stroke," Osborne notes, "the king's power was reduced to the point where his authority scarcely extended beyond the palace."[41] The *ordonnance royale* of 11 July 1897 regularised this position and confirmed that no decision of the king had legal standing unless it was countersigned by the resident superior; the king's control over official appointments was therefore severely curtailed.

Until 1887, Cambodia was administratively linked to Cochinchina. That year, the Indochinese Union, the first step towards unification of France's colonial possessions on the peninsula, was established by decree. The position of governor-general was created, along with the *Conseil Supérieur de l'Indochine*, an advisory board for the general budget. The department of civil affairs now supervised a federated administration system. The Cambodian Protectorate's administration was headed by the resident superior in Phnom Penh (the title *résident général* was dropped in 1889) with residents in the provinces. By 1894 there were ten residencies: Phnom Penh, Kampot, Kompong Thom, Kompong Cham, Kompong Speu, Kratie, Banam, Takeo, Kompong Chhnang, and Pursat.[42] Each residency reflected a rationalisation of the boundaries of the *srok*, and small boundary adjustments continued intermittently throughout the period of the Protectorate. By the early 1920s, there were 14 provinces, or *khet*, corresponding to the 14 residencies.

Perhaps the most significant administrative reform of the Protectorate was the creation of the commune, *khum*, by the *ordonnance royale* of 5 June 1908. The function of the *khum* then, as now, was to form the administrative link between the moral law of the village with its selected chief, an honourable and capable leader acknowledged as such by his fellow villagers, and the bureaucratic commands of the *chauvay srok*, the district chief who was appointed by his provincial governor. From its inception, the commune council was to be an elected body; men and women on the head tax register had the right to vote. Elections did occur, in different communes at different times, according to Henri Locard, although whether or not they sowed the seeds of early democracy is debatable.[43] The organisation of the commune was the object of numerous reforms; Locard notes that there were changes in 1919, 1925, 1931, 1935, and again in 1941 — "an indication that things were not running as smoothly as hoped. French administrators were continuously trying to simplify the intricacies and meanderings of the bureaucracy of the metropolis they were attempting to transplant into the Protectorate." Perhaps this interpretation is correct, or perhaps the Protectorate Administration understood the crucial importance of the *khum* as both supervisor and mobiliser of the villagers, not to mention tax assessor and collector, just as later regimes would, and needed to get the format right.

From the beginning, French rule in Indochina suffered from a lack of consistency, a direct result of the turbulent history of the Third Republic. Virginia Thompson counted 52 transmissions of power in Indochina between 1886 and 1926, observing, "Each new governor has brought his own policy."[44] Cochinchina had 38 changes in that time, with interim governors frequently lasting longer than the titular heads. During those 40 years, Cambodia had no fewer than 22 residents superior. A ministry for colonies was created in 1894, a post held by 46 colonial ministers by 1930, or more than one per year. Even worse, Thompson pointed out, they interfered constantly in colonial affairs.[45] There was a general confusion of laws and sovereignty caused by multiple legislators: the French parliament, the president of the Republic, the minister for colonies, the governor-general of Indochina, and the local governors. The confusion in the delegation of colonial legislative powers, she argued, was matched only by their juridical set up. By way of example, she wrote, "Certain provinces of Cambodia — Battambang, Sisophon, and Siem Reap — are *de jure* colonies but *de facto* protectorates."[46]

Governor-General Sarraut whose three-year term commenced in November 1916 introduced provincial councils, in Cambodia's case, the *Conseil de Résidence*, an elected body with a male franchise restricted to local elites, graduates of the French schools and registered businessmen. Paradoxically, these local representative bodies preceded any form of representation for the *colons*; the European settlers did not receive satisfaction for their long-held demands for representation until 1928, when Pasquier created the *Grand Conseil des Interêts Economiques et Financiers*. Federal in structure and purely advisory in function, it nevertheless gave the taxpayers a voice that was shared equally by French and local representatives following amendments that were made subsequent to the Yenbay revolt of 1931. As the name implies, the council's role was limited to economic and financial matters but at the time of world economic depression, the implementation of important labour legislation initiated by the former governor-general, Alexandre Varenne, and the strong opposition coming from the rubber planters' lobby, the role was a crucial one. In 1930, for example, it adopted in principle the government's labour reforms, including making arbitration of differences between capital and labour compulsory.

As significant as these reforms may have appeared to a liberal European audience, most Cambodians would not have known that they existed, nor could they have comprehended their meaning. Virginia Thompson took some delight in reporting that when the provincial councils were set up, Cambodian representatives were reluctant to attend because they thought it was some new form of *corvée*.[47] The implementation of the labour code was monitored and supervised by Administration authorities, sometimes with the assistance of provincial local officials, but its concerns were largely for immigrant labour employed on the foreign-owned rubber plantations where very few Cambodians were involved. A decree of 29 April 1930, promulgated on 20 June, set up an arbitration council in Indochina. Hereafter, commissions consisting of employers and workers were to reconcile parties in conflict over work contracts and commercial, industrial and agricultural matters. In Cambodia, an order of the governor-general of 16 October 1930 resulted in a single commission for Phnom Penh and Kandal but no issues were submitted, at least during the first two years of its existence.[48]

The French Protectorate had a major impact on the forms, structures and institutions that modern Cambodia would build on, but this impact stopped short of the mass of the people, the villagers who had little contact with the French and who went out of their way to avoid them. The villagers regarded the French the way they had regarded the Vietnamese, as oppressive tax-gatherers and threats to their culture. The French saw the villagers as timid and indolent, yet given to sudden outbursts of rage when provoked as in the case of the assassination of Résident Bardez in Kompong Chhnang in 1925.[49]

In part, this minimal contact was simply a matter of numbers. In 1931, no doubt alarmed by the revolts and street demonstrations of that and the previous year, Governor-General Pasquier sent a circular to the heads of local administration throughout Indochina.[50] He had just completed a tour of the colony and was concerned that in some places there was scant contact between the Administration and the people, "insufficient to permit government representation to take account of the evolution of the thinking of our *protégés*, of their wishes, of practical means to employ to maintain their spirits in the happy state of equilibrium." He continued,

> The basic law of direct contact seems to have been lost by some.... It is important that the Indochinese people have proof that the French representatives, in all circumstances in liaison with them, are good at guiding their efforts and bringing them moral comfort of which they have need in the presence of subversive propaganda which solicits them.

He called on the *chefs de province* to establish frequent, direct contact. In the protectorates, he recognised that the exercise of government had to be performed "in competition with the provincial mandarins." This, however, was to the advantage of both parties, having "the double benefit of maintaining local authorities in their exact role and assuring them of visible collaboration, official and efficacious between the French provincial authority and the native provincial authority." The resident and the provincial dignitaries should examine together, he wrote, "the diverse problems — economic, social and administrative — which are brought to his attention."

The Cambodian resident superior replied promptly in a confidential note, pointing out the obvious fact that there simply were not enough French officials to do the job the governor-general required of them.[51] He appended a table comparing the number of French functionaries of the department of civil affairs in 1914 with the number present in 1931. These figures are for the main provinces only:

Table 1.1 Number of Functionaries of the Civil Services (residents, adjoints and commis européens) in the Main Provinces of Cambodia, 1914 and 1931

Province	1914	1931
Kandal	3	2
Kompong Cham	4	3
Kompong Chhnang	3	2
Kompong Thom	3	2
Prey Veng	4	2
Stung Treng	2	1
Takeo	4	2
Battambang	7	3
Kampot	3	3
Phnom Penh (R.S.)	10	5
Cabinet	4	3
Total	47	28

While the number of French bureaucrats had declined, their volume of work, he complained, had grown and become more complex. Not only were they occupied with the development of provincial services including public works, education, veterinary services, cadastral surveys, agricultural extension and so on, the many residential tribunals, involving mainly the Vietnamese and Chinese sectors of the population, were very time-consuming. In 1930, there were 400 hearings for complex litigations. These matters were as demanding in the provinces as they were in Phnom Penh. The *résident-juge* of Kampot, for example, dealt with 31 criminal procedures in 1930, three more than the regular tribunal of Phnom Penh. These affairs, the resident superior argued, consumed long hours of delicate and fastidious work, continually interrupted by interventions for which the doors of the residencies remained open. Therefore, he stressed,

"There is little time left, in these conditions for the *chef de province* to leave the *chef-lieu* and make contact with the population of the interior, especially in Cambodia where the distances between villages is far ... so he only goes for a specific reason."

There is endless debate about the efficacy of colonial administration and the rights and wrongs, in general, of the colonial system as it operated in the former French Indochina. Colonialism was, of course, abhorrent. It trampled on the historical paths of militarily weaker states, exploited their natural resources and subjected their populations to harsh taxation and the impost and destiny of Western capitalism. On the other hand, the peoples of the states that made up this French construct were the beneficiaries of the policies and practices of some truly visionary and humane governors-general, especially Varenne and Pasquier, and in Cambodia, even at the provincial level there were residents like Desenlis who toiled tirelessly to bring justice to the small people, especially the Tonkinese coolies who laboured on the rubber plantations of Kompong Cham. Centuries of occupation and control by Siam and Vietnam had left little trace; the 90 years of the French Protectorate, on the other hand, would change Cambodia irreversibly.

Population

From the reports of Mouhot and de Carné, the total Cambodian population when the Protectorate Treaty was signed in 1863 was between 750,000 and one million. These estimates presumably did not include the inhabitants of the *srok* under Siamese jurisdiction (roughly 300,000 in 1907), but may have included those of Kampuchea Krom (326,000 in the late 1930s).

The first reliable census was not conducted until 1962. In the intervening years, the French compiled "official statistics" (for taxation purposes) and in 1937 a more thorough population count was undertaken. French economist, Rémy Prud'homme took the results of the 1962 census and, with the help of those available official statistics from the Protectorate Administration, he compiled a population growth chart for the years 1900 to 1975. He started with the figure of 5,740,000 inhabitants, representing the Cambodian population on 1 June according to the 1962 Census and, taking account of immigration, with variable rates of annual growth, he offered the following figures.[52] He rated the results of his method as "doubtful" but reasonable. According to these figures, when Cambodia achieved full independence in 1953, the Cambodian population was around 4.5 million.

Table 1.2 Population of Cambodia, 1900–55

Year	Rate of Annual Increase (%)	Population
1900	1.0	2,057,000
1905	1.0	2,163,000
1910	1.2	2,274,000
1915	1.2	2,414,000
1920	1.4	2,562,000
1925	1.4	2,746,000
1930	1.6	2,944,000
1935	1.8	3,187,000
1940	2.0	3,485,000
1945	2.2	3,847,000
1950	2.4	4,289,000
1955	2.6	4,829,000

It is too simple to say that the Cambodian population more than quadrupled under the French Protectorate. The territorial changes make it difficult to give assessments of this kind, and we do not know if the earlier estimates included all ethnic groups. Most assuredly, however, the Cambodian population grew quite strongly during the ninety years of political and economic stability that the Protectorate provided.

The available literature on Cambodia offers a variety of population estimates. The promotional text *L'Indochine Française Pour Tous* gives the population of Cambodia in 1911 as a very precise 1,634,252 (far lower than Prud'homme's estimate) and again in 1921 as 2,402,585; the source of these figures, however, is not cited.[53] In 1924, it noted, Phnom Penh had a population of 77,000, including 1,145 French; a third of all Phnom Penh's citizens were Chinese and a quarter were Annamites (that is, Vietnamese). Statistics from the Cabinet of the Resident Superior support both the 1921 figure above and Prud'homme's rough estimate, but strengthen them with an ethnic breakdown of Khmer (2,120,000), Chinese (91,000) and Annamite (140,000).[54] There were large groupings of Vietnamese and Chinese in most administrations in that year and especially in Kandal, Svay Rieng, Prey Veng, Takeo, Kampot and Kompong Chhnang. In Phnom Penh itself, the report noted, Cambodians were on the periphery. Demographer Jacqueline Desbarats, referring to (uncited) French administrative records, also puts the total population of Cambodia at approximately 2.5 million in 1921.[55] Her figures for ethnic minorities, however, are different, particularly for the Vietnamese living in Cambodia: 40,000 Chams, 80,000 Annamites and 100,000 Chinese (half of whom were farmers). The population of Phnom Penh, she added, was then estimated at 60,000 and there were some 200,000 Khmer Krom in the western part of Cochinchina.

The census of 28 January 1937 was the first based on individual returns. There is more than a hint of the European concern with eugenics in the way Charles Robequain reported the results. "It would be very desirable," he wrote, "to determine precisely the proportions of these different groups [referring to 'creoles,' 'half-breeds' and those of 'mixed blood']. An estimate of the number of creoles, in particular," he thought, "would make it possible to determine to what degree the white race has been able to take root and establish families in the colony."[56] The number of "pure whites" was approximately 30,000, not quite three-quarters of the category of "European and assimilated" throughout the whole of French Indochina where the total population was 23,030,000.

Cambodia's population had reached 3,046,000 according to the 1937 census.[57] Density was 17 inhabitants per square kilometre although there were major variations according to province. Kandal and Takeo were the most populous provinces with 88 and 83 inhabitants per square kilometre. After them, in order of density were Kompong Cham, Prey Veng and Svay Rieng, with 60, 59 and 52 respectively. Battambang had only 13 people per square kilometre. Throughout the whole country, there were 2,534 Europeans and *assimilés* (that is, with the legal status of Europeans although not necessarily of European origin). There were also 6,000 "Asiatic foreigners" throughout Indochina but mainly in Cochinchina and Cambodia. They were mostly Indians (and thus British subjects) who originated in Madras and the Sind and earned a living through money-lending and brokerage.

In 1937, the vast majority of the population were Khmers (2,596,000), followed by Vietnamese (191,000), Chams (150,466), and Chinese (106,000). When *de jure* independence was granted in January 1949, official statistics recorded 3,750,000 inhabitants in Cambodia.[58] Rémy Prud'homme's estimate was approximately half a million higher than this figure.

Human Development

Strong and steady population growth throughout the 90 years of the Protectorate might merely have reflected the absence of war and the recovery of a people from a long, dark period of uncertainty. A similar "resurrection" as the colonial officials termed it, would occur again in the 1980s under Vietnamese occupation. For genuine development to occur, however, population growth has to be accompanied by lasting improvements in living standards.

Paul Collard lived in Cambodia continuously and worked as a high official for the Administration for 24 years, starting in 1900. Public works, particularly road-construction, was a major activity of his era and he believed that the communication network changed more than just the landscape. "The Cambodian villager of our time no longer shows astonishment or naiveté," he wrote. "He is no longer confined to the corner of the earth where he was born."[59] Bright red laterite roads did crisscross the country by 1924; the road-building programme provided 1,173 kilometres of black-topped *routes coloniales* and 2,220 kilometres of provincial roads.[60] Dykes were dug, maps were charted, a railroad was built from Phnom Penh to Battambang (although the line from Phnom Penh to Saigon was never realized), and the Phnom Penh port was opened. The port represented, for Collard, the commercial emancipation of Phnom Penh. "Cochinchina could not invoke indefinitely its rights to oversee this country," he wrote. "It had enjoyed this situation sufficiently. The benefit that it drew was becoming abusive."[61] There were French dreams of building a seaport on the Gulf of Siam at Ream.

By 1924, it took only five hours to drive from Phnom Penh to Saigon, but the telephone lines between the cities provided almost instant access. There was a telephone network within Cambodia too, although in Collard's time it was still small and limited to just a few southern provinces. Cambodia, via Saigon, was in easy reach of the rest of the world. In 1922 a supplementary steamship service ran between Bordeaux and Saigon; two years later, a new wireless (telegraph) station linked Indochina to France, and in 1929, Saigon was linked to Paris by an air route.

Progress in the health sector was far less spectacular. Charles Robequain commented on changes in the mortality rate in Annam, but whether we can extrapolate from those figures and assume the same result for Cambodia is risky. He noted that French occupation had raised the standard of living in Annam and along with that, the establishment of law and order, and mass vaccination programmes had lowered the mortality rate. In Hanoi and Saigon, in 1937, the birth rate was 40 per 1,000 and the death rate 30 per 1,000. Children under the age of 15 accounted for half of all deaths. The infant mortality rate accounted for between 25 and 30 per cent of all births in those two cities.[62] We can only assume that the infant mortality rate was higher in the countryside. Paul Collard thought that infant mortality in Cambodia was considerable, "one of the reasons why there are so few inhabitants in the kingdom which could easily feed ten times more."[63] He thought there was no indigenous medical science, and no idea of "rational" medicine at all. In 1906, each residency in Cambodia had a medical centre and a native ambulance; one French doctor was assigned to each residency.

The Protectorate is generally reviled for its failure to provide even rudimentary health care for the general populace, but it seems that rural Cambodians were also reluctant to trust Western medicine. In Kompong Cham, for instance, the French doctor at the health centre there lamented that once the Tonkinese workers from the surrounding rubber plantations were admitted to the single building that made up the infirmary's facilities for the sick, the Cambodians deserted it, "even though it had started to get their confidence."[64] This was in 1927, more than 20 years after the provincial health system was established.

Similarly, the Protectorate Administration achieved poorly in the field of education. Early efforts at public schooling, in fact, catered only to the ruling elite. It was not until the appointment of the associationist, Albert Sarraut as governor-general in November 1916 that serious efforts were made to extend formal schooling based on Western principles of education to the general population. The system that evolved in Cambodia was indigenous to the extent that it retained the "native" education that the pagoda schools had provided, but it was supplemented with reforms synonymous with "modern" French education. A teacher-training programme piloted in Kampot province in 1924 was found to be successful and from that point, the new system was expanded throughout the country.[65] Collard thought that the Cambodian education system was well adapted to the political and administrative conditions of Cambodia, observing that "the village corresponds to the primary school or to the pagoda; the secondary school to the provincial capital; the residential school to the residency."[66] Starting in 1925, he added, each Cambodian village would have a school which all Cambodian children would attend for eight to ten years and they would learn, apart from religious study of the sutras, to read, write and count in their national language.

Such optimism was ill-founded. The statistics relating to education are as varied as they are for other sectors of the Administration, but Rémy Prud'homme offers the following table with reference to modernised pagoda schools and private education in Cambodia, using figures from the statistical yearbooks for selected years between 1931 and 1950:

Table 1.3 Education in Cambodia, 1931–50[67]

Year	Primary		Secondary		Technical		Higher	
	Schools	Pupils	Schools	Students	Schools	Students	Schools	Students
1931	3,014	65,000	2	310	2	400	–	–
1936	1,072	56,200	3	370	2	260	–	–
1940	1,300	72,000	3	390	2	320	–	–
1945	1,369	89,000	3	680	3	280	–	–
1950	1,928	183,000	4	1,570	5	280	2	240

Full secondary education was first offered in 1935, and although some technical and administrative education was available in Cambodia, indigenous students wishing to pursue higher education had to travel to Saigon, Hanoi or Paris.[68] These fortunate few were usually the children of the royal families or other members of the elite. By 1950, the year after the granting of *de jure* independence, there were approximately one hundred Khmer students studying in France. Most of them returned to positions of further privilege in the new indigenous government or the business community. A few were caught up in the fervour of leftwing student politics which caused them to question the social system into which they had been born. These radical students, including Pol Pot, Ieng Sary and Khieu Samphan would lead the vanguard revolutionary party that took power in 1975.

It was not only the French education system that nurtured elites. All colonial or other occupying administrations relied heavily on the services of language interpreters. Those Cambodians with the requisite linguistic skills found themselves at great advantage during various episodes of political change in modern Cambodian history. Nicholas Tarling argues that colonial rulers provoked nationalism by providing education but not opportunity. "Education they had to provide," he argues, "if only in the interest of modernisation; but they were less ready to share power with the educated."[69] The rulers' heavy dependence on those educated into the language of the occupying force, however, opened up tremendous opportunities, opportunities which those lucky few would never have been offered in the traditional society. They formed the new elites of colonial societies, and they were generally ambitious, intelligent and modern in their outlook, but committed more to personal advantage than to goals of national development.

Economic Activity

Agriculture, Land and Concessions

Cambodia's economy at the turn of the twentieth century was characterised overwhelmingly by subsistence agriculture. There was, of course, trade in goods, and profits were also made by lending money against future harvests. Trade and usury, as commercial activities, were usually conducted by Chinese Cambodians. Private wealth most certainly existed; high officials, the *okhnya*, were made rich by taxing the surplus product of the farmers and others in their domains or *apanages*, but wealth served the twinned purposes of prestige and power, not the creation of capital. The French Administration regarded the power of the *okhnya*, and the cost of that powerful display as the main impediment to growth:

> The farmer, the sole producer, is crushed under the charges; and the burden becomes for him so pressing that it condemns him to the meanest share while giving means to feed the covetousness of the functionaries. Why should he irrigate a large rice field? Hasn't the lion's share of his crop gone already to the mandarins? All he asks of his soil, however fertile it might be, is subsistence, no more. There is no lack of free land but he keeps himself to the land he cultivates since to increase the size of his land does not increase his revenues.[70]

There was much truth in this interpretation. The Cambodian villager knew instinctively that to hoard wealth was to invite disaster. James Scott has famously described this habit as the "moral economy" of the peasant farmer of Indochina who regards what is left of his harvest as more significant than the amount which must be paid in tax or levy or inflated charges to officials.[71] Over the centuries, however, the officials had also learnt the limits of peasant tolerance. Lines in the sand must have been recognised by both the peasant and the tax-collector alike, and charges were always negotiable, whether for *corvée*, military service, or a portion of the harvest. The official also had to moderate his desire for wealthy display; as explained to the present author in the early 1990s, "We Cambodians accept that an official may own two villas and three cars, but more than that is corruption." The French, on the other hand, could not accept this sort of compromise. Instead, they interpreted the behaviour of the *okhnya* as official corruption and they blamed this corruption for the lack of development, the poor living standards that existed in rural Cambodia, and for the lack of private capital that could be employed for the purpose of economic growth:

There is no need to search elsewhere for the reason of this persistence of the mediocrity of material life that distinguishes the Cambodian of the countryside. It is that which accounts for the total absence of private wealth in the kingdom. The only ones owning some wealth are the functionaries who, placed at the head of very populated provinces, fatten themselves to the detriment of the inhabitants.[72]

Put simply, there was no capital in Cambodia to fund the sort of development envisioned by the French and explained by Paul Collard as: "For its first step, essentially agricultural.... In its second step, transforming its own primary resources. It becomes industrialized. It produces for export and becomes more commercial."[73] Until the First World War, metropolitan capitalists were reluctant to invest in the economic development of French Indochina, even though French capital investments abroad at the turn of the century were second only to those of Britain. Throughout the colony, it was the personal investment of the *colons*, French settlers, and the revenue from taxing the *protégés* which initiated growth. Obviously, given the very small size of the French community in Cambodia and the limits to which subsistence rice-farmers could be squeezed for taxes, alternative sources of capital investment had to be sought in order to develop the country.

In terms of meeting French needs, Cambodia's most valuable natural resource was what the Administration regarded as vacant land. Population density was low, and away from the plains to the south and east of Phnom Penh, density was very low. The solution lay in increasing land values, that is, through capitalised rents. By the time Collard left Cambodia in 1924, however, little had been achieved on this front. The 1884 Convention had made the purchase and transfer of landed property legal but after 60 years of French rule, land registration was still embryonic. The Chinese, perhaps the only section of the society with both the means and the motivation to acquire private property, were prevented legally from doing so by French laws.

This does not mean that Cambodian villagers lacked the notion of land ownership. Land, in effect, belonged to the tiller; as long as he cultivated the land continuously, and had done so for at least three years, he enjoyed usufruct rights and could bequeath the land to his successors. Collard argued that these conditions did not equate with "property" because, in his words:

> If he left it without a crop for three years, he lost all his right to it. He was not then its owner. He had the enjoyment of it, as his children had after him, on the condition of making it produce. This condition met, the land was under the protection of the law and, thus protected,

given to process, sale, and so on. But when this condition ceased to be fulfilled, the field became the pleasure of who took it and cultivated it. It evidently was not property. There is, moreover, a lot of land that is waiting to be developed.[74]

In other words, land had to be commodified, capitalised, in order for development to take place. The concession system had officially begun with Governor-General Paul Doumer's *arrêté* of 26 August 1899 that defined the conditions under which French nationals could apply for rural land concessions in Cambodia.[75] These concessions, awarded provisionally, were for the purposes of agriculture or raising cattle and, as a general rule, were not to be larger than 500 hectares, unless proof was given of the capital needed to develop larger areas. Throughout Indochina, the concession system proved problematic from the beginning. Large areas were awarded provisional titles but lay idle because of insufficient development capital. The Administration lacked the authority required to enforce its regulations until the (second) rubber boom of the mid-1920s made proper implementation of the law essential.

On 19 September 1926, Governor-General Varenne issued a circular containing a series of instructions to accompany his new *arrêté* concerning the *Régime Général des Concessions de Terrains Ruraux en Indochine*.[76] Earlier orders concerning the transfer of public land were no longer adequate in the face of the huge demand. According to the circular, the new general ruling on rural land concessions was in response to the numerous requests for concessions during the previous two years that had been made in "a rather imperious fashion," pressuring the local administrations "to open to colonisation, without delay, vast regions without communication routes and some even impenetrable." The conditions set down in that *arrêté* were passed into law and promulgated by the Governor-General of Indochina on 16 July 1927.[77] Under this ruling, a single concessionaire was entitled to a maximum of 15,000 hectares of land by provisional title, the only restriction being that these areas could not be grouped into a single concession by a single tenant on an area greater than 6,000 hectares.

The effects of this ruling and the impact of the great land rush of the 1920s are illustrated in the following table prepared by the Cabinet of the Cambodian *Résidence Supérieure* for the annual report of 1927–28.[78] The relevant chapter of the report begins, "The total [land] area of Cambodia is 173,625 square kilometres or 17,362,500 hectares. On an area of 1,354,720 hectares occupied in 1928 by colonization of French, indigenous and Asiatic foreigners, 870,494 hectares have already been developed."

Table 1.4 Land Area under Concessions, 1926–28

Year	Area Conceded	Area Developed
1926	878,155ha	674,167ha
1927	1,120,551ha	697,166ha
1928	1,354,720ha	870,494ha

European colonisation, the report added, represented 138,302 hectares which was only around 10 per cent of the total area conceded.

The major difference between concessions granted to "indigenous and Asiatic foreigner" developers and those awarded to Europeans lay in their size. The year 1928–29, for example, was considered an "average year from the point of view of alienation of crown land."[79] During that year, a further 98 provisional concessions were awarded on a total area of 11,000 hectares. Only two of those concessions were larger than 500 hectares, including one of 4,000 hectares for a rubber company. This means that concessions granted to local people were well below 100 hectares in size. Nevertheless, this still represented a large land-holding compared to the typical rice farmer's plot of land which was between one and five hectares. We know little about these indigenous concessionaires, but perhaps we can safely assume that they were highly placed in the local administration and close to the colonial power.

One of Cambodia's most respected intellectuals of the modern era, Hou Yuon, considered this matter in his doctoral thesis of 1955.[80] In 1905, the *apanages* were abolished, but Hou Yuon wondered about the reality of this:

> How could one suggest that our princes, mandarins and high officials of all categories would so casually divest themselves of what they, at the time, considered was the best basis for fortune and honour! It is very probable that they kept some domains for themselves…. One can be certain that [they] do not just live on their former fortunes of silver and gold, on their retirement pensions or on the salary from their new position.[81]

He claimed that the Protectorate Administration conceded a total of 139,559 hectares [*sic*, and presumably 1,395,590 hectares] in 8,532 land grants. From the figures above, approximately 10 per cent of that area, was awarded to a small number of European *sociétés* and rich individuals for plantation agriculture. European concessionaires were almost exclusively powerful limited share companies engaged in the extensive cultivation of rubber and paddy. Battambang, Kampot, Kompong Cham and

Kratie had most requests for concessions, closely followed by Svay Rieng, then Kompong Thom. The figures below are from the annual report for 1927–28:

Table 1.5 Concessions Held by Large Companies, 1927–28

Company	Area of Concession (ha)	Area Developed (ha)
Compagnie du Cambodge	25,900	15,260
Société Indochinoise des Plantations de Mimot	14,000	2,210
Compagnie Générale des Colonies	6,319	3,500
Société des Plantations de Kratie	4,000	–
Compagnie des Caoutchoucs de Padang	6,000	–

Who claimed the other 8,500 grants of land under the Protectorate? Hou Yuon suggested that these grantees represented a new social stratum because the rural concession system signified "a kind of land redistribution."[82] He noted:

> First, it consolidated the economic and social position of the former mandarins and feudal officials, who were able to add to the property they had inherited from the old regime.... And secondly, it facilitated the ascendancy of the advanced elements ... in particular inhabitants of the urban or rural centres where land was valuable.[83]

Undoubtedly these groups constituted the category of "big landowners" in the table below for the years from 1927 to 1930, representing the great land rush in Cambodia:

Table 1.6 Landownership Classification, 1927–30 – Ricefields

Province	Small Landowners (%)		Medium Landowners (%)	Big Landowners (%)	
	0–1 hectares	1–5 hectares	5–10 ha	10–50 ha	>50 ha
Battambang	18.5	57.8	18.3	5.3	0.12
Svay Rieng	12.9	67.4	16.5	3.0	0.22
Prey Veng	28.3	58.7	10.5	2.4	0.14
Kg Cham	48.6	48.2	2.8	0.4	–
Kandal	64.1	34.9	0.9	0.1	0.002

Source: Yves Henry, *L'Economie Agricole de l'Indochine*, reproduced by Hou Yuon in his doctoral thesis.

Poster for the 1906 Colonial Exhibition in Marseille depicts an iconic Khmer royal dancer

We do not know the purposes to which these indigenous concessions were put. There was no surplus agricultural workforce to engage in extensive cultivation and it is unlikely that indigenous concessionaires would have employed migrant Tonkinese labour as the French-owned plantations did. Members of the ruling elite c. 2000 own relatively large and highly valuable tracts of land which are put to little productive use, either for speculation or for "hobby" cultivation of tropical fruits and other delicacies, including ponds of carp and exotic fish. These *chamcar* are usually tended by family groups of loyal retainers. It is probable that they are following a tradition fostered by the French concession system.

The productive activity of the European rubber plantations, on the other hand, was both hectic and well documented. On the eve of the Second World War, at the peak of French colonisation, Cambodian rubber plantations produced 16,500 tonnes of raw product which represented around one-third of total rubber production for Indochina. In 1938, the plantations received an average price of ten francs per kilogram for their rubber on the international market; the plantations, the Protectorate Administration reported, were doing well.[84] At 31 May 1939, there were 13,921 migrant workers on the plantations, almost all from Tonkin (fewer than 3 per cent of them were from Annam, and under 10 per cent of the total number were women). Before the war, Cambodians were only employed on the plantations for land-clearing or for casual labour.

Rubber and paddy were not the only cash crops. In the 1930s, "people have feverishly cleared all land suitable for maize," the Administration reported.[85] Vast areas of good alluvial land remained unexploited but the problem, French officials recorded, was demographic; in fact, the problem facing extensive agriculture was not so much a dearth of people as a lack of an agricultural labour force in Cambodia. To surmount this obstacle to development, the Protectorate authorities attempted to create agricultural cooperatives, "but timidly and only in the most advanced provinces because the temperament of Cambodians is essentially individualistic."[86] A cooperative on 3,000 hectares of redlands at Chamcar Krauch in Kompong Cham province was established in 1938. In its first year it produced 400 tonnes of maize and 53 tonnes of cotton. A model farm for the production of coffee and diverse crops was set up on 130 hectares within this cooperative. Another cooperative for sugar palm production was established in Kandal in December 1938 and a third was planned for paddy production in Battambang.

There is no doubt that cultivated land areas increased during the time of the Protectorate, in line with the increase in rural population. There were also some attempts at diversification and experimentation with introduced crops and animal stock as well as new methods of cultivation. The cash incentives system encouraged small-scale development of both agricultural and domestic animal production. Starting in 1905, amounts were fixed annually, by an *arrêté* of the resident superior according to budget availability.[87] Incentives were tied to good practice, extension of cultivation and for results proportional to the area cultivated. These incentives, and the experimentation that went along with them, however, applied only to farmers with holdings of ten hectares or more and stopped well short of the traditional rice farmer. Reporting on Cambodian agricultural production in 1922, that is, before the boom, Collard provided the following statistics:

Table 1.7 Main Agricultural Products and Exports, 1922[88]

Product	Quantity Produced	Quantity Exported
Paddy	450,000 tonnes	
Cotton	5,000 tonnes	
Maize	8,000 tonnes	8,000 tonnes
Tobacco	600 tonnes	
Palm sugar	6,500 tonnes	2,500 tonnes
Kapok	350 tonnes	306 tonnes
Indigo paste	1,500 tonnes	
Groundnuts	4,500 tonnes	
Legumes	5,500 tonnes	
Sesame	68,440 kg	
Soybeans	339,856 kg	

At that point, just before his departure from the country, Collard noted that an irrigation study had been conducted for drought-prone areas of Kompong Speu and Kandal using water from the Prek Thnot; in those provinces, demonstration farms had been set up to popularise the use of chemical fertilisers and to study plant diseases. Despite the positive rhetoric of Administration reports, however, it seems that there was little genuine change in the methods of agriculture practised by the vast majority of the population. Productivity in paddy production changed very little, if the following figures are any indication:

Table 1.8 Paddy Cultivation, 1900–50[89]

Year	Area Cultivated (hectares)	Workers	Production (tonnes)	Yield (tonnes/hectare)	Yield (tonnes/worker)
1900	400,000	935,000	560,000	1.40	0.59
1905	450,000	980,000	540,000	1.20	0.55
1910	500,000	1,010,000	550,000	1.10	0.60
1915	570,000	1,040,000	627,000	1.10	0.60
1920	620,000	1,080,000	682,000	1.10	0.63
1925	700,000	1,120,000	735,000	1.05	0.66
1930	800,000	1,160,000	816,000	1.06	0.70
1935	920,000	1,220,000	920,000	1.00	0.76
1940	1,100,000	1,280,000	1,012,000	0.92	0.79
1945	1,100,000	1,340,000	935,000	0.95	0.70
1950	1,660,000	1,400,000	1,580,000	0.95	1.13

From these figures, it is clear that the cultivated area certainly grew but yield in terms of product actually declined. We can excuse the figures after 1940 on the basis of insecurity, but if, as Prud'homme claims the figures for 1930 are highly reliable, then the overall record is not a shining one. Referring to rice farmers and merchants throughout Indochina, Virginia Thompson judged, "Up to the [Second World] War it may be said that they made almost no effort to better the quantity and the quality of their rice, nor to remedy its lack of homogeneity by improved methods of seed selection or classification."[90] The failure to increase rice production, she noted, was disguised by rises in the price of paddy that were not immediately followed by increased living costs. Except for Cochinchina, the purchasing power of "the natives" remained unchanged until the Great Slump brought matters to a head in 1931–32.

Cambodia achieved full independence from France in November 1953. In terms of agriculture, the vast majority of the farming population was still engaged in subsistence rice cultivation; some farmers supplemented their income with the sale of cash crops including maize, pepper and soybeans. Rubber was a major foreign exchange earner but there was no family-scale rubber production; technically speaking, there were no rubber smallholdings that were below 100 hectares in size. The rubber industry remained foreign-owned and most profits from the sale of the rubber crop were also exported.

The first harvest of independent Cambodia, for the 1953–54 season was estimated at around 1,463,000 tonnes by the Direction of Agriculture. Areas harvested and paddy production in the rice-growing provinces of Cambodia for the years 1952–53 and 1953–54 are tabulated below:

Table 1.9 Area Harvested and Production of Paddy in Cambodia, 1952–54[91]

Provinces	Area Harvested (hectares)		Production (tonnes)	
	1952–53	1953–54	1952–53	1953–54
Battambang	140,000	143,000	238,000	240,000
Pursat	29,000	36,000	46,400	57,000
Kompong Chhnang	108,000	113,000	140,400	147,000
Kompong Thom	70,000	69,000	91,000	80,000
Kandal	72,000	74,000	86,400	80,000
Kompong Speu	81,000	81,000	89,000	89,000
Takeo	144,000	158,000	155,000	185,000
Kampot	101,000	103,000	131,300	103,000
Prey Veng	170,000	181,000	204,000	208,000
Svay Rieng	105,000	117,000	115,500	152,000
Kratie	12,000	11,000	14,000	15,000
Siem Reap	40,000	46,000	48,000	56,000
Stung Treng	2,000	2,000	2,000	2,000
Total	1,116,000	1,175,000	1,411,000	1,463,000

Source: Ministry of National Economy/reproduced in the *Bulletin Bi-Hebdomadaire, Chambre Mixte de Commerce et d'Agriculture du Cambodge* (hereafter BCMCAC), June 1955.

Between the outbreak of the Second World War and the granting of full independence, Cambodian agriculture suffered setbacks, particularly regarding the cultivation of cash crops. Maize, for instance, which farmers had feverishly planted in the 1930s, was in 1953 grown on a much smaller scale and production then was less than 200,000 tonnes. Cambodian cotton recovered briefly from the sharp decline of the Great Slump of the early 1930s and benefited from the demand created by the Second World War, but annual production was only 200–300 tonnes per year by the time the French left. Other important crops and their production figures in 1953 are listed below:

Table 1.10 Areas Cultivated and Production of Main Crops of Cambodia, 1953

Crops	1953		
	Area (hectares)	Production (tonnes)	Yield (t/ha)
Rice (paddy)	1,175,000	1,463,000	1.24
Maize (red, white)	120,000	180,000	1.5
Beans	50,000	20,000	0.4

Table 1.10 continued

Crops	1953		
	Area (hectares)	Production (tonnes)	Yield (t/ha)
Soybeans	13,000	80,000	0.61
Cotton (unginned)	230	350	1.5
Groundnuts (in shell)	6,000	4,500	0.75
Castor (seeds)	350	250	0.7
Tobacco (dried)	8,000	5,500	0.68
Pepper (black)	300	1,200	4
Kapok (ginned)	5,000	3,500	0.7
Mulberry (raw silk)	30	20	0.6

Source: Ministry of National Economy/BCMCAC, June 1955.

Fisheries

The concession system extended to the freshwater systems in the form of fishing lots. The domestic annual fish harvest was enormous: 130,000 tonnes per year, of which around 80,000 tonnes was processed, mainly dried. In 1941, a freshwater fisheries cooperative was created in order to centralise the collection of dried fish destined for export, especially to the markets of Southeast Asia. The following tonnages of dried fish were gathered from various companies. Once again, the figures reflect the instability caused by the First Indochina War and the year of diplomatic struggle with Thailand, 1950–51:

Table 1.11 Dried Fish from Freshwater Product, 1940–53

Years	Tonnes	Years	Tonnes
1940–41	10,087	1947–48	4,770
1941–42	11,092	1948–49	4,857
1942–43	15,353	1949–50	4,175
1943–44	6,774	1950–51	17 (*sic*)
1944–45	4,739	1951–52	7,729
1945–46	6,190	1952–53	7,647
1946–47	9,342	1953–54	10,150

Source: BCMCAC, June 1955.

The same source refers to an annual production of between 20,000 and 30,000 tonnes for the maritime fishing industry. Most of the catch was consumed locally, some was sold to Thailand, Indonesia and Singapore and a small amount, between 3,000 to 6,000 tonnes, was dried. A further small quantity was used for the manufacture of *nuoc mam* (fish sauce), shrimp paste and dried shrimp.

Before independence, a European processing factory with around 60 workers was set up near the fisheries in the bay of Kompong Som. During the period of insecurity it halted production.

Forestry

The wealth of Cambodia's forests is not only in its tropical hardwood timber. Zhou Daguan listed some of its precious products: the resins, perfume oils, dye woods, lacquer wood, and so on. In 1924, just before thousands of hectares of lowland forest were felled to make way for rubber plantations and other agro-commercial ventures, Paul Collard made an intricate list of the raw materials that flowed from the forest. "The Cambodian forest is no longer an unutilised fortune," he boasted. "Between 1 July 1922 and 30 June 1923, it brought to the budget 604,204 piastres being, at the average rate of 10 francs to the piastre, 6,042,240 francs."[92]

Collard's forest products were far more pedestrian than those Zhou had described, but they were obviously just as valuable. Hundreds of thousands of bundles of firewood powered the steamboats, fuelled the distilleries, brickworks, furnaces and new factories. "Also leaving these forests," he continued, "are 45,000 quintals (100kg) of *bois de taour* which Cambodians turn into excellent charcoal, 50,000 cubic metres of bamboo, 462,000 kilograms of resins, 88,700 *touques* of wood oil, 1,255 kilograms of wild rubber, 490,000 kilograms of rottan, 156,741 kilograms of *noix vomique*, 340,200 kilograms of bark and 40,800 kilograms of various seeds."

The Forestry Service of the Protectorate Administration was also, it seems, committed to good stewardship of the forests. When Collard left the kingdom, there were 167 forestry reserves, and a further 16 were under review. In total, these reserves would have totalled slightly less than one million hectares.

Official figures for the final years of the Protectorate put forest cover at ten million hectares, including dense forest, glade forest and flooded forest. In the following table are the figures for forestry production during the years 1952 and 1953, with annual averages calculated for the period 1944 to 1953.

Table 1.12 Forestry Production, 1952–54 with Annual Averages, 1944–53

Foresty Product	1952	1953	1954	Annual Average (1944–53)
Timber, cubic metres, of which	247,390	217,911	248,000	190,272
– luxury timber	1,653	2,310	–	2,371
– first category	51,621	36,964	–	44,517
– second category	181,802	169,213	–	126,022
– third category	3,340	3,598	–	6,276
– fourth category	8,974	5,826	–	11,085
Fuelwood (in bundles)	496,724	394,439	400,000	470,045
Coke from wood (in tonnes)	24,391	30,736	24,000	14,559

Source: Service des Eaux et Forêts du Cambodge/BCMCAC, June 1955.

It is interesting to note that the annual average cut of around 200,000 cubic metres during the last decade of the Protectorate remains the optimum yield from Cambodia's remaining forests that is recommended by international sponsors such as the World Bank.

Industry and Services

Industry lagged far behind agriculture when the French finally left in 1953. Paul Collard had envisioned the second stage of development as the processing or manufacturing of the country's own raw materials, that is, adding value to the primary product. There was a little of this type of economic activity, as has been demonstrated above with relation to fish processing and some forest products, but this industry differed little from the artisanal trades which had existed when the French arrived. It is fair to say that the French ignored industry, preferring to concentrate all their efforts on agriculture, locked as they were into a stagist approach to development.

The industrial establishments that existed in 1953 were recent, some of them dating only from the Second World War. For the most part, they were oriented towards the manufacture of consumption items from materials produced in the country, such as the rice mills and distilleries. A few industrial enterprises, however, were working with primary materials imported from abroad with a view to transforming them into products destined to be sold in the country. For example, the weaving factories imported silk or cotton thread and made woven cloth for local consumption; printeries imported paper and the foundries worked foreign metals.

The table below presents the main industries in Cambodia in 1951 and 1952. The figures for the number of establishments appear to be highly unreliable, but they do give some idea of the scale of industrial activity occurring in Cambodia on the eve of full independence.

Table 1.13 Main Industries in Cambodia, 1951–52

Type of Industry	No. of Establishments 1951	No. of Establishments 1952
Rice milling and de-husking	47	285
Distilling	12	–
Palm sugar refining	22	31
Sawmilling (manual, mechanical)	178 (170 manual)	158
Charcoal burning	335	64
Electricity generating	17	
Brick and tile manufacture	208	88
Food paste preparation	21	
Tanning	5	2
Soap making	14	3
Fish preservation	19	3
Soy sauce production	5	10
Syrups	4	
Printeries	11	
Glassworks	1	
Paper mills	1	
Silkweaving factories	2	
Foundries	3	
Mechanical repairs	16	2
Electrical repairs (and rewinding)	5	
Nickelplating	3	
Button making	1	
Working in tiles, brick and cement	2	1
Potteries	11	
Chandlery	10	2
Shoe repairs	16	1
Dyeing	6	3
Lapidary	7	
Jewellery	116	
Carpentry	20	8
Smithies	4	
Tinsmiths	17	3
Koh Sautin blanket-making	1,000 (approx.)	
Tailors/dressmakers	9,000	
Marble sculptures	25	
Leatherwork	15	
Iceworks	6	54
Soft drinks	7	

Source: *Bulletin Mensuel de la Banque Nationale du Cambodge,* March 1955, reproduced in BCMCAC, June 1955.

Not all of these industries were foreign-owned. Local Chinese businessmen owned the distilleries and usually also owned and operated the rice-mills and the ice works that were spread throughout the country. Silk weaving and cloth dyeing, however, were traditional Khmer family industries. Khmer artisans also excelled in carving marble, working leather and silversmithing.

Apart from traditional occupations, it is irrelevant to discuss the division of labour on the eve of independence. There was no labour force that was distinct from family farming or the small workshops and mills which were owner-operated and run on family lines or with hired workers who identified more with a patron-client relationship than with formal labour relations.

As noted in the section on agriculture, the chief (perhaps sole) employer of contractual labour in Cambodia was the rubber plantation industry. The first world rubber boom occurred in 1910 and this necessitated the introduction of a labour law which applied to the whole colony and remained in force until the end of the First World War. The boom years of the 1920s, and the alarming stories of abuse on the plantations which scandalised metropolitan voters, gave rise to Varenne's *arrêté* which was issued on 25 October 1927. The legislation was applicable "to all indigenes of both sexes from the various countries of Indochina or foreign Asiatics who, recruited in Indochina or their country of origin, sell by contract their services for salary to a public administration or an establishment engaged in agriculture, industry or mining. It is equally applicable to those who hire them." (Article 1)[93] A federal Labour Inspectorate oversaw the implementation of the conditions set out in the ruling. In 1933, the legislation was completed by regulating the status of free labour. This very important *arrêté* remains the basis of the current labour law in Cambodia. There was, however, one very important gap in the legislation that was never filled. The law only ever applied to labour relations between foreign employers and their workers. There was, apparently, never any attempt to regulate contracts between local employers and their staff.

In 1937, *corvées* were finally and unconditionally abolished throughout the Union. The Labour Code was thus completed and promulgated in January 1937.

Foreign Trade, Aid, Investment and Debt

The Indochinese Union was formed in 1887 as French economic theories were tending towards protectionism and to the creation of a close tariff union. In 1892, Indochina was declared an "assimilated" colony and the economic principle of *l'exclusif* was applied to all foreign trade. Under this tariff arrangement, products of the *Métropole* could enter the countries of the Union free of charge while those of other countries were subject to the same tariffs as in France. In return, Indochina could export to France without being charged a tariff.

While this arrangement suited the planters who were guaranteed a market for their rubber, it was totally unrelated to the needs of indigenous commerce and industry which, naturally, was bound up with the markets of East and Southeast Asia, particularly China which was a major rice market. The colony was placed in the invidious position of being "protectionist as exporter and free trader as importer" and in both cases, Virginia Thompson noted, "she came out at the small end."[94]

Exports from Indochina were almost entirely raw materials. Rice was the main export, chiefly from Cochinchina, followed by minerals, maize, fish and rubber. On the eve of the Second World War, the countries of the Far East, particularly China, rivalled France as the leading customer for these goods, but Chinese goods were charged the 15 per cent tariff when they entered the colony rendering them uncompetitive. The principal imports at that time were food and drinks, perfume, textiles, medicines, machinery and petrol, luxury items consumed by French settlers or the wealthy local elites. "The tariff regime has succeeded, throughout its Protean forms, in reserving whole-heartedly to France 58 per cent of the import trade of the colony. France sells much more to the colony than she buys from it," Thompson recorded.[95]

Philippine trade protectionism severely harmed one under-reported export from Cambodia, that of live cattle. Cambodia has long been unique in Southeast Asia for its cattle herds, most notably on the plain to the south and east of Phnom Penh, in Takeo, Kandal and Prey Veng provinces. The main market was the Philippines and exports reached their peak in 1910 with about 40,000 head. Tariffs closed the Philippine market in 1911 and sales to Singapore and Hong Kong were insufficient to make up the shortfall. By 1937, exports had dropped to only 15,000 head.[96]

In 1937, the total value of Cambodia's exports was a modest 78.9 million piastres but growing. Maize was the most valuable export earner that year, closely followed by paddy, fish and rubber. The following year, the last before the outbreak of the war in Europe, Cambodia's exports were worth 94.1 million piastres.[97]

We are warned not to read too much into figures describing the export of food crops such as paddy and fish, and rice in particular. Virginia Thompson, for one observed, "One curious phenomenon of Indochina's commerce is the slight apparent relationship between the country's productivity and the statistics of its commercial prosperity." By way of example, she wrote of a drought that ruined the rice crop in Tonkin in 1887, yet exports increased appreciably that year. "A rise in imports," she wrote, "may simply mean that the number of functionaries has increased, or that the public works department has ordered materials which have been covered by a loan."[98] Hou Yuon shared this scepticism and made light of statistics published in France in 1948 concerning the volume of paddy exports from Indochina before the Second World War and the commentary that read in part, "The exportable surplus comes from the difference between production and internal consumption."[99] He argued that the exportable surplus reflected the difference between production and what he called "solvent internal demand." "For how else," he asked, "can both the undernourishment of the masses of the people and the existence of a large export quantity be explained? The latter is only possible because the peasants remain underfed and financially destitute."[100]

By 1953, while the First Indochina War was still raging, only Cambodia and Cochinchina were exporting rice and derivatives. One part of those exports was needed to make up the deficit in Northern and Central Vietnam, and then Laos; the remainder was available for export abroad. The following table describes neither "surpluses" nor "exports", but simply movements of paddy out of Cambodia in the three years before full independence was won. The figures are derived from various sources and are not exact:

Table 1.14 Movement of Paddy, Rice and Derivatives from Cambodia, 1951–53 (in '000 tonnes)

Destination	1951	1952	1953
South Vietnam	184	102	20
North and Central Vietnam	11	20	13
Vietnam	195	122	33
Abroad	53	88	100
Total	248	210	133

Source: BCMCAC, January 1954.

The trend signifying greater independence for Cambodia away from the big markets of Cochinchina and towards foreign markets of its own choosing is quite marked in these figures. A further trend, not shown, was that from exports in the form of paddy to value-added milled rice.

What is more, exports were leaving directly from the port of Phnom Penh rather than via the ports of Saigon. On the other hand, export volumes were noticeably reduced. "This important reduction," the source notes, "reflects the various difficulties that commercialization of Cambodian rice has met both domestically and abroad."[101] Nonetheless, this small level of commercial independence was important for Cambodia which was about to take full control of its own affairs. Rubber, however, continued to be transported to Saigon before it was classified and exported abroad. It was only in mid-2004 that Cambodian rubber was finally regarded internationally as a product separate from that of the former Cochinchina and marketed directly from Phnom Penh.

Virginia Thompson estimated that in a normal pre-depression year, 40 million piastres were sent out of Indochina. Some of that represented profits made by French companies in Indochina and repatriated to pay stockholders, while a further amount was exported to China as commercial profits. An annual sum went directly from the general budget to the French budget to pay for the military defence of Indochina. In rough perspective, the sum of 40 million piastres represented approximately half the total value of Cambodia's exports in 1937.

Altogether, five main loans were raised in France to fund the public works programme in the colony but the public debt was fairly light by the time Indochina ceased to exist.

Public Finance, Banking and Credit

When Paul Collard retired as a colonial official in 1924, the French Protectorate of Cambodia was 60 years old. He left before the brief, but spectacular economic boom that preceded the Great Slump which affected the colony rather late, in 1931 or 1932, and the confusing years of the Second World War when Vichy French officials maintained colonial rule despite the presence of the occupying Japanese military forces, and the final bitter years leading up to full independence for Cambodia in November 1953. Those first 60 years were by no means a smooth ride for the Administration, although it can be argued that they represented a period of bureaucratic consolidation.

One important battle in that consolidation process involved wresting control of public finances from the court and the high officials and placing them firmly in the hands of the Administration. "Taxes," Hou Yuon wrote, "strike the same terror in the heart of the peasant as plague or cholera."[102] The taxes that the Administration collected from the villagers were the tax on produce, that is, paddy, the harvests from the market gardens (*chamcar*) and palm sugar, and the personal or head tax. In addition to these taxes, the villager owed 90 days' labour in *corvée* to the court. In 1890, the king was forced to surrender the tax on rice exported from each of the provinces and these revenues were returned directly to the treasury. Two years later, all taxes were centralised, in theory at least, in the *Trésor Unique du Royaume* according to the terms of the contract of 1 January 1892. The king was placed on a civil list and the *okhnya luong*, the high provincial officials, were required to direct all revenues to the treasury. In fact, there were insufficient French authorities in the provinces to oversee the contract and old practices prevailed, much to the disgust of officials like Collard:

> How is this tax assessed? The royal envoy (*okhnha luong*) does it as arbitrarily as he can ... with the complicity of the *bamro khet*, the [provincial] governor's delegate. They are both skilled at subtracting an important part of the total estimate of the tax from the Treasury. So as not to reduce the king's part too much, they have to levy the burden more heavily on the *réas* [the ordinary people]. The *réas* are always the victims, the eternal victims. And what of the *corvées* demanded by the palace? The governor calls for the *corvée*, offers exemption to those who can pay, shares the sum thus raised with the royal envoy and sends to the king only those people without resources who cannot find the means to exempt themselves.[103]

The head tax was assessed and collected by the commune. Collard praised at length the honesty and transparency of the *mésrok* who was elected to the position of commune chief, "thus escaping the caprices of the provincial governor."[104] The 1908 administrative reform that created the commune council, the *krom-chomnum*, according to Collard, greatly increased the revenues of the budget. Other income was earned through customs and excise, registration, and industrial exploitation; the last mentioned surely included those capitalised rents already discussed from the sale of land concessions and fishing lots.

The revenues thus collected were spent mainly on administration and public works, especially the construction of roads and bridges of which the Administration was very proud. Just before he left the colony, Collard remarked, "If it has been possible to achieve a great material effort, it is thanks to a corresponding financial effort. Expenses in 1922 by the territorial jurisdiction of Cambodia, by the local budget and the general budget of Indochina was 3,902,255 piastres which represents at the rate of 10 francs, the sum of 39,022,550 francs."[105] As we have seen, very little went into services for the majority of the taxpayers, the villagers, least of all in the form of public health and education.

Throughout the whole of Indochina, it was only in Cochinchina that local merchants and large landowners had the capacity to save. These incipient capitalists were generally involved in industries related to rice, its production, transport, milling and export. Credit services, offered by banks or by individuals, represented a further opportunity for profit. Nevertheless, capital accumulation was very restricted. Virginia Thompson estimated that in a normal year, such as 1931, "the country's possibility of self-enrichment could be valued at only 30 million piastres."[106]

The Bank of Indochina was founded in 1875 with monopoly privileges. In 1927, *Credit Populaire Agricole* was established with loans financed by the Bank of Indochina that were backed by the guarantee of the governor-general. Finally, in 1942, the Office of Popular Credit was formed, consisting of five sections (rural, craft, maritime, small industries and rural settlement). A local Committee of Popular Credit operated in each country of the Union. The credit services, however, were very limited both in terms of accessibility (there were only seven outlets for the whole of Cambodia) and also in terms of the amount of credit available. Hou Yuon complained that the loans that were advanced by the Office of Popular Credit were used for commercial speculation rather than for productive investment.[107] He argued that the loans from the agricultural banks went to merchants, small industrialists and to landlords. "In effect, the size of the average loan (510 piastres in 1950 and 757 piastres in 1951) leaves no doubt about its destination."[108] In any case, he added, the advances made by the Office of Popular Credit were smallest during the season of heavy work, May to July, the time when most investment was needed by the peasant farmer. "There is no investment of funds," he stressed. "Modern capitalists deliberately shun productivity in favour of more secure and lucrative commercial speculation and usury."

Conclusions

Until the Second World War reached its eastern borders, the Cambodian economy benefited from the protracted period of peace and stable governance provided by the Protectorate. The restitution of territory and formal recognition of the boundaries of the Cambodian state allowed the French Administration to extend its jurisdiction (and its tax collectors) to its farthest reaches. This reach, however, was more in distance than in depth. The residencies were so poorly staffed and over-worked that whatever power and influence the French exerted at the local level was mainly bureaucratic and fell far short of the village where the vast majority of Khmers lived. The villagers resentfully paid their taxes, but otherwise had little contact with the French. Such contact might have come through the education system or at the provincial hospital, but these social services were vastly under-funded and poorly attended by ordinary Cambodians. Public works came to Cambodians mainly in the form of roads which must have benefited the villagers, both in terms of security and in access to markets, but whose immediate impact would have been in burdensome *corvée*.

Certainly the area under cultivation increased substantially, at least in line with population growth. Distribution of those lands brought under cultivation, however, was skewed by the foreign owned and operated plantation system, particularly the rubber plantations which averaged between 4,000 and 6,000 hectares in size. Paddy production increased substantially and Cambodia was exporting rice at the end of the Protectorate period, although not in great quantities.

At the same time, methods of production and marketing changed very little. At the end of the Protectorate, the typical Cambodian rice farmer still cultivated only that area of land which could be tilled by his family unit and which, in turn, produced sufficient rice for his family's immediate needs. According to the law, the farmer could own his land outright, not simply enjoy usufruct rights, but the cadastral system was embryonic when the French left. Land titles, then as now, existed to protect and benefit the rich, and it is unlikely that a common rice farmer possessed any proof of ownership of the land he worked. Chronic indebtedness to the local money-lender was still the rule rather than the exception, despite some small attempts by the state to provide agricultural credit. Rural living standards changed very little. If Cambodian farmers were not actually starving, neither were they prosperous. Infant mortality, that critical indicator of socio-economic change, remained very high.

The elite class, made up of high officials who derived their power from the court, suffered few setbacks under the French, although it must be said that the French did attempt by various ways and means to curb their power and the excesses of their power. Corruption, however, merely found new avenues to thrive. It can be argued that the Protectorate provided those novel opportunities and nurtured a new elite class. About eight per cent of Cambodia's land surface was granted in concessions under the Protectorate, and 90 per cent of that area was awarded to "indigenous and Asiatic foreigner" concessionaires. These applications would, necessarily, have been made via interpreters and locally hired officials. The concession system must have represented the "pot of gold" for these men.

The concessionaires, in turn, profited from the cash incentives scheme put in place by the French to develop the land or, alternatively, from speculation in the land itself. Their children, in turn, benefited from French education and scholarships to advance themselves in the administration. As noted previously, a handful of these scholarship recipients would later use their education in modern Western political thought to question and even overturn their own society's institutions.

For the most part, the Protectorate left those existing institutions intact and there was minimal change in social property relations. Despite very liberal labour laws enacted in the late 1920s and the 1930s, and their effective implementation on the rubber plantations of Kompong Cham, indigenous labour relations were not changed from their traditional patron-client pattern. Industrialisation was a second, perhaps even a third stage in the Protectorate's scheme of modernisation for the Cambodian economy. The French reasoned that agriculture should develop first, but apart from plantation agriculture which was foreign-owned, for foreign industrial purposes, and for the profit of foreign shareholders, there was little capital investment in local agriculture. There was, therefore, no industrialisation of the local economy and, by corollary, there existed no industrial proletariat. Because agriculture hardly moved beyond the subsistence level, there was no surplus agricultural workforce even to supply labour for the rubber plantations. The Second World War saw the repatriation of approximately half of the imported Tonkinese labour on the Cambodian rubber plantations and their replacement with Cambodian labour, but it was far too late in the history of the Protectorate to speak of an indigenous labour force.

By the end of the Protectorate, therefore, we cannot speak even of incipient capitalism in Cambodia. A very small sector of the economy, that represented by the rubber plantations, was capitalised, but there was almost no local participation in that sector.

French officials like Paul Collard were captivated by the charm of rural Cambodian life and seemed reluctant to affect it in any fundamental way. For all their rhetoric about *mise en valeur*, colonial economic development was reserved for the benefit of French investors and almost deliberately confined to isolated, gated spaces like the rubber plantations of the eastern plateaux. Some Cambodians who actively fought for their country's independence intended to change all that.

(Front view)

(Reverse view)

Five hundred riel note of the Sangkum period, in circulation 1953 to 1974

(*Front view*)

(*Reverse view*)

One riel note of the Sangkum depicting shipping

Fifty riel note of the Sangkum depicting fishermen

CHAPTER

2

Post-Independence Economic Change, 1953-69

[The monarchy and the Buddhist religion] are the irreplaceable factors of unity, but they must be complemented by the birth or rebirth of a constructive dynamism permitting the country to engage in the mode of modernisation.

Prince Norodom Sihanouk[1]

Between 1947 and 1954, Cambodia, like the other countries of French Indochina, was wracked by political insecurity. Much of the insecurity was caused by brigandage and warlordism and some of it by Viet Minh activity in collaboration with a few Khmer *Issarak* (independence) groups of similar political persuasion. Jean Delvert was conducting his seminal study in Cambodia at the time and he gave eyewitness accounts of the impact of the war between the French expeditionary forces and the Khmer Viet Minh on human settlement patterns. Rural populations in the eastern rice-growing provinces of Cambodia, especially Kampot, Takeo and Kompong Cham, were displaced and then regrouped along major roads. The typically dispersed habitat of the Cambodian farmers gave way, Delvert wrote, to very grouped habitat and once peace was restored it was rare for the farmers to return to their former dwellings. "The main advantage in their eyes," he suggested, "is not from regroupment in itself as groupment on a communication route; in future, they will benefit from all the advantages of travelling."[2]

Generally speaking, the struggle for independence was not a widespread or mass movement. King Norodom Sihanouk claimed that it was his "royal crusade," a series of diplomatic manoeuvres, that won political and military independence for Cambodia in November 1953, about eight months before the political settlement achieved at the Geneva Conference ended the First Indochina War. On 1 January 1955, independence was completed when Cambodia won full sovereignty in monetary, commercial and financial affairs, and before the end of that year, the currencies of Cambodia, Laos and Vietnam were effectively separated from the piastre.

By 1954, it was not only the member states of *Indochine* that had regained their independence; throughout South and Southeast Asia, as well as in Africa and the Middle East, former colonial possessions were demanding, and winning or still fighting for freedom from foreign domination. Consequently, by 1960, apart from the main contenders in the Cold War arena, there was also a "Third World" consisting of some forty newly independent states with a total population of 800 million that united with older nations like those in Latin America with a shared colonial past in demanding equal participation in global economic prosperity and social justice for their citizens. In the tense Cold War environment, instability caused by rapid decolonisation made the threat of social revolutionary movements loom large. Modernisation, those on the right argued, would contain the threat of communism. Michael Latham notes, "Theorists placed Western, industrial, capitalist democracies, and the United States in particular, at the apex of their historical scale and then set about marking off the distance of less modern societies from that point.... [T]hey stressed the ways the United States could drive 'stagnant' societies through the transitional process."[3]

At the beginning of 1955, King Norodom Sihanouk abdicated in order to take full executive control of the government. Former contending political parties were brought together under one umbrella political movement, the *Sangkum Reastr Niyum* (Popular Socialist Community), led by the now Prince Sihanouk. By shrewdly manipulating the official foreign policy of neutrality, the prince tried to steer the economy towards modernisation while avoiding his country being drawn into the increasingly complex political and military conflict that had developed across the border in South Vietnam. These efforts would inevitably fail, but for about a decade, the Sangkum delivered both progress and hope for a peaceful future. For the people, it restored the prestige of their country within the international community. Among older Cambodians, the Sangkum is regarded nostalgically, if not entirely accurately, as Cambodia's aspirational model for economic prosperity.

Policies

Although Cambodia was politically and commercially independent of France by the end of 1955, foreign trade and the banks were still in foreign hands, largely French and British. The production of electrical energy, the supply of petroleum products and the water supply were controlled by foreigners, as were the few major industrial establishments. The big rubber plantations, the principal source of foreign currency revenues, were the property of foreigners. National infrastructure, including roads, bridges and irrigation systems, had been neglected during the period of insecurity and was in need of repair. The French had never realized their plan for a deepwater port on the coast, and Cambodian exports from the port of Phnom Penh still had to transit an increasingly unstable South Vietnam.

Genuine independence required that administration and services should be staffed by Cambodian personnel, but higher and technical education had been neglected by the colonial authorities so that local engineers, doctors, agricultural scientists, and so on could be counted in single figures in 1955. Cambodia would need to depend on foreign personnel for some time until its own education system could take up the slack and train sufficient cadres and specialists for its modern economy. There were, however, no financial means to undertake national reconstruction and economic modernisation.

As deliberate interim policy, therefore, Cambodia accepted "economic coexistence" with foreign interests.[4] This policy applied to technical assistance, that is the hiring of foreign personnel with the expertise to maintain and manage those posts formerly staffed by the French Administration, as well as to continued recognition of foreign-owned businesses, including the rubber plantations. "Our ... principle," the Director-General of Plan explained, "has been to conduct this economic decolonisation firmly but equitably for foreigners. In all our previous steps for taking the economic reins, we have avoided being accused of illegal dispossession and we will not break the confidence in us of foreigners who continue to work in our country."[5]

For practical reasons, he acknowledged, Cambodia had to rely on foreign aid to finance its modernisation goals, especially "to achieve rapidly the large-scale works necessary to free us from our constraints *vis-à-vis* Vietnam for our foreign trade and especially to undertake economic construction of an independent state."[6] At the same time, there was awareness of the political perils of aid dependency, particularly in the Cold War environment, so the principle of self-help was employed to mobilise national energy and resources through manual work, community development schemes, voluntary contributions, and so on. Local private capital also had to be generated for the cause of national development.

The key term that defined policy during the era of the Sangkum was "neutrality." Neutrality in foreign policy, it was believed, would both protect Cambodia from external threats and guarantee external assistance from a multiplicity of sources. Neutrality was synonymous with balance or equilibrium. While *sangkum niyum* translated as "socialism," spokespeople for the government repeatedly stressed that its meaning did not imply Marxist socialism or communism. The economic policy of the Sangkum was explained in an official communiqué in 1961 in this way:

> Our socialism, it must be repeated, differs profoundly from Marxist socialism or communism.... Neutrality in the political domain consists of staying outside blocs, between capitalism and communism. On the economic plane, it suggests a balanced adaptation of the two systems for the organisation of the country.[7]

It was state policy to foster a stable equilibrium between public action and private action. The concrete application of this policy was the "mixed-economy enterprise" which merged individual capital and enterprise with state capital and supervision, thereby safeguarding national interests against what the communiqué termed "privileged capitalists, national or foreign." The state reserved full control over the key economic sectors, including energy, transport and mines, but mixed businesses were preferred to private businesses in all other areas of industry, agriculture and commerce. The licence granted to these businesses, it was hoped, would stimulate collective and individual savings to generate growth. The policy applied at both private and state levels of industry, the important stipulation being that Cambodian capital had to represent a majority share in all mixed enterprises. There were, for instance, Khmer-Yugoslav projects for the fishing industry, a Khmer-Czech tractor-assembly plant and rubber tyre factory, Khmer-Chinese enterprises for maritime navigation, and so on. The state created its own enterprise, OROC (*Office Royal de Coopération*), in an attempt to break the centuries-old monopoly of local Chinese merchants in purchasing agricultural products and selling consumer goods to villagers. State cooperatives in the countryside would also eventually operate their own credit programmes, thus breaking, it was hoped, yet another Chinese monopoly.

Essentially, this policy permitted state intervention in every sector and at every level. Foreign observers were understandably confused about the actual nature of the *Sangkum Reastr Niyum*. Some referred to it as "state capitalism," although capitalism, in the common sense of the term, had little to do with the sort of economy envisaged by Prince Sihanouk and the Sangkum leaders. They believed they were creating or reviving an idiosyncratic Khmer or Buddhist socialism, which was essentially agrarian socialism leavened by traditional practices of mutual support.[8] With regard to agriculture, Sangkum policy was encapsulated in five points:

> to assure each peasant family full ownership of the lands which they can develop and the free disposal of the fruits of their work;
>
> to give all rural communities the means to improve their yields by helping each farmer to acquire better equipment and each village to access the minimum means for the mechanisation of agriculture;
>
> to help rural populations to develop resources other than agricultural resources (artisanal trades, forestry exploitation, animal production, fishery, and so on);
>
> to guarantee farmers the best conditions for sale of their products; and
>
> to guide peasant collectives in the improvement of their lifestyle through a rationalisation of the 'social space' of the village in the framework of community development, in particular by helping them to manage the environment, the health infrastructure, schools, and so on.[9]

State policy was implemented in two five-year plans.[10] The plans were supposedly drawn up by the *Conseil Supérieur du Plan*, with Sihanouk presiding as head of state with other members representing the National Assembly, chief ministers in charge of the technical programmes, the governor of the National Bank of Cambodia, the director of the *Office des Changes*, and the president of the Cambodian Chamber of Commerce. In actual fact, Rémy Prud'homme noted, the plans were drafted by a handful of functionaries and experts without real powers of decision-making, so the role of the Council in the elaboration of the plans was very small and the role of the private sector was nil.[11] Prud'homme thought this might have been the reason why the documents were rarely consulted.

The main objective of the first plan, 1960 to 1964, was community development. The plan aimed for a rather modest three per cent annual GDP growth rate and targeted remedying "the serious imbalance created during the war and the period of insecurity between the incomes of urban populations (which have grown considerably) and those of rural populations which increase only very slowly."[12] The plan relied on private investments to the extent of 33 per cent but, as Prud'homme pointed out, "The plan does not seek to influence the behaviour of private entrepreneurs and outlines no real instrument to assure the achievement of its predictions.... The first five-year plan is thus a catalogue of anticipated public investments."[13] He thought that the first five-year plan represented "a grave technical imperfection" because the means were not adapted to the end. In any case, the plan was not respected in its execution. In 1962, for instance, more than half of public investment was outside the plan, and the trend increased in the remaining years of the Sangkum. Unplanned projects included the Olympic Stadium, the Phnom Penh to Sihanoukville railway, the Sangkum Lycée, and hydroelectric dams while most of the less prestigious planned projects were abandoned. Therefore, in a real sense, the economy was not planned at all.

The second plan, 1968 to 1972, was less ambitious and more realistic than the first but, in the event, it did not have time to run its course and, in fact, by 1968 the Cambodian economy was in serious recession. The Sangkum policy was deemed a failure well before the monarchy was overthrown in a *coup d'état* in March 1970.

Administration and Governance

The French Protectorate had organised Cambodian territory into 14 provinces. The Kingdom of Cambodia reorganised its administration and strengthened its borders by creating five new provinces: Mondolkiri and Ratanakiri in the northeast, Oddar Meanchey and Preah Vihear in the far north, and Koh Kong on the Gulf of Siam in the southwest.

Before independence, the northwestern provinces of Battambang and Siem Reap were returned to Cambodian sovereignty under the terms of the 1946 Treaty of Washington. Border disputes with Thailand continued, however, specifically over ownership of the Angkorian temple, Preah Vihear. In 1958, when Thai police occupied the temple, Cambodia briefly cut off diplomatic relations and took the case to the International Court of Justice that ruled in Cambodia's favour in 1962. The remote northern region was the scene of another international incident in 1958 when South Vietnamese forces crossed the border in pursuit of Viet Cong guerrillas. This so-called Stung Treng incident was the most serious in a string of similar incursions. Security over the northern boundary was strengthened by the creation of four provinces: Ratanakiri and Mondolkiri, in 1959 and 1960 respectively, Oddar Meanchey in 1962, and after the International Court ruling, Preah Vihear in 1964. Koh Kong province in the far southwest was instituted by a *kram* of 13 January 1958, when it consisted of two districts, including Kompong Som where the municipality of Sihanoukville, Cambodia's deepwater maritime port, would later be built.

The terminology of Cambodia's administrative structure was also clarified. Under the French, the word *srok* had been variously applied to provinces and districts. By way of further confusion, Paul Collard had referred to the commune chief as a *mésrok* who was "the village chief."[14] Now the *khet* (province), was divided into *srok* (districts), and subdivided into *khum* (communes). The village (*phum*) was not an administrative unit but was tied, however loosely, to the *khum* for administrative purposes.

As previously noted, the political insecurity of 1947–54 had caused large populations of rural dwellers in the rice-growing plain to the south and east of Phnom Penh to be regrouped along the main communication routes. The formerly dispersed habitat typical of the Cambodian rice farmer gave way, in this heavily populated zone, to relatively large, grouped settlements. This affected the administration, particularly that of the communes. Jean Delvert thought that the communes had become too big. "Most of the communes have more than 3,000 inhabitants," he complained, and this had severe administrative repercussions because the commune chief (*mékhum*) was usually illiterate and incapable of conducting a census or supervising anything like a local civil service.[15] The very existence of the commune seemed to annoy Delvert. It did not correspond, he thought, "to any human reality." At the whim of the central government or for administrative ease, it could be carved up or doubled in territorial size:

> All this shows how artificial this commune is, created out of nothing fifty years ago. The French Administration of the Protectorate found itself in front of the void: an unorganised peasant mass, even inorganic, in the vague historical framework of the *srok* (at that time called *khet*) which was a feudal principality led by a high mandarin or given in *apanage* to a member of the royal family.... In Cambodia, the basic cell does not exist; it still does not exist. This is perhaps the most serious problem of political life in the country.[16]

The much-amended 1947 Constitution of the Kingdom of Cambodia made no mention of the commune.[17] In accordance with the existing law, however, Cambodian peasants elected deputies (between 8 and 16 councillors in proportion to the number of villages) to the commune council, but the commune chief was appointed by the provincial administration, "without exception," according to Delvert. An effort was made to give a bigger life to the commune, but these reforms faced major difficulties. Delvert thought this failure was due to the fundamentally artificial character of the commune.

Elections were held for the first National Assembly in December 1947 and again in September 1951. In June 1952, citing Article 21 of the constitution that all power emanated from the king, Sihanouk dismissed the elected government, named himself Prime Minister and formed his own cabinet. In March 1955 he abdicated, placed his father on the throne and assumed full executive authority in order, he explained, to remodel a political system that was bogged down in unproductive rivalries and squabbling.[18] The *Sangkum Reastr Niyum* was created the following month. It was a broad political movement and it had initial success but, as Milton Osborne observed, it lacked cohesion "and was shot through with the perennial Cambodian problem of political factionalism."[19] There were nine ministries between the September 1955 general elections and those of March 1958 in which women voted for the first time. The Sangkum gained 99 per cent of the vote in those elections; the leftwing economists, Hou Yuon and Hu Nim, were among the successful candidates. In 1960, Sihanouk's father died. In a deft political move to avoid a constitutional crisis, Sihanouk had himself sworn in as chief of state while his mother "symbolised" the throne.

The next three years represented modest prosperity and witnessed the construction of large-scale infrastructure works, thanks to the infusion of foreign aid. The road network was extended, most importantly with the construction of Route 4, the all-weather highway that ran between the capital and the new sea-port of Sihanoukville. The highway was built with American aid, and the port with French funding. French and German loans helped to build the railway to Sihanoukville. An international airport was opened in Phnom Penh, the airstrip at Siem Reap was upgraded to handle heavy aircraft and small airports were built around the country. Phnom Penh was "beautified" (as it would be again c. 2000), and new bridges in the city spanned the Tonle Sap and the Bassac rivers. A hydro-electric dam was built at Kirirom and another commenced construction at Kamchay. In the countryside, schools were built and clinics were opened. From 1963 onwards, however, Sihanouk's control began to slip. Osborne argued that this was largely because the prince lacked an understanding of economic issues and also because the economy was subjected to what he called political "manoeuvring."[20]

Spending foreign aid and grants on showcase projects like the Olympic Stadium and Route 4 had undoubtedly contributed greatly to Sihanouk's prestige and popularity, but he began to fear that his country's political independence was being put at risk by the scale of foreign ownership and control of the country's major commercial and industrial businesses and that Cambodia's reliance on American aid would reduce his country to client status, as had already befallen South Vietnam. In November 1963, he renounced U.S. aid and nationalised the import-export business, the banks and insurance companies, and bought back some big industries, including two French distilleries which were formed into the SKD (*la Société Khmères des Distilleries*), with monopoly rights. The economy, always riddled with corruption, could not cope with these radical changes. Sihanouk's reforms never had a chance of success.

Corruption was the "hot issue" of the remaining years of the Sangkum. On 17 March 1967, the Sihanouk-sponsored newspaper, *Bulletin Contre-Gouvernement du SRN*, published the opinions of a functionary employed at the Phnom Penh Post Office.[21] Corruption, he wrote, was "this social scourge which we have had the misfortune to inherit from the regime of the Protectorate." He listed some official bodies that had been created in order to rid the society of this scourge, among them the National Purification Committee, and departmental committees for Defence of Honour. All measures had proved fruitless, he argued, because "more often than not [the functionaries responsible for the clean-up] themselves do not have clean hands.... To my knowledge, except for a few, they already have sumptuous villas, luxury cars and lead an enviable life. Armed with a fortune whose origin is equally questionable, can they have a clear conscience to undertake the hunt for the 'dishonest'? I doubt it." In 1957, he recalled, it was decreed that officials should declare their assets on taking office, but he considered this a waste of time: "... alas the declarations went calmly to fill up the archives and to sleep there."

There was a more sinister aspect of corruption. In 1968, as the economy sank into recession and the war in South Vietnam spilled across the border, General Saukam Khoy explained to that newspaper's readership that the revolutionary war in Cambodia had already begun.[22] "Knowing [this]," he wrote, "the nationalists should be able to organize themselves to counter-attack effectively and prevent the Khmer Rouge from winning this great and long battle whose stake is Cambodia." He warned that the battlefront would be lost, however, if the rear could not or would not support it. The "weak points" included corruption, aggravated by gambling, contraband, and scandals among the elite, all of which were being exploited by the Khmer Rouge. He acknowledged that cleaning up the society was a Herculean task but it was a vital one:

> If we do not succeed in cleaning up our rear, our front will not be able to rely on it because you cannot rely on something rotten. The Maoist enemy is, by definition, untouchable on the matter of corruption because they own nothing. Everything superfluous and luxurious is forbidden by them. They envy nothing and have no interest in winning fortunes.

Our struggle on the front will not be won if our psychological action on the popular masses can be easily contradicted by our enemy who exploit our weakest point, which is corruption.

The warnings were prescient. Lemming-like, however, the corrupt circles ignored all appeals to common sense and moved the Cambodian population ever closer to the cliff edge.

Population

Jean Delvert lamented the lack of accurate population statistics when he began his study in 1949. He disregarded the results of the 1937 population count and took instead the official figures from 1921 as a benchmark, but his scepticism remained. "The population is generally assessed by the local authorities by multiplying by four the number liable to tax (men aged over 18)," he complained. "The civil service does not exist in practice; births and deaths are only rarely registered."[23]

He estimated the total population in 1958 was 4,600,000.[24] This estimate represented an average of the 1956 official estimate and a demographic study of April 1958. Of the 4.6 million people in the kingdom, around four million were ethnic Khmer. Among the minorities, the Chinese community numbered about 220,000, half of whom lived in Phnom Penh. Under the Protectorate, they had been grouped into five clans whose leaders dealt locally with the authorities, but this system was abolished in 1958. The number of Vietnamese was around 230,000; almost half of them, or 100,000, lived in Phnom Penh, while the same number were spread throughout the provinces, and a further 30,000 lived in villages in and around the rubber plantations of Kompong Cham and Kratie. The First Indochina War had caused what Delvert termed "political difficulties" between Vietnam and Cambodia and many Vietnamese had repatriated themselves. The Khmer Islam, by far the largest majority of whom were the Cham, numbered around 90,000. There were also various ethnic minorities including the Kuy (roughly 3,000 people) in the communes to the south of Phnom Dek, the Pear (only 1,500 in 1936) in Pursat, former slaves of the king and harvesters of cardamoms, and the Phnong (*Khmer Leu* in official terminology, numbering around 30,000) in the eastern highlands.

The countryside was still sparsely settled. Hardly more than 300,000 people inhabited the vast regions of the north, northeast and southwest, which together constituted two-thirds of the total area of the country.[25] Populated Cambodia amounted to only 55,000 square kilometres that supported 4.3 million inhabitants; thus, 90 per cent of the population inhabited only 30 per cent of the total area of the country.

The road from Kompong Cham to Angkor Wat constructed with corvée and coolie labour during the French Protectorate

Tapping rubber on a plantation in Kompong Cham province

Delvert estimated that the urban population, in 1958, was around 600,000, about half of whom were Khmers. During the period of insecurity between 1947 and 1954, and with the development of education and transportation in the post-independence years, Phnom Penh's population had grown considerably. In 1942, Delvert noted, the city had only 120,000 residents (of whom 47,000 were Khmer), and in 1958 there were around 450,000 city dwellers.[26] The Khmer population in the city, made up of functionaries, refugee peasants, and temporary working peasants, was growing.

On the night of 17 to 18 April 1962, a general census of the Cambodian population was conducted in accordance with international norms.[27] The total population was found to number 5,740,115 with a sex ratio (men per 1,000 women) of 992.6. Density was 31.7 on a total area of 181,035 square kilometres, including an area of 3,000 square kilometres for the Great Lake. According to the census findings, Phnom Penh's population was 403,500, being by far the largest of the four municipalities that also included Kep, Sihanoukville and Bokor. Their combined populations numbered only 14,646 people. Prud'homme used the term "mono-urbanisation" to describe the status of Phnom Penh, which accounted for about 70 per cent of all urban dwellers in the country.[28]

The 1962 census took account of 17 provinces (the northern provinces of Preah Vihear and Oddar Meanchey had not yet been established). The most populous province was Kompong Cham (819,223 inhabitants), and the most densely settled was Kandal (186 per square kilometre). At the other end of the scale was Mondolkiri with only 14,650 people, or one individual for every square kilometre. The age pyramid was regular by age and symmetrical according to sex; just over half of the population, 53 per cent, was under 20 years of age.

Nationality and mother tongue were counted separately by the census. According to these criteria, there were 206,100 Vietnamese nationals in Cambodia on the night of the census, and 240,500 inhabitants of Vietnamese mother tongue.[29] The French had employed many Vietnamese in junior administrative roles, but laws passed in 1956 and 1957 forbidding access by foreigners to certain professions largely excluded them from these jobs. Nevertheless, the Vietnamese continued to make an important contribution to the economy through fishing and artisanal trades, as they had before the arrival of the French. The census gave the figure of 208,000 inhabitants with Chinese as mother tongue, but figures for Chinese nationality were unreliable. Traditionally, Sino-Khmers and Chinese in Cambodia have claimed Cambodian nationality because it buys them important economic advantages. Chinese private schools and Chinese language newspapers operated freely, particularly in Phnom Penh.

A salt farm in Kampot province

A ricefarmer uses the traditional light plough to turn his field

Prud'homme tentatively placed the number of Chinese at 380,000 in 1966, or a little more than five per cent of the total Cambodian population. In 1967, he estimated more confidently, there were 250,000 Vietnamese in Cambodia, being a little more than four per cent of the total population.[30] In that year, there were around 150,000 Chams and perhaps 50,000 *Khmer Leu*.

The economically active population in 1962 accounted for 44 per cent, or 2.5 million people. Of them, 81 per cent were engaged in the primary sector, 15 per cent in the tertiary sector, and only 4 per cent in the secondary sector. More than 80 per cent of those employed in the primary sector (almost 1.7 million people) were engaged in rice production. In 1962, there were only about 70,000 workers engaged in manufacturing, another 20,000 employed in construction and public works, and a few thousand who worked on the production of electricity, water and gas.

Proportionately there was little change in the composition of the labour force until the end of the regime. Quoting figures from the Ministry of Labour for 1967, Prud'homme demonstrated that the tertiary sector continued to employ three or four times the number engaged in manufacturing; of the 400,000 tertiary sector employees that year, 64,500 were engaged in religion.

Human Development

The Asian Development Bank (ADB) published its economic report on Cambodia in March 1970, the same month as the *coup d'état*. The report based most of its analysis on figures for 1966, the last year for which there were official estimates of GDP. The annual growth rate that year was exactly the same as that given in the report for population growth, 2.2 per cent. The economy had clearly stopped growing and it continued to decline after 1966. Changes in the GDP during the five years, 1962 to 1966 inclusive, at 1966 prices were as follows:

Table 2.1   Gross Domestic Product at 1966 Prices[31]

Year	Value (billion riels)	Annual Growth (%)
1962	27.7	–
1963	29.9	7.9
1964	29.9	–
1965	31.3	4.7
1966	32.0	2.2

Source: Ministère du Plan, *Comptes Économiques*, 1966.

The bank reported that per capita income in 1966 was 4,200 riels, or US$120 at the official exchange rate of 35.07 riels. For the average rice farmer, of course, such a figure was simply fanciful. In 1958, Delvert estimated the average annual personal income of the peasant was 1,700 riels, plus small earnings from fishing and forestry. He believed that a peasant family of five or six people survived on 8,619 riels per year (60,000 francs in 1958).[32] Given urban-rural wealth disparities, not to mention the declining purchasing power of the riel after the economic reforms of 1963, it is fair to say that the peasant's living standard in 1966 was not higher than it had been in 1958, and individual income was nothing at all like US$120. Between 1964 and 1967, as a direct result of restricted imports and growing demand from a rapidly increasing population, some measure of inflation was inevitable. The consumer price index for those years is given in the following table:

Table 2.2 Consumer Price Index by Class, 1964 and 1967[33]

Class Year	Working	Middle	European
1964	306	316	373
1967	314	341	419

Note: Base year, 1949 = 100.
Source: Statistics of the Ministry of Plan, National Institute of Statistics.

The distribution of income was poorly accounted for in national figures, but Rémy Prud'homme thought that personal distribution was "extremely unequal" in Cambodia.[34] Those employed in the non-agricultural sectors of the economy represented less than 20 per cent of the economically active population, but they enjoyed 60 per cent of the national income. Moreover, he argued, there was considerable inequality within those sectors. "It seems," he noted, "that the 125,000 richest people in the country (representing five per cent of the active population) account for more than 30 per cent of the national income."[35] According to his calculations, average per capita income was around 3,300 riels in 1962, or US$94; it fell to 2,600 riels (US$74) in 1963, and rose again to 3,800 riels (US$108) in 1964, but on his own admission, "[these figures] do not signify much."[36] On the other hand, even though rice still represented nearly one-quarter of total household expenses throughout the country, he believed that there was no lack of food or malnutrition in Cambodia.[37]

Rural living standards were an almost permanent topic for debate in the national arena. The prince was very sensitive to criticisms of lack of social progress under the Sangkum. In a heated response to his political opponents, he wrote:

> The Sangkum can only protest against the accusation that the masses "live in misery" and "bleed themselves" for the profit of capitalists.... According to the calculations of the United Nations, since the coming of the Sangkum, annual per capita income has risen by 3.4 per cent (instead of the three per cent foreseen in the 1960–65 Five-Year Plan), taking into account a fairly explosive demographic increase. In our country, even in the countryside, there is hardly anyone who does not have trousers and a white shirt. Most boys have a wristwatch, transistor radio and a *vélo*. A lot get around on motorbikes.... Thatched huts are giving way to wooden houses and wooden houses to ones of bricks and cement.[38]

He pointed to other factors indicating improved living standards and general well-being, including "infrastructure, industrialisation, diversification of agriculture and water policy, public health, democratisation, education — and especially the national union, the consolidation of independence, the recovery and preservation of territorial integrity, neutrality, peace...." He was not wrong to claim credit for all those socio-economic and cultural achievements, but, as history would prove, they were hastily built and without strong foundations.

Health

The French Protectorate may have left little in the way of medical infrastructure or trained medical personnel, but it did begin the battle against the major diseases and epidemics. During the Sangkum, there was a rapid expansion of clinics and hospitals and despite the lack of locally qualified personnel, there were positive changes in the health status of the population. Jean Delvert, who observed rural life very closely in the decade after 1949 judged that epidemics had virtually disappeared from central Cambodia. There were still a few minor outbreaks of cholera and bubonic plague each year, but they were contained. Malaria had virtually disappeared from the plain, but in the northeast highlands and the rubber plantations, the population was still decimated by malaria. Tuberculosis persisted but it was more prevalent in the towns than in the countryside. Delvert's overall assessment of the health of Cambodians, therefore, was very positive: "Altogether, the rural Cambodian population is perfectly healthy, young, and growing rapidly (two per cent per year)."[39] Infant mortality, according to an estimate by the 1958 demographic study was 127/1000, but maternal mortality remained very high.

Based on the findings of the 1958 study and the 1962 census, Prud'homme cautiously proposed a crude birth rate of 44/1000.[40] He thought that the mortality rate of 20/1000 given by the 1958–59 study was high, given a population that did not suffer from malnutrition and in a country where major epidemics had practically disappeared; malaria and tuberculosis, he argued, did not suffice to explain this rate. He concluded, "If the birth-rate is actually 44/1000 and the mortality rate 18/1000, it follows that the rate of population increase is actually 26/1000."[41] He estimated that the Cambodian population would be around 8 million by 1975.

Education

Education provision is almost always held up as the Sangkum's most thorough and determined effort to modernise Cambodia. It cannot be denied that many schools were constructed, around 2,000 primary schools alone, and thousands of children throughout the whole country were enrolled. Secondary education grew spectacularly; in 1955 there were ten high schools in the country, but by 1968 there were two hundred. The French Protectorate had left Cambodia without any tertiary education institutions, but by 1968 there were nine universities. The educational statistics were dazzling. The following table briefly illustrates this:

Table 2.3 Education Indicators, 1955 and 1968[42]

Education Indicator	1955	1968
Primary School enrolments	300,000	1,000,000
High School enrolments	5,000	100,000
Universities	–	9 (with 11,000 students)

The reality behind these dazzling statistics, Osborne contends, was low educational standards and the inability of the Cambodian state to provide jobs for the graduates of its education system.[43]

The 1962 census found that more than half of the population over the age of ten could neither read nor write. The illiteracy rate was much higher among women (more than 80 per cent) than among men (30 per cent), as the pagoda schools had traditionally offered basic education only to boys. Two per cent of the population had a primary school certificate, and only 300 Cambodians had graduated from upper secondary school.[44] Literacy campaigns and the development of schooling after 1962 did raise the standard of literacy and education in general, but outcomes were disappointing.

Prud'homme blamed the curriculum which was poorly adapted to the needs of development. "Primary, secondary and higher schooling only prepares students for the career of a bureaucrat," he wrote. "Agronomists, technicians, accountants, engineers, economists and entrepreneurs who play an important role in economic development are not very numerous in Cambodia."[45] Higher education received both technical and material support from abroad, especially from France and the USSR. The universities had faculties of law, medicine, pharmacy and the arts, and technical education to engineering level was offered at the Khmer-Soviet Institute. Most university students, however, graduated with arts degrees. The majority of them aspired to be officials; few wanted to be engineers or technicians. Like so many of the Sangkum's socio-economic achievements, the expansion of education services had more to do with form than with content, with political gain and personal prestige rather than genuine social development.

Economic Activity

Agriculture, Land and Concessions

Given that the year 1962 represented the peak of the Sangkum's economic success and 1966 its plateau, the following table from the Ministry of Plan provides an interesting statistical synopsis of the economy in the intervening years:

Table 2.4 Industrial Origin of GDP at 1966 Prices[46]

	1962 (%)	1966 (%)
Agriculture (incl. plantation crops)	30.7	30.3
Animal husbandry	4.3	4.9
Fishing	2.4	2.3
Forestry	3.9	3.5
Salt mining	0.1	–
Manufacturing	8.6	10.5
Energy and water supply	0.9	1.1
Construction	6.8	5.3
Transportation	2.0	2.1
Commerce	23.8	22.2
Public administration, defence and financial institutions	13.1	14.4
Other services	3.4	3.4

Source: Ministère du Plan, *Comptes Économiques*, 1966.

As the table shows, there were small gains in the secondary sector during the Sangkum, but the Cambodian economy remained overwhelmingly dependent on agriculture. The primary sector maintained a 41 or 42 per cent share of GDP, but productivity barely changed. On average, agricultural production per person grew by one per cent annually, too little to sustain progress in manufacturing and services. Yields for the wet season harvest were generally 1.3 tons per hectare. When paddy production actually diminished during the three seasons after the 1963–64 harvest, it triggered a slide in related industries including rice milling, transportation, distilling and so forth and sent the economy into a downward spiral.

The agricultural sector seemed stubbornly resistant to growth of the kind needed to support a modern economy. At the same time, despite claims to the contrary by contemporary economists such as Hu Nim, there really was no acute agrarian problem in Cambodia during the Sangkum. The cultivated area continued to grow regularly in line with the population. Prud'homme's calculations showed that the paddy growing area increased steadily at a little more than two per cent annually. "The cultivated area per economically active individual has not diminished and has even slightly increased," he noted.[47]

The total cultivated area was roughly divided into three major regions: the populous rice-growing region of the centre and southeast, the more sparsely settled but equally productive rice-growing region in the northwest, and the market gardens on the banks of the Mekong and the Bassac, especially south from Kompong Cham province. In the mid-1950s, Jean Delvert estimated that average property size was just under two hectares in the central plain, and smaller than that (between one and 1.5 hectares) in those parts that coincided with the most intensive sugar palm production.[48] These areas were in the provinces of Kandal, Kompong Speu and Takeo, along with Banteay Meas District in Kampot and four populous districts of Siem Reap province. The densely settled riverbank region was supported by holdings of only one hectare or less. In the rest of inhabited Cambodia, average property size ranged from two to five hectares. Delvert included the important rice-growing provinces of Svay Rieng and Prey Veng in this category. In summary, Delvert found that 92 per cent of Cambodian property owners had less than five hectares of land and 80 per cent had less than two hectares.[49] Big property was rare: there were only 1,191 owners with holdings larger than 20 hectares, but Delvert also believed that there were commensurately few landless peasants.[50] Even around half of the Cambodian coolies working in the rubber plantations, he found, owned some land.

The small Cambodian ox is used for transport in central rural parts of Cambodia

A rice harvest in the Cambodian countryside

Hand-weaving of cotton and silk fabrics makes an important contribution to household incomes throughout the countryside

A silversmith at work in a village in Kandal Province

Teams of buffalo plough a paddy field in Kompong Thom

Metal-workers in the rural provinces provide essential services to farmers

Proportionately, there was little change in this pattern throughout the Sangkum. The ADB reported in 1970, "Cultivated land totals 2.8 million hectares, while land holdings per farm family average 2.3 hectares. About 80–90 per cent of total cultivated land is owner-operated, while the remainder is under tenancy. Tenancy is predominant in such fertile areas as Battambang province, the rice granary of Cambodia."[51] Distribution of agricultural landholdings in 1962 is shown in the table below:

Table 2.5 Number and Distribution of Agricultural Landholdings, 1962[52]

Size	Number of holdings (%)	Area covered by the holdings (%)
Less than 1ha	31	5
1–2 ha	22	10
2–5ha	33	38
5–10ha	10	25
10–20ha	3.4	16
More than 20ha	0.6	6

The fertile riparian market gardens accounted for most of the holdings under one hectare in size. Otherwise, as the figures above show, almost half of the cultivated area (48 per cent) was divided into farms, mainly rice-producing, of between one and five hectares that were heavily parcellised. Compared with income, land was expensive. Prud'homme quoted an average price for farmland of 5,000 riels per hectare.[53] In the better rice areas, Delvert calculated, in 1956, for example, one hectare would return 2,400 riels, but he warned that figures like this were "soft."[54]

Paddy was not the only crop that Cambodian farmers produced, but it was by far the main crop and many farming households devoted themselves, as nowadays, solely to the cultivation of rice, supplementing their income from the harvest by raising a pig or a few chickens and by selling their labour in the city during the dry season. In the heavily populated plains region, including the provinces of Kompong Speu, Kandal and Takeo, palm sugar also made a contribution to family income.

Results for the seasons between 1963 and 1968 of some of the main crops, including paddy, are listed below. Relevant figures for 1954–57 are included for purposes of comparison.[55] It should be noted that the 1967–68 rice harvest was exceptionally good, thanks to near-perfect weather during the growing season. The following year, the crop was affected by a severe drought and estimates were for a decline in production in the order of 700,000 tons.[56]

Table 2.6 Principal Crops Grown in Cambodia (production in thousands of tons)[57]

Crops	1954–57 (average)	1963–64	1964–65	1965–66	1966–67	1967–68
Paddy	1,528.0	2,760.0	2,500.0	2,376.2	2,457.2	3,251.0
Maize (red)	110.0	170.0	110.0	107.9	134.1	138.2
Cotton (unginned)		3.5	5.4	5.1	2.7	2.5
Jute (fibre)		2.3	2.4	1.5	1.5	4.0
Groundnuts	3.5	7.0	19.2	24.1	20.8	21.1
Sesame	2.0	12.3	10.0	8.0	9.8	4.9
Palm sugar		40.0	50.0	50.0	37.7	56.0
Fruit crops		259.0	280.0	260.0	236.5	304.0
Market-garden produce		397.7	430.0	430.0	169.0	196.0
Tobacco	5.5	6.9	10.5	10.5	10.1	11.8

The market gardens along the rivers produced a rich variety of cash crops for sale in local and foreign markets. While praising the polyculture of the riverbanks for their adaptation to the soils, the climate and the rise and fall of the Mekong, Delvert thought the cultivation of these crops was unscientific. "They do not give perfect products for commercialisation," he noted. The red maize was poorly dried and the tobacco was hardly consumable outside of Cambodia and South Vietnam.[58] On the other hand, they had a lot of market potential, superior to that of rice, in Delvert's estimation.

How could this potential and that of agriculture in general be tapped? Given the severity of droughts and floods that visit Cambodia regularly, lack of access to irrigation is readily understood to be the main cause of low farm productivity. The French Administration had built a barrage for irrigation purposes at Bavel, in Battambang Province, but Delvert observed that it was not operational in the mid-1950s. American aid projects were planned in order to irrigate 20,000 hectares in both Siem Reap and Kompong Cham, but "nothing recalls the admirable hydraulic works of the Angkor kings," Delvert wrote. "A real water policy is indispensable."[59]

From the official propaganda, one might assume that there was a high level of public investment in agriculture during the Sangkum. Sihanouk claimed that his water policy delivered megalitres of irrigation water to the farmers. From a starting point of just 29,000 hectares of irrigated ricefields when the Sangkum started, he boasted, "Today, 30 May 1969, ricefields which irrigate with imported water amount to 171,443 hectares." In 1955, he argued, "there were practically no irrigation channels, but by May 1969, there were 1,077 kilometres of channels, nine important barrages and 63 big reservoirs." When severe drought hit the 1969–70 harvest, he wrote, "Thanks to irrigation, the people did not suffer a lack of rice and were able to export 400,000 tons."[60]

In fact, the drought was so severe that Battambang and Kompong Thom, major rice-producing provinces, lost 50 per cent and 51 per cent respectively of what they cultivated and the Department of Agriculture predicted there would be a 700,000-ton drop in production compared with the previous year's harvest.[61] The farmers hardly had access to irrigation. Even if the prince's figure of 171,443 hectares of irrigated paddy land in 1969 was correct, it still constituted only a tiny fraction of the total paddy area. The ADB team reported that three per cent of paddy land was irrigated compared with 2.1 per cent in 1953/54, which was no cause for celebration:

Table 2.7 Irrigated Paddy Area[62]

	Crop Year	
	1953/54	*1967/68*
Paddy area (hectares)	1,700,000	2,473,000
Irrigated paddy area (hectares)	34,872	79,926
Irrigation ratio	2.1%	3.0%

Commenting on the irrigation projects that had been constructed, the ADB report noted, "The maximum use of these irrigation projects is hampered by the lack of terminal networks which were expected to be built by the farmers themselves." The farmers apparently saw no advantage in completing the system. In light of the fact that every post-independence regime in Cambodia has harped on the importance of irrigation to develop agriculture and to raise rural living standards, and that each regime has attempted, in varying degrees, to implement an irrigation policy, we can only assume that the farmers, or at least the influential majority of them, do not want a centralised irrigation system. Cambodian farmers have long employed their own manual (or pedal) methods to irrigate crops from channels that they choose to maintain. Large-scale systems, on the other hand, have frequently been neglected and even vandalised. In terms of access and cost of maintenance, public irrigation systems are a source of dispute and conflict in rural communities everywhere. Perhaps Cambodian farmers simply opted for peaceful coexistence with their neighbours and placed that value above profit. If local government, typically the commune council, was not strong enough or trusted sufficiently to mediate water disputes fairly between individual farmers, even the popular Sangkum could not successfully implement a water policy.

In the 1960s, rice and rubber were considered the twin pillars of national development and economic independence. Other commercial plantation crops such as cotton and mulberry paled into insignificance when compared with the value of rubber to the national economy. The export figures below are for the month of December in consecutive years towards the end of the Sangkum:

Table 2.8 Exports of Agricultural Products: December 1967 and December 1968 (volume in tons and value in riels)[63]

Export Product	1967		1968	
	Volume	Value	Volume	Value
Rice and derivatives	227,446t	1,332,770,737r	268,238t	1,525,642,803r
Rubber	48,574t	690,103,841r	50,195t	716,231,266r
Maize	76,100t	167,527,303r	78,444t	134,801,735r

In line with the policy of co-existence of foreign and local enterprise, the big French companies continued to run the plantations they had developed on concessions in the redlands of Kompong Cham, Kratie and Kompong Thom during the 1920s and 1930s, but no new concessions were granted to foreign investors after independence. In 1945, during the few months of independence declared at Japan's bidding in March and before the Allied victory in August, then King Sihanouk had promulgated a law (*Kram* No. 79-NS, 14 July 1945) which abrogated the *ordonnances* which had given the French Administration the authority to award rural concessions. In 1956, this *kram* was revived in its essence and foreigners were forbidden by law to acquire new concessions on rural land. On the other hand, many Cambodian citizens were awarded concessions, particularly after 1960 when the Royal Government offered incentives that exempted "hevea land" and other rural properties from land tax for a specified number of years depending on the crop planted.[64] The law, promulgated by *Kram* No. 376-NS of 29 January 1960 and implemented according to a *prakas* that was issued in June 1961, was intended to encourage the production of crops for export, or other crops where local demand was currently not met; rubber, tea, coconut, mulberry, and cashews were the crops which presented "an exceptional interest" for the Kingdom's economy. Most applications were for 200 or 300 hectares, usually to grow hevea, in areas where rubber plantations were already well established, such as in Mimot, Stung Trâng or Krek.

As the French Administration experienced problems with its concession system, so did the Royal Government. In mid-1964, the Ministry of Agriculture issued a circular "On the Control of Developing Rural Lands."[65] The circular noted that there had been abuses of the terms on which concessions were granted; land had been cleared before the formalities had been completed by some applicants whose aim, it became clear, had been to sell the timber from the land, not to develop agriculture there, and some of the land had been the subject of speculation. A special commission was created to monitor the minister's stipulations for future concessionaires. Disputes concerning these rural land concessions, however, continued. In January 1967, the minister issued another lengthy circular setting out the procedure for granting permits to cultivate.[66] "Where more than a year passes before the land in question is cleared and cultivated," the circular warned, "this may be considered as speculation. The administration is resolved not to tolerate such activities and measures will be taken with a view to revoking these authorisations when they occur."

In line with its policy of economic co-existence, the Sangkum government cooperated with the French rubber plantations and also established state rubber plantations. In 1958, the French donated Tapao plantation in Kompong Cham, complete with operating installations, on an area of 242 hectares almost all of which was in full production. The mixed-economy enterprise at Tapao, SKPH (*La Société Khmère des Plantations d'Hévéas*), started with a 60 per cent government share of 12 million riels, and it was intended that this share would eventually be sold to Cambodian private investors.[67] Another Franco-Khmer company was established near Sihanoukville on a total area of 648 hectares where tapping commenced in 1967 with production that year of 42 tons; another at Christianville in Kompong Thom Province produced 35 tons.

By 1968, public investment in state rubber plantations was 233 million riels.[68] Their total area was 4,540 hectares, or less than one-tenth that of the French-owned plantations. The largest of them, named in honour of the prince, was established in 1959 at Labansiek in Ratanakiri Province, extending over 3,000 hectares. To attract a workforce to this remote, malarial part of the country, the government advertised the attractive conditions and benefits migrant worker families would receive.[69] Apart from free accommodation, water and medical care, each (male) worker would be paid 800 grams of rice and a guaranteed wage of between 20 and 25 riels per day, plus a bonus of 100 riels every three months. After three years of satisfactory service, workers would be able to request five hectares of land near the plantation. By 1977, the plantation at Labansiek expected to have a population of 15,000 workers and their families.

Because of the time required to establish plantations and then to bring the hevea trees into production, the state plantations contributed very little to total rubber exports during the Sangkum. By 1967, there were also around two thousand family-scale plantations with an average size of about five hectares, but they produced less than two per cent of Cambodia's total rubber output. Most rubber was still produced by the five big foreign-owned companies that tapped around 50,000 hectares of heveas in Kompong Cham, Kratie and Kompong Thom. In 1969, the plantation at Mimot owned by *Société des Plantations Réunies de Mimot* was seriously damaged by defoliants sprayed by US military aircraft as Cambodia was drawn ever deeper into the Second Indochina War.[70]

Fisheries

Commercial fishing remained important to the economy throughout the Sangkum, contributing about 2.4 per cent of GDP. Official figures from the National Bank of Cambodia suggest a fairly steady annual harvest of around 120,000 tons from the freshwater fisheries, particularly the Great Lake. Between 1955 and 1968, the lowest catch was 95,000 tons in 1956 and the highest was 138,000 tons, a bumper catch, in 1960. Marine fishing was less important; the annual catch was 35,000–40,000 tons.[71]

Fish is the main source of protein in the Khmer diet and a considerable proportion of the freshwater catch was consumed locally. Approximately ten per cent of total production was exported, mainly in the form of dried or salted fish. Prud'homme noted that fish exports to Thailand were banned due to the protracted diplomatic strife between the two countries in the 1960s, although clandestine exports continued.[72] The value to the formal economy of fish exports, in consequence, declined dramatically from US$1.3 million in 1955 to only US$200,000 in 1968, or from 10,000 tons to just one ton.[73]

Forestry

The ADB reported in 1970 that forests covered more than half of Cambodia's land area and that the exploited forests were concentrated in an area of 13.5 million hectares that included Battambang, Pursat, Kompong Chhnang, Kompong Speu and Kampot provinces.[74] The sector's annual contribution to GDP was around 3.7 per cent. The forest was a rich source of diverse products. Apart from timber, forest products included firewood, charcoal, honey, resins, rattan, bamboo, cardamoms and bark. Revenue from all these products, in thousands of riels, for the years 1964 to 1968 is as follows:

Table 2.9 Revenue from Principal Forest Products (Supervised Production) (thousands of riels)[75]

1964	1965	1966	1967	1968*
48,217	69,160	110,973	131,584	109,628

Note: * The 12th month of the year is excluded from the total.
Source: Service of Water and Forests, charged with the conservancy of Fisheries and Game (based on the results of extensive surveys carried out during the years 1960–64).

The Sangkum is remembered as a time of good stewardship of the nation's forests. National reserves and protected areas were monitored by the Service of Water and Forests in accordance with the 1965 Forestry Code that was based on an *arrêté* of 1930, with amendments. The Statistical Year-Book for 1968 provided the following figures showing the areas of the various types of forest that were under national reserve or had been declared protected forests.

Table 2.10 Area Covered by Different Types of Forest (thousands of hectares)[76]

Type of Forest	National Reserve	Protected Area	Total	Percentage
Sparse	1,023.1	4,273.6	5,296.7	40.04
Dense	1,683.1	2,272.2	3,955.3	29.90
Semi-dense	639.7	1,864.3	2,504.0	18.93
Pine	13.0	4.8	17.8	0.13
Evergreen scrub	113.6	175.1	288.7	2.18
Mangrove	11.4	26.9	38.3	0.29
Secondary mangrove	10.9	46.6	57.5	0.43
Inundated	246.2	435.2	681.4	5.15
Bamboo-cane	193.8	193.6	387.4	2.95
Total	3,934.8	9,292.3	13,227.1	100.0

Source: Service of Water and Forests, charged with the conservation of Fisheries and Game (based on the results of extensive surveys carried out during the years 1960–64).

There were also teak plantations, but their total area was too small to rate a mention in the official statistics. In 1960, there were 1,851 hectares of teak growing mainly in Kompong Cham, on the outskirts of the rubber plantations. As the reserves of secondary growth forest set aside for provisioning the latex treatment factories with firewood were exhausted, teak forests replaced them. Their growth was small, between 100 and 150 hectares per year.[77]

Industry, Services and Labour

During the time of the Protectorate, the French largely ignored local manufacturing and processing. At independence, domestic industry was owned mostly by ethnic Chinese merchants and it included rice and sawmills, kilns producing tiles and bricks, ice works and drinks factories, along with some outlets for the generation of electricity; there were two weaving factories and a little tobacco processing. Commerce involved the collection and export of agricultural products, including animals, timber and fish. Foreign trade was controlled by the big European houses, and mediated by Chinese compradors. The transportation industry was also in the hands of the Chinese.

In his dissertation, Khieu Samphan argued that the further development of Cambodian industries at the time of independence depended absolutely on external conditions. The capitalist enterprises that existed were directly owned by corporations whose head offices were offshore, local industry and small enterprises depended on foreign suppliers for their raw materials and supplies, and local enterprises were so bound to foreign-owned industries that even the cigarette companies processed foreign tobacco and the soap factories relied on imported copra. "So, while agriculture slumbers under a profoundly pre-capitalist structure," he concluded, "the elements of industrialisation born of the international integration of the economy are designed to be extensions of industries in the advanced capitalist countries."[78] He believed, nevertheless, that Cambodia could industrialise, "but responsibility for industrialisation must be accepted by the government whose policies must be translated into rigorous control of foreign trade within a planned framework of structural reform."[79] After 1963, this was very much the industrialisation policy that the Sangkum government addressed.

In the 1950s, modernisation was synonymous with industrialisation. To be modern, therefore, Cambodia needed factories and an indigenous skilled workforce. In line with Sangkum policy, industrialisation would both support and contribute to agricultural development. Cotton, jute, rubber, timber, bamboo, sugar cane, palm sugar, tobacco and other locally-grown produce would be processed in state and mixed-economy factories, thereby saving foreign exchange, creating jobs and giving an impulse to Cambodian technology and skills.

The Battambang Jute Factory was a model for the sort of industrialisation that the Sangkum envisaged. Hou Yuon was the secretary of state for the Ministry of Plan who presided over the setting up of the mixed-economy enterprise for the manufacture of jute bags. The company had starting capital of 50 million riels, divided among 50,000 shares of which 40 per cent were state-owned, 30 per cent foreign-owned and the remainder were available for local investors to purchase, no single local investor being allowed more than one thousand shares.[80] The company intended to be involved in the whole process from cultivation of jute to the sale of the bags produced by its factory.

According to the official propaganda, by 1968, there were 29 mixed-economy factories in the country, as well as 28 state factories and 3,700 private factories and small industrial enterprises.[81] To meet industrial demand for power, state capacity for electrification expanded from 11,055 kilowatts in 1955 to 80,000 kilowatts in 1969, 10,000 kilowatts being produced by the Kirirom hydroelectric plant which had been constructed with a US$8 million loan from Yugoslavia.

Like agriculture, the reality behind the statistics was not as spectacular as the official reports would have the reader believe. Too often, it seems, politics intervened to thwart sound economic intentions. In June 1963, the bulletin of the Chamber of Commerce published a faintly damning article from the *Far Eastern Economic Review* entitled "The New Factories of Cambodia."[82] The author made the point that in developing countries like Cambodia, a factory might be built "in a terrain for which it is not prepared, to play a role for which it is not foreseen." Such was the case with the plywood factory built with Chinese aid and run by the government through Ofenet (*Office des Entreprises de l'Etat*) at Dey Eth:

> The site, rather uninhabited and without importance, seems to have been chosen rather for political motives: a factory in Kandal Province was needed. It is far from the source of the wood it needs. It has lots of problems.... The plywood of Dey Eth sells for around three times more than plywood of the same quality imported from Hong Kong. The importation of competitive products is now prohibited but despite that, there are still large quantities unsold in the factory store. It is obvious that the market for the factory's products was never seriously studied since production greatly exceeds the local demand; in fact, production is three times greater than consumption.

The paper mill at Chhlong, a small market town on the Mekong in Kratie Province was more suitably located in terms of access to supplies of water and bamboo, the main material used by the factory. Production, however, fell far below its annual capacity of 5,000 tons. The problem was management, not lack of technical skill, according to the journalist, mainly because managers of state factories had neither financial nor administrative autonomy. The Chinese textile factory in Kompong Cham was more successful. In less than three years, it had almost reached its maximum capacity, producing 1,450 tons annually from raw cotton grown in the province and purchased directly from the farmers. About half the product was exported to reserved markets. China was also constructing a cement factory at Chakrey Ting in Kampot to produce 50,000 tons of cement annually. Three other projects were completed with Czech aid: a palm sugar refinery in Kompong Speu, a tyre factory at Takhmau in Kandal, and a tractor assembly plant in Sihanoukville. Unlike the Chinese, who made gifts of their factories, the Czechs gave loans of 80 per cent of the total cost at 2.5 per cent interest repayable in five or eight years.

State intervention extended to the composition of the workforce. In March 1956, *Kram* No. 83-NS was promulgated, making it illegal for foreigners to take part in 18 specified professions. Otherwise, all enterprises had to employ at least 70 per cent of Cambodian nationals among its workers in the categories of office personnel, specialised and non-specialised workers. Temporary arrangements could be made to hire foreign personnel only when they were judged to be indispensable to the enterprise.[83]

Despite the forced pace of industrialisation and restrictions on the hiring of foreign workers, there were not sufficient new job places to cope with the demand from graduates of Cambodia's modern education system. The Ministry of Labour's *Bureau de Placement* noted an exceptional increase in demand for jobs after 1963: 12,520 applications, compared with 2,551 in 1961 and 3,083 in 1962.[84] In 1967, the bureau was preparing itself for the Sangkum's second wave of school leavers, but there were few jobs waiting for those without skills. The unemployment problem in the city was exacerbated by a "rural exodus" from the infertile yet densely populated regions of the countryside.

The pace of economic growth slowed after 1963. The consumption of electricity stagnated, construction slowed and figures for several industries, including food, textiles, printing and paper, and mechanical industries declined in each successive year. The structural reforms had not worked. Rémy Prud'homme pointed out the obvious fact that despite all the attention paid to state and mixed-economy enterprises, the progress of industry in Cambodia was mainly due to the efforts and the investment of private capitalists who had continued to operate in their usual fashion which Prud'homme considered "rather disorderly.... The private capitalist, by definition, looks for his profit *à tâtons*, without being guided by a total plan."[85] The public authorities, meanwhile, lacked the means to extend their plan to the private sector. They also obviously lacked the authority to tax these private entrepreneurs. Their percentage share of the national tax burden for the year 1964 is indicated in the table below:

Table 2.11   Share of Sectors in Industrial Activity, 1964[86]

	Public Enterprises	Private and Mixed Enterprises	Individual (Private) Enterprises	Total
Value added	2.2	32.8	65.0	100
Salaries paid	5.1	53.1	41.8	100
Taxes paid	2.8	82.2	15.0	100
Gross revenue	0.5	15.1	84.4	100

What is most apparent from these official figures is the extent to which industry was dominated by the private sector, contrary to popular perception. The public sector that year was making only a very small contribution to both the GDP and the national coffers. The private sector, on the other hand, although very important in terms of production, paid lower salaries than the other sectors and, as already noted, very little tax. The mixed-economy model was fairer for workers and the state, but the scale of their profits would seem to offer few incentives to new investors.

That year, 1964, marked a dramatic downturn in the economy. In mid-November the previous year, American aid had been cancelled, and banking, insurance and foreign trade were nationalised. A policy of austerity was initiated to try to cope with the repercussions of these changes. The policy, however, proved to be ineffectual. Inflation started to bite and the (unofficial) value of the riel fell to 48 against the American dollar. In that year, too, the population officially passed the six million mark.

Foreign Trade, Aid, Investment and Debt

Foreign trade, aid and investment were practically indivisible throughout the Sangkum. At the height of the Cold War, a developing country's choice of trading partners or source of foreign assistance identified its affiliation with one political bloc or its nemesis. In accordance with the policy of neutrality, therefore, Cambodia maintained its pre-independence trade partnerships, but it also signed commercial agreements with a host of socialist countries including the People's Republic of China, Czechoslovakia, the USSR, Poland, North Vietnam, Yugoslavia, Bulgaria, North Korea, and Hungary. While Cambodia sought membership in the GATT (General Agreements on Tariffs and Trade), the Colombo Plan, and the Asian Development Bank, during the Sangkum it chose not to join the International Monetary Fund or the World Bank.

Two dates mark the beginning of very different episodes in the economic history of the Sangkum. On 1 January 1955, Cambodia regained full sovereignty over its monetary, commercial and financial affairs, and for almost nine years the new state enjoyed generous external support. On 15 November 1963, the National Assembly voted for the bill on state intervention in exports and imports. The Royal Government nationalised foreign trade by granting the monopoly of import-export operations to a mixed-economy company that was created for the purpose, *la Société Nationale d'Exportation et d'Importation*, or Sonexim. Banking and insurance were similarly nationalised. A few days later, Cambodia renounced U.S. economic and military aid; subsequently, diplomatic relations with the U.S.A. deteriorated rapidly and in May 1965 they were suspended for four years. Until the end of 1963, state coffers had been constantly replenished by generous infusions of grant aid. The remaining years of the Sangkum, conversely, were ones of enforced self-reliance and increasing austerity, at least for the majority of the population.

Cambodia's export trade at independence was totally dependent on its primary sector. Figures for the second quarter of 1954, for example, showed that rice and its derivatives accounted for almost 55 per cent of the value of total exports, followed in order of importance by rubber, timber, fish, palm sugar, lentils, animals (including both live exports and hides), maize, pepper, and kapok.[87] Vietnam was the main destination for every product, but other countries were already significant trading partners, including Singapore, Hong Kong, and European countries other than France, especially the Low Countries. In that quarter, more exports were going to the U.S.A. than to France. America was the first customer for Cambodian rubber, while the countries that made up the franc zone, Senegal, for instance, were important consumers of Cambodian rice.

Basically, Cambodia's exports continued to rely on rice and rubber throughout the whole of the Sangkum period. Depending on the weather, sometimes rice was more valuable than rubber, but these products together always represented more than half the total value of Cambodian exports. Below are figures for the years 1955 to 1957, inclusive:

Table 2.12 Percentage Value of Rice and Rubber to Total Cambodian Exports, 1955–57[88]

Year	Rice and Derivatives	Rubber	Total (%)
1955	8	45	53
1956	21	43	61
1957	37	32	69

During those years, the trading bloc formed by France and the other members of the franc zone resumed its priority position among customers for Cambodian exports, buying 35 per cent of the total, followed by the U.S.A., Malaya, Hong Kong, South Vietnam, and Japan. The balance of trade figures for those years suggest a high degree of fiscal responsibility. The figures are expressed in millions of riels:

Table 2.13 Balance of Trade, 1955–57 (millions of riels)[89]

Year	Imports	Exports	Balance
1955	1,521 (*1,600*)	1,402	–119
1956	1,242 (*2,000*)	1,282	+40
1957	1,618 (*2,148*)	1,798	+180

The figures in italics record the actual cost of imports.[90] In fact, these extremely favourable official results were largely due to aid, mostly American, which allowed Cambodia to pay for imports without having to use its own foreign currency reserves.

American aid to Cambodia, before it was suspended in November 1963, took various forms. The type of assistance that allowed Cambodia to pay for its imports, and effectively to balance its trade, was delivered by USAID's Commercial Imports Programme (CIP) operating on the principles of open dollar credits or triangulation. According to the dollar credits system, suppliers of goods from all over the world were paid in dollars on behalf of Cambodian importers. The importers then paid for these dollars in riels, at the official rate, which were placed in a special fund for technical and economic aid projects and for the army. The imported goods included basic consumption items (54 per cent), essential equipment for production (21 per cent) and mechanical equipment (25 per cent). For the most part, they were textiles, petroleum products, iron and steel goods, industrial machines, motor vehicles, pharmaceutical products, electrical equipment, and cement. Imports under the CIP constituted around one-third of total Cambodian imports between 1955 and 1959. During those five years, this type of assistance was worth US$135.7 million, which translated into 4.75 billion riels for aid projects and much of the budget of FARK, the Royal Khmer Armed Forces.

Triangulation also had benefits for the exporter. For example, the U.S. government sold its raw materials and food products such as cotton and maize to France at special rates. The French government paid in francs. Washington transferred these francs to South Vietnam or to Cambodia to allow those countries to import from member states of the franc zone. In 1956, more than 60 per cent of French exports to Indochina were made on dollar credits, and in 1957 with triangulated francs. The purpose of this special aid was to generate riels so that Cambodia would be able to fund its own development projects.[91]

The director of the American Economic Aid Mission to Cambodia who explained those details about the CIP to the Phnom Penh Rotary Club in 1959, noted that in the four years following Cambodia's commercial independence, foreign exchange reserves of the National Bank of Cambodia almost trebled, amounting to 3.366 billion riels at the end of December 1958. This increase, he believed, would give Cambodia the monetary guarantees it needed to obtain international loans in the future.

The programme was too generous for any newly-independent and developing nation to refuse. At the same time, it was very taxing for a young administration to manage such a complicated system of trade and currencies. The Department of Economic Affairs tried to exercise its authority over the burgeoning import-export industry through a complicated system of licences, taxes and rules on exchange. In March 1957, for example, there were 763 import licensees of whom 319 were nationals and 444 were foreigners.[92] The latter were the long-established big European firms and the Chinese exporters and importers. They discovered many ways to turn the official system to their own advantage. Foreign currency earned through the export of Cambodian products had to be submitted to the *Office National des Changes*, but a fixed percentage (around 13 per cent) of the registered amount of sales was automatically transferred to a separate account which was left to the free disposal of the exporter who could, not illegally, sell this foreign exchange on a parallel market and make a handsome profit.[93] Alternatively, the foreign trader could take advantage of the procedure called *échanges compensés*, whereby the export of one product was tied to the import of another, allowing him free disposal of the foreign exchange earned.[94]

On 15 November 1963, the Royal Government declared, "[I]mportation and banking will be taken over, for the most part, by the state, with eventual control. The modalities will be applied without delay.... Our compatriots know that this measure is entirely dictated by the noble concern of accelerating the development of the national economy, orienting private investment towards the most useful sectors of the nation, and raising the living standards of the *petit peuple*."[95] The declaration stressed that the government decision did not amount to nationalisation of private enterprises; plantations, industries, hotels, clinics, private schools and so on, it assured investors, were unaffected by the government action.

Three weeks later, Prince Sihanouk invited Khmer and foreign businessmen to a meeting at Kep, a coastal resort in Kampot Province. He wanted to reassure them that the reforms were not undertaken to cause them trouble but rather to avoid "the revolution which will surely break out one day if we are complacent in capitalism or even semi-capitalism."[96] He continued:

> American aid, which has been given to us for ten years and which is only conceived to consolidate capitalism in Cambodia, has enriched the wealthy class and not the nation which has only progressed by itself, by its own means. It has naturally resulted in economic and financial problems that have become more and more serious, year after year. Our trade balance and our budget slide further into deficit.... Our job now is to bring alive and develop our economy without American aid, a job that will be difficult at the beginning because there has to be some time for adjustment. It will be necessary for our rich *sahachivin* (notables) and my foreign capitalist friends to turn themselves towards new activities, to produce more in the domain of agriculture and industry, to increase our exports and reduce imports more and more. For those concerned with agriculture, I stress that the government will provide assistance in awarding to individuals or companies that are financially capable vast free concessions (long applause). The concessionaires will only pay relevant fees, conveyancing, for example.... I want to assure our farmers that their enterprises will not risk being nationalized. The government has no interest in becoming farmers. That is very evident. We will practise a policy of autarky and protectionism. I promise you rigorous measures of protectionism. The government will have to make an appeal to the private sector to get the cadres needed for its state or mixed-economy enterprises because this is the best means of guaranteeing the good functioning of these enterprises. Experience has already amply demonstrated that our bureaucrats are absolutely incapable of becoming good managers of commercial or industrial enterprises....[97]

The law on state intervention in exports and imports was definitely a move against the "privileged capitalists" who had obstructed the prince's efforts to institute his Sangkum's economic reforms, but it was also a genuine effort to protect Cambodia from the sort of client status to which South Vietnam had been reduced by its over-reliance on American aid.[98] The law was promulgated by *Kram* No. 149-CE of 16 November 1963. It stated categorically, "The role of exporter and importer is exercised by the State." Participation by private national capital could be authorised, but the state's part could not be less than 60 per cent of the capital needed to establish the agency to exercise this task.[99]

According to official figures, the trade deficit continued to fall: from 1,631 million riels in 1962, to 635 million riels in 1963, and to just 200 million riels in 1964. Initial improvements were due to both increased exports and reduced imports. The longer-term results, however, were far less encouraging, according to historian Milton Osborne who was an eyewitness to events in Cambodia at the time. The foreign European firms no longer found Cambodia a profitable place to work, but the Chinese and Sino-Khmer import-export firms soon found ways to evade the state mechanism so that after an initial reduction in imports of luxury goods, the level soon rose again "to a point where external trade deficits reappeared."[100]

More ominously, state control over rice exports was circumvented and customs revenue lost as more and more of the harvest was sold clandestinely to Viet Cong forces both inside Cambodia and across the border. At the end of November 1966, the government announced that it would collect at the farmgate all paddy, milled rice and by-products from the cooperatives and other groups that came under official inspection: "The cooperatives and state organisations working under the careful supervision of the provincial governor and incorporating all the merchants will do whatever is necessary not to let the merchants gather the rice directly — seeking the highest bidder," Prime Minister Lon Nol declared.[101] When even state-sanctioned violence failed to prevent breaches of the law, a new *prakas* was issued by the Ministry of Industry and Commerce on 12 April 1968 that required rice merchants to declare all their rice stocks on the 15th and 30th of each month. Another order, just five days later, made permits compulsory for the transportation of paddy and rice in quantities above one ton by land, river or by sea. By then, however, the situation was out of control.

Until 1965, thanks to foreign aid, particularly of the type already referred to in relation to American aid, the balance of payments remained stable. The inflows of foreign exchange more than compensated for losses registered in foreign trade and other payments. Until 1963, Cambodian stocks of gold and foreign reserves actually increased. Foreign aid quite literally paid for the first five-year plan. In percentage of total expenses, the contribution of foreign aid was as follows:

Table 2.14 Source of Aid and Contribution to First Five-Year Plan (January 1960–December 1964)[102]

Source	%
American aid	57
Chinese aid	23
French aid	17
Cambodian budget	2
Undetermined	1

Even before the first five-year plan, U.S. aid was substantial and almost three times greater than French aid.[103] Between 1955 and 1959, American aid that was given for public works, agriculture, education, public health, civil police, communications and national defence was worth a total value of US$178.8 million. More than half of that total amount (US$90.2 million) was allocated to the Royal Armed Forces.[104]

The Royal Government's cancellation of American aid had a severe impact on foreign reserves and that naturally jeopardised economic plans for further industrialisation. The government responded to the challenge with two key strategies. Firstly, high tariffs meant that local industries were practically forced to rely on local products, even when their quality and price were less competitive than imported products. By way of compensation, the government banned the importation of foreign products likely to compete with those that were locally manufactured. This was termed "integrated protectionism."[105] The other strategy involved a drive to increase capital investment. In August 1967, the minister of state responsible for national economy, Chau Seng, announced that his government would look favourably on requests for investment, particularly in agriculture and animal production, in full conformity with the generous *kram* of 1958 concerning foreign investment and the repatriation of profits. Guarantees of non-nationalisation would be given for 10, 15 or 20 years, depending on the nature of the investment.[106]

This investment policy was consistent with that declared on the day of signing the quadripartite accords in Paris on 18 May 1955, when the royal government, at the instigation of Prince Sihanouk, published a declaration assuring foreign capitalists, especially the rubber companies, that their investments were safe.[107] The *kram* (No. 102-NS) of 31 May the following year permitted existing investors the ongoing right to repatriate net profits, as well as to transfer ten per cent of net assets for the divestment of old capital which had been invested in foreign currency. Authorisation for new investments was the responsibility of the Ministry of Finance, in consultation with the governor of the National Bank concerning the nature of the currencies that were acceptable. Participation of Cambodian capital, as well as the percentage of Cambodian personnel employed by the new enterprises was determined on a case-by-case basis. Article 4 of the law was the forerunner of the liberal investment law of the 1990s. Enterprises deemed to have an exceptional interest for the economic development of the Kingdom, were free from tax where profits were reinvested, and free from customs duty on imported equipment. They enjoyed total or partial exemption of taxes and charges during the first years of exploitation. Two laws of 13 September 1957 completed this *kram*, further clarifying conditions of tax and transfer of profits. Reassurance that equitable compensation would be paid in case of the transfer of ownership for reason of public utility (Article 7) was given when the government bought out a French water and electricity company whose concession had neared its end.

By August 1967, however, the political climate in the country was no longer conducive to foreign investment. Agrarian unrest over government control of rice harvests and the violence used to enforce that control continued in the northwest where the Samlaut rebellion had been harshly put down by government troops. Unrest among minority groups in the northeast highlands rivalled that on the other side of the country. Shockwaves from the cultural revolution in China were being felt in the high schools and colleges of Phnom Penh. The prince's policy of neutrality was in tatters. In 1969, in an effort to forestall his enemies on the left, he renewed diplomatic relations with the United States of America. In hindsight, Milton Osborne judged, "[H]e was taking up a foreign policy option that strengthened the hands of those on the right who were ultimately to depose him."[108]

Foreign Debt

Until 1963, Cambodia had little debt, apart from the very soft loans associated with aid from some socialist countries like Czechoslovakia. During the period 1964 to 1969, according to the Ministry of Finance, capital repayments and interest on external loans totalled US$17.2

million.[109] In the second half of 1969 several loans were contracted and at the end of that year, external credits were worth US$86.9 million.[110] The most important creditor was France which supplied US$34.7 million for transport and industrial projects and in January 1970 promised new loans worth around US$22.5 million. In addition to France, East Germany lent US$12 million, Belgium gave US$7 million and Denmark, US$4 million. These loans were for a cement plant, a sugar factory and for various agricultural, power, transport and tourism projects.

The Asian Development Bank reported that at the end of 1969, Cambodia's external debt was US$69.7 million and debt service payments amounted to US$7.5 million, being 8.7 per cent of the estimated receipts from exports in 1968.

Public Finance, Banking and Credit

The Bank of Indochina, since 1875, had issued the piastre, the currency that was shared by the five members of the Indochinese Union. The piastre was based originally on a silver and then a gold standard, but in 1936 it was placed on a fixed rate of exchange with the French franc. After the Pau Conference of 1950, the *Institut d'Emission* of the renamed Associated States (1945–55) assumed this function of the Bank of Indochina. The piastre then had an official value of 17 francs; on 11 May 1953, it was devalued to 10 francs. On 1 January 1955, as already noted, the newly independent states of the peninsula took full control of their monetary systems. The National Bank of Cambodia then reserved the right to issue the riel, which was based on the value of a gold weight (25.3905 grams) and backed by the bank's reserves of gold and foreign exchange. The official value of the riel was ten francs; one United States dollar could buy 35.07 riels.

In theory, at least, the official value of the riel against the American dollar remained steady until August 1969 when it was devalued to 55.65 to the US dollar. By then, the Royal Government was in panic mode. That month, merchants were warned that those among them who were found to be hoarding imported products, illegally increasing prices of imported products, or refusing to sell products at "normal" prices would be accused of profiteering from the devaluation of the riel in order to sabotage the Cambodian economy and they would be severely punished. The following month, residents holding foreign currency bills were ordered to submit them to the authorities before the end of December or to suffer penalties.

Prior to all this, the riel had remained remarkably stable and inflation was not a major problem. There was corruption on a grand scale, but there were also ministers like Son Sann and Keat Chhon, names that would recur throughout Cambodia's economic history in the latter part of the twentieth century, who were respected for their capable and honest management of the country's finances. National budgets were never too much in deficit, although the deficits became more worrisome after 1964.

Despite this reputation for sound management, however, Rémy Prud'homme thought that it was extremely difficult to know precisely what the receipts and expenses of the Cambodian state were during the Sangkum because they were not all registered in the national budget. Foreign aid, for instance, was not accounted for, and because provinces, even communes, had their own sources of revenue and their own expenditures, what was expenditure for one agency of the state was revenue for another. These details were not explained by the budgets that are still available for study, that is, those for 1967, 1968 and 1969. They represent austerity budgets and should not be considered typical of the whole period. Nevertheless, they give an indication of sources and distribution of both income and expenditure for the Sangkum regime.

Government revenues, estimates that exclude domestic and foreign borrowing and the drawing down of treasury cash resources, for the years 1967–69, were as follows:

Table 2.15 Government Current Revenues (million riels), 1967–69[111]

Source	1967	% of Total	1968	% of Total	1969	% of Total
Income and business taxes	2,040	36.4	2,150	35.9	2,400	37.5
Customs and excises	2,100	37.5	2,387	39.8	2,350	36.7
Administrative income	582	10.4	659	11.0	700	11.0
Public domain	155	2.8	160	2.7	180	2.8
Extraordinary receipts	335	6.0	320	5.3	400	6.2
Misc. receipts	390	6.9	320	5.3	370	5.8
Total	5,602	100.0	5,996	100.0	6,400	100.0

Source: Ministère des Finances, *Budget National*, 1968 and 1969.

About 30 per cent of total budget expenditures for the years 1968 and 1969, were on defence (including national police), no doubt in response to increasing civil unrest and the constant threat of war spilling over from South Vietnam. The extravagance of the education budget, however, in comparison with the spending on other sectors, health and public works, for instance, let alone on agriculture, is difficult to understand at this point in the Sangkum's history.

Table 2.16 National Budget Expenditures, 1968 and 1969 (million riels)[112]

Department	1968	1969
National Assembly	27.4	29.2
Council of the Kingdom	7.1	7.6
President of the Council and Sports	73.1	71.6
Labour	9.8	–
Social Action	18.3	24.7
Plan	14.6	14.6
Industry	7.0	7.8
Post and Telecommunications	74.9	78.3
Foreign Affairs	124.9	129.1
Interior	126.4	138.7
National Security	77.1	83.2
Defence (Constabulary)	406.2	463.8
Information	55.6	56.6
Tourism	16.1	15.8
National Education	1,523.6	1,675.9
Commerce	10.4	9.6
Agriculture	240.7	261.9
Justice	42.9	44.8
Religious Affairs	19.6	21.0
Public Health	355.0	367.2
Public Works	226.3	234.7
Finance	1,822.1	2,005.5
National Defence	1,720.9	1,823.4
Total	7,000.0	7,565.0

Source: Ministère des Finances, *Budget National*, 1969.

From the revenue figures quoted in Table 2.15 above, the overwhelming importance of taxation, that on businesses and personal incomes as well as customs and excise, is evident. These taxes were established by a *kram* of 88 articles that was promulgated in 1954, namely *Kram* No. 900-NS, *Impôt sur les bénéfices, industriels, commerciaux, non-commerciaux, agricoles et fonciers*.[113] Essentially, tax assessed annually on the gains made during the preceding 12 months was set at 18 per cent of net profit for companies, and according to a progressive scale for personal incomes. Those with earnings of 0–20,000 piastres were taxed at the rate of 13 per cent, while those at the top of the scale, that is, 500,000 piastres and above, paid a maximum of 62 per cent in tax.

Despite the official rhetoric, it was a widely held public view that tax evasion was practised universally. In fact, as demonstrated in Table 2.11, the tax share paid by private enterprises was far smaller than that of public and mixed-economy enterprises even though the gross income of private businesses was about five and a half times greater than that of public and mixed-economy enterprises combined. Tax evasion with the full complicity of state agents charged with tax collection, therefore, represented a serious loss to the state budget, as one contributor to the *Bulletin du Contre-Gouvernement* pointed out:[114]

> The state decrees that every industrial enterprise should pay a tax on revenue and profit according to a pre-determined percentage. Few industrialists, in practice, sincerely respect this law. Moreover, very often, the tax is falsely set on a base fixed according to the industries and the state agents who are supposed to collect the tax.... The state is thus frustrated each year by the failure to gather several million riels.

Banking and Credit

The National Bank of Cambodia was established at the end of 1954 as a mixed-economy enterprise. In fact, no private entrepreneur ever had a share in the bank's capital and it functioned entirely as a public institution from its inception. Until the major reforms of November 1963, there were also around a dozen private banks operating in the country. Following nationalisation, these were replaced with just two state banks: *la Banque Khmère pour le Commerce* (BKC) and l'Inadana Jati (IJ) or *Crédit National*. The sudden closure of the private banks, however, was not as destabilising as one might expect. The National Bank set up funds for the BKC to cover exigencies, particularly for the 1963–64 harvest, but otherwise the BKC and the IJ simply assumed the roles the private banks had played. Prud'homme thought that this relatively smooth transition was due to the special nature of banking in Cambodia:

> The essential function of the banking system evidently consists of facilitating exchanges, or of maintaining a degree of liquidity in the economy sufficient to assure the financing of commerce [mainly foreign trade].... On the domestic market, a good part of exchange takes the form of barter or personal credit.[115]

In the state banking system, deposits were essentially state revenues and they were used to finance the operations of foreign trade, imports and exports which came under the control of another state authority, Sonexim. The banking system, therefore, played a negligible role in development. There were no institutions to mediate between savings and investment, no financial market, no savings banks, and no business banks. "There are no specialized organisms which, in a country like France, for instance, give medium and long-term loans," Prud'homme noted.[116] While average household savings were above 10 per cent of household income, they were usually invested in the form of personal jewellery, expensive homes, or smuggled abroad.

Short-term credit, on the other hand, was only too readily available. "The short-term loan is absolutely a general practice in the whole kingdom," Delvert stressed. "The sale of credit is a general practice; it is, in reality, a usurious loan."[117] Delvert paid special attention to the credit system that operated in the market gardens beside the rivers. Here, he noted, polyculture allowed the farmer to avoid losses through market fluctuations and usually it was the local merchant-cum-moneylender who gave loans for crops with high market value. There was, Delvert judged, a symbiotic relationship between the local moneylender and the farmer. "The Chinese," he considered, "gives the Cambodian economy life. Without him, the peasant would have difficulty assuring his livelihood."[118]

Interest rates, however, were exorbitant. In Delvert's time, they were more than 10 per cent monthly, and normally around 12 per cent. For the paddy farmer, this translated into between three and five *thang* of paddy (worth then 120–200 riels) for every 100 riels borrowed. State-administered agricultural credit began during the French Administration and popular credit banks had been operating in Cambodia since 1942, but the scale of their operations was so small and peasant access so limited, that they played a negligible role in agricultural development. Hou Yuon made a strong case to prove that the loans issued to farmers through the Office of Popular Credit were "basically subsistence loans to needy farmers through the critical hungry period," that is, the two or three months before the harvest.[119]

In 1956, the Royal Government created two credit organisms which offered short and medium-term loans to the agricultural sector: the *Caisse Nationale d'Équipement*, and, more importantly as far as the individual farmer was concerned, *l'Office Royal de Coopération* (OROC). The latter effectively replaced the Office of Popular Credit but greatly expanded its mission. OROC's mission was "to create and organize cooperatives in the various agricultural and economic domains of the Kingdom in relation to credit, production and consumption, to supervise and coordinate all the activities of the cooperatives attached to it, to supply them with essential financial and material needs, and to conduct the operations of purchase and sale, export and import in the interest of the cooperatives."[120] Rémy

Prud'homme considered OROC to be "the principal means by which public authorities intervene in the main sector of the Cambodian economy."[121]

Rural cooperatives started forming in 1956 but their numbers did not grow much before 1964. In 1966, existing cooperatives were re-grouped into around 400 "multi-purpose" cooperatives. In turn, they were divided among 13 provincial credit cooperatives or one per major participating province; the remote area provinces were not included. Nominal membership in 1966 was 323,000, or about one-fifth of the 1.7 million farmers numbered in the economically active population.[122]

From the start, the rural cooperatives faced serious problems. Local merchants, naturally enough, resisted their development and this proved to be an obstacle, but they were developed too quickly and suffered from the same defects as the state factories, namely a failure of sound management and close supervision. Official corruption was also a factor, as was a lack of genuine understanding and commitment from the farmers themselves, the targeted beneficiaries of the cooperative system. Unlike the factories, however, the cooperatives also lacked investment, or at least sufficient investment to lift agriculture from its normal level of production. OROC began in 1956 with total capital of merely 200 million riels, half of it state-subscribed and the rest in the form of a reimbursable long-term loan.

In those heady days of national debate, much criticism was levelled at OROC. Even those who were sympathetic to the cooperative system in theory could find little to defend in practice. In February 1967, Tan Kim Huon, *recteur* of the University of Agricultural Sciences, wrote in the *Bulletin du Contre-Gouvernement* (BCG), "In the face of multiple social and economic problems, this organism is incapable of finding satisfactory solutions on a national scale. Therefore, its usefulness is itself in doubt."[123] He thought the causes of failure were basically two: "the intrinsic causes inherent in the actual organisation of OROC, and the extrinsic causes found in the economic and social structure of the country."

Even though OROC was the main agricultural credit agency, the Asian Development Bank team found that only 10 to 30 per cent of farmers got loans through the cooperative system. "The vast majority of the cultivators still borrow from such sources as moneylenders, middlemen, traders, and village shopkeepers," they reported.[124] Given OROC's inherent problems and the "symbiotic relationship" that had formed over generations between the local moneylender and the farmer, this should not be surprising. What is surprising is the actual scale of the informal credit industry and the central role it played in production and consumption in the national economy.

Delvert found it difficult to get the farmers to admit their indebtedness. "An inquiry among the Cambodian coolies on the plantations was negative. Among 1,308 coolies," he noted, "none had a debt. But this is certainly false."[125] He quoted OROC estimates that in 1952, three-quarters of rural households had debts and that the total personal debt in the agricultural sector was a little over 4 million riels. Given the scale of debt and the chronic state of indebtedness among Cambodian farmers, the level of investment in agriculture, both public and private, was obviously negligible. Despite the political rhetoric, state irrigation works supplied only two or three per cent of the total paddy area and the annual national budget for agriculture came a poor third after other development sectors, education and health, for instance.

A clear exposé of agricultural credit during the Sangkum was provided by Tan Kim Huon.[126] The individual farmer, he explained, required short-term consumption credit to cover the subsistence needs of his family, mid-term production credit for his crop and to finance equipment, livestock or repairs, as well as long-term credit in the case of, say, family-scale rubber cultivation or for the needs of the rural collectives engaged in road-construction, electrification or irrigation. There were, in 1968, three sources of credit. Public credit was offered by the two commercial banks that gave short-term loans but were not involved in loans to peasants, and the *Caisse Nationale d'Équipement* that lent to the big industrialists and planters. Cooperative credit was dispensed by OROC through the intermediary of the provincial credit cooperatives and increasingly by the "multi-purpose" cooperatives. This credit was only for cooperative members who represented less than one-third of the total number of agricultural households, and only those who had collateral. Farmers without collateral could not take part in the cooperatives. There was, finally, usurious private credit from the merchant-cum-moneylender. Tan Kim Huon judged, "One can no longer remain silent about the fact that the provincial credit cooperatives function very badly ... and that OROC does not have at its disposal much credit for usefully financing agricultural activity." He calculated that total investment annually to cultivate 2.5 million hectares of paddy using intensive methods, including fertiliser and pesticides but not counting the cost of irrigation, would cost seven billion riels. Actual investment was about half that figure, mainly at the cost of scant savings and expensive private credit. The role of OROC was negligible. "OROC and all the cooperatives affiliated with it contribute in a good or bad year 160 million riels in the form of advances, but this amount is not used solely as credit for the production of rice," Tan Kim Huon wrote.

The only solution, he believed, lay in the establishment of an agricultural bank that offered short, medium and long-term credit to cover the varied activities of rural life. In September 1969, the government did indeed establish such a bank, the *Banque Agricole Paysanne*, capitalised at 100 million riels subscribed entirely by the government and state-owned financial institutions.[127] The established method for borrowing from the bank was that still used in the Cambodian countryside c. 2000 by the various NGO credit agencies: groups of five to ten members, in theory (but rarely) from the poorest and most needy families in the village, could borrow at an annual rate of seven per cent (to guarantee funds and to pay the costs of the village committee).[128] Had the *coup d'état* and civil war not intervened six months later, perhaps the Farmer's Bank could have made an important contribution to the rural economy.[129]

Conclusions

Given the catastrophes that befell Cambodia after 1970, analysts can sometimes forget the enthusiasm and optimism with which ordinary people embraced the *Sangkum Reastr Niyum* and its plans for modernisation that promised all Cambodians a fair share of the prosperity that would grow from it. At the same time, it is too easy to blame the Second Indochina War alone for the Sangkum's failure to deliver on the promises contained in its policies. Of course, the war played a major part in the downfall of the regime, but it was not the only factor.

The main aim of Sangkum economic planners was to generate local savings, both collective and private, in order to stimulate growth. National development was state-directed and even the leftists like Hou Yuon and Khieu Samphan recognised the need to capitalise the economy and to transfer the capacity for capital earnings from the big foreign firms and the ethnic Chinese traders to local manufacturers and entrepreneurs. For seven or eight years, the policy seemed to succeed. In a broad sense, there were personal savings and there was national growth as a result of Sangkum policy, but because one was not intrinsic to the other — because private wealth was generated more by graft than by economic growth and those personal assets were not reinvested in local enterprises such as agriculture — development was not sustainable and after an encouraging "lift off" stage, the rate of growth soon levelled out and the economy stagnated.

The Sangkum employed a variety of strategies to drive growth. Ongoing close cooperation with longstanding foreign investors and guarantees that their investments were safe from nationalisation served to attract further investment which enjoyed very liberal, even generous terms. Foreign aid was spent on infrastructure works that were essential to industrialisation and to attracting new investment: for instance, the seaport at Sihanoukville and the road and rail links between the port and the capital, the hydroelectric plant, bridges linking the capital with key provinces, and so on. Whereas the French Protectorate had permitted the employment of foreigners for certain administrative and other roles, the Sangkum took affirmative action to provide jobs for Cambodians, particularly the graduates from a vastly expanded and extended education system. There was public investment in state-owned enterprises and experimentation with mixed-economy enterprises and rural cooperatives. Meanwhile, the rate of growth was kept at a manageable level, the currency remained relatively stable and inflation was not a serious problem, nor was the balance of payments or the trade deficit. The external debt was low.

These achievements were not insignificant. As a developing country Cambodia was considered by many to be a model of successful decolonisation. It should also be remembered that economic theories of development at that time supported the policies adopted by the Sangkum. Modernisation was about adding value through domestic manufacturing and processing of local resources and primary products and then profiting from their export or sale. Protective tariffs were the norm globally to ensure that domestic industry did not suffer from foreign competition. The world market was still divided into zones, not simply the ideological ones of communism and liberalism, but also currency zones with colonial ties, such as the sterling zone and the franc zone. Decolonisation was a lengthy process, and adopting a balanced, neutral approach to foreign assistance seemed reasonable, even courageous, for an emerging nation at that time.

Big business that was still largely controlled by Chinese and European interests prospered during the Sangkum era. Importers, contractors and local firms that provided services and materials were the most successful beneficiaries of foreign aid. The state, on the other hand, collected far less than its legal share of resulting business profits through taxation, and too few of the remaining profits were returned to the Cambodian economy through investment in the type of enterprise favoured by state policy. Widespread official corruption allowed profits to be under-taxed and too much of the remainder was either smuggled abroad or legally transferred under the generous terms provided by the investment law. Some profits were invested in non-productive consumables such as lavish villas and expensive imports, primarily vehicles. Meanwhile, private investment in rural development and agricultural diversification was virtually non-existent. The coercive power of the state was far too weak, and the private sector far too powerful *vis-à-vis* the public and mixed-economy sectors for this situation to change.

Institutional development lagged far behind economic development. There were no mechanisms, for instance, to mediate between savings and investment. There was no stock exchange or other financial institution that offered incentives for those who saved to invest in national growth. The small banking sector existed principally to facilitate foreign trade and occasionally to provide credit for big and medium private enterprises. Least of all did it provide credit to individual farmers.

In order to sustain growth, the government had to ensure that a surplus existed in order to continue funding state-sponsored development projects. Foreign aid receipts should have provided the government space to allow sources of that surplus to develop. When American aid was cancelled, however, and private industry proved elusive to taxation, the government was forced to fall back on the agricultural sector to make up the shortfall in revenue.

The peasantry, despite official claims to the contrary, benefited little from the economic reforms of the 1950s and 1960s. While the cultivated area grew, more or less in line with rural population growth, there was already a noticeable trend towards increasing numbers of workers per hectare of land. Productivity changed very little and paddy yields stubbornly remained at an average of 1.3 tons per hectare. The irrigated area amounted to only three per cent of the total area cultivated with paddy in the 1967–68 season, hardly different from that of 2.1 per cent in 1953–54. Conditions for the sale of farmers' products barely changed. The cooperative system, including the provision of agricultural credit, had very little effect on rural incomes and living standards, largely because public investment in the management body, OROC, was too small. Consequently, there was little agricultural diversification during the Sangkum and the national economy remained dependent on the same crops as during the French Protectorate, namely rice and rubber. Natural rubber was already coming under intense competition from synthetic rubber, but the state continued to establish new plantations, despite increasingly organised resistance from among indigenous groups like those around the Labansiek plantation in Ratanakiri.

Fundamentally, the nature and structure of the Cambodian economy in 1969 was little different from what it had been when independence was declared in 1953. Cambodia had active markets but it did not have a market economy. The term "pre-capitalist" is commonly used to describe the sort of economy that persisted in Cambodia, the assumption being, as Ellen Meiksins Wood notes, that the "seeds of capitalism" are contained in any form of trade or market activity.[130] Market activity, however, is an insufficient requirement according to her definition of capitalism as "a system in which goods and services, down to the most basic necessities of life, are produced for profitable exchange, where even human labour-power is a commodity for sale in the market, and where all economic actors are dependent on the market."[131] The peasants, who still make up the vast majority of the economically active population of Cambodia, were not dependent on the market for their livelihood, in the sense that they did not have to enter market relations to gain access to the means of production. Social property relations remained little altered, except for the plantations and even there, as Delvert found, at least half of the Cambodian rubber coolies he interviewed owned land in their home villages. The typical rice farmer considered himself to be the owner of the land he and his family worked; together they produced what they needed for food, plus a small surplus to provide for essential cash needs and to cover the state's share as well. The local merchant-cum-moneylender took the lion's share of many peasants' output but it would be wrong to define this relationship as a capitalist one. The rice merchant was and still is more like a medieval pawnbroker than a modern capitalist. Khieu Samphan thought that local artisanal trades also had more in common with those of the Middle Ages than with the modern market. The capitalist laws of motion — laws of competition, profit-maximisation, and capital accumulation — that "uniquely compel people to enter the market, to reinvest surpluses and to produce 'efficiently' by improving labour productivity" had very little to do with the market place that typified the Cambodian economy in the 1950s and 1960s.[132]

Apart from big business which remained in the hands of the large European firms, the post-independence economy still functioned according to the old laws of trade: buy cheap and sell dear. Essentially, GDP growth was driven by the sector that was capitalised but it was largely foreign-owned so, when the government withdrew incentives from the foreign-owned sector, the Cambodian economy simply stopped growing. In March 1970, therefore, it was the economic crisis, as much as the worsening political situation, that triggered Cambodia's first revolution, the transfer of power from the ancient monarchy to a new republic.

(Front view)

(Reverse view)

One hundred riel note of the Khmer Republic depicting weaver

(Front view)

(Reverse view)

Five hundred riel note of the Khmer Republic

(Front view)

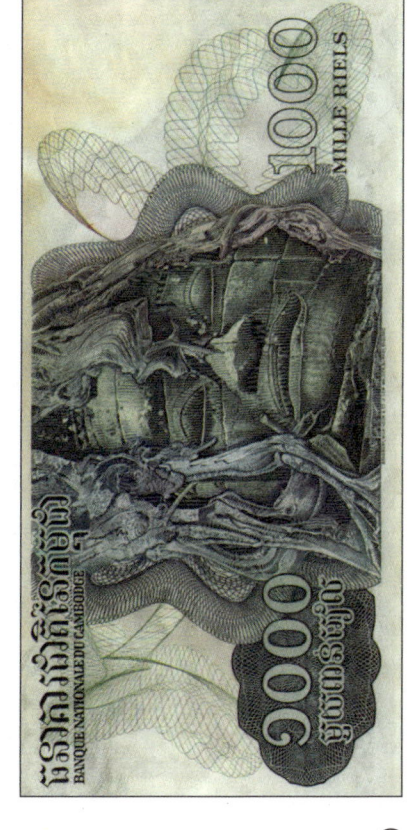

(Reverse view)

One thousand riel note of the Khmer Republic depicting education

(Front view)

(Reverse view)

One hundred riel note of the Khmer Republic

CHAPTER

3

The Wartime Economy, 1970–75

> We are at a decisive turning point in our history. A radical change in almost all domains is being made. The time of improvising, of making decisions without reflection, of temper tantrums, of irresponsible advice is gone. Something solid, reflective, and studied should take its place. A certain stability ... in the political economy is desirable.
>
> Sim Thai Pheng[1]

On 18 March 1970, at one o'clock in the afternoon, the plenary session of the National Assembly and the Council of the Kingdom voted unanimously for the dismissal of Sihanouk as Cambodia's head of state. Cheng Heng, president of the National Assembly and interim head of state during the prince's absence from the country since January that year, was sworn into the post. The Cambodian elite had chosen to cast off two thousand years of monarchy and launched the ship of state into very perilous seas. Given the sharp escalation of the American War in neighbouring Vietnam and the growing presence on Cambodian soil of North Vietnamese troops for the purposes of sanctuary and transit, it is probable that there was U.S. involvement in the coup that overthrew Sihanouk, who had tolerated their presence in his country. The nature and extent of that involvement, however, has never been publicly revealed. Nevertheless, the critical factor that precipitated the coup was dissidence from powerful conservative elements within the state, political elements that were almost certainly backed by the small but very influential business elite.

Since August 1969, the "national salvation" government had been led by General Lon Nol, who concurrently held the post of Minister of Defence, and his deputy, Prince Sisowath Sirik Matak whose outspoken opposition to many Sangkum policies had kept him abroad in ambassadorial posts for much of the previous decade. These men were given wide authority to revive the stagnating economy. Sirik Matak was a vocal advocate for the resumption of U.S. aid to ease the problems of the economy, especially the mounting budget deficit. He had also opposed the nationalisation programme and, while the still vacillating Lon Nol was outside the country for a couple of months at the end of the year, he devalued the currency, removed state control over foreign trade and banking and set about implementing a policy of disengagement, or reducing state involvement in economic enterprises.

Sirik Matak was undoubtedly the driving force behind the coup, but he had little popular appeal and, more significantly, he lacked the essential *khsae*, the strings of patronage, to influence the military. Lon Nol had the necessary credentials but he proved to be an inept leader, driven by a strange mix of occultism and ruthless ambition. In the first week of March 1970, anti-Vietnamese demonstrations, almost certainly orchestrated by Lon Nol himself, broke out in Phnom Penh and provincial towns. The embassies of North and South Vietnam were sacked and youths stormed unchecked through the Vietnamese quarter of the capital, looting and smashing for three days. Quelling the disturbances was the immediate excuse for the coup which itself was bloodless and, strictly speaking, was only a *coup de chef d'état* since the legislature, popularly elected on 2 December 1966, remained virtually unchanged and the administration also stayed more or less intact. Some analysts argued that the coup plotters never intended that Cambodia should become a republic. The motive, it seems, was to remove Sihanouk, not to abolish the Khmer monarchy. Following a near-unanimous vote in the National Assembly on 5 October, however, the republic was proclaimed. The urban middle-class, Justin Corfield notes, were "quickly buoyed with a new sense of patriotism and national identity."[2]

During the last week of April 1970, the American War in Vietnam escalated into the Second Indochina War. In a bitter riposte to his enemies in Phnom Penh, Sihanouk, now in exile in Beijing, had granted legitimacy to the communist guerrillas, the Khmer Rouge, by joining forces with them in the FUNK (National United Front of Kampuchea). Six weeks after the coup, on 29 April, U.S. and South Vietnamese forces crossed the border into Cambodia to destroy the Vietcong sanctuaries. The Cambodian government was not forewarned of the invasion by 12,000 ARVN ground troops, accompanied by the terrifying firepower of American air support. The effect of the invasion was to drive the North Vietnamese forces farther inside Cambodia where they joined with the Khmer communists to mobilise and organise thousands of peasants who joined the FUNK at the summons of their king. Thus, when the main forces of the U.S. invasion withdrew on 30 June that year, a brutal civil war had already begun and the Cambodian government had lost control over approximately half of the countryside. It was a civil war that the republican government never admitted until the final year before defeat. As far as the government leaders were concerned, they were locked in battle with troops of North Vietnam and the Vietcong; the army of Sihanouk, they deluded themselves, was an "imaginary" one.[3]

A state of martial law would commence on 1 June, Cambodians were warned via a radio broadcast delivered by Lon Nol approximately one week before the decree was implemented.[4] Later that month, the government issued a further decree-law on general mobilisation. This did not, however, amount to official conscription. The new regime, lacking legitimacy, hardly had the authority to enforce such draconian measures. Nevertheless, thousands of students left their studies to volunteer for Lon Nol's "holy" war against the *thmils*, the unbelievers. At the beginning of the dry season in December, Lon Nol launched the first of two major offensives against the North Vietnamese forces in Cambodia. The Cambodian troops, many of them raw recruits, were no match for their adversaries and the 1971 dry season offensive was also the last. David Chandler believes that the government survived for a further four years, "largely because of U.S. military assistance and heavy bombing and because the Vietnamese Communists were unwilling to help their Cambodian colleagues take Phnom Penh before they managed to liberate South Vietnam."[5]

Given the precarious military situation, the economy faltered, foreign trade dwindled, almost all the rubber plantations stopped tapping, the tourist industry built around the ruins at Angkor was no more, and plans for investment loans were shelved. On the other hand, corruption flourished. Justin Corfield reported an incident in January 1972 when a colonel was charged with attempting to sell a truckload of medical supplies to the insurgents.[6] Far from this being an isolated incident, it was part of a flourishing illicit trade with the enemy. The most widespread form of corruption within the armed forces was the enlistment of ghost soldiers whereby officers added extra names to their unit payrolls and pocketed the salaries. The foot soldiers then paid the real cost by having to fight in under-strength units.

Despite suffering a debilitating stroke in 1971, Lon Nol, now promoted to marshal, increased his power over the republic at the expense of

Sirik Matak and Cheng Heng, the nominal head of state. Sirik Matak's resignation from a brief, five-day term as Prime Minister was accepted on 15 March 1972; in May, he was appointed "special adviser" to the president, a position still reserved for those who represent a potential threat to ultimate power holders in the Cambodian polity. The government dissolved further into tragi-comedy or farce with the appointment as Prime Minister of Son Ngoc Thanh, Sihanouk's old nemesis, who had spent the previous 27 years in the political wilderness. The constitution of the Khmer Republic was eventually approved by popular referendum on 30 April 1972 and on 3 July, Lon Nol was invested as president. In September that year, elections were held for the National Assembly as well as for the Senate, the legislative review chamber, formerly called the Council of the Kingdom.

By 1973, the Khmer Republic barely existed outside of Phnom Penh, plus a narrow corridor along Route 5 to Battambang and the Thai border, and a few provincial towns. The rest of the country was either already firmly in communist hands, or insecure and contested. That year began with the signing of the Paris Peace Accords between North Vietnam and the United States of America on 27 January. The Khmer Rouge refused to participate and they suffered the consequences of their intransigence. Their inevitable victory over the republican forces was delayed by massive U.S. aerial bombardment of the Cambodian countryside, some of it in the most densely populated regions. In a little more than six months, until 15 August, over 100,000 tons of bombs rained down, almost incessantly. This was the climax to years of saturation bombing. Craig Etcheson calculated that between May 1969, when American bombing of Cambodia began and mid-August 1973, a total of 539,129 tons of ordnance fell on the country, equivalent to 15,400 pounds of explosives for every square mile of Cambodian territory (or almost three tons per square kilometre).[7] Phnom Penh swelled to bursting point with refugees fleeing from the bombs.

With the end of U.S. air support, however, the forces of the Khmer Republic could not hold. Despite the government's three desperate and unheard appeals to the other side for unconditional negotiations throughout 1974, Phnom Penh fell to the communists on 17 April 1975.

Policies

The influential Chamber of Commerce immediately threw its support behind the republic, declaring in the first re-issue of its bulletin after the coup:

The continuity of the Khmer state has not been put at risk.... If this bulletin can appear in the present exceptional circumstances, it is thanks to the support of H.E. General Lon Nol who thus manifests his wish to promote the economic and social progress of the country.... The *Chambre Mixte de Commerce et d'Agriculture* will do all in its power to assist the Government of Salvation to relaunch business and to restore confidence by trying to erase the stagnation born of the ill-considered 1963 economic reforms.[8]

This close collaboration was confirmed on 9 April 1970, when the secretaries of state for labour and social action (Chau Seng Ua), and for commerce and industry (Prom Thos) addressed the Chamber of Commerce to explain key policy issues affecting the economic and social situation in the country.[9] They declared that the republican government's goal was that economic expansion should benefit the whole population, not just a narrow clique as in the past. The immediate objective, however, was to ensure the regular provision of vital supplies for Phnom Penh and the areas threatened by insecurity. In the medium-term, some sectors of the economy would be transformed into a "war economy" for the production of national defence needs, precautions would be taken to protect local food products from black marketeering or bottlenecks in supply and distribution, and special attention would be paid to protect the cultivation of export crops such as maize, rubber and beans.

The government, the officials said, was seeking the cooperation of the private sector to achieve its long-term policy goals. The Sangkum objective of providing farmers with manufactured goods at reasonable prices was still a priority, as was identifying favourable markets for agricultural produce. Small private enterprises would be created to supply potable water and electricity for the countryside. For the industrial sector, the government envisaged enterprises where the employees, workers or technicians could become shareholders, in fact, part-owners of their own workplaces. In addition, "associations" of technicians would be created, and "leading cadres from the great schools" would be attached to enterprises in order to improve production, create new jobs and "to elevate the prestige of the private sector."[10] Merchants and industrialists were reassured at the meeting that the government would proceed with further liberalisation of foreign trade, "allowing merchants to carry out their own commercial operations."

The 1963 reforms, when foreign trade, banking and insurance were all nationalised, had left the Phnom Penh business elite deeply resentful. Confirmation that the policy of economic liberalisation initiated by Sirik Matak and enacted into law by two *kram* (numbers 425 and 426) issued on 12 February 1970 would continue was really all that the Chamber of Commerce wanted to hear.[11] Sirik Matak's address to the National Assembly on the occasion of the investiture of the first republican government on 6 May 1971 gave that assurance, but he emphasised that the government's priority was winning the war:

> Our first objective will be to defeat our aggressors (Vietcong/North Vietnamese).... Secondly, we will accelerate the work of elaborating the constitution of the Khmer Republic so it can be promulgated with the shortest possible delay in order to establish progressively republican foundations.... Thirdly, we must solve our economic, financial and social problems by finding an acceptable equilibrium that does not compromise our war effort, which remains essential for the survival of our nation. In this regard, we will perfect the application of the policy of economic liberalisation taken in August 1969. The government, however, will not hesitate to take over management of some industrial and commercial sectors if, for the war effort, the liberal mechanisms are not functioning in a satisfactory manner. The government will not hesitate to take measures to protect domestic industries when the too rapid application of liberalisation measures puts them in peril. In the economic domain, I must stress the importance of prices. The government will do all in its power to improve the system of supply and transportation. The price of products of first necessity will be fixed and controlled. Severe sanctions will be taken against speculators. We will use foreign aid effectively so that it profits the masses. In the social sphere, we will deploy all our efforts to raise the standard of living of the population and protect workers ... our final aim being, without doubt, social justice.... In these exceptional, grave circumstances ... we ask the National Assembly to honour us with its confidence by awarding us full powers.... In foreign policy, the new government will continue to respect the principles of active neutrality: we will collaborate frankly with those who declare themselves to be our friends. We affirm our will to develop regional cooperation.... In ending this brief speech, I solemnly declare before the nation that our soldiers and civil servants should all fulfil their roles with order and discipline. That is an absolute necessity if we want to have victory over our aggressors and then organize a republican society where our children can live in security and prosperity. Everything that contravenes this elementary rule of discipline constitutes treason against the Khmer Republic.[12]

State coercion was probably the only means the government had to enforce its economic policies under war conditions. Given its tenuous legitimacy, however, the government of the Khmer Republic rarely used coercion, except against minority ethnic groups like the Vietnamese. Despite official rhetoric, therefore, there were no sustained efforts to adhere to policy. Even more than during other regimes, the gap between stated policy and actual practice assumed the dimensions of a bottomless gulf during the Khmer Republic. The appeals to merchants to be satisfied with honest and reasonable profits fell on deaf ears. Greed and corruption ruled the Khmer Republic and sealed its fate, in equal measure with the cynicism of the Nixon Doctrine and the determination for victory by the other side.

Administration and Governance

Almost immediately after the coup, the government was at war. In these exceptional circumstances, it may be harsh to judge the fledgling regime as incompetent and misdirected. Some analysts excuse the failure of the Khmer Republic on the grounds that Sihanouk had never allowed his ministers and officials to learn the ropes of good governance, to make independent decisions and to follow through on established policies. To some extent, this was true. On the whole, however, the regime proved unwilling to cope with the war or to accept responsibility for its economic, financial and especially its social consequences. It was a regime that wore blinkers for fear that it would be startled by the reality of a situation that was spinning rapidly out of its control.

The new constitution was two years in the drafting. Sirik Matak had given the constitution his second priority after ensuring victory in war, and a month or so after his investiture speech, on 16 June 1971, a special committee was charged with the task of preparing the constitution. Lon Nol refused the first draft and dissolved the committee. He then decreed constituent powers on the National Assembly, but its draft went the way of the first. On 10 March 1972, Lon Nol unilaterally proclaimed himself president, dissolved the Assembly and two weeks later set up a new committee for drafting the constitution. A draft was finally approved and it was put to popular referendum on 30 April. The constitution of the Khmer Republic was promulgated by Ordinance No. 19/72 on 10 May 1972.

It was a constitution that reflected the events surrounding its formulation. The preamble declared, in part: "We, the Khmer people ... are determined ... to defend our republican system against any attempt to restore the monarchy and against any establishment of personal power."[13] The first article defined Cambodia as "an independent, democratic and social republic," but the democratic rights enshrined in the constitution were limited, in almost every case, by a proviso. Political parties, for instance, could be freely organised, "[h]owever, the state shall encourage every effort to reduce the number of political parties in order to achieve a two-party system." Capital punishment was abolished except when the nation was deemed to be in danger. Freedoms of expression, association and assembly were granted, but they were all conditional and proved easy to revoke. Similarly, economic freedom as such was not guaranteed; only the state's protection of that freedom "in the artisanal trades, agriculture, commerce and industry" was assured. Article 16 declared that the state had "the duty to regulate that freedom with a view to co-ordinating the national economy for social ends and preventing monopolies or any attempt at monopoly in commerce and industry."

The constitution provided for several new institutions including the Supreme Judicial Council, a Constitutional Court, a High Court of Justice with the power to judge the president, the vice-presidents, cabinet members, national assembly deputies and members of the Supreme Court, a Council of State, and separate councils for education and culture, the armed forces, economic and social affairs, as well as two offices: the Government Comptroller's Office with power to examine and investigate personnel implicated in abuse of their positions, and the General Mobilization Office. All of these bodies were decreed into law, but it was not the time for institution building. Nevertheless, the careful system of checks and balances that institutions such as those defined in the constitution might, in different circumstances and given the necessary political will, have helped the Cambodian political system to evolve in the way that some republican supporters envisaged. The political system c. 2000 was still grappling with the complexities of instituting some of those watchdog bodies that the true republicans valued.

In the chaos of war, refugees, inflation, destruction of communication routes, and an ever-shrinking food resource base, the old habit of official corruption thrived and fed itself like a glutton on massive offerings of American aid. As the Sangkum had blamed the French Protectorate for the legacy of official corruption, so the Republic blamed the Sangkum; the ruling elite never held themselves to account. In fact, it was generally known that high-ranking military officers, even Lon Nol himself, either directly or through their families were involved in the transport of contraband supplies and munitions from China to the Vietcong via the maritime port at Sihanoukville well before the coup.[14] Graft and corruption were long-entrenched habits of the administration. During times of peace, a measure of corruption was tolerable. In war, however, corruption represented more than just a financial threat to the state. One of Sirik Matak's first circulars from his office as first vice-president of the Council of

Ministers was addressed to public servants concerning their duty to serve loyally and to serve well:

> In my circular No. 10-PCM/AP/C of 27 March 1970, I asked all functionaries to adopt the motto: "To serve loyally and to serve well." I invite you to apply the rules strictly so that our country can free itself definitively from the rotten regime and become a modern state equipped with a healthy, efficient and devoted administration. The sacred duty of all functionaries is to bear themselves as servants, representatives of the state, animated with new ideas complying with the aspirations of the people.... I count on you to punish all forms of corruption and all activities judged dangerous for the security of the country.... Our country has to confront a mortal threat. It is more than ever imperative that all functionaries, of whatever level, are conscious of their responsibility, and that they have the heart to work to re-establish justice in the spirit of genuine democratic freedom for the happiness of our dear Kampuchea.[15]

Where there are no independent institutions with the power to enforce a code of conduct such as that ordered by Sirik Matak, corruption continues to rise with the level of opportunity. Rarely have opportunities for corruption been as plentiful as they were in Cambodia during the few brief years of the Khmer Republic. The United States government provided economic and military aid in increasingly generous quantities. Both forms of assistance were exploited for private gain but military assistance was the most lucrative. The American academics Hildebrand and Porter noted, "By some estimates, fully half of the $350 million in U.S. military aid provided in 1974 was never used for military purposes but was sold by the generals, colonels, and majors for private profit."[16] Ammunition, weapons and other military supplies, as well as medicines, and rice were sold by the military to merchants who resold them on the free market or to Cambodian and Vietnamese revolutionary forces. This trafficking in goods became so important to the governing elite that there was an unspoken understanding that individuals in the most lucrative posts would be rotated every few months. Thus Phnom Penh observers spoke of the "merry-go-round" of executive positions.[17]

Consequently, while thousands of refugees and the urban poor of Phnom Penh were starving, the elite indulged their taste for luxury as never before. The hypocrisy of the regime whose constitution declared its firm commitment to social justice for all citizens reached one of many peaks in August 1971 when two merchants, both of Chinese ethnic origin, were sentenced to death by firing squad for harming the economy and aiding the enemy. Specifically, they had trafficked in vehicles and profited from the deterioration of the economy by sharply increasing their prices. Lon Nol had ordered that these "traffickers" be taken before a military tribunal as an example to others.[18]

In March 1972, Lon Nol gave an order to his government to examine the possibility of organising general elections for a new legislature. The Khmer Rouge would be invited to take part, he declared, and the signature of a formal ceasefire agreement was not a condition for their participation. The minister of information, Keam Reth, reconfirmed that the government was continuing its efforts to bring about a ceasefire. "But so far Hanoi has not responded to proposals for negotiations with Lon Nol," he said, "while the absence of a recognized leader of 'Khmers on the other side' and the different factions among them renders contact difficult."[19] The elections were set for 3 September. The country was divided into 61 electoral districts, and each district would have two seats in the new National Assembly. This arrangement allowed for an enlarged assembly, in line with population growth, but it ignored the fact that much of the country was no longer under the republic's control.

The elections proceeded without incident, and later the same month elections were also held for the Senate. The new government was led by Hang Thun Hak, but like his predecessors, he was unable to deal with corruption and his administration was doomed almost as soon as it was formed. Hang Thun Hak's was the fifth government of the Khmer Republic and four more would stumble before the surrender on 17 April 1975.

Population

The Cambodian demographer, Ea Meng Try, made the interesting observation that although Cambodia's involvement in the Second Indochina War caused greater insecurity, the birth rate actually increased during the first years of the war.[20] The increase, he argued, was due to "a relaxation of social mores, parental insecurity prompting early marriage of daughters, and the decline of unemployment as a result of military recruitment. The fall in the birth rate began in 1973."[21] Generally speaking, however, demographic estimates show that the rate of growth of the Cambodian population was depressed by the war. In view of rapidly declining fertility and the simultaneous rise in mortality, Jacqueline Desbarats argues that the growth rate fell to within the range of one to two per cent.[22] Of the various estimates, she found those of the U.S. Census Bureau the most plausible, that is, a growth rate declining steadily from 2.7 per cent in 1971–72, to 2.3 per cent in 1973, 2.1 per cent in 1974, and finally only

1.5 per cent in early 1975. In her opinion, "A period of absolute population decline began in 1974–75."[23]

The first official 1962 census had enumerated the population as 5.7 million. This figure was ruled to be an undercount and was later adjusted to six million. Population growth rates were subsequently revised to 2.83 per cent for the early 1960s and to 2.95 per cent for the late 1960s, indicating an accelerating growth rate. The United Nations put the average annual increase at 2.8 per cent for the period 1965–70, whereas World Health Organization projections prepared in 1968 used a rate of 2.2 per cent for the low-growth assumption and of 3.0 per cent for the high-growth assumption. An annual growth rate around 2.6 per cent would have yielded a population of about 7 million by 1968 and 7.3 million in 1970. Jacqueline Desbarats offers the following table to illustrate these various estimates of the Cambodian population up to 1974, the last full year of the Khmer Republic:[24]

Table 3.1 Estimates of the Cambodian Population, Selected Years, 1921–74

Year	Population (millions)
1921	2.40
1948	3.75
1962	5.70
1968	7.00
1970	7.30
1974	7.92

Life expectancy at birth, which had been around only 35 in 1945, rose to 45 by the early 1960s. International organisations then reported a crude death rate of between 18 and 20 per 1,000, which remained virtually unchanged until 1970. After that year, according to Jacqueline Desbarats, mortality levels are largely a matter of conjecture. Ea Meng Try estimated that the rate was as high as 28 per 1,000 by 1975, due in part to the very high levels of infant and child mortality in the period leading up to the fall of Phnom Penh and the concomitant drop in life expectancy to 35 years in the early 1970s. Nevertheless, Desbarats suggests, this and other mortality rates, which did not take into account an estimated 600,000 victims of violence during that period, are likely to be too low. She supports the United Nations proposed average mortality rate of 22.5 per 1,000 for the whole period 1970–75, which was about 1.5 points above the arithmetic average of Ea Meng Try's estimates. "This figure is probably closer to the truth," she noted, "implying as it does a total of about 750,000 deaths over the five-year period for a population around seven million, a figure compatible with the generally accepted estimate of 600,000 war casualties during the Lon Nol period."[25]

Estimates of war casualties for the period 1970 to 1975 range from a very low 200,000 to a very high one million. The table below was collated by Craig Etcheson and apart from the extremes, it shows that estimates from both sides more or less concurred that between 600,000 and 700,000 Cambodians lost their lives as a direct result of the war. The number of deaths caused by U.S. bombing, however, remains very controversial, as the table suggests. Furthermore, given the nature of civil war, it is practically impossible to give separate figures for civilian casualties and those of combatants.

Table 3.2 Death in Kampuchean War[26]

Estimates for 1970–75	Millions of Human Lives	Causes of Death 1970–75	Millions of Human Lives
W.J. Sampson	0.20	Combat:	
		– combatants	0.10–0.80
		– non-combatants	0.05–0.30
Ieng Sary	0.60	U.S. Air Power	0.03–0.50
Norodom Sihanouk	0.60		
U.S. State Department	0.60		
Saloth Sar	0.80		
Khieu Samphan	1.00		

Apart from war casualties, the Cambodian population also suffered a significant migratory deficit during this period. The most substantial loss was due to the forced repatriation of about 200,000 Vietnamese, or around half of the total Vietnamese population in Cambodia, soon after the coup. In the final months before the Khmer Rouge victory of April 1975, many more Cambodians, especially those of Vietnamese and Chinese origin, left the country for fear of reprisals. Rémy Prud'homme put the number of Vietnamese residents in Cambodia at 250,000 in 1967, or four per cent of the total population. Jacqueline Desbarats believes the real number was probably closer to twice that figure; as the level of insecurity increased in neighbouring South Vietnam more and more Vietnamese took shelter inside Cambodia.

By 1975, Cambodia's Vietnamese community barely existed. Lon Nol employed traditional Khmer hostility towards Vietnamese to rally popular support for his regime and for his anti-communist campaign. "Vietcong" was used as a derogatory term and applied indiscriminately to all Vietnamese residents. There were selective arrests, detention camps sprang up in the city and the countryside, and there were massacres. In one incident, 800 Vietnamese men, most of them skilled labourers from the community at Chrui Changvar on the peninsula directly opposite the centre of Phnom Penh, were herded onto boats, shot and their bodies were dumped in the river. On 27 April 1970, the Lon Nol regime admitted that more than 3,500 non-combatants, many of them Vietnamese civilians had been killed in the preceding month.[27] The persecution of Vietnamese continued with the seizure of their homes, mandatory detention and the threat that those who remained would be assumed to be communist sympathisers and shot. Hildebrand and Porter noted that between 100,000 and 150,000 Vietnamese Cambodians either fled the capital or were deported after the April massacres.[28]

The reprisals taken against Vietnamese Cambodians also panicked the local Chinese population. Discrimination was practised against the Chinese, but not nearly on the same scale as that suffered by the Vietnamese. Chinese schools and newspapers were shut down and Chinese citizens were harassed by the police and charged with being Khmer Rouge sympathisers. A Sino-Khmer butcher from Kompong Cham province told Penny Edwards that after the coup, the Lon Nol government gave Chinese special identity cards and charged them a special tax.[29] Therefore, she added, "While Chinese names figured prominently in the daily list of donors of funds on behalf of Lon Nol's defence forces and some Chinese took advantage of their business networks to turn the war to their profit, a great number of Chinese in Cambodia were unsympathetic to Lon Nol." Many ethnic Chinese students moved to the liberated zone and many Chinese in rural areas responded to Sihanouk's call for resistance to the republican regime. As noted previously, many wealthy Chinese Cambodians left the country before the final victory of the Khmer Rouge, but, despite this, Jacqueline Desbarats estimates that by 1975, the Chinese population had grown to about 425,000.[30]

The most significant migrant flow was from the countryside to Phnom Penh. The escalating war, the U.S. bombing, and the increasingly strict rule in the liberated zones sent perhaps as many as two million rural people fleeing for the relative safety of the city. Phnom Penh was radically changed by the war from the proud, multi-ethnic "Pearl of the Orient" with a little over 400,000 citizens at the time of the 1962 census, to a city around five times that size, the majority of the inhabitants being provincial and rural Khmer refugees.

Human Development

The World Bank reported per capita income of US$130 for an estimated Cambodian population of 7,692,000 at 30 June 1971. Meanwhile, in reality, the government in Phnom Penh was grappling with an ever-worsening food situation in the capital and the provincial cities.[31] That month, the Mixed Economic Commission was given the task of forming convoys to supply the urban population with rice and other provisions. During its first year, 149 convoys were organised between the capital and Battambang (117 convoys) and Kompong Som (32 convoys), delivering over a million sacks of milled rice to the capital, as well as more than half a million sacks of rice derivatives and 75,870 tons of various merchandise.[32] From Kompong Som, trucks and remorques transported salt, beer, cement, sawn timber and tons of imported goods. Convoys at the rate of three per month also came up the Mekong bringing important supplies of petroleum products. During that first year, the convoys returned with 26,888 metric tons of exports destined for Hong Kong and Singapore.

Despite the convoys and the government appeals to the population not to stockpile food, market prices rose at a staggering rate. From 10 riels per kilogram in December 1971, within two years the price of rice had risen to 125 riels.[33] By the middle of February 1975, a kilogram of rice cost 340 riels on the free market. The government aimed to provide subsidised rice to Phnom Penh residents at the rate of 15 kilograms per family every ten days; in August 1972, a kilo of subsidised rice cost 117 riels and by then the number of needy families in the capital had risen to 216,936.[34] Just two months before Phnom Penh fell, the maximum that could be obtained at the subsidised price was just 270 grams per person daily, which was only 60 per cent of the minimum nutritional requirement set by the World Health Organization.[35] In fact, even that tiny amount was not reliable because corrupt officials diverted subsidised rice to the black market.

In these circumstances, inflation was unstoppable. In October 1971, Sok Chhong, the second vice-president of the Council of Ministers responsible for financial and economic affairs acknowledged that the consumer price index for the middle class had risen from 354 at the time of the coup to 770 by August 1971.[36] Hildebrand and Porter claimed that the small middle class was virtually wiped out by runaway inflation that reached 280 per cent in 1974.[37]

The cost of the war was not borne equitably, as the republic's last Prime Minister, Long Boret, acknowledged in his first speech to the two chambers of parliament on 28 December 1973. "It is essential that the cost of this war imposed on us by the North Vietnamese aggressors be supported equitably by all social classes," he said, "but at present it is the opposite. The elite, which consumes a large part of imported merchandise, have suffered rises in the cost of living far less noticeable than the middle and working classes."[38] The highest cost of all was paid by the refugees.

The tide of refugees into Phnom Penh was so vast that in 1972, in an effort to manage the flood, the city planners undertook an administrative subdivision into 8 *khan* (municipal districts) comprising 30 *sangkat* (municipal communes).[39] Each *khan* was advanced half a million riels for administrative purposes and awarded a provisional budget of between one and two million riels according to the size of its population. The main function of the *khan*, at this critical point in the republic's history, was to cope with the problem of refugees. At the same time, Lon Nol made an international appeal for humanitarian assistance for Cambodians displaced by the war. While the plight of refugees in Phnom Penh was severe, the worst-affected regions were in the south and the southeast of Cambodia near the border with South Vietnam. There, he said, the North Vietnamese forces and their Vietcong auxiliaries had displaced the population, forcing the inhabitants of many villages to follow them and be regrouped in the forested zones.[40] He added:

> Thousands of Khmer inhabitants have been displaced under inhumane conditions and thousands of others have taken flight to escape the invaders and their constant exactions. This is particularly the case in Svay Rieng where the provincial capital has already grown with more than 47,000 refugees since the beginning of the general offensive.... But it is not only in this province where the number and the misery of refugees is increasing day by day. Refugees are flocking to Phnom Penh and other towns.... This influx poses problems that are becoming more and more difficult to resolve.

In his speech to the two chambers at the end of 1973, Prime Minister Long Boret spoke of the "great misery" that had settled on his country and of the "almost insupportable and excessively complex socio-economic problems" that continued to grow despite the efforts of the government in cooperation with some international aid organisations. "The government is taking charge of this problem in its entirety," he told the parliament. Journalist Elizabeth Becker, who was an eyewitness to this misery, described government policy towards its civilians as "criminal neglect."[41] Wartime

Phnom Penh, she wrote, was a seedy city where army officers and their subordinates fleeced refugees at roadblocks, confiscated anything of value and bought young girls to stock their brothels. "By 1974," she noted, "the U.S. had delegated the task of caring for the homeless to private American charities which had to plan, build, staff and purchase everything for the expanding population.... Malnutrition was commonplace among the children."

Health

The escalation of the war after March 1970 led not only to a rapid decline in the nutritional status, but also to the deterioration and destruction of many health facilities. During the Sangkum, there had been a highly satisfactory development of the health sector. A WHO estimate in 1969 had put the number of hospitals throughout the country at 40, and the number of hospital beds at close to 5,500. Within six months of the outbreak of hostilities, however, only 27 hospitals remained in operation and this number had fallen to 13 one year later.[42]

Given the widespread starvation that came to be associated with the regime of Democratic Kampuchea after 1975, the severe malnutrition and death from starvation, particularly among young children in the refugee camps in Phnom Penh and other centres after 1972 is usually forgotten. The average daily calorific intake fell from an already meagre 2,190 in 1972 to just 1,884 in 1974.[43] The average body weight of a two-year-old child in January 1975 was 27 per cent less than it had been before the war. During the last five months of the war, Hildebrand and Porter believed that 250 deaths per day from starvation was a conservative estimate.[44] Many other malnourished children were stunted both physically and mentally.

Education

The provincial universities in Battambang, Kompong Cham and Takeo had to close because of the war, and public instruction in many parts of the country was similarly affected. Nevertheless, for obvious reasons, education remained as important to Lon Nol's regime as it had been to Sihanouk's.

As Sihanouk had declared the ideology of Buddhist socialism to be a fundamental element of his state development policy, so Lon Nol formulated his beliefs into the state ideology termed, in official French

Table 3.3 Planned Exports for 1971[53]

Rice and derivatives	120,000 tonnes	607,634,000r
Rubber	20,000 tonnes	55,860,000r
Total planned exports		795,212,000r

In fact, there was little cause for optimism. The cultivated area had not fallen below 1.8 million hectares since 1955, the first year of the Sangkum, and the estimated 1970–71 harvest was actually less than that for 1963–64. In general, the ministry's policy was to maintain current yields and production by ensuring that farmers received essential supplies and that there was sufficient protection for the work of harvesting, collecting and transporting produce. In and around the main centres, there would be intensive production and stockpiles had to be built against foreseen difficulties of supply. Draught animal stocks had to be protected from illegal exports and thoughtless slaughtering, and there would be a relaxation of forestry regulations in order to facilitate the transport of forestry products. There was also thought for the future and development plans were established for all branches of the ministry because "[it] will be called to play a very important role once the war is over."[54]

After the failure of the 1971 dry season offensive, the course of the war only worsened for the republican side and more and more of the important rice-producing regions fell outside government control. By the end of 1973, when Kompong Thom and Takeo had also fallen, the government could rely only on parts of Battambang province to supply its food needs. In 1974, Hildebrand and Porter estimated, the total cultivated paddy land had fallen to about 500,000 hectares.[55] "Primarily because of loss of control over productive land," they noted, "and secondarily because of lower yields in the remaining areas, paddy production in the Khmer Republic zone fell from a high of 3.8 million tons in 1969–70 to 493,000 tons (at a highly favourable estimate) in 1974–75 — an 87 per cent decline. Thus Cambodia, which had exported some 230,000 tons of rice in 1968 had to import 282,000 tons during calendar year 1974 under the PL-480 program."

Industry

The most significant change in industrial policy was the disengagement of the public sector and the resumption by private enterprise of its role as the motor of commercial and industrial development. The law of 12

February 1970, *Kram* 425/70-CE, reserved only the production and distribution of electricity above 500KVA and the production of arms and munitions as monopolies for the public sector; rail transport and the post and telecommunications services were also state preserves. The private sector therefore believed that apart from these areas, free enterprise should have unrestricted access.

The mixed economy companies, however, remained a structural feature of the republican economy and they presented a challenge both to private entrepreneurs and to the government. The Chamber of Commerce argued that the state's original role in these businesses was a temporary one, to be cast off once the enterprise was able to stand alone. "The state was supposed to play just the role of a go-between and progressively the enterprises would be able to work alone, keeping only a percentage or a sufficient authority to safeguard the national interest against speculative activities by some greedy capitalists," the editor of its bulletin wrote in January 1971.[56] After 1963, however, "impromptu statisation of some mixed economy companies and the eviction of private shareholders, put an end to the harmonious marriage of public and private capital." In fact, by the end of the Sangkum, many of the mixed economy companies were *de facto* state companies and they were run by state functionaries who, Michael Vickery argues, ruled them like the *apanages* of pre-colonial Cambodia:

> Under royalist-Buddhist socialism the state industries and nationalized enterprises after 1964 became in effect appanages for Sihanouk's favourites, who grew wealthy while the account books showed red. Periodic scandals served to spread the wealth around, placing some in temporary eclipse while others took their turn at the trough. It was a continuation of the traditional practice of officials extracting a percentage of what they collected for the state and no one in the elite was ever severely called to account or forced to repay what he had collected from the public till.[57]

The Chamber of Commerce claimed not to be opposed to the existence of the mixed economy companies, only to their management practices. "Undoubtedly, mixed economy is not the best formula, but in a developing country like ours, it is perhaps the least bad formula. The essential point is that things move freely and that management is organized according to private norms."[58]

The economic liberalisation policy of the republican government met its first test over the ownership of *l'Electricité du Cambodge* (EDC), one of the most profitable companies of the national economy. Officially,

EDC was a mixed-economy enterprise and according to the Commercial Code (Article 386b), private investors were entitled to at least a 20 per cent share of the ownership. In fact, under the Sangkum, the state had run the company as a monopoly. The Chamber wanted the state to recognise its own law in this regard and suggested, "It would be very desirable if the private participation rate could be increased ... because the state has to use what little capital it has at its disposal for the imperatives of national defence."[59]

While economic liberalisation served to benefit the handful of big investors in the country's economy, as far as the small industrialists who constituted the vast majority of those engaged in the industrial sector were concerned, liberalisation had few advantages. Almost 90 per cent of the estimated 1,480 industries were small and they operated on very little capital. The removal of protective tariffs at the end of 1969 hurt them badly because they could not compete with imported products in terms of either quality or price; they were also severely affected by inflation, as well as rising costs and salaries for their workers.

Towards the end of 1972, Khuon Chhiek, secretary of state for industry, discussed some of the problems of industry caught between war and peace, of trying to meet the immediate needs of the army and the civilian population while also preparing for post-war reconstruction.[60] "When the war is over," he said, "there will be many things to do — jobs for youth, for those who left the countryside because of war and do not want to return, and for the demobilized soldiers who may want to stay in the towns. With what [little industry] we have, it is not possible to envisage absorbing 5,000 new workers and technicians each year." He said he was helping to prepare a government plan for reconstruction with a view to creating economic development zones in Phnom Penh, Kompong Som and Battambang.

The Labour Law of the Khmer Republic was promulgated by Ordinance No. 2/72 on 14 January 1971 but it was never implemented. Galloping inflation and rising food prices created worker discontent, especially among civil servants whose salaries, always disproportionately small, rapidly lost purchasing power. In July 1972, Lon Nol made a national radio broadcast, promising them higher wages. In part, he said:

> I know that the small salaries in the public services have not seen an improvement in those workers' situation. I must find money to improve the situation for those whose salary is below 2,500 riels. For them, their salary will be increased to 3,500 riels. For those whose salary is between 2,500 and 3,500 riels, it will be a small increase. For those

whose salary is above 3,500 riels, I ask them to be patient because the country can do nothing in their favour at the moment. For "floating" workers, I have decided to award them a minimum of 80 riels per day. This measure will take effect from 1 July 1972.[61]

The official exchange rate was then 159 riels to one American dollar and the black market rate was well in excess of that; at the end of 1971, when rice was still only 10 riels per kilogram at the official rate, one dollar fetched 370 riels on the black market. Two years later, the cost of a kilogram of rice had increased more than ten times and labour strife had grown commensurately. Following demonstrations and then a general strike at the beginning of 1973, the government finally fixed and paid a minimum wage of 3,500 riels per month to take effect from January that year.[62] The striking workers had also demanded administrative reforms, family allowances, improved accommodation, social security and a 40-hour week, demands that were in line with the government's own labour code. In response, the Ministry of Labour and Social Action promised them a 40-hour week "after the war."

Foreign Aid and Trade

In July 1969, Cambodia restored diplomatic relations with the U.S. and Ambassador Emory Swank presented his credentials in September the following year. By then, diplomatic relations had also been restored with Thailand, South Korea and South Vietnam. In 1969, Cambodia also completed all the formalities for joining the International Monetary Fund and the World Bank (then the IBRD) and had regained its membership in the Asian Development Bank. Subsequently, the National Bank, in its report for the 1969–70 fiscal year announced that in order to consolidate its economic independence and in view of the country's increasing defence needs Cambodia was actively seeking external finance.

The Ministry of Finance was convinced that large-scale international collaboration would soon resolve the economic and financial difficulties that Cambodia was experiencing. In May 1970 the ministry issued a communiqué promising that "the diabolical plan of the communists to paralyse our economy will not be achieved."[63] The IBRD mission had concluded that Cambodia's economic and fiscal situation was "relatively good," so the ministry could report, "Our country will be able to count on annual aid of US$10 million from friendly countries and an annual loan of a further US$10 million at five per cent interest reimbursable in 12 years, including two years of grace, without any inconvenience because the level of our foreign debt is low and the conditions of self-regulation are very favourable."

Economic assistance, however, was not immediately forthcoming once diplomatic ties were restored with the U.S. The Asian Development Bank approved a US$1.6 billion loan funded mainly by Japan and the U.S. for hydroelectric and other infrastructure work and by June 1970, some military aid had been received from the U.S., Thailand and South Vietnam, but the first shipments of U.S. economic aid did not start arriving until after 23 June 1971. According to William Rosoff, "Washington, it seems, was putting pressure on Phnom Penh to de-nationalise the economy as a prerequisite for receiving [economic] aid."[64]

The second of the two laws of economic liberalisation issued on 12 February 1970, *Kram* No. 426/70-CE, allowed the private sector "to exercise competitively with the public sector the profession of exporter and importer."[65] According to this law, the state retained its exclusive monopoly over exports of rice and derivatives, maize, rubber, and precious or semi-precious stones, and the commerce ministry would continue to regulate goods that could be imported with foreign currency, but otherwise the private sector could compete equally with the public sector in trade operations. The revised legislation must have satisfied the U.S. because in August, three weeks before the new ambassador presented his credentials, the State Department announced that it had approved an aid programme for Cambodia worth more than $100 million per year. This aid would be delivered in a variety of forms: as direct financial support to the Cambodian budget, as credit for Cambodian purchases from the U.S. (under the Commodity Import Programme, CIP, as before 1963), and as technical assistance. An extra $40 million was added to military aid for the 1970–71 fiscal year in the form of light arms, munitions, communications equipment, training and uniforms.[66]

No doubt reassured by the promises of economic and military assistance, the National Assembly, on 14 October, voted for an additional bill to liberalise the export of rice and its derivatives and maize. The government press release concerning the new law explained, "The measures of liberalisation respond to the current need: we must end blind statism and *l'économie en vase clos* imposed on the country by the catastrophic experiences and so-called socialisation of the dictatorial Sihanoukist regime, responsible for the severe economic and political crisis which endured for years and from which we still suffer the effects."[67] The end of state monopoly over the export of grains and cereals saw the dissolution of the state companies Sonaprim, which had been responsible for the distribution of imports, and Magétat, which ran the state food shops.

The Chamber of Commerce members naturally responded to the law with satisfaction and the added hope that removal of the remaining state monopolies on the export of natural rubber and precious stones would represent the last stage of full liberalisation.

The further liberalisation of the economy received the endorsement of the U.S. Senate Commission on Foreign Affairs, which approved $255 million in aid to Cambodia on 29 December 1970. This figure represented almost half of the total American aid commitment to Southeast Asia that year. Australia had also promised A$3.7 million in aid under the Colombo Plan, and Cambodia had requested US$20 million from Japan as special grant aid for humanitarian purposes, for communications, and for ambulances and medical supplies.

Thus, by the end of 1970, the Lon Nol regime was securely hooked up to the drip-feed of aid. Hildebrand and Porter calculated that the Khmer Republic received a total of almost $1.9 billion in U.S. assistance.[68] Like an addictive drug, however, the aid that the regime received from the U.S. only served to weaken it. Most analysts are scathing in their assessment of the role the Nixon government played in the destruction of Cambodia in the 1970s, not only by aerial bombardment but also by the way it delivered aid. Elizabeth Becker observed that Lon Nol's belief that the U.S. commitment to the war effort was a "blank cheque" was one of his most serious errors:

> Lon Nol never received public, long-term support from the United States, there was not even a common agreement on goals.... American troops but not American money would be withdrawn. The U.S. would support its allies' war effort until American objectives had been reached ... [but] Nixon and Kissinger had no intention of fighting a war against Asian communism to the finish.... A dance of deceit and manipulation ensued between the American president and the U.S. Congress, and between the president and his ally Lon Nol in Phnom Penh.[69]

The aid, she wrote, was sent first to the military where it could be best disguised and where U.S. interests were centred. On the other hand, the U.S. gave no humanitarian aid until 1971, "and then not nearly enough to care for the growing number of refugees, the wounded in crowded hospitals, and the thousands going hungry as rice fields became battlefields."

It is difficult to track and calculate this aid because, as Elizabeth Becker said, it came in many guises. The Commercial Imports Programme, the main form of U.S. aid to Cambodia before November 1963, was resumed. Under the CIP, Cambodian importers could repay the U.S. in riels (at preferential exchange rates) for goods purchased with foreign exchange such as petroleum, spare parts, machinery and chemical products, and these riels were then placed in a special fund for technical aid projects or for the army. Agricultural products, including cotton, tobacco, vegetable oil and flour, were imported under PL-480, Public Law 480, which in America funded a programme to provide free food for the poor. In Cambodia, according to Hildebrand and Porter, it too was used to generate Cambodian riels for the army.[70] There were also categories for technical aid, humanitarian aid, and aid to the Exchange Support Fund. All of this was termed "economic assistance" to distinguish it from "military" aid, but it hardly mattered because most Western observers agreed that all but a tiny fraction was diverted to support purchase of military equipment or to pay military salaries.

Humanitarian aid amounted to almost nothing compared to the total aid budget. For the 1974 fiscal year, for example, the total amount of non-military aid provided by the U.S. was $236.5 million. That year, humanitarian aid accounted for only a little more than half of one per cent of the total but, according to Hildebrand and Porter, the unspoken understanding was that "the U.S. provided military and economic aid and it was the policy of the U.S. to encourage other countries to assist Cambodia with humanitarian needs."[71] The following table shows how the total disbursement was broken down that year:

Table 3.4 U.S. Civil Aid to Cambodia for the 1974 Fiscal Year[72]

Programme	Amount (millions of U.S. dollars)
Commercial Imports Programme (CIP)	52.0
Public Law 480 (PL-480)	170.7
Refugees (humanitarian aid)	1.6
Technical Assistance	0.7
Exchange Support Fund (ESF)	11.5
Total	236.5

By 1974, the area of the country still controlled by the Khmer Republic had shrunk drastically. This amount of non-military aid, therefore, was destined only for the population of Phnom Penh and a few provincial towns, or around half of the highest total population estimate of just under eight million Cambodians. Hildebrand and Porter calculated a total U.S. civil aid bill of $748 million for the previous fiscal years (1971,

1972 and 1973).[73] Therefore, the total amount spent on non-military aid to the regime of the Khmer Republic was close to one billion dollars, from the U.S. alone. The fact that children starved to death in the Phnom Penh slums and that civil servants had to strike in order to draw attention to their plight only highlights the scale of official corruption.

The amount of military aid, so termed, was greater than the total amount of civil aid, but it was not vastly greater. The following table is based on figures provided by General Sak Sutsakhan, a respected republican and a resistance leader throughout the 1980s. According to his figures, the total amount was almost $1.2 billion:

Table 3.5 Disbursement Schedule, U.S. Military Assistance Programme, Khmer Republic[74]

1971	1972	1973	1974	1975
180	220	131	414	254

Note: All figures are approximate amounts in millions of current U.S. dollars per fiscal year.

The amounts reported by the Chamber of Commerce bulletin are a little different. The following table is a composite derived from various issues between 1970 and 1975, inclusive; it calculates that a total of $904.8 million was given as economic assistance. The figures for military assistance, unfortunately, are incomplete, but are roughly consistent with those above for the three financial years, 1972 to 1974.

Table 3.6 U.S. Economic and Military Assistance to the Khmer Republic (for fiscal years, 1 July–30 June, in millions of U.S. dollars)

Assistance	1970–71	1971–72	1972–73	1973–74	1974–75
Economic	78.5[1]	110	226.8	253	236.5
Military	Not Given[2]	185[3]	161.6	196 + 200[4]	Not given

Notes: [1] $70m under CIP and the remainder under PL-480.
[2] On 24 August 1970, the State Department gave an "extra" $40m in military aid. In December 1970, a global figure of $255m in aid to Cambodia was announced.
[3] Sirik Matak told reporters in September 1971 that the figure was $200m. On 2 June 1972, the U.S. Senate Commission on Foreign Affairs fixed a limit of $275m in military assistance to Cambodia (not including the cost of aerial operations).
[4] In December 1973, U.S. Under-Secretary of State, Kenneth Rush, requested an extra $200m for munitions, matériel, transport and distribution, and maintenance for the Lon Nol government.

Therefore, it is not an exaggeration to claim that the government of the Khmer Republic received, from the United States of America alone, two billion dollars in combined economic and military assistance between March 1970 and April 1975, the bulk of it in just two years. Far from aiding the war effort, this level of support destroyed political will along with the national economy. An unknown quantity of this aid was diverted by corrupt military officers to support the enemy side.

Trade

In May 1970, the atmosphere was still positive. From the perspective of Phnom Penh, the combined U.S. and ARVN operation in the south and east of the country was engaged in driving out the Vietnamese communist troops from Cambodia. This was supposed to be the prelude to peace, not war. Meanwhile, the excellent 1969–70 wet season harvest had been successfully collected and stored. The Ministry of Finance anticipated earning 5,255 million riels from exports in 1970, with rice exports accounting for almost half of that amount.[75] In the first quarter of 1970, in fact, exports had already earned about one-fifth of the plan. Export earnings were needed to help reduce the budget deficit that had risen rather alarmingly from 945 million riels in 1968 to 1,505 million riels in 1969.[76] Due to the hostilities, there had been a few difficulties getting the export products to the port in Kompong Som, but the government was confident that all would proceed normally, despite a recent fall in rubber stocks. The 1970 annual plan estimated that total imports would be worth 3,703 million riels, excluding imports for the needs of the *Forces Armées Nationales Khmères* (FANK). Military imports were considered a priority, the finance ministry advised, and were confidential. Between April and June, however, the situation changed dramatically. The export plan was halved, the security of Route 4 leading to the maritime port was in jeopardy and traffic along the Mekong to the port at Phnom Penh was possible only with the protection of armed convoys.[77]

The general impression of foreign trade during the time of the Republic is that of a one-way traffic of massive stocks of imported agricultural products and war matériel arriving at Kompong Som port, or of petroleum products reaching Phnom Penh by armed convoys along the Mekong from South Vietnam, with very little going the other way. In fact, Cambodia continued to export rubber, for instance, at least until the middle of 1973. Stocks of rubber sheets and crepe had been transferred out of the conflict zone before the outbreak of major hostilities, and there were also small plantations that continued to operate around

Kompong Som after the plantations in the east were no longer viable. Therefore, Cambodia was able to fill orders for rubber for some time after the main supply of latex dried up. During the first half of 1973, for example, Sonexim shipped 10,641 metric tons of rubber worth US$3.674 million. Most of this rubber was sold to Singapore, followed by Malaysia and France.[78]

Nevertheless, export revenue declined drastically as a result of the war. The government of the Khmer Republic had to seek alternative sources of income to cover its rapidly increasing costs.

Public Finance

The war, along with the massive amounts of foreign assistance that were supplied to pursue it, destroyed the productive base of the Khmer Republic. The economic assistance programme known as CIP was supposed to maintain the supply of commodity imports and to replace losses of production caused by the war. In this way, the CIP should have helped to avoid excessive inflation and other major economic problems. The habit of official corruption, however, destroyed any hope of that. As noted previously, many of those imports were diverted to the private sector and sometimes even sold directly to the enemy forces. Consequently, there were insufficient stocks of food and other supplies for distribution by government agencies, and inflation was the unavoidable consequence of demand exceeding supply.

Seven months before the coup, on 18 August 1969, the riel was devalued from 35.07 riels against the U.S. dollar, to 55.65 riels, or, in gold terms from 25.3905 milligrams to 16 milligrams. This devaluation was not entirely unforeseen or unwelcome. The official rate of around 35 riels had not been adjusted since the riel was first issued in 1955. The National Bank of Cambodia, in its report for the fiscal year ending 30 June 1970 noted with satisfaction, "This new definition of the riel compared with gold and its new parity is closer to the real value of the national currency by comparison with other foreign currencies."[79] Furthermore, the report added, "Reserves in gold and foreign currency of the [bank] can thus be estimated at their real value, being 3,500 million riels rather than 2,600 million riels, and the rate of cover of the riel has gone from 42 per cent to 56 per cent."

The years of the Khmer Republic coincided with years of uncertainty in the international money market. In the two years between August 1971 and August 1973, the U.S. dollar was devalued twice, the price of gold trebled and strong currencies such as the deutschmark were revalued three times. None of these fluctuations, however, compared with the collapse of the riel. On 28 October 1971, the National Bank of Cambodia ordered the commercial banks to suspend all foreign exchange operations pending measures to stabilise the economy, including establishing a "flexible" rate for the riel which had to be "realistic and reasonable."[80] At that point, some optimists believed that the riel would settle at 150 riels to the dollar, but already, while the official rate was 140 riels, the dollar was selling for between 200 and 370 riels on the black market.[81]

By late 1971, the Cambodian economy was showing deep scars from one and a half years of war. The level of budgetary expenditure had risen sharply from 8,391 million riels in 1969 to 14,324 million in 1970 and 18,700 million in 1971 in order to finance war needs and soldiers' salaries for an army which was six times larger than it had been in March 1970. At the same time, Sok Chhong, second vice-president of the Council of Ministers, responsible for finances and the coordination of economic and financial affairs, admitted that the dislocation of domestic production, the shrinking of trade and other important economic activities had resulted in a substantial loss of budgetary receipts.[82]

Various measures were taken to stabilise the economy. The only way to combat inflation, according to Sok Chhong, was by reining in monetary growth and increasing the supply of consumer goods on the market.[83] The success of the stabilisation programme, he admitted, would depend on external assistance to a large degree, but he also called for sacrifices on the part of the people. "The measures are classic ones," he said, "limit the deficit by reducing expenses and increasing normal receipts." He added:

> We will issue treasury bonds to finance part of the budget deficit. We will have bank credits only for essential operations of production, export, import and distribution. It will be forbidden to use these credits to finance losses by state enterprises and public services. We will substantially increase interest rates and strengthen control the National Bank has over commercial banking operations through the introduction of minimum obligatory reserves for the banks.... Instead of price control, we will introduce special official programmes to ensure the continued supply of essential food items at reasonable prices.

Sok Chhong advised that the government would introduce new taxes, guided by the principle of asking those who could afford them to pay the heaviest price. For instance, imported rice and salt was now to be charged the minimum tariff, while import taxes on less essential items were raised from 35 per cent to 60 per cent.

The commodity aid programme, the CIP, accounted for almost two-thirds of total imports. It had proved difficult to administer, however, and the long delays between ordering and delivery had made importers reluctant to utilise the programme, despite the preferential credit facilities that it offered. The government tried to introduce lists of import items that were available exclusively under the CIP, but the private sector demanded full liberalisation of trade. Aware of the U.S. stand on free trade, the government eventually abandoned its lists and instead opted for a preferential exchange rate for commercial aid imports purchased in the donor country.

The Exchange Support Fund for the Khmer Republic made up the budget shortfall to try to secure the economy. Twelve countries: Australia, the Republic of Korea, U.S.A., U.K., Indonesia, Italy, Japan, Malaysia, New Zealand, Philippines and Thailand, along with IMF representatives, took part in a conference held in Phnom Penh in January 1972 to discuss pledges to this fund. Sok Chhong explained the broad features of the government's economic stabilisation programme since its inception at the end of October 1971.[84] These included, he told the participants, the decentralisation of economic management, the lifting of direct import and exchange controls, and the introduction of a flexible exchange rate. These strategies, he claimed, had succeeded in restraining growth in the consumer price index (CPI) for the working and middle classes, figures for which had risen alarmingly by around 100 per cent for the whole of 1971. Fluctuations in the CPI were admittedly seasonal, but in December 1971, at least, the CPI had remained stable, which was an encouraging sign. Nevertheless, he noted, "We do not believe that lasting price stability will be attained quickly ... and the prospects are for continued monetary expansion on account of the 1972 budget deficit."

During the first year (January to December 1972) of operations of the Exchange Support Fund, it was estimated that the Khmer Republic would require US$35 million to support its budget. The total Khmer contribution for 1972 would amount to US$15 million, including $6.25 million borrowed from the IMF. The Exchange Support Fund was indeed "extremely precious aid" as Prime Minister Long Boret told the U.S. *chargé d'affaires*, Thomas Enders, at the ceremony signing the agreement for 1974.[85] It would be used, he said, to arrange the budget and "regulate some social problems resulting from lack of salaries." Thomas Enders said the aid was intended to allow the Khmer Republic to buy imports it needed to combat inflation and to reduce the budget deficit.

By 1974, according to Hildebrand and Porter, the military budget was half as big again as the total liquid assets in the hands of the public at the end of December 1973.[86] By then, they added, 95 per cent of domestic revenues were drawn from U.S. assistance. The March budget of 1970, the first budget of the government of the Khmer Republic, had anticipated that aid funds, grants and loans would represent only 7.3 per cent of total government revenue.[87] When that budget was brought down, of course, the war had not yet begun.

The mounting deficit, commonly given as an excuse for the coup of March 1970, rose from 8,889 million riels in 1970 to 10,107 million riels in 1971. Ironically, between 1968 and 1969 it had risen from only 945 million to 1,505 million riels, an increase that had given cause for great alarm at the time.[88] In December 1971, the economic commission of the Asian Parliamentarians Union presented a report on the situation in Cambodia to its general assembly. The report noted that monetary mass had increased by 123 per cent since March 1970.[89] It included an inventory of war damage, completed in July 1971, still very early in the war, that already amounted to US$300 million; of this, basic infrastructure had suffered $85 million worth of damage, the rubber industry $46 million, and private industries $40 million. In those circumstances, no amount of foreign assistance could put the economy together again.

Conclusions

It is not possible to judge the economic performance of the Khmer Republic as anything other than a failure. Despite massive inputs of foreign assistance, it could neither feed its people nor defend them. By the end of the regime, the population growth rate had halved and life expectancy had fallen to only 35 years, the level it had been at the end of the Second World War. Damage to the nation's economic infrastructure during the civil war, which began only one month after the coup, was massive. By its final year, the national budget was almost totally dependent on foreign aid. The regime left future generations of Cambodians with an external debt of around $300 million owed to the U.S. alone. Repayment of this debt was still being negotiated c. 2000.

It is tempting to dismiss the five years of the republic as an anomaly in Cambodian history, a failed experiment to govern without the traditional, perhaps essential, synergy between the monarch and the people. The removal of the king from executive power, however, seems to have had little effect on the political economy. In fact, if the war had not intervened, the transition from kingdom to a republic might have represented merely a further stage in the evolution of the Cambodian state. As far as urban dwellers and the middle class were concerned, the coup signified the fulfilment of the modernisation process that started with independence from French colonisation; it was a "turning point" in Khmer history as the Chamber of Commerce chose to call it. There were, certainly, demonstrations in the provinces against the coup and thousands of peasants joined the communist insurgents in the *maquis* at Sihanouk's call for them to do so. On the other hand, thousands of young people in the city and towns, especially students, rallied to the republican side during the Chenla offensives in the dry seasons of 1970 and 1971. The government ordered a general mobilisation, but force was not generally necessary to conscript the people, even though the army grew six times in size.

The coup was popular in Phnom Penh. As Justin Corfield noted, the citizens there were buoyed with a new sense of patriotism and national identity. Big businesses, both foreign and locally owned, backed the republic from the outset. The policy of economic liberalisation was for their benefit, although small industrialists and artisans suffered from the removal of protective tariffs and competition from cheap imports. The big businesses also stood to gain from the policy of disengagement of the state sector from those enterprises that had been created under the Sangkum. Some mixed-economy enterprises, including Sonexim and *l'Electricité du Cambodge*, survived but only under sufferance from the big private entrepreneurs. It is not an exaggeration to claim that the coup of 18 March 1970 represented a victory for big business and the indigenous capitalist elite over efforts by Sihanouk and leftist elements to promote local industries and to encourage private domestic savings.

The private sector soon realized that its demands for more and more economic liberalisation were backed by the U.S. government which faithfully rewarded the government of the Khmer Republic with ever larger quantities of economic and military assistance for each step it took towards full deregulation. As the government was financially dependent on this assistance for its very survival, to the extent of 95 per cent by 1974, whatever plans it had for managing a war economy or for post-war reconstruction had to be scrapped.

The government of the Khmer Republic had to rely on foreign assistance because it quickly lost the traditional source of the surplus it needed to fund itself. The republican government lost control of half of the Cambodian countryside within the first few months of the regime. After that, despite some minor military reversals, more and more of the food-producing resource base fell outside its administration until, by the end, fewer than half a million hectares of paddy were still producing rice for the republic. The war was disastrous for the whole agricultural sector.

Rice fields, as Elizabeth Becker wrote, turned into battlefields and a once proud rice-exporting country, within a few short years, became a rice importer. By the end of the regime, imported rice was being dropped from aeroplanes to feed urban enclaves that were besieged by communist armed forces. Natural rubber, the other mainstay of government receipts was also an early war victim. The big French-owned plantations were severely damaged by defoliation and aerial bombing, and their location in the far east of the country made them ideal sanctuaries for enemy forces. Tapping there stopped in the first month of the war, in April 1970. The forestry and fisheries sectors also suffered from the expanding war.

Generous foreign assistance was provided to support the war effort, to compensate for losses in production caused by the war, and to combat inflation. During the five years of the Khmer Republic, the U.S. alone provided around two billion dollars in combined military and economic assistance. Economic assistance was offered in the form of commodity imports supplied at preferential exchange rates, food aid, humanitarian relief, technical assistance, and budgetary support through the Exchange Support Fund. Much of this "economic" assistance was also diverted to pay for the growing military budget, and an unknown, but presumably large amount of all foreign assistance was stolen for private gain. Corruption was endemic in official and military circles and at all levels. There were new political institutions, but no political will, to deal with corruption.

As an urban phenomenon, the Khmer Republic stimulated new ideas and discussion about governance, the economy, and the future direction of the country. Its constitution was radically different from that of the Sangkum. Despite the limitations it imposed on genuine civil liberties, constraints which may be understandable in terms of the war, it was a liberal document which focused on the rights of the people rather than on the privileges of the ruler, as the previous constitution had. It introduced political concepts of human rights and social justice, and it provided for institutions to protect those rights. In practice, however, most glaringly in relation to the treatment of refugees, workers and the urban poor, these concepts had little application. Institutions that guaranteed constitutional rights and protections were decreed into law, but there is little evidence that they ever did the job for which they were intended by the constitution.

The republicans believed that they had made revolution in their country's polity. Little, however, genuinely changed. Despite the Americanised constitution and liberal flourishes in official rhetoric, the political and economic leaders proved that they were unprepared to forego the old habits and privileges on which they relied for their wealth and status.

It was difficult for Westerners to understand, Prime Minister Son Ngoc Thanh told a journalist in 1972. "The Khmer revolution is not like Western politics," he said, "it is not strictly logical, it is more like a complex piece of Angkor sculpture that unfolds slowly to the viewer."[90]

The real Cambodian revolution, of course, was already taking shape in the countryside and it had little in common with the delicate traceries of Angkorian sculptures.

(Front view)

(Reverse view)

Smallest unit of currency prepared for Democratic Kampuchea but never issued

(Front view)

(Reverse view)

Smallest unit of currency prepared for the People's Republic of Kampuchea, circulated in 1980

(Front view)

(Reverse view)

One riel note prepared for Democratic Kampuchea depicting workers digging an irrigation channel

(Front view)

(Reverse view)

Five riel note prepared for Democratic Kampuchea, 1975, depicting Angkor Wat

(Front view)

(Reverse view)

Ten riel note prepared for Democratic Kampuchea, depicting soldier working with peasants

(Front view)

(Reverse view)

Fifty riel note prepared for Democratic Kampuchea, depicting peasants transplanting rice

(Front view)

(Reverse view)

One hundred riel note prepared for Democratic Kampuchea depicting industry

(Front view)

(Reverse view)

Note worth half of one riel, the People's Republic of Kampuchea

(Front view)

(Reverse view)

Ten riel note of the People's Republic of Kampuchea depicting pepper farming

(Front view)

(Reverse view)

Fifty riel note of the People's Republic of Kampuchea

CHAPTER
4

The Revolutionary Economy, 1975–89

> Cambodia can industrialize, because there is no vicious cycle of poverty that cannot be shattered by conscious human effort. But responsibility for industrialization must be taken by the government, whose policies must be translated into rigorous control of foreign trade and a planned effort at structural reform.
>
> Khieu Samphan[1]

Sir John Clapham's advice to economic historians about repeatedly asking "how large? how long? how often? how representative?" is rarely as difficult to follow as when discussing the consequences of economic policies and practices of the Cambodian revolution.[2] Despite the paper mountain of internal documents, transcripts of propaganda broadcasts and interviews with refugees, survivor memoirs, academic papers and monographs concerning the period, the first stage of the revolution, the regime of Democratic Kampuchea (DK), remains a highly contentious field of study because there are no reliable, verifiable statistics.[3] Most of the record of that regime remains anecdotal. Perhaps the only point of common agreement is that the experimental economic policies and plans that were implemented between April 1975 and December 1978 failed. This assessment is based on the overwhelming evidence that the regime did not adequately feed its people, and the population deficit at the end of that period bears out survivors' claims that vast numbers of people died of overwork, maltreatment and starvation, apart, that is, from the thousands of the regime's own supporters who were executed for political motives.

The final victory over the Khmer Republic came quickly for the forces of the Cambodian communist movement. When the Khmer Rouge troops entered Phnom Penh on 17 April 1975, the territory of the Khmer Republic had already shrunk to an area that included only the capital, some towns in the northwest including Battambang, Pailin and Poipet along with around 500,000 hectares of rice fields there, and a further small area near the maritime port in Kompong Som. These scattered population centres had been fed by U.S. airlifts of rice since February 1975 when the Mekong was closed to river convoys.

The evacuation of Phnom Penh began within hours of the surrender. Three days later, the city that had swelled with the influx of nearly two million refugees from the war in the countryside had been reduced to just a few thousand inhabitants consisting of upper echelons of the party and those workers and technicians needed to maintain water and power supplies. Later, an industrial workforce for factories producing agricultural tools and other essential items, as well as the staff employed by a handful of foreign delegations, increased the population to perhaps 100,000.[4] For all intents and purposes, however, Phnom Penh was no longer a city.[5]

In this first large-scale migration, residents of the towns returned, where possible, to their native districts. A second major relocation occurred in September 1975, mainly of long-term Phnom Penh citizens who had first made their way to the already populous south and southwest of the country. They were transferred to the less populated northwest that had had little direct experience of communist rule because it remained under nominal control of the Khmer Republic until the end of the war, so it may have been lack of administrative experience, coupled with the urban deportees' poor agricultural skills, that made conditions in most of the northwest cooperatives particularly harsh. Much of what is recorded about the regime of Democratic Kampuchea is drawn from accounts of refugees from the northwest region, that is, from those who were relocated to the provinces of Pursat, Battambang, and what is now Banteay Meanchey.[6]

Most evacuees went to the liberated zones where the revolution had been in force for some time. Kratie, for instance, had been under communist rule since March 1970. Until 1973, villagers in the zones retained private property and lived as normally as war conditions allowed. Ith Sarin, a former schools inspector, spent nine months in the *maquis* in 1972 and described his journey through the countryside first south and then northwest of Phnom Penh where some villages were already silent and empty, and the big houses of Chinese merchants had been locked up and abandoned. The landscape he described resembled a tropical *Guernica*, "We saw houses broken, burnt and bombed, coconut and sugar palm trees shattered by rocket fire, bamboo clumps and mango trees dried up and withered with shrapnel. It was a scene of war painted with great pain."[7] On crossing into a liberated zone in Takeo province, however, he noted farmers doing their work "as normal" and observed trading in food taking place along the road. The houses on either side of Route 3 had been destroyed and the highway itself had been "gouged out and cut up" by constant raids of T-28 aircraft piloted by the republican air force. Many wats along the way were crowded with displaced villagers who had taken refuge there.

In May 1973, at the height of the American B-52 saturation bombing, when conditions in the countryside must have been intolerable, the Khmer Rouge initiated efforts to create a nationwide system of cooperatives. This would take time to effect, but gradually ownership of the means of production, including draught animals, was collectivised. At first, membership in the collectives was voluntary but by 1974 harsh coercive measures were being reported by peasants fleeing from them to the towns. Market activity ceased and money was no longer used for transactions. Each collective was urged to attain self-sufficiency. The structure of the collective that had developed during the period of people's war served as the model for reconstruction as, in one giant leap after 17 April 1975, the Cambodian revolution passed from the phase of national revolution directly into that of democratic or social revolution.

The radical economic policies of Pol Pot, the revolutionary leader of Democratic Kampuchea, might have eventually achieved their aims of mastery and self-reliance, perhaps along the lines of North Korea. Deep factional rifts within the Communist Party of Kampuchea, however, and hysterical xenophobia directed against Vietnam together wrought such violence that, as the revolution turned on itself, the party ranks were depleted by bloody purges and counter-productive raids on Vietnamese territory. Future key players, among them Heng Samrin, Hun Sen and Chea Sim, defected to Vietnam and plotted the downfall of Democratic Kampuchea.

By late 1978, a counter-revolutionary front had formed in the refugee camps in southern Vietnam. In the last week of December, with the massive support of the People's Army of Vietnam (PAVN) in a military effort funded largely by the USSR, the National Salvation Front forces, led by Heng Samrin, moved against Democratic Kampuchea and drove the Khmer Rouge towards the northwest border with Thailand. There, and later safely ensconced inside Thailand in refugee camps supported by western governments and multilateral aid agencies, as well as with ongoing diplomatic and matériel support from the People's Republic of China, the Khmer Rouge regrouped and fought alongside Khmer royalist and republican contra-style troops in a bitter decade-long war against the Vietnamese-backed regime installed in Phnom Penh.

The People's Republic of Kampuchea (PRK) was founded a few days after the liberation of Phnom Penh on 7 January 1979. While heavily dependent on Vietnam's ongoing military presence and Soviet technical and financial assistance, the new revolutionary regime committed itself to national defence and nation-building, as Democratic Kampuchea had, in the name of social revolution. Factional infighting was kept relatively in check and despite the ongoing war against the regrouped Khmer Rouge and the severe restrictions imposed by the U.S. embargo on international trade, aid and credit which it shared with Vietnam, Cambodia was slowly rebuilt.

The ten-year struggle for hegemony in Cambodia was the last battle of the Cold War and it ended without a clear victory, moral or military, for either side. Major political and economic changes taking place in the Soviet Union, along with demands arising in Southeast Asia for freer regional market and trade conditions put pressure on the Cambodian warring factions to resolve their differences. Following a protracted diplomatic process, peace was negotiated and settled according to the Paris Peace Agreements signed on 23 October 1991.

By then, the Cambodian revolution was long over. Market liberalisation had already commenced in 1985 and relaxation of rural policies concerning the organisation of labour, and access and control over land had continued throughout the PRK regime. In 1989, the revolution formally ended with the transformation of the People's Republic of Kampuchea into the ideologically neutral State of Cambodia, which opened sufficient diplomatic space for resolving the country's longstanding conflict prior to United Nations-sponsored general elections in May 1993.

Policies

When the revolutionary movement triumphed in April 1975, Cambodia watchers believed, with good reason, that the new regime's economic policies would more or less follow the general principles argued in the theses of the three leftwing economists who had all held government posts during the Sangkum: Khieu Samphan, Hou Yuon and Hu Nim. They had all fled to the *maquis* in 1968 and had played active roles during the people's war period. Hou Yuon, for instance, was the GRUNK, or United Front's government minister for the interior, charged with "preparing the countryside and associations," according to Ith Sarin.[8] Hou Yuon disappeared in August 1975 and it is generally assumed that he was executed for holding counter-revolutionary views, as was Hu Nim, DK's minister for information and propaganda, in 1977.

Khieu Samphan, however, not only survived but fulfilled the role as head of state. While this was a ceremonial post with no executive power, by his own admission, he was also "a simple member" of Office 870.[9] This office was what was variously called the Department of Government, or Department of the Central Committee, or the Cabinet of the Council of Ministers during the following PRK regime. It was the central office from which emanated the most important circulars and regulatory orders for implementation by all levels of administration throughout the country. The political wing of Office 870 would most certainly have held more power than its executive wing, but Khieu Samphan was not the political chief; his party history and his class background prohibited that. Nevertheless, it is difficult to read the biography of Khieu Samphan and not believe that at least some of his ideas about how the Cambodian economy should develop affected policy decisions made by the revolutionary regime. He denies this, arguing that after the fall of Phnom Penh it was Pol Pot who made all the decisions. "One thought of a development programme in the genre of economic reforms of the *Sangkum Reastr Niyum* with appropriate restructuring," he said. "But Pol Pot thought revolution, not reform...."[10]

Those revolutionary policies were explained by Pol Pot during a meeting held in September 1975.[11] All economic restructuring had to revolve around agriculture, the bedrock of national rehabilitation and economic development. According to the general plan, within 10 to 15 years, Cambodia's backward agriculture would be transformed and modernised by mastering the water problem, by mechanisation, use of fertilisers and pesticides, by electrification, and by supporting scientific research and technical development. Productivity was fixed at three tonnes of paddy per hectare, per seasonal crop. Industry and commerce, in their turn, had to develop in order to serve the needs of agriculture, to provide for the immediate needs of the people, and to improve their living conditions. Thus, existing industries manufacturing mosquito nets and blankets, thread, soap, bicycle tyres, milk, dried fish, buttons and clothes had to be consolidated and diversified. Cigarettes, bricks, tiles, writing paper, pens, ink and so forth were added to the list of basic needs. The party's role was key. "We had to have a proper line to lead and mobilize the masses," Khieu Samphan explained, adding:

If at the end of fifteen years, we had not achieved our objectives, it would be not because of external factors but rather due to internal factors, that is, the leadership of the party ... [that] had to establish detailed plans with manageable figures for each domain of activities: production of machines, of fertilizer, electricity, and so on.... Once the strategy and the tactics were established, everybody had to throw themselves into the work without hesitation.... We had proceeded in this manner, with success, during the war. It would be easier for us to do it now. It was sufficient only for the party to elaborate a proper line of management and clearly fix the objectives to reach.[12]

Policy concerning the introduction of the new riel, already printed and awaiting circulation, was still undecided at the time of that meeting. Khieu Samphan merely notes that a decision about using money was not urgent "for the simple reason that our state did not have many products to sell or to buy." He argues further that the young administration lacked experience for maintaining the currency's stability, that "the enemy would not fail to sabotage our money," and that the introduction of money would affect the "essence of our state." Above all, it seems, money was regarded as a threat to the pure society that the revolution had created.

Whether or not it circulated currency, the new state still needed capital. The urgent need to accumulate capital through savings was a constant theme in post-colonial Cambodian economics. Hou Yuon had argued for a rural credit programme to boost savings, while the economists of the Republic complained that the absence of private savings blocked national development. Khieu Samphan could hardly deny the importance of capital but he stressed that capital should serve the state. "Capital," he argued, "should serve to ameliorate the living conditions of the people, to finance the efforts of development in all domains: national defence, agriculture, industry, culture, social affairs. Capital comes from production. Our capital is the rubber, rice, maize and fish that we produce." To achieve production goals, in July–August 1976, the party launched its "Four-Year Plan to Build Socialism in All Fields."[13] In fact, the introduction to the plan declared that socialism had already been achieved since the society was basically already a collective one so Cambodia was "in the process of continuing our revolution." The plan harped on the theme that with plenty of agricultural capital, industry could be strengthened and expanded. Economic independence would provide the regime with the capacity to defend the country. Nation-building had to serve the ends of national defence.

Mastery and self-reliance subsumed in conscious human effort was the key to economic development. Given the Khmer Republic's complete and willing dependence on foreign aid, Democratic Kampuchea's ringing calls for mastery and self-reliance must have appealed to Cambodian pride. Moreover, agriculture-based economic development was hardly a new theme; nor was identifying the lack of water as the main inhibiting factor to improved productivity in the rural sector. All post-colonial governments had the same goals with regard to agricultural modernisation. The novelty of DK economic policy lay not in its goals but in the paranoid haste with which they were pursued.

The ease with which the PAVN and the Salvation Front forces invaded Cambodia during the last week of 1978 and put the Khmer Rouge troops to rout proved the failure of DK economic policy. Autarky was an extreme and unnecessary approach that served merely to weaken further the economic base that was still adjusting to decolonisation.

The Salvation Front central committee, forerunner to the government of the People's Republic of Kampuchea, set out its policy position in an eleven-point programme announced on 2 December 1978, just weeks prior to the invasion.[14] Accordingly, the new economy would be "both planned and market, meeting the needs of social progress." Collectivisation, in the modified form of mutual aid and cooperative organisations, would be "assisted and encouraged" on the basis of the free consent of the peasants with a view to boosting production and raising the living standards of the population. The Front promised to open a bank, circulate currency, and develop the movement of goods and produce. Domestic and foreign trade would resume "on the basis of equality and reciprocal advantage."

State planning commenced in 1982 with short-term, annual plans. Until the first five-year plan, 1986–90, the eleven-point programme acted as a checklist for government action. The *krom samaki*, or solidarity groups for increasing the harvest, were first organised on an *ad hoc* basis in 1979. This institutionalised system of mutual support in the countryside suffered from many of the same problems that had plagued the Sangkum cooperatives, especially incompetent management by poorly-trained cadres and a general unwillingness on the part of the farmers to work ricefields collectively or to repay their loans. The following year, the riel was reintroduced and a rural credit programme commenced. The credit scheme had the aim of extending circulation of the new currency and of increasing the provision of essential commodity items to the farmers. The purchasing power of the farmers remained low, however, as did the supply of manufactured items from the towns.

Agricultural policies achieved rather poor results throughout the PRK and rural reconstruction was very slow. On the other hand, the mutual support that the *krom samaki* provided, however irregular their form and management, did provide an essential level of organisation and security, including food security for the most vulnerable groups who might otherwise have drifted to the city where there was no support at all. Conversely, markets in the city revived very quickly on the basis of private exchange. The urgent demand for food and essential commodity items in the towns as residents returned from wherever they had spent the Pol Pot years made it impossible for the state to regulate the market. Bands of "smugglers," petty traders on bicycles, crisscrossed the country with goods purchased at border points in Thailand and Vietnam with gold and gems they had kept on them throughout the DK period or had buried prior to the evacuation in 1975. Large-scale, organised smuggling was already being conducted through the southern ports by *towkays*, big merchants, some of whom had continued to prosper in this fashion throughout the Pol Pot regime, despite the official rhetoric.

At the fifth congress of the People's Revolutionary Party of Kampuchea, held in October 1985, the private sector was formally recognised as playing an essential role in the national economy.[15] In fact, the private economy was the only sustainable sector by then. The Prime Minister, Hun Sen, explained the complexity, or general unruliness, of the Cambodian economy by 1989 in these terms:

> Over the past ten years, in Kampuchea, we have created two markets and three prices: they are the state market and the free market, prices for provisions, prices to ensure livelihood and prices of the free market, [a situation] which has created severe difficulties for market management.[16]

His objective was "one market, one price." The market of choice became apparent in February 1989 when the already defunct *krom samaki* system of collective agricultural production was officially abandoned and individual property rights were formally recognised.

At the end of April that year, the National Assembly adopted numerous amendments to the constitution, including recognition of private property and free market economy. The new State of Cambodia (SoC) was still governed by the same single party, but the constitutional changes and their enactment were sufficient, particularly after the final withdrawal of Vietnamese troops in September that year, to make the new regime and its economic policies significantly different from those of the People's Republic of Kampuchea.

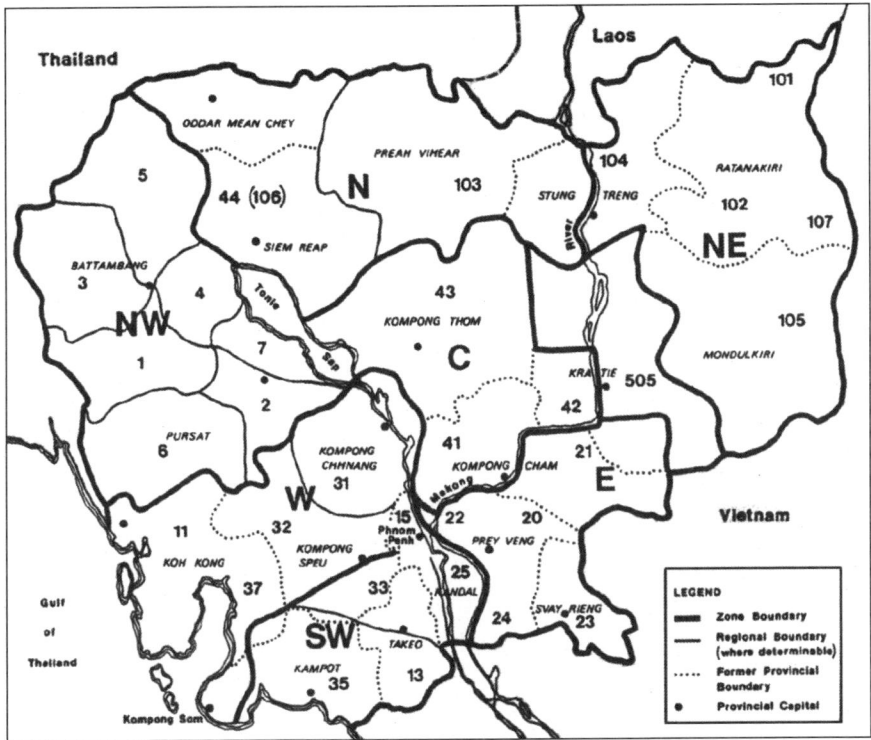

Figure 4.1 Administrative Divisions of Democratic Kampuchea[17]

Administration and Governance

For administrative purposes, Democratic Kampuchea was divided into six zones named simply Northeast, North, Northwest, West, Southwest, and East, plus the Centre, and the special region of Kratie. The zones were subdivided into numbered regions. The pre-revolutionary units of district (*srok*), commune (*khum*) and village (*phum*) remained, but the most important rural administrative unit was the cooperative (*sahakor*), which was roughly equivalent in size to a commune and incorporated several villages.

Building the cooperatives commenced in May 1973 during the U.S. aerial bombing. After liberation, the plan was for the cooperative system to grow from the base level with cooperative committees replacing the village committee first, then upwards through the other levels to the Centre itself. Before 1977 the cooperatives were small units involving between 50 and 500 members, but during that year of the "Great Leap" the pace of collectivisation was matched by the growth in size and uniformity of the collectives. According to Twining, "By late 1977, Pol Pot reported that 20 per cent of Cambodia's cooperatives consisted of seven hundred to one thousand households, 30 per cent had four hundred to six hundred households, and 20 per cent were made up of one hundred to three hundred households.... A reasonable estimate of a typical cooperative's population is about 2,000 persons."[18]

Each level of the administration was governed by a three-person committee and as Michael Vickery notes, the governance structure was extremely decentralised "with a very great degree of autonomy for each vertical administrative unit and virtually total compartmentalisation of units horizontally."[19] This degree of autonomy had grown out of practical necessity. When armed struggle began in the 1960s, the communist movement had very loose coordination and local leaders inevitably formed their armies according to different party lines. The three-person committee also fitted with the original size and structure of party cells, designed for complete secrecy and therefore security. It was only after liberation in April 1975 that the exercise in power and control over the movement began, when the Centre led by Pol Pot in alliance with the Southwest zonal leadership and troops moved against the others to form one army and one party line.

The party, the government and the army were synonymous. Party leadership controlled all areas of the state. As Timothy Carney argues, "In reality, the party formed not only the leadership core, but, to very nearly the lowest level, the only real organisational structure in the country. From the organisation of ten-family groups to the central committee, in each platoon and brigade, at each ministry and office, a party committee sought full control. At the top, the central committee, as of August 1978, had about thirty members.... Most were regional and sector secretaries and deputy secretaries or, presumably, senior commanders."[20]

The DK regime issued no laws or decrees apart from the constitution that was promulgated on 5 January 1976. The constitution made provision for a People's Representative Assembly of 250 members that was responsible for legislation and for defining the domestic and foreign policies of the regime. The Assembly was also supposed to elect the "administration" or executive body, appoint the judges at all levels of the people's courts, and choose the state presidium. In March 1976 national elections for the People's Assembly were held in a number of places throughout the country, and Nuon Chea was appointed president of its standing committee of ten members. The Assembly seems to have met in plenary session just once, for only three days, in order to approve the elections and to establish its method of organisation. The following month, the central administration was formed with Pol Pot as Prime Minister and, if Khieu Samphan and other surviving leaders of that regime are to be believed, all decisions and authority emanated from his office alone.

In terms of organising and administering the economy, there were six committees: agriculture, industry, commerce, communications, energy, and rubber plantations with each committee chairman holding the equivalent of ministerial rank. Charles Twining believes that it is fair to assume that these economic administrators were inexperienced in running a centrally planned economy so the simplest method was to place everyone in the same basic agricultural organisation. "It is doubtful," he noted, "that local conditions were allowed to influence the uniform application of revolutionary policies." Thus, while the committee system did allow for a high degree of decentralisation, decentralisation did not equate with flexibility in decision-making.

Consequently, at a very basic level, DK policy failed because the administration of their plan did not respect the adaptations that Cambodian rice farmers had learnt to make to subtle variations in soil quality and topographical and climatic conditions to ensure their livelihood, regardless of the political storms that blew across the land with almost monotonous regularity. The villagers had trusted the Khmer Rouge throughout the years of civil war because their organisation and defence ensured that a sufficient harvest could still be gathered. After 1977, when the peasants were forced to suffer the same harsh food rationing as the urban evacuees, they withdrew their support and quickly transferred it when the new regime offered them a more pragmatic form of government.

The People's Republic of Kampuchea was ruled by a provisional eight-member revolutionary council until the constitution of 1981 provided for a regular distribution of legislative and executive authority. Its constitution was approved in June by the National Assembly, under the presidency of Chea Sim, following general elections held in May. In accordance with the constitution, the Council of State, with a legislative review function led by President Heng Samrin, and the Council of Ministers, the executive body headed by Prime Minister Pen Sovann, replaced the People's Revolutionary Council.

The pre-1975 provincial administrative divisions in the countryside were restored. In the original redistribution there were 18 provinces (Siem Reap and Oddar Meanchey shared the same administration) and two municipalities, Phnom Penh and Kompong Som. Late in 1986, the new province of Banteay Meanchey was formed by removing five districts from Battambang and one from Siem Reap/Oddar Meanchey. This new

Vietnamese troops parade before dignitaries and officials at the final withdrawal ceremony in September 1989

The young foreign minister, Hun Sen, casts his ballot in the 1981 elections for the National Assembly

provincial administration helped to share the burden of defending the border against increasing incursions by the anti-PRK forces after the formation of the Coalition Government of Democratic Kampuchea (CGDK) in 1982, and proved to be crucial for the maintenance and supervision of the K5 campaign of border defence that commenced in 1985.

The provinces were divided into 122 districts which acted as intermediaries between the provincial centre and the most important administrative base, the commune (*khum*). During the PRK, the function of the district (*srok*) was ill-defined. The commune, however, finally came into its own. This structure that Jean Delvert had scorned as artificial, "created out of nothing," proved to be the mainstay of the PRK administration and of the party's relations with the village masses. The communes were responsible for overseeing the functioning of the *krom samaki*, the solidarity production groups, and were also responsible for collecting the "patriotic contributions," the agricultural tax, ensuring that the farmers sold their produce to the state and repaid their loans, as well as mobilizing "volunteers" for border defence work and the militias. General elections were held for commune councils in 1981, prior to the elections for the National Assembly, but insecurity prevented people from voting in some places. Nevertheless, the fact that the regime even staged those elections gave the communes the stamp of legitimacy.

If the PRK administrative structure and its operations had much in common with the system that operated in Vietnam, this was not true of the village. The Cambodian village, as always, remained largely autonomous. Each village had a three-member village committee and a militia of between 10 and 50 men, but the village leaders appear to have been chosen in the traditional way, that is, by other villagers and for qualities that were not narrowly political ones. A party central committee decision of 1979 advised simply, "[I]n any village where there still is not a state authority, we must monitor and grasp the state of affairs within the village and then make a plan to mobilize the masses to select and appoint people with a good attitude and qualities to join the state authority."[21] There were no Vietnamese experts with administrative responsibility at the village level and fewer than 20 per cent of all villages had a permanent Vietnamese troop presence at that time.[22]

The party, officially the Kampuchean People's Revolutionary Party (KPRP) following the fourth congress in 1981, took precedence over all forms of governance and of the judiciary. Administration at all levels, apart from the village, was supposed to reflect that of the centre. That is, the party committee of three to five members acted as the point of reference, while the people's revolutionary committee of five to seven members conducted the work of government, and the mass organisations (trade unions, youth and women's associations) of the Salvation Front were responsible for mobilising the masses, for maintaining popular support for the regime and for finding new party recruits. In fact, however, because there were so few party members in 1979 the party committee and the people's revolutionary committee were usually one and the same thing. Party membership was very small until decisions taken at the fifth party congress in 1985 resulted in rapid growth. For instance, in 1986, the KPRP was reported to have 10,000 members but two years later, at the end of 1988, that number had more than doubled and there were almost 3,000 party branches throughout the country.[23]

Therefore, when the Vietnamese made their final withdrawal in September 1989, the administration was on a firm footing. By any measure, Cambodia was still a poor country, but it had rebuilt its key institutions and redeveloped the basic human capacities and skills to run them. Meanwhile, old habits of official corruption had resurfaced in line with the increase in opportunities. Cambodia had not been revolutionised, but neither was it the same country it had been before 1975.

Population

The Cambodian population suffered severe shocks between 1970 and 1980, but to what extent, to whom, where and why remain controversial questions. Like most aspects of the revolutionary era, population estimates tend to be viewed through an ideological prism. The most reliable sources of information about Cambodian population trends are the two censuses conducted in 1962 and 1998 according to international norms. Unfortunately, they are rather distant from either end of the revolutionary era. Another important tool is the 1996 Demographic Survey of Cambodia (DSC) which, by reverse projection, allowed verification of the results of the population count carried out by the government of the People's Republic of Kampuchea in 1980. The most unreliable figures are also the most essential — those for 1974 or the final year of the Khmer Republic.

As discussed in the previous chapter, in addition to a sharp decline in fertility by 1974, there were many "excess" deaths, or deaths above the normal rate, due to war casualties suffered by both sides of the conflict throughout the period of the Khmer Republic. A total of 750,000 deaths (600,000 war-related and the remainder due to natural mortality) seemed to be accepted by most researchers, whether demographers, historians or political scientists. This figure, however, was revised by demographic experts who tried to calculate the cost in human lives of the Democratic

Kampuchea regime. They took the number of war-related deaths and applied it to total population loss between 1970 and 1975, allocating it in roughly equal thirds to war casualties, emigration, and natural causes.[24] Without explanation, then, the number of war casualties was suddenly revised down from the formerly accepted figure of 600,000 to 200,000. Consequently, much controversy still surrounds the scale of atrocities committed in the Pol Pot regime.

Before civil war intervened, the most optimistic projection for the population in 1974 was 7.92 million; most observers now agree that the Cambodian population in April 1975 was somewhere between 7.1 million and 7.3 million. That population was divided more or less equally between the two parties in the civil war, despite the fact that practically the whole country was in rebel hands by 1974. The republic had fewer than half a million hectares of rice-producing land, all in Battambang province, under its nominal control by then. Given rough averages for family size and size of family land holdings, the non-urban population of the Khmer Republic was, therefore, at most 1.5 million. Phnom Penh's population had grown rapidly to around two million and other urban centres' populations still in republican hands were also swollen with war refugees from the countryside. The population under the regime of the Khmer Republic, therefore, was mainly an urban one, although not necessarily urban in origin.

In April 1975, Phnom Penh and a few provincial towns, specifically Battambang, Poipet, Pailin and Ream, were emptied of their populations. As "new people," the evacuees generally suffered from harsh work and living conditions, poor and increasingly inadequate food rations, and consequent physical and psychological debilitation. The "old people," rural folk who had remained in the countryside and participated in the revolution, also suffered from inadequate diet, particularly after the policy on communal eating was enforced in late 1976, and most particularly in those regions that were heavily purged in 1977 and 1978. These purges, firstly of the North and Northwest and then of the East, as well as the increasingly hostile war against Vietnam, took a heavy toll of lives from among the ranks of party cadres and the military. In addition, there were mass executions of former Khmer Republic administrative and military staff at the commencement of the regime, and other killings often termed "assertive" or "revenge" killings which were carried out throughout the almost four years that the regime continued. In total, it is thought that excess mortality during the period of Democratic Kampuchea, from April 1975 to December 1978, was around one million, but this is a "loose" figure.[25]

The Finnish Inquiry Commission which published its findings in December 1982 estimated that altogether — and presumably "altogether" means a total of normal deaths and excess deaths — nearly one million people died during the regime of Democratic Kampuchea. They based their findings on an April 1975 population of 7.3 million and a growth rate of 2.8 per cent or slightly lower which should have resulted in a population of between 8.3 million and 8.5 million in 1981. The mid-1980 population count of the People's Republic of Kampuchea, readjusted to include some groups that had not been represented in the count, was only 6.7 million. This figure, plus the 300,000 refugees then in Thailand and a further 100,000 already living in Western countries, in addition to a (returned) Viet-Khmer population then estimated at 250,000, brought the total Cambodian population, at home and abroad, to around 7.4 million. "Thus," the commission concluded, "approximately one million died during the Pol Pot period. On the other hand, if one assumes that the natural growth in population of 2.8 per cent fell during 1975–79 — which is quite probable — then the number of people who died during the Pol Pot period would have been lower than one million.... Examining the whole of the decade of the 1970s shows that the total loss in Kampuchea's population including refugees amounted to nearly two million people. This means a loss of almost 30 per cent of the entire population."[26]

The birth rate did indeed decline to an unusually low level during the second half of the 1970s. Demographer Jacqueline Desbarats quotes CIA fertility estimates for the period of Democratic Kampuchea, considering the "new people" and the "old people" separately. According to these estimates, among the latter, the birth rate dropped from 43 per 1,000 in April 1975 to 30 in late 1975, and was about 28 at the end of 1978. The decline was far more marked among the evacuees, where during the same period the crude birth rate fell from 32 to 15 during the first year and further to just 10 by late 1978.[27] In general, she accepts Cambodian demographer Ea Meng Try's proposal that birth rates for the whole country were between 20 and 25 per 1,000 for the period 1976 to 1978. "These rates," she summarises, "imply a decline of almost fifty per cent relative to pre-1970 fertility."[28]

If we accept that fertility levels are directly related to material living conditions, then the 1998 census not only confirmed these proposed figures but also provided an interesting synopsis of how conditions must have varied from province to province at that time. The age cohort, 20 to 24, that is, of those men and women born between March 1974 and 1978 inclusive, accounted for 6.5 per cent of the total population in

Returning home from the catastrophe of the Democratic Regime, 1979 (Agence Khmère de Presse archive)

An irrigation system in Takeo province, reconstructed with foreign assistance after 1979

1998; the cohort below, children born after the DK, were 11.8 per cent, while the cohort above, born at the end of the Sangkum and in the early years of the civil war, were 7.7 per cent. The province with the lowest proportion of its population in the 20 to 24 age group in 1998 was Pursat (only 4.1 per cent); Kompong Chhnang and Battambang were also low, with 5.2 per cent and 5.7 per cent respectively. At the other end of the scale, Kratie had eight per cent of its total population in this age group.[29] These figures bear out the existing evidence that living conditions were worst in the Northwest zone. In eastern parts of the country, especially in Kratie, conditions were far less onerous. This was also true for much of Kompong Thom province where the impact of the regime on birth rates was more severe than in Kratie but certainly less drastic than in most other places.

The other significant gap that the 1998 census results revealed was in the 40 to 44 year group, that is, those aged from 17 to 21 during the DK. Again, results for all provinces showed a marked population deficit in this cohort, particularly among males. This was the age group of soldiers. Their mortality rate must have been very high, and the morbidity rate even higher. Those tolls will never be known, but Jacqueline Desbarats suggests that life expectancy at the end of the 1970s was only 31 years, one of the lowest in the world and it was compounded by an infant mortality rate of 263 per thousand live births, perhaps the highest in the world at that time.[30] Applying the United Nations' suggested average annual death rate of 40 per 1,000 to a Cambodian population assumed to range between 5.5 million and 7 million over the 1975–80 period, she estimated that the annual death toll was 200,000 on average, "or a total exceeding one million."

For some months after the National Salvation Front-PAVN invasion of December 1978 there was confusion and a scattering of the population as the Khmer Rouge pushed whatever population groups they could manage towards the Thai frontier, while the others fled to escape them and to return home, or to Phnom Penh or wherever might be safe. There was, too, a rather brief period in 1979 when people in some parts of the country lacked food but, as the Finnish Inquiry Commission found, the crisis was not "overwhelming." The commission concluded that deaths from warfare and famine in that period did not exceed "some tens of thousands."[31]

In 1980, the People's Republic of Kampuchea organised a population count, with communes reporting their populations to districts and so on up the administrative levels to the central government. The population in mid-1980 was estimated to be 6.4 million. This official total was later adjusted to 6,590,000 with reference to the end of 1980, perhaps to include some unreported groups. That population by sex and age is presented in the following table:

Table 4.1 Population by Broad Age Group and Sex, as Counted at the End of 1980[32]

Age Group	Both Sexes	Males	Females
Total	6,589,954	3,049,450	3,540,504
0–15	3,092,083	1,556,526	1,535,557
(Under 1)	274,764	137,833	136,931
(1)	216,850	109,077	107,773
(2–5)	600,442	302,830	297,612
(6–15)	2,000,027	1,006,786	993,241
16	125,893	58,569	67,324
17	121,701	52,891	68,810
Male 18–60 Female 18–55	2,865,055	1,234,647	1,630,408
Male 61+ Female 56+	385,222	146,817	238,405

Source: National Institute of Statistics, Ministry of Planning.

This reported population was, of course, only that within Cambodia's borders. Cambodians in the camps, in refugee centres and those who had already emigrated abroad were not counted. This result was more or less confirmed by a demographic survey of Cambodia conducted in March 1996 by the National Institute of Statistics with the assistance of the United Nations Population Fund (UNFPA) using reverse projection methods. The survey results put the mid-1980 in-country population at 6.55 million.[33] This figure, then, represented a slightly higher revision of the total derived from the PRK's population count which was for the end of that year.

As the table shows, almost half the total population at the end of 1980 was under the age of 15; the number of infants (0–1 year) was almost twice the total number of adolescents aged 16 and 17. The sex ratio in that 16 to 17 age cohort was severely imbalanced. Indeed, for all age groups 16 and over, there were considerably more women than men. The 1996 demographic survey showed that the sex ratio (the number of men per 100 women) for the 40 to 44 age group, the cohort suffering the most severe imbalance, was just 65.5. Therefore, in 1980, when that age group was 24 to 28, in the peak reproductive stage, there were half again as many women as men.

The extent of the demographic shocks suffered in the decade of the 1970s can be seen in the table below. It continues from the one presented in the previous chapter where Jacqueline Desbarats compiled estimates of the population for selected years from 1921 to 1974. In view of consistent underestimates in previous surveys, she selected the highest estimate for each year. As the figures suggest, the population did not reach the highly inflated estimate given for 1974 until after 1987. If, as is generally accepted, the 1974 population was in the range of 7.1 to 7.3 million, then the population of Cambodia had recovered only to this point by 1984. Cambodia had indeed lost a decade of population growth.

Table 4.2 Estimates of the Cambodian Population, Selected Years, 1974–89[34]

Year	Population (millions)
1974	7.92
1979	6.70
1980	6.70
1983	7.00
1985	7.40
1986	7.67
1987	7.90
1988	8.11
1989	8.40

The Cambodian population revived strongly, especially during the first half of the decade of the People's Republic of Kampuchea. By international standards, the figures that represent that recovery are poor, but they compare very favourably with the era of Democratic Kampuchea. The crude death rate, for instance, declined rapidly from around 40 per 1,000 during the previous regime to half that during the early 1980s and then back to pre-war levels of 17 to 19 per 1,000 by 1989. Life expectancy, as low as 30 for men and 32 for women during Democratic Kampuchea, was around 45 and 48 respectively by the late 1980s. The United Nations Children's Fund (UNICEF) estimated that the infant mortality rate, which had risen above 200 per 1,000 live births by 1980, had dropped back to between 120 and 134 by 1987.[35] Despite differences of opinion about exact fertility levels in the 1980s, the 1998 census was able to confirm that a baby boom did indeed occur after 1980. Until 1986, the crude birth rate was estimated at between 41 and 43 births per 1,000 and it then fell gradually to level out around 38 by 1988.[36]

The figures for urbanisation confirm that the *krom samaki* provided the rural poor with enough support to keep them in the village. Urbanisation was estimated at 12.6 per cent of the population at the end of 1980 and Phnom Penh's population then was reported to be 368,000. Despite rapid population growth throughout the decade, the rate of urbanisation remained constant at around 12 per cent until the end of the PRK.[37] In 1982, the Finnish Inquiry Commission noted that the capital city's population had risen to nearly half a million and most of the residents were newcomers; only about a third of them having lived there before 1975.[38] "They lacked any connection with the area's earlier traditions," the report continued, "as a result of which the face of the cities has deteriorated, and the material resources to repair the cities have not been available."

Migration

Between 1970 and 1992, there were mass movements of Cambodians leaving and returning to their country. During the war throughout the 1980s, there was also a considerable population of internally displaced people, particularly in the northwest provinces, who fled active fighting in their home districts. The severe dislocation of people's lives during those 20 years or so contributed greatly to the confusion over the size of population losses during the whole period.

The final major migration event began in March 1992 when, under the auspices of the United Nations High Commission for Refugees (UNHCR), Cambodian residents of the border camps were resettled inside Cambodia in preparation for registration and participation in the UN-sponsored general elections of May 1993. At that time, there were 370,000 refugees in Thailand, and a further 25,000 were reported to be refugees in Vietnam. Among those who would never permanently return were 152,000 Cambodians who had resettled in the U.S.A. and another 90,000 or so living in other countries, mostly in France, Canada and Australia.[39]

The huge border camp population was not a static one. There was always considerable cross-border movement to and from the camps, for the purposes of petty trade, for temporary shelter from government efforts to mobilise the population for defence purposes, or, in the case of the resistance forces, for guerrilla raids on the PRK administration and territory. Banister and Johnson offer a detailed picture of the cross-border and international movements of Cambodian refugees in the following table.

Table 4.3 International Migration Assumptions, 1970–89[40]

Year	Number	Directions
1970	200,000	Vietnamese citizens of Cambodia expelled to Vietnam
1971–74	34,000	Cambodian refugees to Thailand
	120,000	Refugees (mainly Vietnamese residents) to Vietnam
1975–78	34,039	Cambodian refugees to Thailand
	150,000	Chinese and Khmer Cambodians to Vietnam
	10,400	Refugees to Lao PDR. All were returned by 1987.
1979–80	100,000	Cambodian refugees return from Vietnam
	172,380	To Thailand. Figure includes 12,000 ethnic Chinese.
1980–91	500,000	Vietnamese to Cambodia. Figure includes many of those who had migrated to Vietnam 1970–78. Annual estimate of 41,666 returnees.
1984–85	208,995	In dry season offensive, refugees living in camps on Cambodian side of the border were pushed into Thailand. Figure includes an estimated 70,000 Khmer Rouge and associated civilian population.
1985–89	92,112	Refugees to Thailand. The vast majority (70,000) entered Thailand in 1985, the first year of mobilisation for the K5 (border defence) programme.
1984–91		Natural increase in Thai camps (exclusive of migration) of 57,000.
1986–91		A great deal of movement across the border for trade and warfare, or just seeking UN-provided food.

Despite the cross-border movements into and out of the Thai camps, the populations there were so long-lived and camp life so thoroughly aid-dependent and therefore so different from the reality inside Cambodia that a separate culture, however temporary, seemed to emerge. Camp life, paradoxically, was the antithesis of the new society the Khmer Rouge leadership had sought to create. By late 1989, more than 90 per cent of the entire Cambodian refugee population in Thailand were housed in three camps, all assisted by the United Nations: Site 2, Site B and Site 8.[41] In 1982, the United Nations Border Relief Operation (UNBRO) was created to coordinate relief efforts while a host of international non-government organisations provided health, education and skills training services. Each camp was affiliated with one or another of the rebel factions making up the Coalition Government of Democratic Kampuchea (CGDK) that formed in June 1982. The camp called Site 2, affiliated with the republican Kampuchean People's National Liberation Front (KPNLF) was the largest with 182,000 people, or more than half of the total Cambodian refugee population in Thailand. This population consisted of 40,000 families, each with an average size of 4.6 members. A point of interest, but one not discussed, was that approximate parity existed between males and females in all age groups in Site 2, a population feature which was markedly different from the situation inside Cambodia. Further data showed that close to 60 per cent of the family heads at Site 2 claimed to be literate, but three-quarters of them had received only three years of primary education. About half of those surveyed had previously been farmers, while a third had been children or still at school when they had fled their homeland. Obviously, by 1989, the early refugees to Thailand who had represented Cambodia's urban middle class — merchants, teachers and civil servants — had already been resettled abroad. Those remaining in the camps had little or no chance of ever permanently entering a third country as legal migrants.

Ethnic Groups

From early times, long before the French Protectorate, Cambodia had counted ethnic minorities among approximately ten per cent of its total population. These ethnic groups included the Khmer Leu, the diverse tribal groups of the upland regions and the Kuy and Pear in the lowland forests, the Khmer Islam, especially Chams, along with the Vietnamese and the Chinese. By 1981, their proportion of the population was reported to have fallen to only three per cent.[42] In September 1988, a UNICEF document reported a minority population of five per cent, of whom half were Chams and other indigenous minorities.[43] This was undoubtedly an underestimate, especially given the bitter controversy over the size of the Vietnamese population inside Cambodia, both military and civilian. Resisting the Vietnamese presence in Cambodia was the only point of common interest shared by the unlikely marriage of republican, royalist and communist forces that constituted the CGDK. Furthermore, the so-called Vietnamese occupation of Cambodia guaranteed them Chinese, U.S. and other Western bloc support for their resistance cause. It was therefore in the interest of the contra forces to exaggerate the number of

Vietnamese residents in Cambodia. Equally, it was in the PRK government's interests to underestimate Vietnamese immigration in order to corroborate its nationalist credentials.

In September 1989, the PAVN made a final withdrawal of its troops from Cambodia. There had been, on average, around 180,000 troops stationed in Cambodia throughout the PRK and, in the normal course of events, some married Khmer women and stayed while others found opportunities in Cambodia that were not available to them at home and remained. These numbers were probably not great. It is generally assumed that most of the Viet-Khmers who had been expelled by the Khmer Republic and Democratic Kampuchea returned after 1979. The push-pull factors of poverty and population pressure on land along with the perception that conditions for earning a living were easier in Cambodia encouraged many Vietnamese from the southern provinces to cross the border and settle. Banister and Johnson believed that by 1992, the Vietnamese population in Cambodia was about 500,000. They acknowledged that a wide range of estimates existed but thought that their "arbitrary" estimate was reasonable.[44]

If the Vietnamese population quickly revived after 1979, the ethnic Chinese population did not. Until the mid-1970s, the Chinese minority had closely rivalled the Vietnamese population in size. During the regime of Democratic Kampuchea, their population was halved. As Penny Edwards notes, "[P]ositions of former commercial advantage translated into instant and potentially fatal disadvantage in Democratic Kampuchea. Approximately two-thirds of ethnic Chinese in Cambodia were city-dwellers at the time of the KR takeover in 1975."[45] She refutes the argument, however, that Chinese were singled out for persecution by the DK regime. She found that the Teochiu (Chaozhou) dialect group, the majority Chinese group as far as trade and big business was concerned before 1975 and those who ran the most and largest Chinese schools in Cambodia at that time, survived the DK regime with the least proportional loss. "This statistical anomaly," she records, "undermines the theory that Chinese victims of DK rule were automatically persecuted on the grounds of capitalist or intellectual backgrounds."[46] It is more likely that many city-dwellers simply could not endure the rapid transition to rural life under the particularly harsh conditions of DK rule and perished from hunger and over-work.

Unsurprisingly, Cambodian Chinese also chose to emigrate in large numbers after 1979. The ideological rift between Vietnam and China, erupting into short-lived but furiously fought border battles between the two states in early 1979, meant that Cambodian Chinese suffered ethnic discrimination during the PRK regime, at least until 1985. They were excluded from government administrative posts and certainly from positions within the Party; shop fronts were not allowed to display Chinese characters, the traditional festivals were banned and their community newspapers and schools were outlawed. In the mid-1980s, according to official sources, only about 61,000 Chinese remained in Cambodia.

Early estimates of losses in the Cham community provided the first grounds for charges of genocide against the leaders of Democratic Kampuchea. The Finnish Inquiry Commission reported that the number of Chams had fallen from around 200,000 to just 50,000.[47] This latter figure, however, was later proved to be a gross misrepresentation. The Cambodian Cham community did indeed suffer serious losses, like the rest of the population and more or less in line with general losses. Historian Michael Vickery calculated that the surviving 1979 Cham population, allowing for an estimate of 30 births per 1,000 throughout the four-year period, was 180,727. According to these figures, the number of deaths over normal was 31,290, or 15.47 per cent of the total 1975 population.[48] These calculations were confirmed by demographer Jacqueline Desbarats who noted, "Estimates of the pre-1970 Cham population ranged between 153,000 and 200,000. After an actual count in 1982, PRK officials put the Cham population at 182,000, a number estimated to have grown to 200,000 by 1988 and to 240,000 by 1993."[49]

Human Development

Whereas living standards had been measured by annual per capita income during the Sangkum and the Republic, in revolutionary Cambodia it was measured by food intake, in measures of grams of milled rice per day.

Under normal conditions, Cambodian farmers consume around 700 grams of rice daily. In the countryside in Battambang province before April 1975, that is, in those rural areas still under Khmer Republic control, they were living on about half that amount, or 400 grams per adult, which is considered adequate but minimal.[50] There are no figures for the zones under Khmer Rouge control. However, the diversion of young farm labour to the war effort, not to mention the persistent air raids, must have disrupted the rice harvest and the distribution of the harvest so that a figure of 400 grams per adult is also conceivable for the liberated zones. Villagers who worked on the construction of the Mkak dam in Chikreng district of Siem Reap between 1973 and 1975, for instance, told this author that many workers were made vulnerable to workplace accidents and illness by a lack of food. The families of the massive workforce of around 20,000 did not, or perhaps could not supply them with sufficient food for the two years it took to complete the project. On the other hand, they judged the whole period to 1977 as "not too bad."[51] From interviews Charles Twining conducted with refugees, he concluded that between 1975 and 1977 food supply decreased and many people were surviving on only 250 grams or less.[52] With other supplements, the daily diet would have provided about 1,500 calories.[53]

Once again, we have to remember that there are no firm figures and it is now agreed that conditions varied considerably from region to region, even from one cooperative to the neighbouring one. The Chikreng villagers, however, remembered clearly that they were eating barely enough in the first quarter of 1977 and it was hunger that drove them to revolt. A woman villager said, "They (the demonstrators) were angry because they didn't have enough food ... eating rice soup with banana stalk, sometimes just the banana stalk, sometimes nothing for two or three days. If we had just been the base people, there would have been enough, but with us and the *chunleas* (the deportees from the towns) together, it was difficult."[54]

When the invasion by PAVN-Salvation Front forces began in the last week of December 1978, the drought-affected wet season harvest was well advanced in many areas. During the Khmer Rouge retreat, it is reasonable to expect that some ricefields were deliberately burnt so that the invaders would not have the benefit of the harvest. The first few months of 1979 were chaotic as people criss-crossed the country, returning to their homes or in search of relatives. There were also pockets of resistance, particularly in the northwest where the security situation remained poor for the whole decade.

Debate remains over whether or not there were further deaths from starvation inside Cambodia during 1979. Certainly in April that year, President Heng Samrin sent a request to the provincial People's Revolutionary Committees urging them to take precautions against deaths from starvation by planting a late rice crop and encouraging the cultivation of fast-maturing root crops. The new regime had already received food aid from Vietnam, other socialist countries and from an aid effort mounted by the international community, but non-producers were put on rations and authorities were ordered to monitor the situation carefully.[55] By the end of that year, each person in Phnom Penh was estimated to be consuming around 450 grams of rice a day; in the peri-urban areas it was 270 grams and slightly less in the rest of the country where supplementary root crops and wild food was available.[56]

Increases in food production throughout the 1980s brought about a gradual improvement in the people's nutritional status and a United Nations' agency report of 1985 estimated that the daily individual intake had finally surpassed 2,000 calories.[57] Nevertheless, demographer Jacqueline Desbarats noted, chronic marginal malnutrition remained widespread and serious malnutrition was thought to affect over half of the population in some areas.

Health

Given the high mortality rate during the regime of Democratic Kampuchea, many analysts have concluded that the health system suffered from malevolent neglect or worse, along the lines of this observation:

> The Pol Pot regime intentionally killed the doctors and pharmacists, laid waste the hospitals and clinics, and almost completely destroyed what little preventive and primary health infrastructure had existed before their rule. Under the Khmer Rouge, [s]o-called medical care was given by 'the barefoot doctors,' teenagers from 12 to 15 years old who had three months of training.[58]

Positive experiences like the one related to the present author by a medical graduate of the PRK regime received little attention in the propaganda-prone years after 1979. She said that as an urban deportee to Kompong Thom she did not suffer hunger, but her appetite was never fully sated either until she became ill and had to go to hospital where she was treated well and could eat as much as she wanted. A factory worker who had escaped to the refugee camps from Phnom Penh told Charles Twining that there was good Chinese medicine available and Chinese physicians were stationed about the city.[59] The Nestlé milk factory in the city continued to produce condensed milk specifically for hospitals and clinics.

Why would a regime that was almost totally dependent on manual labour power deliberately destroy its health system and personnel? The obvious answer is that it did not, but as the previous chapter demonstrated, it inherited a system that was severely stressed by war, by the destruction of health infrastructure and especially by the flight of many of its doctors. The Finnish Inquiry Commission noted that over 200 doctors had left the country before 1975, representing almost half of the total number of doctors at that time.[60] The paranoid fear of enemies and an unreasonable insistence on self-reliance may have compounded the situation and denied many people the medical assistance that might easily have saved lives throughout the DK regime.

A rudimentary health system had been operating in the liberated zones from as early as 1972. A GRUNK official told Hildebrand and Porter that it consisted of "one or more hospitals in every province, a fully trained doctor for each district, a medical committee for each village, and two male nurses with three years of medical training for each hamlet."[61] This was surely more a utopian dream than the reality in the field at that time. On the other hand, some doctors from the city had reportedly joined the anti-republican cause by then and there were also paramedical teams — the barefoot doctors — which each year received three months' training and then served in the villages, teaching people the fundamental rules of hygiene and preventive medicine. The renowned Dr Thiounn Thioeun, formerly the dean of the Faculty of Medicine and director of the Soviet-Khmer Friendship Hospital was in charge of health.

Apart from the barefoot doctors, the medical system as related to Michael Vickery by someone who had been hospitalised twice during the Pol Pot years was not vastly different from the system that operates in rural Cambodia today. There were medical centres at cooperative level, and referral hospitals at the district (*srok*) and sub-regional (*damban*) levels. Medical personnel then were "youngsters of poor peasant background trained by a revolutionary doctor who had studied with Vietnamese guerrilla medics before 1975."[62] Most medicine, he said, consisted of traditional preparations and at the hospitals foreign medicine was occasionally available.

Khieu Samphan described the DK public health strategies as falling back on traditional medicine and buying modern medicine from abroad, if possible, by exchanging it for rubber and rice. The Chinese, he said, promised to help with the production of pharmaceuticals. There were campaigns to eradicate specific diseases. An anti-malaria campaign, for instance, began at the beginning of the dry season in 1975. "Malaria is a curse," the leadership declared. "It is necessary simultaneously to treat the sick and to eradicate the illness. There are also other sicknesses to combat such as leprosy, tuberculosis and goitres. For each sickness there must be a strategy to combat it."[63]

International aid, most importantly from Vietnam but also from Cuba, Czechoslovakia and other Soviet-bloc countries, as well as from UNICEF and non-government institutions like World Vision International, helped to rebuild the health system after the Pol Pot regime was overthrown. Much was made of the poor figures for the surviving members of professional groups, particularly doctors. Only 50 or, at most, 55 doctors trained before 1975 survived the Pol Pot era in 1979 and almost half of them had fled to the Thai camps and, presumably, from there to another destination in the West by 1981. Jacqueline Desbarats noted that when the Faculty of Medicine reopened in 1980, only 728 of its 3,400 students returned to continue their studies and chronic shortages of trained medical personnel continued to limit the people's access to proper health services.[64] Despite the re-establishment of health facilities in most districts, she notes, these were accessible to just over half the population. By 1990, there were only 18,000 beds in hospitals and rural clinics for a population of over 8 million, or one bed for every 450 citizens. There were already substantial disparities in medical access between Phnom Penh and the rest of the country.

Although the number of physicians had grown from 50 to 705 by the end of the PRK and there were a further 15,180 medical support personnel (medical assistants, nurses, midwives and pharmacists), the demand for health services had also greatly increased, due not least to the ongoing conflict, landmines, and the malaria epidemic spread by "volunteers" for the K5 border defence programme. Nevertheless, by 1990, estimates for the crude death rate were reduced to between 12 and 14 per 1,000 and life expectancy at birth may have exceeded 50 years. Infant mortality, however, although it had declined significantly, remained among the highest in the world.[65]

Education

In the previous regimes, education had received very high priority in the national budget. Education promised ambitious students social advancement and other rewards. From the outset, however, the DK neglected the education system. Khieu Samphan's recollections hint that this neglect was deliberate in order that Cambodia could undergo far-reaching cultural revolution. "The war has taken all our time," he noted. "Our children and youth spent all their time making war and gathering food.... Let us not forget that later we will need a more advanced technology. But scientific education and technology should obey this orientation: our technicians and scientists should first forge themselves in the mass movement."[66]

Basic literacy and numeracy was taught to children over the age of five but, as Michael Vickery observes, "[W]here living conditions were very bad, or where local cadres distorted the policy, such schools may never have been organized."[67] David Ayres agrees that rudimentary schooling was provided in almost every *damban* or region but there were districts where there was no education at all; he adds that "the provision decreased throughout the life of the regime and markedly so after the second migration of 1976."[68]

The level of consistency throughout the country, David Ayres argues, indicates that there was a central education policy in Democratic Kampuchea.[69] The schools catered to children of approximately primary school age, almost all adopted a study-work routine and used identical self-made materials and taught a similar curriculum of basic literacy and numeracy, revolutionary songs and, through slogans, revolutionary morality. There was a ministry of education although little is known about its activities apart from the production of texts to guide teachers.

The People's Republic of Kampuchea, by contrast, made formal and non-formal education a priority and primary schooling commenced almost immediately after 7 January 1979. The Law on General Education was ratified in 1986 and its articles described a system that had already been in place for several years.[70] It defined a curriculum based on "political consciousness, revolutionary morality, and basic knowledge for competency in modern labour skills, production, agriculture, artisanry and industry appropriate for the real situation of the Kampuchean revolution." Education, it said, had to follow the principles of theory tied to practice, education tied to labour and production, and schools tied to the society. Attending school was not compulsory under the PRK, although the state aimed to provide all children with five years of basic education. The target was to have all primary school graduates proceed to lower secondary school by 1992. State authorities and the mass organisations had to make provision for the employment of high school graduates either in the production units, the armed forces, or by sending them to do vocational skills training.

Illiteracy, always high, had risen to extreme levels by 1979. The PRK officially launched its first three-year campaign to eradicate illiteracy in June 1980 but by then the Department of Adult Education had already started classes for more than 60,000 participants. The first campaign involved 33,597 volunteer "teachers," many of them barely literate themselves.[71] A second campaign was initiated by a government directive in January 1984. Together, the two campaigns claimed to have "liberated" about one million illiterates.

Teacher training institutions were already operating in Battambang and Kandal by mid-1980 and others were preparing to open. Also by then, the Curriculum and Textbook Writing Centre had manually prepared and then printed books for all primary grades. Complementary schools allowed cadres, soldiers, and factory workers whose schooling had been interrupted in 1975 to complete their education. Even after the University of Phnom Penh reopened in 1988, many of its students continued to attend complementary school classes at night in order to get their senior high school certificates.

The reconstruction of the education system was a major achievement of the PRK. By 1988, according to Grant Curtis, most school-aged children had access to at least primary schooling and one of every four Kampucheans was enrolled in some part of the education system.[72] In general, however, education standards remained low and infrastructure and materials were in short supply throughout the regime. There were also disparities between provision to urban and rural children; in Phnom Penh, 90 per cent of school-aged children were enrolled, but the figure dropped to only 50–60 per cent in rural areas, and lower than that in areas of ethnic minorities.[73] Despite official claims to the contrary, illiteracy remained the norm in the countryside.

Economic Activity

Agriculture and Land Tenure

In 1968–69, national statistics for agricultural production recorded 2.427 million hectares of paddy land producing, on average, 1.3 tons per hectare.[74] Total paddy production for that year of almost unparalleled drought was 2,523,000 tons; the following season, however, was a good one and paddy production was expected to reach 3.3 million tons or approximately what it had been before the drought.[75] Where irrigation and fertiliser were used, the yield increased to between 2 and 2.5 tons per hectare, although this area of intensified rice production was relatively small. In the 1967–68 crop year, for instance, only 10 per cent of the total paddy area was fertilised and three per cent or just under 80,000 hectares were irrigated.[76]

There are no verifiable statistics concerning paddy production for the next ten years. Some American academics well-acquainted with Cambodia before 1975, however, provided useful observations. Allowing for war conditions, the 1974–75 harvest, gathered a couple of months before the final communist victory, was reasonbly good. Hildebrand and Porter estimated that it was 2.2 million tons.[77] In the country's rice bowl, the northwest, still more or less under the Republic's control, the rice merchants were said to be stuck with a surplus because the security situation made it impossible to transport purchases. In the southeast provinces as well as in the communist-controlled area of Kompong Thom, the harvest was also said to be good. There may, then, have been sufficient stockpiles of rice throughout the countryside to cope with the waves of forced migration across the country in 1975. The 1975–76 harvest, given these exceptional conditions, was not large but better than Cambodia watchers had expected, according to Twining. Good rains promised a particularly good crop for the following year also, particularly in the southern half of the country, and the 1977–78 harvest was better than expected, despite late rains and then severe floods. The final DK wet season crop, however, was hit by one of the worst droughts in living memory, although the regime was over before the harvest was gathered.

The leadership of Democratic Kampuchea concentrated all national resources on rice production. The major decision of the party congress of January 1976 was to develop modern agriculture within 10 to 15 years. Taking rice as the staple, the party set a minimum target of six, later revised to seven tons per hectare for the whole country. This target was based on two and where possible three crops per year: a wet season crop, a recession crop and a dry season crop. The key to achieving the target was mastering the water problem. Large-scale hydraulic projects had started in 1973 and in his speech to commemorate the anniversary of the party in September 1978, Pol Pot claimed that the dams, reservoirs and canals constructed since then had provided for 700,000 hectares of irrigated land, or almost ten times the area irrigated in 1968.

Subsequent to the decisions of the 1976 party congress, large co-operatives were established to permit the organisation of vast labour surpluses. All remaining private ownership of chickens and livestock as well as family fruit and vegetable gardens was abolished. Communal eating was enforced in most places in the last quarter of that year. Construction brigades of thousands of workers toiled day and night to construct dams, reservoirs and irrigation canals. A more rational distribution of rice fields based on kilometre-square units divided into single hectare sections, it was believed, would one day facilitate the full mechanisation of rice cultivation.

The result was the complete opposite of the plan. Rice production, in the northwest zone at least, actually seems to have halved as a direct consequence of these decisions.[78] Both the "old" and the "new" people reported that hunger, even starvation, started at this time. Nevertheless, in March 1978, Pol Pot told a visiting Yugoslav press delegation, "[W]e have succeeded in solving the agricultural problem particularly with regard to growing rice ... [and] we have enough rice to feed our people ourselves. As a result, our people's living conditions have improved and we still have rice available for export."[79]

Many survivors reported seeing large quantities of rice being taken away on trucks, presumably to depots and later for export. Pol Pot told the Yugoslav journalists that his regime was exporting rice in return for "all the necessary commodities." It is worth remembering Hou Yuon's warning at this point never to compare the level of rice exports with actual rice production. It was usually at times of greatest hunger, he said with reference to an earlier period of Cambodia's modern history, that rice exports reached their peak.

The jute factory that Hou Yuon had helped to establish in Battambang during the Sangkum continued to operate throughout the Democratic Kampuchea period. Michael Vickery found that the old workers at the factory were replaced by peasant workers in 1976, in line, it seems, with general policy for industrial establishments.[80] Otherwise, the jute factory functioned normally until 1979 and beyond. In his September 1978 speech for the party anniversary, Pol Pot claimed that jute production that year had exceeded the plan, as had cotton. "[W]e keep on developing industrial crops and export crops such as corn, groundnuts, beans, soy beans, sesame, tobacco, and so on," he said on that occasion, "in order to increase capital for the building up of our industry."

The rubber plantations were nationalised in June 1974.[81] As always, rubber production was a priority for regime economic planners. Despite extensive damage caused by defoliants and aerial bombardment, the plantations under rebel control had continued to operate throughout the war, although obviously on a much reduced scale. United States intelligence agents reported the exchange of rubber by the communist-front forces for gasoline from Vietnam at that time.[82] After the revolution, Cambodian rubber began appearing in Thai border markets in 1976. It was generally a "dirty, inferior product," according to Charles Twining and it was not known what part of Cambodia it originated from or whether it was new product or from old stocks.[83] Later the same year, there were reports of rubber being exported in greater quantities through Kompong Som. A refugee who had worked on the Mimot plantation told Twining that the DK regime had maintained the rubber plantations relatively well.

Within a few short weeks at the beginning of 1979, everything changed. The cooperative system collapsed like a house of cards as the Khmer Rouge withdrew ahead of the advancing PAVN-Salvation Front forces. As far as the people were concerned, the socialist experiment had failed. Far from creating a workers' paradise, the DK regime had resulted in a life of endless toil without remuneration, not even sufficient food. Terror and extreme violence in some areas had left thousands dead.

Attempts by the new regime to reinstate some form of collectivist organisation in the countryside, therefore, met with at best passive resistance. Given the level of economic destruction and social dislocation, however, the government needed control over the rice surplus to save the state from disintegrating entirely.

By August of that first chaotic year, only a third of the paddy land, or around 875,000 hectares had been planted.[84] Immediate food relief was provided by Vietnam, the Soviet-bloc countries and a special international NGO effort. Meanwhile, the PRK administration set about implementing its policy of agricultural collectivisation. Many incentives were built into the system. For instance, there were no taxes on the first four harvests and, in theory at least, there was no compulsion to sell to the state. The farmers were free to sell their rice in the market or to the state or to save it for their family's needs. The state guaranteed its purchasing price would match the market price. The main aim of state procurement, the government argued, was to circulate the new riel and get the economy moving again.

The family economy was encouraged and promoted according to similar incentives. To this end, common land and land surplus to the needs of the *krom samaki* was brought into production for crops other than rice and also for domestic animal production. The family economy was supposed to help achieve the official target of bringing two million hectares of arable land back into production as soon as possible. By the end of 1980, around half that target had been reached. Three years later, the PRK could claim with some justification that although living standards were still very low, it could sustain people's lives. This excellent result, however, had little to do with socialism. By then, perhaps no more than ten per cent of the *krom samaki* were collectives and more than half were working according to the traditional method of mutual support. The remainder were *krom samaki* in name only where the *krom* chief managed the land but it was worked on an individual basis. A last ditch effort was made in 1984 to stimulate the development of the *krom samaki*. Hundreds of model villages were set up but, in fact, the government did not have the resources to provide them with adequate fertiliser, quality rice seeds, water pumps and so on. In any case, once a certain degree of normalcy and security had been established in rural areas not directly affected by the ongoing civil war, the farmers simply reverted to the style of farming they knew would ensure a sufficient harvest for their needs.

The PRK never did achieve its goal of cultivating 2.5 million hectares of paddy land, or the magical target of three million tons of paddy, including both wet and dry season crops, figures that the Sangkum had established as benchmarks. This was due in part to the ongoing civil war, particularly in the northwest, where the war escalated seriously after 1985. Total rice production, however, did eventually rebound to levels not too far below the Sangkum optimum figure and by the end of the regime in 1989, as the following table shows, Cambodia was almost self-sufficient in rice. Yields were as they had been in 1967.

Table 4.4 Paddy Production, 1980–89[85]

Year	Area Planted ('000 hectares)	Average Yield (tons/ha)	Paddy Production ('000 tons)	Shortfalls ('000 tons)
1980	1,441	1.16	1,670	692
1981	1,493	1.00	1,490	213
1982	1,681	1.18	1,990	357
1983	1,740	1.17	2,040	222
1984	1,418	0.89	1,260	267
1985	1,517	1.18	1,790	423
1986	1,618	1.29	2,090	117
1987	1,418	1.28	1,815	145
1988	1,878	1.36	2,560	259
1989	1,890	1.36	2,570	51

Sources: Ministry of Agriculture Statistical Office, *et al.*

Despite persistent concerns expressed by Prime Minister Pen Sovann about appalling working conditions, the rubber plantations were also restored and by the end of the PRK regime rubber was the second export earner after timber. In 1988, the last full year of the regime, Cambodia exported almost all the rubber it produced (26,700 of 27,403 tonnes) and earned around US$20 million in foreign exchange.

Fisheries

Cambodia's forests and fisheries, from a conservationist perspective, benefited from the isolation of the DK regime. Commercial fishing in the inland waterways and the Great Lake was principally a Vietnamese industry and after the expulsion of the Vietnamese in 1975 the fisheries restocked naturally. There were fishing production solidarity groups during the DK, as recounted by eyewitness May Someth, and Hildebrand and Porter noted that groups also existed for marine fisheries in the Koh Kong region.[86] There are, however, no statistics remaining about the extent of fish production during that period. Hildebrand and Porter simply recorded, "In the past Cambodia exported 45,000 tons of dried fish to Thailand and Singapore, and the resumption of this trade is planned." Charles Twining noted that fish sauce and fish paste were bartered on the Thai border in the summer of 1975 "and it was universally agreed that the source had to be the Tonle Sap."[87] Marine fish were also bartered with the Thai for products needed in the Koh Kong area.

Freshwater fisheries recovered spontaneously after 1979. That year the catch was only 20,000 tons but by 1982 it had grown more than three-fold to 68,700 tons. The following year, the PRK government formed *krom samaki* for both fishery and forestry exploitation and put regulations in place in order to boost production for export. The industry was eventually organised into three sectors, namely state fisheries enterprises, fishing solidarity groups, each involving from six to ten families, and family fisheries. The restructuring appears to have an almost immediately negative effect on production. According to official figures, output dropped in 1983 and even further in 1984 when only 56,000 tons were produced.[88] At the fifth party congress in October 1985, Heng Samrin declared that as a "spearhead," fisheries would reach annual production of 130,000 tons by 1990. By 1986, however, results were far below that year's target of 90,000 tons.

It seems far more likely that production remained very high but that illegal sales and exports were flourishing. The National Assembly's Commission for the Economy and the Budget investigated the problem and in 1987 reported that there was "chaos" on the fishing grounds, "especially when the fish are spawning and when fishing is prohibited."[89] According to the commission's report, "[T]he fish stock in Kampuchea has dropped by more than fifty per cent and some fish have almost disappeared. From ancient times, our country has not had to raise fish. However, if this anarchy continues, and we have no firm measures, then one day Lake Tonle Sap will have no fish at all."

The commission's complaints must have been heard because the following year, the Prime Minister's budget report announced that fisheries production was back on target, although marine fisheries were very weak.[90] A UNDP report of 1989 also referred to the slow recovery of marine fisheries' production which, it noted, "seems now to have stabilized at 12,000 metric tons, far below the 40,000 tons of the 1960s."[91]

Forestry

The Food and Agriculture Organisation (FAO) of the United Nations completed an inventory of Cambodia's forests in 1970.[92] It showed that forests then covered 73 per cent, or 132,200 square kilometres of Cambodia's territory. Official figures recorded that timber production in 1967 was 400,000 cubic metres, exclusive of farmers' self-consumption. Of this amount, a little over one-third was fuelwood, including wood for charcoal, and the remainder was industrial wood.

Little is known about forestry throughout the 1970s although decreases in forest cover were said to range from 75,000 hectares to 130,000 hectares due to heavy bombing and defoliation, as well as destruction of portions of the flooded forest and increased shifting cultivation. The volume of logs extracted annually fell to around 100,000 cubic metres.[93] Twining notes, however, that there were as many as 500 small sawmills that probably became operational again after 1975.[94] In fact, it is impossible to know how the forests fared during the DK regime because there are no statistics or even survivor memoirs about this sector.

Throughout the PRK, annual production amounted to an average of about 140,000 cubic metres of round logs and a further 2.4 million cubic metres of fuelwood, which was a steady and sustainable cut in line with policy and the Department of Forestry and Hunting's awareness of stewardship which it inherited from the Sangkum. In 1983, apart from establishing the solidarity groups for forestry production, the government also introduced a tax on forestry products. Like the agricultural tax, it was disguised as something else. The *krom samaki* and other units that had permits to harvest and take by-products of forestry were required to contribute payments for the maintenance of a fund for the protection and care of forests. The transportation of logs within and across provincial boundaries was regulated by official permits. There were, however, many abuses of the system either by provincial authorities acting alone or by Vietnamese military units that stole logs and defied the government monitors. Large-scale abuse and theft began during the 1984–85 dry season when the PRK government implemented the K5 Plan to seal the border against incursions by resistance troops. This necessitated a massive programme of forest clearing with the aim of denying the enemy sanctuary bases once they had infiltrated the defence line of mines, trenches and metal spikes that eventually stretched for 1,000 kilometres along the northwest border with Thailand. In preparation for that major dry season offensive, 500 square kilometres of forest were cleared.

According to the first five-year plan, 1986–90, timber production was supposed to reach an annual output of 200,000 cubic metres. The target set for 1987 was 150,000 cubic metres of which 35,000 cubic metres would be for export. Demand for Cambodian timber increased significantly that year and the target was exceeded. As a memo from the cabinet of the Council of Ministers recorded, "These days, all friendly socialist countries want to buy our Kampuchean timber."[95] Production in 1988 exceeded 200,000 cubic metres. More than one-quarter of that was exported to the USSR, Vietnam, Czechoslovakia, Bulgaria and the German Democratic Republic; a small amount, only 2,700 cubic metres, was sold to Western countries.[96] Despite, or rather because of this commercial success, the level of abuse was starting to alarm some officials. The same Commission for the Economy and Budget that had reported so vehemently on the fisheries sector had this to say about the illegal cutting and transportation of logs out of the Kompong Speu forests:

> If this chaos continues, some day our country will meet severe difficulties because our commission has checked and seen some places where there used to be a lot of forests but now they have become cleared fields. We used to say that it was the activities of the enemy that caused us to encounter difficulties in cutting and protecting the forests. However, in reality, we see that the people who can cut the trees know only how to continue cutting without stopping.[97]

The commission condemned this behaviour as "national destruction" and noted further that replanting was still only "in principle" and that the policy was not being implemented well at all.

In response, the Council of State issued a lengthy decree-law of 42 articles in June 1988 concerning management of the forestry sector. Over the next decade, this law would be sorely tested. That year, for the first time, the government made direct contracts with non-socialist countries and realized the high prices that Cambodian timber could command on international markets. Before the end of the PRK, contracts were made with foreign countries for logging concessions in Cambodia's forests. Vietnam won a concession on 75,000 hectares in Kratie province, giving Cambodia a return of half of the proceeds from the timber, and in May 1989, contracts were signed with Thai companies through individual provincial agreements.[98]

Industry, Services and Labour

The Finnish Inquiry Commission in 1982 found that Cambodia's small industrial sector had suffered heavy damage as a result of the war, especially during the U.S. bombing in 1973. These findings included the following:

> Of the 1,400 rice mills that had been in operation only 300 were still working in 1974 and only 65 of the previous sawmills were in use. The

country's only phosphate plant and only paper mill were completely destroyed. Similarly, cement and textile production facilities suffered serious damage. Of the roads, 40 per cent were entirely unfit for use and one-third of the country's bridges had been blown up.[99]

Damage to national infrastructure by the saturation bombing of 1973 was on a massive scale, as quantified in the previous chapter. Khieu Samphan in his biography, however, mentions none of this. He refers only to the industrial landscape of Phnom Penh and he claims that there was a high level of activity there from the beginning of the DK regime. "Immediately after our entry to Phnom Penh," he said, "we started up the railways, the tyre factories, textiles mills, mechanical workshops, and factories for tiles and soap. We also started the drinks factories, one per month, to supply the state. We also had the petrol refinery to serve local consumption and export, distilleries to produce alcohol (to serve drinks for foreigners) and chemical laboratories for our pharmaceutical production, perfume, vinegar, and so on. What we lacked were raw materials."[100]

The comprehensive interviews that Michael Vickery conducted with refugees in Thailand in 1980 confirmed these claims. After quoting the evidence supplied by his informants, he noted, "We also have additional evidence from refugees and confessions of arrested officials, that in 1975–6 the tempo of industry and the skilled personnel of many factories were maintained, and in some instances technicians were even called back from the evacuation."[101]

According to the official rhetoric, growth in agriculture would stimulate the development of light industry which, in turn, would lead to progress in heavy industry. This goal was pursued with the same haste as in agriculture and with the same mania for self-reliance and mastery. There were indeed, as Khieu Samphan admitted, few raw materials to feed industrial growth and the skilled personnel including the railway workers, technicians, and foreign trained engineers were not employed for very long. Young workers of poor-peasant background replaced them in 1976 and learnt — or did not learn — theory through practice.

In view of these fundamental constraints, the success claimed by Pol Pot in 1978 was surely exaggerated.[102] The stated achievements included full reconstruction of the textile factory in Kompong Cham, the phosphate factory in Tuk Meas, the plywood factory and the glass factory. The cement factory and the Battambang sugar refinery, it was claimed, had been upgraded and repaired, while a new paper mill, a second tyre factory and four crepe rubber factories were under construction. He planned to build a steel works that could meet a quarter of the country's needs and a factory to produce twelve-horsepower diesel engines. The oil refinery at Kompong Som, he said, was planned for full reconstruction by the end of 1979.

On the other hand, these claims cannot be dismissed entirely. There are no records and the scorched earth retreat of the Khmer Rouge as the PAVN and the Salvation Front forces invaded in late December 1978 destroyed many of the gains that may have been made in the industrial reconstruction of the country. Furthermore, the anarchy of the first couple of months of the new regime allowed widespread damage, looting and theft of state property that was also blamed on the Khmer Rouge.

Some Cambodia watchers believed that, in some respects, the quantity of manufactured output by Democratic Kampuchea might have been greater than that of the 1960s. The encouragement of small-scale local manufacturing probably did result in more agricultural hand tools, fishing boats, food processing machinery and the like, if only because so much manpower was assigned to the industrial effort.[103] Meanwhile, at the central level, facilities were available for medium-scale industry. Rail transport, for example, was revived under the DK and Charles Twining recorded that there was at least one freight train operating in each direction between the port of Kompong Som and Phnom Penh by August 1976.[104] The Phnom Penh to Battambang line was also brought back into operation. Mekong river traffic resumed and the Phnom Penh port facilities were repaired. Pochentong airport was functioning again.

Therefore, it is reasonable to accept the UNDP's assessment that in 1979, both the central government and the provincial authorities inherited a large number of former private and state-owned industrial enterprises in various states of repair ranging from fully operational to completely devastated.[105] The shortage of qualified and trained personnel was a more serious obstacle to reconstruction than the lack of plant and machinery, but the PRK's failure to develop a state industrial sector was due to many factors, not least to a lack of its own political will.

By the middle of 1981, foreign journalists were describing "booming markets" in Phnom Penh and Battambang, stocked with a wide variety of goods smuggled from Thailand. "Every other day Phnom Penh railway station is the scene of a mad rush of traders as the train from Battambang pulls in laden with Thai goods," Nayan Chanda wrote.[106] This private trade, he added, had already allowed hundreds of Chinese or Sino-Khmers to dominate the business scene. Economic disparity between low-paid government workers and the newly rich merchants in the market was already apparent.

The private traders financed their smuggling with personal stocks of gold and gems but obviously this supply would run out sooner or later and the government would have to find revenue to pay for imports or produce those goods themselves in state factories. The government seemed to lack the will to address this issue. "Some officials seem to feel that the problem of the market will solve itself as the private stocks of gold and jewellery which finance it run out," Nayan Chanda concluded.[107] At that early point in PRK's history, 63 out of 85 industrial installations in Cambodia were said to be capable of working, but because the government did not have the means, or presumably even the felt need to import raw materials, only 12 factories were in production. These factories were producing textiles, tyres, plastics and iron tools with materials supplied by international non-government aid agencies.

In 1983, the Council of Ministers gave relative budgetary autonomy to provincial and line ministries. The following year, the industrial sector was singled out for praise as a "model ... that has implemented the system of financial self-reliance in almost all of its enterprises along with starting to pay money into the state."[108] State industrial enterprises were classified on the basis of their dependence on state supply of raw materials. Those independent of state supplies were given the freedom to import materials and spare parts with foreign currency and to retain and reinvest their "profit" or production above the annual target. As the PRK proceeded, this system of self-financing was more and more encouraged as the state showed less and less interest in regulating a centralised market.

Industrial production remained far below pre-war levels throughout the PRK and growth was very slow. Midway through the regime, more than 40 per cent of installations were still inoperative and the capacity of those that were functioning was constrained by lack of materials and an insufficient and irregular power supply.[109] By 1989, around 70 factories and enterprises were back in production. Some 14,000 state workers were employed in six industrial sectors including power, mechanics, textiles, chemicals, food processing, and light industry. In addition, according to the Ministry of Industry's reckoning, there were 4,000 small-scale artisanal enterprises throughout the country and up to 10,000 either private or *krom samaki* industrial enterprises operating sawmills, rice mills, furniture workshops and so on.[110] The reality behind the figures was that the total value of industrial production, including handicrafts, was only US$20 million, representing a tiny contribution to the GDP which in 1988 reached US$1.56 billion or half of what it had been in 1968.[111] Almost three-quarters of the total value of the Ministry of Industry's production came from cigarette manufacturing.

After the total employment of the DK years, Cambodia's economically active population resumed levels consistent with what they had been in the 1960s. In 1987, the Ministry of Planning put that population within a range of three million to 3.7 million, or between 40 per cent and 47 per cent of the total population.[112] Around 80 per cent of the working population was engaged in agriculture, forestry and fishery, and women predominated, making up more than 60 per cent of the agricultural workforce.[113] Despite the large presence of women in the workforce and the public service, they occupied mainly the middle and lower ranks. Even in education, Desbarats observed, women accounted for only 30 per cent of all teachers. Women workers were in a particularly vulnerable position as the move towards a radical free market situation became obvious in 1989.

Foreign Trade, Aid, Investment and Debt

While the impression of Democratic Kampuchea as a self-reliant, hermit state seems to have been generally correct, some official trade continued and smuggling persisted at the usual points, that is, on the northwest border near the Thai town of Aranyaprathet, in the southwest between Trat and Koh Kong, and perhaps also in the southeast with Vietnam.[114] The volume of official trade, however, was very small. In 1978, the last full year of the regime, the U.S. Central Intelligence Agency estimated that exports, including rubber, rice, pepper and wood were worth less than one million dollars and imports of food, fuel and machinery cost less than 20 million dollars. The People's Republic of China was the main client, but Japan purchased kapok, and rice was exported to Madagascar and West African nations like Senegal that had remained steady importers of Cambodian rice since the time of the French Protectorate.[115]

For a very short period of about one month after late September 1976, Pol Pot seems to have lost power. A flurry of liberalisation measures in relation to foreign trade occurred during that time. For instance, DDT was purchased from the U.S. to combat malaria.[116] Trade delegations were sent to other countries in the pro-China bloc: Albania, Yugoslavia and North Korea. Ieng Sary, the deputy premier for foreign affairs, went to Japan to negotiate a contract for steel, and a trading company was set up in Hong Kong to administer trade between DK and non-socialist countries.[117]

Trade in rubber continued. Several Cambodia watchers noted that rubber was shipped to Singapore in rather large quantities of around 35,000 tons following the visit of a Singaporean trade mission to Cambodia in 1978.[118] A Chinese villager who spent the DK years in the Stung

Trâng rubber plantation in Kompong Cham province told Penny Edwards that latex left the plantation en route for China. There were about 40 young Chinese experts at his plantation alone, he told her.[119]

These technical advisers from China and others from North Korea might have represented the bulk of foreign aid to DK. The UNDP needs assessment study of 1989 reported, "No credits were accepted, and aid comprised mainly Chinese technicians who seem to have advised on the construction of infrastructure but only to a small extent on agricultural or industrial production activities."[120] This statement, however, is unfounded. There is no doubt that many Chinese experts worked alongside DK counterparts in the rubber plantations, at Pochentong airport and on other sites.[121] But whether other forms of assistance were given as grants, soft loans, or were directly exchanged for Cambodian produce is not recorded. It is known, for instance, that Chinese and North Korean bilateral assistance was provided for the tractor assembly plant in the northwest and for coastal patrol vessels. Large-scale infrastructure works including a military airstrip in Kompong Chhnang and improvements to Kompong Som harbour were also part of foreign assistance. If it is true that "no credits were accepted," then it is no wonder that the people had to work so hard in the ricefields for so little in return. Khieu Samphan in his biography makes no mention of trade balances or foreign debt.

Long-term debt was, however, a concern for the PRK from early in its history. In July 1981, Pen Sovann addressed the Council of Ministers with a highly detailed list of goods imported since the overthrow of the DK regime on 7 January 1979.[122] The list included 615,000 tons of rice from the USSR, Vietnam and other socialist countries, 5,000 tons of paper, medicine and medical supplies worth 15 million commercial roubles (roughly on par with the U.S. dollar) and 58,000 tons of fertiliser worth 5 million roubles. In addition, there were trucks, light sedans, tractors, water pumps, fishing nets, and large quantities of cloth and thread which, together with "victory goods and chattels" seemed like a lot, according to the Prime Minister, but in fact barely covered the country's immediate needs. More than 90 per cent of those goods had arrived as humanitarian aid, but the USSR had also lent the new government 60 million roubles. Pen Sovann reminded his cabinet that this money had to be repaid. "Therefore," he said, "we must consider how we can do that or beg an extension. At present, we can only import, we cannot export yet."

The major trading partners of the PRK were the USSR and Vietnam. While the relationship with the USSR was a normal bilateral one, arrangements made with Vietnam were special. The first summit meeting between the Socialist Republic of Vietnam and the People's Republic of

Kampuchea was held in Phnom Penh from 16 to 19 February 1979, only five weeks after the PAVN-Salvation Front forces took control of the city. The Treaty of Peace, Friendship and Cooperation between the SRV and the PRK was signed at that meeting.[123] Article 3 of the treaty concerned "beneficial fraternal exchanges ... in the fields of the economy, culture, education, public health, science and technology, and for training cadres and exchanging specialists and experience in all fields of national construction." To achieve this objective, the two parties would sign necessary agreements and increase contacts and cooperation between the state bodies concerned and between mass organisations of both countries.

In this arrangement, provinces and municipalities were "twinned" for the purposes of commercial exchange. The central governments established lists of goods and produce that could be traded as well as those that needed special permits. For instance, Cambodian provinces could export corn, lentils, groundnuts, tobacco, dried fish, and timber and could request their Vietnamese provincial counterparts to provide mechanics, labourers, or even machinery on hire. Products like fertiliser and petrol could not be exchanged without special permission from the Council of Ministers. Rice exports, of course, remained a state monopoly. The provinces were free to establish their own prices according to the market. The commercial rouble was used as a common currency of exchange.

Agreements were also made on a ministry-to-ministry basis. In 1983, for example, the Cambodian Ministry of Agriculture signed an agreement with its counterpart in Vietnam for nine long-term experts as well as 46 short-term experts to assist its departments.[124] Vietnam, at that time, was training 35 Cambodian agricultural technicians. The Vietnamese ministry agreed to supply its Cambodian counterpart with crop seeds, pesticide, animal vaccine and tractor parts in return for agricultural products.

The agreement with the USSR, for the period 1982 to 1985, was for credit as loans as well as for non-refundable assistance.[125] The former, with interest-free credit up to 30 million roubles, included redeveloping the waterworks in Phnom Penh and Kompong Som as well as hotels in those two cities, the fertiliser factory in Kampot, the power stations and electricity grids, and the ports. The agreement confirmed the continuation of work already begun on roads, bridges, telecommunications, and for the supply of equipment and spare parts. The USSR agreed to provide credit for construction of the National Bank of Cambodia, for a technical college (Tuk Thlaa) and an agricultural experiment station. According to the terms of the agreement, this credit was available for 20 years with repayments commencing after a five-year grace period. Non-refundable assistance was provided for the Kampuchea-Soviet Friendship Hospital, four provincial hospitals, 30 mobile health teams and other medical assistance, for the Khmer-Soviet Technical Institute, the Chamcar Dong Agricultural Institute, for repairs to various state buildings and for training. The USSR also offered to build a satellite telecommunications facility in Phnom Penh. Skills training in the Soviet Union for Cambodian technicians and tertiary-level students was built into most items on the list and this support came free of charge. Reciprocally, hundreds of Soviet technicians and specialists were sent to Cambodia. As of 10 June 1982, for instance, there were already 248 of them attached to six ministries. There were many more Vietnamese experts stationed in Cambodian ministries. Cambodia was responsible for the cost of food, accommodation and transport for the Vietnamese experts only. In return, Cambodian cadres could receive free medical treatment in Vietnamese hospitals.

On completion of the first cycle, the PRK and the USSR signed a further five-year trade and aid agreement in 1986. Under its terms, by 1989 Moscow's economic aid, trade, and cooperation with Cambodia was worth around US$130 million a year, representing as much as 80 per cent of total revenue for the national budget.[126]

From very early in its history, the PRK recognised the development of export industries as a life or death matter for the regime. As usual, they fell back on rubber as the first resort and there were few alternatives until 1987 when Cambodian timber started to receive a lot of attention from its Southeast Asian neighbours. Maize, sesame, and soybeans were included in the agricultural products that Cambodia exported throughout the 1980s. Nevertheless, the volume and value of official exports remained very small. The Ministry of Planning reported a 30 per cent increase in the value of exports between 1987 and 1988, thanks to timber exports.[127] Total value of exports in 1988 was US$35 million — one-third of it in latex sold to the USSR — although the actual value may have been half as much again if informal exports in gems, timber and fish had been taken into account.[128]

Imports increased more or less in line with efforts to export. The Ministry of Planning put the cost of imports in 1988 at US$130 million, or almost four times the value of exports. The previous year, imports had cost US$121 million. By then, while the bulk of imports was still coming from the USSR and its allies, some profitable trade was being conducted with Thailand, Singapore, Japan and other non-socialist countries as well as with the former enemy, China. Exports grew slowly and imports remained steady at about four times the value of exports.

In spite of the terrible privations suffered by the people for the unattainable goal of self-reliance, Cambodia's experiment with social revolution from 1975 to 1989 proved to be costly in terms of foreign debt. Robert Muscat offered the following figures to illustrate the external debt of the PRK from 1982 to 1986.

Table 4.5 External Debt, 1982–86 (millions of U.S. dollars)[129]

	1982	1983	1984	1985	1986
Gross long-term debt of which:	368	482	478	508	622
CMEA	128	246	243	269	377
multilateral	3	3	3	4	4
OECD aid	237	233	231	235	241
capital markets	1	–	1	–	–
Short-term debt of which:	2	8	4	6	6
banks	2	3	–	–	–
export credits	–	5	4	6	6

Source: OECD, Financing and External debt of Developing Countries, 1987.

The OECD debt, he believed, comprised what was owed by Cambodian regimes before 1975 and the fluctuations may have been "the result of capitalizing unpaid interest and/or amortization." The significant increase in the debt owed to the Soviet bloc between 1985 and 1986 was almost certainly due to military spending for the K5 Plan to seal the border with Thailand against incursions by the resistance forces. The UNDP needs assessment team thought that the external debt could have been as much as US$1,500 million by 1989, or three times what it had been in 1984.[130] The debt service burden weighed heavily on a country with limited export capacity.

Public Finance, Banking and Credit

The riel had already lost currency in the countryside before the 1975 victory. The suppression of money and the encouragement of barter had been used effectively to destroy the power of the Chinese merchants over rice purchases. This move had been easy because peasants had never had much use for paper money. Nevertheless, the revolutionary movement's leaders had planned to reintroduce the use of money after liberation. Banknotes had already been printed in China and transported to Cambodia. They were in small denominations up to 100 riels and featured designs extolling the labour of workers, peasants and soldiers.

These banknotes were never used. By way of explanation, Pol Pot reasoned that the revolution did not have experts competent enough to understand the workings of the international monetary system, so the riel could have been easily sabotaged by American imperialism.[131] "Personally, I doubted the wisdom of this decision," Khieu Samphan said. "Then, to myself, I made a comparison with cheques commonly used by banks which did not need the actual use of money. Could we be inspired by that to regulate payments between the different ministries and departments of Democratic Kampuchea? The measure seemed to me premature. But I did not offer my opinion because for the moment the vital problem was not about using money. In any case, we could always return to using money because we had not destroyed our new banknotes." When relations with Vietnam became very tense in 1978, Pol Pot sought commercial relations with other Southeast Asian countries and the West in general, he said. A national currency was necessary and Pol Pot went along with the advice of many other colleagues and leaders and decided to return to using money but of course it was too late.

It is not possible to discuss budget deficits or public credit in relation to the regime of Democratic Kampuchea. Public revenue, in Pol Pot's terms, was reduced to the most basic level:

> Our capital comes essentially from the work of our people. Our people, by their work, develop agricultural production.... We have also another important source of capital. That is the fact that we have no salary. The absence of salary constitutes in itself a great source of capital. These accumulated capital [sic] are used for the building up of our agriculture and our industry.[132]

In this way, the state extracted a huge rice surplus relative to outputs. Practically the entire population was mobilised for labour. The dependent population was very small given that even young children were put to work collecting dung and minding cattle, and the urban consumer population was negligible. The army was large but at least half of the military force raised its own rice, according to Twining.[133] Despite the surplus, the people starved. The cost of financing the revolutionary state's plan to develop agriculture and industry exceeded the capacity of human labour to produce and the country's limited resources to supply its needs.

In contrast with the DK, there was little that was genuinely "revolutionary" about the PRK's efforts to restore the basic features of public finance to the Cambodian economy. The capitulation to free market forces that was formally acknowledged in 1989 was, in fact, merely the culmination of a trend that had been established very early in its history. The new riel was put into circulation on 20 March 1980 by the newly restored National Bank of Cambodia. During the previous year, rice had established its purchasing power so the value of the riel was equated with the value of one kilogram of (milled) rice. The value of one ton of rice on the international market was then US$250, so the nominal exchange value of the riel was US$0.25. It was exchanged for three Vietnamese dong. In the first year, between 400 and 450 million riels went into circulation, 250 million riels for salary supplements and 100 million in payment for the farmers' paddy and also to finance the rural credit programme. In turn, this spending had to be backed with a sufficient quantity of goods to the same value. This was a substantial success for the fledgling regime. The new currency was introduced quickly and efficiently, although circulation remained small for many years because the purchasing power of the people also remained very weak.

Given the poverty of the mass of the people, the government moved very slowly to collect taxes from them. In 1979, there were no taxes or other charges. The first agricultural taxes were levied on the 1983–84 harvest. Called "the patriotic contribution," it was a tax on rice fields producing more than one ton per hectare annually, fixed at 100 kilograms per hectare in the plains region and between 60 and 80 kilograms in the less productive coastal regions. The family economy was not taxed and as a further incentive to join military service, the tax was reduced for families of soldiers or the security forces. The state hoped to balance the loss of agricultural tax revenue with efficient procurement of the farmers' rice surpluses, but it took several years of trial and error before this was achieved.

The import tax was decreed as law in November 1982. Within two months of its implementation, it had earned 11 million riels for the state.[134] Collecting this tax was a dangerous exercise. In Kompong Som and Koh Kong, highly organised smugglers were skilled in tax evasion and used bribery and armed threats against officials. Minister for Finance, Chan Phin, estimated that in one month alone the state lost at least 10 million riels on cigarette smuggling by rail. Smuggling was rife but the government persisted and increased the tax rate in April 1984 to between 5 per cent and 60 per cent with no exemptions for essential items.

The first state budget of 1980 was declared a success but the figures showed a dismal state of financial affairs. Total expenditure was 294,546,000 riels compared with total revenue of only 25,477,000 riels.[135] In the next budget, the government expected to spend between 1.4 billion and 1.6 billion riels, against income of one billion to 1.2 billion riels, 70 per cent of which would come from international assistance and the rest from taxation and printing money. In March 1983, Chan Phin submitted his proposed state budget for 1984. At that point, almost mid-way through the history of the PRK, nearly 30 per cent of budgetary income came from printing money. "Generally speaking," he said, "in the past few years aid and loans and the printing of money have amounted to more than 90 per cent of our total income which shows that our economic base does not yet have normalcy and this feature will be protracted if we do not all pay attention to it."[136]

As the budgets indicated, the Cambodian economy continued to grow but tax revenue remained a very small proportion of total income. In 1985, when imports cost five times what exports could earn, total budget expenditure for the first nine months (excluding defence costs) was 3.1266 billion riels. Taxes earned only 179 million riels. The following year, private businesses with a monthly income above 400 riels were taxed on profits, rents and utilities. The annual profits of fisheries, construction, forestry and transport *krom samaki* were taxed between 8 per cent and 26 per cent, while commercial, food and service companies paid almost twice that rate.[137] There was no personal income tax.

The rural credit programme was introduced to coincide with state purchases of the 1980–81 rice harvest. The commune chiefs were responsible for implementation of the scheme which had the aim of extending circulation of the riel while also increasing the provision of essential commodity goods and inputs to farmers. As with every other attempt to implement rural credit in the past, the scheme was plagued by incompetent managers and debtors who were reluctant to repay what they had borrowed. By 1988, the rural credit programme was in tatters. Debt recovery was virtually impossible by then. A circular issued by Prime Minister Hun Sen noted that some loans had not been witnessed, some debts had been passed on to children, "most families have a poor livelihood and have no possibility to repay, while some families have the possibility to repay but do not agree to repay." Alarmingly, he continued, "Some state authorities at the base have taken the debts back from the people already but do not agree to pay it back to the relevant institution and they take it to use for wrong reasons."[138] By 1989, poor villagers were as dependent on the local moneylender as they had ever been.

On 26 July that year, the Council of State ratified the bill to permit foreign investment.[139] The de-socialisation of the economy was complete.

Conclusions

Twenty years of war and revolution were disastrous for the Cambodian economy. When the revolution ended in 1989, the countryside still had not recovered the same level of agricultural production reached by the end of the Sangkum two decades earlier. Industrial output was negligible. Despite a decade of negative growth, however, the population was recovering strongly. All the figures for 1987–88 indicated that Cambodia was desperately poor and possibly already at the stage of being unable to support its population without major foreign intervention, if only to stop the war so that the rich rice-growing region of the northwest could be brought back into full production, young male labour could be diverted from defence to reconstruction, and a brake could be put on the rising external debt.

Some analysts and foreigners sympathetic to the PRK excused its weak economic performance by pointing to the fact that Cambodia was denied international aid and credit by the embargo that was imposed on Vietnam for its intervention in Cambodia in 1979. The lack of international credit may have slowed recovery, but the PRK did not lack foreign assistance. In fact, the terms and conditions of USSR aid were generous and while the national budget had to bear some of the cost of supporting Vietnamese soldiers and technical advisers, this bore no comparison to the actual cost of defence or the organisational support that the advisers gave to restoring the Cambodian administration. Between 1979 and 1989, Cambodia received worthwhile foreign assistance at a rate and of a kind that could be absorbed by an inexperienced government trying to rebuild an economy that had been severely damaged first by war and then by radical revolution. It must be remembered that Sihanouk had terminated the aid programme with the U.S. in 1963 because over-generous assistance was distorting the Sangkum economy.

On the other hand, the post-colonial economy of Cambodia could not survive without a fair measure of external budgetary support. Never before in Cambodia's modern history had the country been so little supported by external assistance as during the regime of Democratic Kampuchea. China and North Korea provided some aid but it seems to have been largely of the "red and expert" kind that served largely to inflame the already over-heated nature of economic policy. Cambodian exports given in exchange for raw materials, machinery, parts and other essential commodities had such low value and had to be produced in such massive quantities that the entire population was reduced to mere units of manual labour. At the very least, this was a highly inefficient way to run a national economy.

The extreme demands made by the DK policy of autarky could never have been met, no matter what cost in human effort. The structure of the economy was not geared to self-reliance and Cambodia lacked the natural resources required for even medium-scale industrialisation, let alone the requisite skilled workforce. What had worked reasonably well during the people's war period because the strategies were a logical response to the immediate situation did not work at a national level after victory was won. Furthermore, the DK regime was too short and far too troubled by internal political strife to produce the sort of structural reform that revolution demands. In any case, it seems not to have been interested in genuine reformulations. The constitution was terse and paid little attention to the matters of governance. There were no laws and no ministries as such. Party power and influence dominated every aspect of the state so that the economic base was also forced to serve ideological ends.

The People's Republic of Kampuchea spent ten years returning the society and the economy to a level that most people would have accepted as normal. It succeeded in this modest goal despite having to pursue the on-going bitter war with the Khmer Rouge and its allies. The new regime attempted to reintroduce a system of collectivised agriculture and communal ownership of the means of production, but there was little state coercion and, it appears, little political will to force its policies on a reluctant rural population.

In the city and towns, market liberalisation proceeded rapidly after the free market economy was officially recognised in 1985. In fact, state industry had never been able to compete with petty traders, smugglers and the big Chinese *towkays* to provide the people with essential and desired commodities. The growth of the informal economy, black market and illegal trade had quickly surpassed the state's capacity to compete. Therefore, surrender to the free market and recognition of private property in 1989 was simply official acknowledgement of a state of affairs that had already existed for several years.

Was the Cambodian economy changed by the years of revolution? While there were significant political changes, it cannot be denied that the nature and structure of the economy remained fundamentally unaltered. Even the usual 20 or so big capitalists who now undoubtedly included those wealthy, gun-wielding smugglers from Koh Kong were ready to exert their influence over the new rulers once the Vietnamese made their final withdrawal. Most Cambodians responded to the new State of Cambodia with practised cynicism, summed up in the often-heard remark, "Same bus, new driver." They never seriously questioned the route the bus was going to take.

(Front view)

(Reverse view)

One hundred riel note of the Second Kingdom of Cambodia, depicting emphasis on education

(Front view)

(Reverse view)

Five hundred riel note of the Second Kingdom of Cambodia, depicting Angkor Wat

(Front view)

(Reverse view)

One thousand riel note of the Second Kingdom of Cambodia

(Front view)

(Reverse view)

Five thousand riel note of the Second Kingdom of Cambodia, depicting King Norodom Sihanouk

CHAPTER
5

Rehabilitation and Reconstruction, 1990–c. 2000

> The main responsibility for deciding Cambodia's reconstruction needs and plans should rest with the Cambodian people and the government formed after free and fair elections. No attempt should be made to impose a development strategy on Cambodia from any outside source or deter potential donors from contributing to the reconstruction of Cambodia.
>
> Declaration on the Rehabilitation and Reconstruction of Cambodia, Article 2[1]

Major changes taking place in the global political arena towards the end of the 1980s affected all four factions involved in the so-called "Cambodia problem." As the Cold War ended, the political props and economic support which had awarded them legitimacy and the means to defend it were withdrawn. The immediate response of the combatants to these changes was consolidation of their defence positions and asset-stripping to pay for the cost of ongoing civil war. In particular, the rich hardwood forests of Cambodia were logged relentlessly until the final battle in the civil war was fought at Anlong Veng in 1998 and the Cambodian communist movement was definitively abandoned. The final decade of the twentieth century, therefore, was as tumultuous for the Cambodian people and their economy as any other had been. While politicians and international peace-keepers spoke grandiloquently about rehabilitation and reconstruction, in reality, this was a faltering process that was still displaying signs of its immaturity as the century ended.

In 1987, Hun Sen, Prime Minister of the PRK, had a cordial meeting with Norodom Sihanouk in France. This event marked the commencement of peace negotiations that culminated in the signing of the Agreements on a Comprehensive Political Settlement of the Cambodia Conflict by Cambodia and 18 other nations, including all the permanent members of the UN Security Council and the ASEAN countries, in Paris on 23 October 1991. The settlement was based on a framework accepted by the four factions: State of Cambodia (SoC), Funcinpec, KPNLF, and the Khmer Rouge at a Jakarta Informal Meeting in September 1990 whereby a Supreme National Council (SNC) would act as the sole legitimate authority in Cambodia during a transitional period to peaceful resolution of the conflict.[2] The Security Council adopted Resolution 668 endorsing the framework, and the signatories to the Paris Peace Agreements then invited the Security Council to establish a United Nations Transitional Authority in Cambodia (UNTAC) with civilian and military components. UNTAC's specific mandate was the organisation and conduct of free and fair elections for a constituent assembly.

This mandate covered seven broad areas: military, civil administration, law and order, elections, human rights, repatriation, and rehabilitation and reconstruction. To guarantee a sufficiently neutral environment for the elections, UNTAC was supposed to have direct control of five key state areas including foreign affairs, national defence, finance, public security, and information. Under the mandate, civil police would maintain law and order as well as protect human rights and fundamental freedoms, while militarily UNTAC would supervise the ceasefire, cantonment and disarming of the factions' forces and take steps towards their demobilisation. In addition, it would facilitate the voluntary repatriation of around 370,000 refugees from the Thai border camps and assist other displaced persons to return to their place of choice inside Cambodia.

In practice, the deployment of 16,000 multinational troops lagged behind schedule and the civil police and civil administration components were even further delayed. As an interim measure, therefore, an advance mission, UNAMIC, of around 400 personnel arrived in Cambodia in January 1992 and it was absorbed by UNTAC in mid-March, or five months after the agreements had been signed. UNTAC was not fully operational until September, and the delay caused increased violations of what had only ever been a very fragile ceasefire agreement. At its peak, UNTAC represented more than 20,000 international personnel, supplemented by three times that many locally recruited staff. It cost more than two billion U.S. dollars, some of which were spent in Cambodia and provided a sudden and reasonably widespread boost to the local economy.

The downside of the huge international presence included inflation, greed, and rampant corruption. Land values skyrocketed and rents became unaffordable to many; the commercial sex industry flourished and HIV/AIDS, while not introduced by the foreign troops, nevertheless spread alarmingly.

There were many breaches of the agreements. Always an unwilling starter, the Khmer Rouge refused to allow UNTAC monitors into their areas in May 1992 to supervise the disarmament of their troops, demanding as a pre-condition that the SoC administrative structures be completely dismantled. Eventually the KR withdrew from the process altogether, so whatever disarmament took place among the four factions before the elections was purely token in effect. The Cambodian People's Party (CPP), formerly the KPRP, complied with the broad strokes of the UNTAC mandate but maintained its grip on the national administration it had built during the previous decade. Funcinpec played the underdog to the international audience, but meanwhile used its association with Sihanouk to very good electoral advantage, especially in the countryside, and quietly maintained its dangerous liaison with the Khmer Rouge fighting forces. The last of the four warring factions now reformulated as political parties contesting a democratic election was the KPNLF which promised much by way of nominating credible contenders for the National Assembly seats, but proved to be hopelessly divided against itself.

The United Nations was generally criticised for moving too slowly to get the transitional authority in place once the agreements had been signed and for not acting decisively against parties that infringed those agreements. Nevertheless, the election process itself was declared a success. Ninety per cent of those who registered to vote did so between 23 and 28 May 1993 and the majority gave their endorsement to Funcinpec. The CPP refused to accept the result. Confronted with a very tense stand-off which threatened to return Cambodia to civil war, Sihanouk proposed a compromise for an executive government led by co-premiers, Prince Ranarridh and Hun Sen, with co-ministers in the strategic ministries of defence and interior, and shared control of other ministries.

On 21 September 1993, the Constituent Assembly that had been elected in May voted to adopt the new constitution. Three days later, Sihanouk signed the constitution and resumed the Cambodian throne as a constitutional monarch, one who reigns but does not govern. The state was once again the Kingdom of Cambodia. The promulgation of the Constitution of the Kingdom of Cambodia brought a formal end to the mandate of UNTAC in Cambodia and the withdrawal of what remained of the operation was completed in the final weeks of 1993.

The tally of ballots cast in the 1993 UN-supervised elections on public display in Phnom Penh

Rural poverty, Battambang province, c. 2003

For most foreign observers still resident in the country, UNTAC's departure was premature. Far from representing reconciliation, the confused power-sharing arrangement it left behind posed an extreme danger to the state. In its preamble, the new constitution declared the "restoration of Cambodia into an 'Island of Peace' based on a multi-party liberal democratic regime." Beyond the rhetoric, however, it was still "the same bus." In fact, Cambodia had settled for an electoral democracy, not a genuinely liberal one, even though several political parties were represented in its legislature. Each of the major parties remained committed to wresting complete control of the state from other contenders, essentially for the benefit of the clientist networks that they patronised. Those interests finally clashed militarily in mid-1997 and the CPP emerged the victor. The following year, the Khmer Rouge, already weakened by major defections, imploded as a consequence of its last bloody purge.

By an unfortunate coincidence, the terrifying "July events" for the Cambodian people coincided with the Asian financial crisis. The slim economic gains Cambodia had made by 1997 were wiped out and GDP registered a near-zero per cent growth rate. The final years of the century saw a faltering return to positive gains. The Cambodians themselves staged national elections in 1998 and again in 2003, still with disputed outcomes but each time with less violence than the previous elections. These political gains were consolidated with the successful staging of the first truly nationwide elections for local government at the level of the commune in 2002. Despite some ongoing "mopping up," the CPP regained its ascendancy over the state apparatus and this historical fact was acknowledged by Cambodia's admittance to ASEAN in 2000, membership that was valued more highly by the general public than that within the WTO in 2004. Cambodia was no longer isolated and despised as a pariah state in its own region. This was an important prestige factor and a valued spur to genuine economic development.

Policies

After 1990, Khmers returning to their homeland after a long exile and international planners alike believed that Cambodia had to be resurrected, not simply reconstructed. The achievements made during the decade following the downfall of Democratic Kampuchea were generally overlooked or considered merely as makeshift and *ad hoc* responses to an emergency situation that had existed after the Vietnamese drove the Khmer Rouge out of Phnom Penh in 1979. There was, therefore, a general misconception that the Cambodian state had been asleep until the Paris Peace

Agreements and UNTAC revived it. This misconception of the somnolent state led many international development planners to believe that they were writing macroeconomic reforms onto a clear slate. Consequently, it should not be surprising that those attempted reforms frequently found strong resistance from entrenched power holders within the Cambodian ruling elite. At the same time, it is fair to say that policy in the 1990s was dictated from outside rather than from within the state, and that the Royal Government of Cambodia was involved more at the level of strategic implementation than at that of decision-making; this was a direct consequence of having committed itself to a Structural Adjustment Programme (SAP) with international creditors in 1994.

The Declaration on the Rehabilitation and Reconstruction of Cambodia was the last of four documents signed in Paris in October 1991. This slim document consisting of 13 points gave the United Nations an important role in this effort. According to the agreement, during the rehabilitation phase, particular attention would be given to food security, health, housing, training, education, the transport network and the restoration of Cambodia's existing basic infrastructure and public utilities, while the reconstruction phase should promote Cambodian entrepreneurship and make use of the private sector, among other sectors, to help advance self-sustaining economic growth. The final point of the document called for the formation of a consultation body, to be called the International Committee on the Reconstruction of Cambodia (ICORC) which would be open to potential donors and other relevant parties. The United Nations would support ICORC by ensuring a smooth transition from the rehabilitation to the reconstruction phase.

This role was coordinated by the United Nations Development Programme (UNDP) which returned to Cambodia in late 1990. With the technical assistance it provided, the newly established Royal Government of Cambodia (RGC) prepared its National Programme to Rehabilitate and Develop Cambodia and presented it to the international donor community at the ICORC-2 meeting in 1994. The programme, David Ayres notes, clearly reflected the agenda of the international community as well as providing evidence of the extent to which Cambodian leaders had embraced the ideology of the New World Order pursuant to the end of the Cold War:

> The underlying themes of the "fields of operation" were market-based economic reform, a powerful private sector, overcoming institutional restraints, capacity building, and economic diversification and regionalization. In short, they are the themes of the economically oriented modernisation model of the New World Order. Formulated by foreign

experts, they were enthusiastically rubber stamped by the co-prime ministers and constituted, at least in terms of policy, the central tenets of the state ideology of the post-election Kingdom of Cambodia.[3]

In short, the Cambodian government promised to reform state institutions and the public service, rely on private entrepreneurship and the market as engines of growth, double GDP by 2004 in real terms, extend social services, improve rural livelihoods, ensure sustainable development, and strengthen domestic self-reliance.[4] This declaration of national policy for the economy was intended to prove Cambodia's preparedness to adhere to the ruling Washington Consensus on international borrowing at that time. As one of the world's poorest countries, Cambodia was eligible for the International Monetary Fund's Enhanced Structural Adjustment Facility (ESAF) that provided especially low interest loans and generous repayment terms. As a condition for receiving ESAF loans, Cambodia was required to adopt a three-year SAP, 1994–96, which set clear targets for public finance reform in order to reduce the budget deficit, for liberalisation of trade and investment, and public sector reform.

It is fair to say that the Cambodian economy, in terms of overall GDP grew substantially as a result of economic policies adopted in 1994. There were several shocks, some exogenous and others related to domestic political events, which stalled economic progress at points throughout the decade, but according to World Bank calculations, the Cambodian economy in 2006–7 achieved double digit growth at a regional rate second only to that of China. This growth, however, was lopsided and by the turn of the century, the wealth gap between city and the countryside, and between the urban rich and the urban poor, was vast and still growing.

The SAP may well have been on track towards achieving the long-term aim of economic growth and development. What was never explained in its agenda, however, was how the wealth thus created would reach the poor and vulnerable or those otherwise lacking the means and opportunities to access the benefits of the newly liberalised market. In reality, the reduced responsibility of the state and restrictions placed on public spending put education and health services even farther out of reach of Cambodia's poor, particularly the rural poor. Although the statistics may not be entirely reliable, the percentage of Cambodia's population living below the poverty line changed very little between 1993–94 and 1999 from 39 per cent to somewhere between 36 and 38 per cent of the total population. About 90 per cent of those living below the poverty line were rural dwellers.

In 1999, the IMF and the World Bank replaced the Structural Adjustment Programme with the Poverty Reduction Strategy Paper (PRSP),

Poster for the 1998 general election showing CPP leaders Chea Sim, Hun Sen and Heng Samrin

allowing poor countries to qualify for concessional loans on condition they developed a strategy to deal with poverty. According to its PRSP, the Cambodian government committed itself to reducing the number of people living below the poverty line to 19.5 per cent by 2015.[5] Progress, however, was slow. In March 2003, the UNDP released an independent report which stated unequivocally, "To date, the macroeconomic framework established under guidance from the IMF has not succeeded in addressing the key elements of poverty in Cambodia.... Even during high growth periods, poverty reduction either did not occur or was minimal."[6] The study recommended some radical departures from IMF dogma including encouraging moderate inflation and taking on more debt. It suggested that the government should borrow locally from domestic private banks to increase budget allocations for rural and agricultural development.

Administration and Governance

The State of Cambodia (SoC) which came into being when the National Assembly adopted numerous changes to the 1981 constitution on 29 and 30 April 1989 is usually conflated with the PRK regime both in popular memory and by journalists writing on Cambodian affairs after the UNTAC intervention. It is true that the single party, the Kampuchean People's Revolutionary Party, renamed the Cambodian People's Party in 1991, continued to govern in much the same fashion as before. There were, however, changes that were more fundamental than those to the name of the nation and the flag. In the new constitution, Buddhism was re-established with prerogatives similar to those before 1975, private property and the free market were officially recognised, and Article 35 of the new constitution guaranteeing citizens their rights to "physically inviolability" under law was an important provision for later persistent efforts to establish human rights standards in national institutions during the 1990s.

In the aftermath of the UN-supervised general elections, Norodom Sihanouk signed the new constitution on 24 September 1993 and, 52 years after his first coronation, once again ascended the throne, this time as the first constitutional monarch of the Kingdom of Cambodia. The constitution provided for a legislature, the National Assembly of at least 120 members elected for five-year terms by free and universal elections, while the executive body, the Royal Government of Cambodia, was incorporated in the Council of Ministers, presided over by the Prime Minister, assisted by deputies, state ministers, ministers and state secretaries. According to the constitution, the president of the National Assembly recommends and the king then designates someone from the successful party at the elections to form the government. This prime ministerial nominee must have a vote of confidence from the Assembly before assuming office.[7]

Under Article 113 of the constitution, the king is the guarantor of the independence of the judiciary and in this role he is assisted by the Supreme Council of the Magistracy. This Council and the Constitutional Council were deemed critical for the independence of the judiciary and adherence of the state to the declared national policy of "Liberal Democracy and Pluralism" as set out in Article 51 of the 1993 constitution. Their establishment, however, was long delayed and their relevance and effectiveness severely curtailed by the efforts of the dominant political party, the CPP, to rule without opposition. The Supreme Council of the Magistracy finally convened in December 1997, its function being to make proposals to the king on the appointment of judges and prosecutors and to decide on disciplinary action to be taken against them. By 2002, this body had met infrequently and had examined fewer than two hundred cases of possible corruption by court officials; none of those cases resulted in prosecution.

The question of political interference in the Supreme Council of the Magistracy affects the Constitutional Council since the former appoints three of its nine members, the others being appointed in equal measure by the king and the National Assembly. The National Assembly voted overwhelmingly for the Constitutional Council Law on 19 March 1998, in time for that year's general elections since, according to Article 117, it has the right "to examine and decide on contested cases involving the election of Assembly members." While the main role of this Council is to examine draft bills for constitutionality before their promulgation and to provide oversight on any proposals to amend the constitution, the international donor community at that time regarded it as a guarantor of acceptable election results. From its inception, the Constitutional Council proved to be highly controversial; the king's three appointees, all very elderly and highly respected Cambodian dignitaries, boycotted the Council's first meeting, claiming that the remaining members had been appointed illegally and that the meeting was therefore invalid.[8]

The Constitutional Council approved the constitutional amendments of 4 March 1999 that created a Senate. Something like a bicameral parliamentary system had operated in most previous regimes, with an legislative chamber, the National Assembly, that debated and passed bills and another that performed the role of legislative reviewer. The Senate

Cambodian NGOs raise awareness of official corruption

assumed this latter role, although it also has the right to initiate legislation. Constitutionally, the number of senators is fixed at not exceeding half the number of National Assembly deputies. The king has the right to nominate two senators, the Assembly elects a further two by majority vote and the others are supposed to be universally elected for a five-year term. By 2005, however, the Senate was still an unelected body.

Even though the Assembly, the Senate and the Prime Minister all have power to initiate legislation, virtually all legislation presented to the National Assembly is drafted at the ministerial or Council of Ministers level. Throughout its history since independence from France, the Assembly has failed to assert its independence and it is still regarded as little more than a rubber stamp for decisions made by the government, and more specifically by the Prime Minister himself.

At the same time, however, it would be wrong to deny that there have been important efforts to improve governance since UNTAC and, indeed, since the significant constitutional changes of 1989. These efforts were made largely in response to demands of major creditors and donors and the conditions tied to loans and aid. Cambodia was re-admitted to the global economic community just as the U.S. launched its drive to liberalise markets around the world, "not as a well-intentioned effort to promote reform," Francis Fukuyama claims, "but as an American attempt to impose its own antistatist values on the rest of the world."[9] Thus, the push was not only for liberalisation and privatisation in the economic sector, but also for decentralisation of political structures and radical down-sizing of the state bureaucracy.

The key concept and justification for administrative change in Cambodia throughout the 1990s was "good governance," defined as "the manner in which power is exercised in the management of a country's economic and social resources for development."[10] States with good governance, those authors explain, exercise powers based on the rule of law through state institutions and organisations that are accountable and transparent to the general public. Five areas with implications for good governance and sustainable development are identified as: public finance reform, public administration reform for the civil service and armed forces, decentralisation, legal and judicial reforms, and regional integration. All came under close scrutiny and pressure from external donors and local civil society groups following the formation of the first Royal Government of Cambodia in September 1993.

Although laws were successfully enacted to permit restructuring of the banking sector and the privatisation of remaining state-owned companies, attempts at public administration reform, struck at the very heart of the patronage networks that have traditionally defined the workings of the Cambodian state. During the UNTAC period, before the May 1993 elections, UNDP was invited to help the Cambodian authorities draw up a national programme of administrative reform and its implementation. The goal was institution-building and the strategies included establishing the legal framework for restructuring public administration, strengthening the management of line ministries and reforming civil service management, developing capacity, and strengthening provincial administration. The matter took on some urgency when the government signed the structural adjustment agreement with the IMF in 1994, committing itself to a 20 per cent reduction of the civil service by 1997. The process began with a count of those on the national payroll in 1995 in order to remove "ghosts." Resistance and subversion, however, proved to be overwhelming obstacles to reform efforts. In mid-1998, the resident representative of UNDP in Cambodia admitted that the sole achievement of the public administrative reform efforts was a database of laws enacted in the previous decade:

> I must state that the results of the national programme of administrative reform so far — to which UNDP has contributed $3.5 million — are disappointing. We have not seen the emergence of a clear independent public administration; we have not seen the establishment of a clear independent judiciary; we have not seen a clear delineation of authority and delegation of responsibility from the centre to the provinces and below; we have not seen a thorough assessment of the existing public servants to test their capabilities and response to their training needs; and perhaps above all, we have not seen a reform of civil service conditions and salary scales, designed to motivate the servants of the state and to enable them to work independently and full time on their designated tasks.[11]

In defence of his government, the minister of state and co-chair of the interministerial commission for administrative reform, Sok An, argued that the momentum of the reform had been constrained by the destabilisation of the coalition government from March 1996 until the July 1997 fighting. The nature of the coalition government had, in fact, made it impossible for either of the main parties to reduce the number of positions available to their clients within the bureaucracy. Actual downsizing was only possible after the 1998 elections. He promised that the RGC would achieve the modernisation of the Cambodian public administration between 1998 and 2002 and that there would be six axes of reform including "deconcentrating state offices towards the provinces so that the administration is close to the needs of citizens."[12]

Deconcentration, or decentralisation, took the form of the elected commune council. The Law on Commune/*Sangkat* Administrative Management was passed by the National Assembly in January 2001, making way for elections the following year for 1,621 councils of between five and eleven members depending on the size of the commune.[13] The commune had developed its political function during the previous regime by mobilising troops and militias for defence and extending the authority of the party to the village; its administrative function had been to control, regulate and record the affairs of the commune. In its new form, it would be responsible for development of the commune, reducing poverty and improving the quality of life. In order to provide basic health services, education, roads, sanitation, potable water, power, and so on to its constituents, the commune council was required by the law to prepare development plans and budgets.

During their first five-year term, most commune councils did not live up to the expectations of international observers. A survey conducted in 2003 found that councillors did not understand their duties, did not communicate well with their constituents and did not have adequate resources.[14] Meanwhile, approximately three-quarters of the constituents said that they never communicated with their councillors. It seemed the fundamental problem was that councillors were elected on a party ticket and party loyalties divided the councils, limiting their ability to make independent decisions and to attract funding. After the first elections, the CPP controlled all except 23 of the 1,621 councils.

Cambodia emerged from protracted civil conflict with large defence and security forces. In 1993, the Armed Forces General Staff, under pressure from UNTAC and donor embassies, agreed to form a national army from those of the SoC, Funcinpec and the KPNLF of 128,000 soldiers. The merger did nothing to reduce the overall size of the armed forces, and a year later the national payrolls registered close to 160,000 men.[15] By April 1994, there were 2,000 generals and 10,000 colonels in the army. It was, as William Shawcross observed, "nothing short of grotesque."[16] In 1998, military personnel were counted at 143,000, or 12.5 per thousand of the total population and together with the security forces consumed almost half of the government budget.[17] Under pressure, the following year, the RGC presented international donors with a comprehensive draft of its plans to demobilise the army. Two years later, it reported that it had demobilised 15,000 soldiers, many of them ill, disabled or elderly, and that it had removed the same number of "ghost" soldiers, along with almost 160,000 "ghost" dependants for whom unnamed individuals were collecting wages, and announced that it had set a goal of reducing the armed forces to about 100,000 by the end of 2002.[18] Donors were asked for a further US$42 million to complete the demobilisation. In 2003, following acrimonious exchanges between the government and the major donors over misprocurement, bribes paid to get onto demobilisation lists and complaints about the poor quality of compensation package goods, the World Bank demanded the return of US$2.8 million from the government and passed sanctions against a number of Cambodian firms for fraudulent practices. The process of demobilisation then stalled for lack of funding.[19]

Corruption dogged almost every effort to reform Cambodia's institutions. This should have been anticipated by the reformers. Several experts on Cambodian affairs have analysed the fundamental contradiction that exists within the post-independence Cambodian state between efforts to modernise, to appear modern, and the traditional habits of patronage and absolutism in the realms of power. As David Ayres notes, "Cambodia's official embrace of modern political institutions and a modern, development-oriented state ideology were sharply at odds with a firmly reasserted and entrenched traditional political culture."[20] A patrimonial political style including clientism and personalism, Grant Curtis agrees, "[is] not only in the style of doing politics but also in the style of governing."[21] In other words, what donors and the international community who supported the peace process in Cambodia regarded as corruption, was only business as usual for those who had achieved high positions of influence. "The organisers of the Paris Peace Agreements," David Roberts argues, "attempted to implant equality and individual choice in a society governed, and financed, through hierarchical inequality and group loyalties. That is, it could not be meaningful to vote altruistically for a personality if that leader could not return the favour in the traditional manner."[22] Without requisite economic restructuring, according to his argument, persistent efforts to democratise Cambodia in accordance with Western standards could put the poor at greater economic risk.

By international standards, corruption in Cambodia is rife. In 2006, Transparency International ranked Cambodia 151 out of the 163 countries it surveyed, awarding it only 2.1 points out of a possible 10, a ranking that was 21 places lower than the previous year.[23] With the exception of Burma, it was judged the most corrupt member nation of ASEAN. A government-commissioned survey of 800 business establishments in 2004 found that 82 per cent of them paid bribes and 71 per cent responded that they paid frequently.[24] They regarded corruption as a major constraint on their business operations in addition to weak laws, bureaucratic costs, unfair competition from well-connected rivals, and unnecessary inspections. Of government institutions, the judiciary and customs were viewed the most negatively. A World Bank report in 2004 estimated that businesses paid US$120 million each year in "bribe taxes" to operate in Cambodia.[25] Financial losses to state revenues as a result of these corrupt practices were considerable. The same World Bank study found potential annual losses of US$226 million to GDP due to "market and administrative distortions."[26] These distortions, including huge military-run smuggling schemes, cost the state around US$28 million in revenue each year.

Corruption also puts a heavy burden on the provision and efficiency of state services. By the turn of the century, civil servants' wages had improved a little since 1990 but they still remained far below what an average family needed to subsist. The consequence was high absenteeism, ubiquitous illegal charges and the drift of civil servants towards the private sector or the NGO community where foreign aid donors support salaries. Perhaps the most pernicious effect of official corruption is the huge disparity in wealth between those who have access to the means of corruption and those who are forced to pay or suffer the consequences of not paying in terms of worsened poverty, health and ignorance.

In post-UNTAC Cambodia, international creditors and foreign donors used the regular supply of aid as a weapon against corruption to little effect. In 1997, for example, the IMF cancelled US$60 million in loans to the Kingdom in response to widespread official collusion in illegal logging and the government's failure to return logging revenues to the state. Lost government revenue from the logging industry that year was approximately US$309 million, equivalent to 73 per cent of the total national budget of US$419 million that year.[27] Funding, however, was typically resumed when the government granted some measure of compliance with donor demands. One donor demand, however, remained stubbornly unfulfilled. A National Anti-Corruption Law was first drafted in 1994, but ten years and several versions later, it still had not been passed into law.

At a purely administrative level, the Kingdom of Cambodia added one province and two *krong* or municipalities, namely Pailin and Kep, to its sovereignty. These changes were a direct consequence of the defections of Khmer Rouge factions and then their final defeat at Anlong Veng in 1998. Subsequent to that defeat, Oddar Meanchey, where Anlong Veng is located, was officially re-created as a separate province in June 1999. It enjoyed full provincial status from 1962 to 1970 during the Sangkum period, but under the following regimes it had existed as an *anukhet*, a sub-province administered by the governor of Siem Reap province.

Population

The 1990s were years of only relative peace for the Cambodian population. Major dry season offensives fought by the Royal Cambodian Armed Forces against the Khmer Rouge in the northwest created large temporary settlements of internally displaced people, and the bitter fighting in July 1997 between the forces backed by the CPP and those belonging to Funcinpec sent as many as 40,000 refugees back across the Thai border into Surin province. Presumably, a good number of those fleeing the fighting had been repatriated from the Thai border camps during the year prior to the May 1993 elections. By the end of the decade, however, with the resolution of the major conflict with the Khmer Rouge, and with what appeared to be a lasting coalition of CPP and Funcinpec in government, there was a positive outlook for lasting peace.

Population figures for the decade indicated strong population growth of about 40 per cent. The UNHCR-sponsored repatriation of around 370,000 refugees in time for the 1993 elections resulted in the abnormally high 6.1 per cent growth figure recorded by the Socio-Economic Survey of Cambodia (SESC) 1993–94; this was the first of four such reports during the 1990s conducted as part of a special training project sponsored by the ADB and UNDP in order to generate a socio-economic database to serve the needs of macro-economic planning and management in Cambodia. These surveys also provided statisticians with preparatory training for the general population census of 1998. The National Institute of Statistics (NIS) compiled results from the four reports and the general census into the following table:

Table 5.1 Population of Cambodia by Gender (in millions)

Year	Total Population	Male	Female	Average Annual Growth (%)	Sources of Data
1989	8.3	3.8	4.5	2.5	
1990	8.6	4.0	4.6	3.6	
1991	8.8	4.1	4.7	2.3	
1992	9.0	4.1	4.9	2.3	
1993	9.3	4.3	5.0	3.3	NIS Provincial Reports
1994	9.869	4.714	5.156	6.1	SESC93-94
1995	10.2				
1996	10.340	5.0	5.4		SESC96
1997	10.368	4.932	5.436		CSES97
1998	11.437	5.511	5.926	2.5	GPCC98 (based on census)
1999	11.599	5.608	5.991		CSES99

Source: National Institute of Statistics, *Cambodia Yearbook 2000*, 1.

When the census was conducted on 3–4 March 1998, enumeration covered the whole country with the exception of a few insecure areas including Anlong Veng, Samlaut, Veal Veng, and one village in Pursat province whose combined population was estimated to be about 45,000. The refugees from the July 1997 fighting who were still in Thailand were not included in the census.

According to the National Institute of Statistics, the Cambodian population will reach 15.5 million by 2010 and surpass 20 million in 2021.[28] In that latter year, the sex ratio should reach parity again for the first time since 1962, and the annual population growth rate will fall below two per cent for the first time. These predictions were made on the basis of total fertility, which, while it remained high in 2000, had generally declined in the preceding decade; the national average was then four children per woman.

The 1998 census showed that national population density was 64 persons per square kilometre but the population was unevenly spread, with the large majority inhabiting the central plains region. The following table suggests that the pattern of distribution has not changed much since Delvert made his observations in the 1950s:

Table 5.2 Regional Population Distribution (in thousands)[29]

Region	1968	1980	1990	1993	1998	Density [per km²] 1998
Lowland	3,797	3,563	4,632	5,018	5,898	235
Tonle Sap	2,039	1,945	2,528	2,668	3,414	52
Coastal	474	426	553	670	816	49
Mountain*	685	656	854	951	1,189	17

Note: * Kompong Speu province is counted in the mountain region for all years.

As the figures above illustrate, demographic renewal affected the country as a whole during the period 1980–93 and there was a 41 per cent population gain. Phnom Penh experienced spectacular growth; the city's population was 691,000 in 1993 and by 1998 it was very close to one million. Population growth rates in the northwest of the country, where most provinces are grouped in the Tonle Sap region, also increased markedly. Most of the refugees indicated their wish to return to that part of the country and, in fact, Battambang province's population increased by almost 40 per cent between 1993 and 1998.

The 1998 census showed that 30 per cent of the population was aged between 5 and 14 years, almost twice the size of the cohorts above them to age 24, and noticeably larger than the 0–4 age group. This demographic bulge represented a high age dependency ratio throughout the 1990s and subsequently created and will continue to create high demand for jobs and also for productive land until 2015 at least. It also guarantees that the population growth rate, which registered 2.49 per cent on the night of the census, will remain high until 2020 at least.

A further trend is towards urbanisation. The 1998 census recorded that 15.7 per cent of the total population lived in urban areas, while the 1999 CSES recorded a total urban population of 2.13 million or 18.4 per cent of the total population.[30] Thus, while the Cambodian population remains overwhelmingly rural, there is a growing migratory trend towards the city and municipalities. The 1962 census noted that 10.3 per cent of the population lived in the municipalities and provincial towns and throughout the PRK regime, urbanisation remained at a fairly steady rate of about 12 per cent. Phnom Penh accounts for the vast majority of the urban population, being more than six times larger than the second municipality, the port of Sihanoukville.

Phnom Penh is a vastly different city from the one it was before 1975, and it would surely be unrecognisable to the French colonial settlers. Apart from its size, the most noticeable change is to its ethnic mix. The old French, Chinese and Vietnamese quarters have largely disappeared and Phnom Penh is now very much a Khmer city with sizable Chinese and Vietnamese populations. Khmers are also prominent in the city's commercial life, unlike before, and are strongly represented in the new working class that is composed largely of young female employees of the many export-oriented, foreign-owned garment factories located in and around the city. The uneven pace of development between that of Phnom Penh and the rest of the country, however, is beginning to have seriously divisive consequences for Cambodian society as the burgeoning city economy exerts a strong attraction for internal migrants in search of paid employment to support relatives who are trying to cope with a flagging rural economy.

While the 1998 census found that most migration (57 per cent) was rural to rural, an increasing number of people are seeking regular paid work either in Phnom Penh or abroad and sending remittances to the village. Of all migrants who had left their villages less than one year before the census date, 29 per cent said their principal reason for moving was unemployment. Population pressure on land, possibly for the first time in Cambodian history, with consequent increasing landlessness, unemployment and poverty, is forcing more and more rural Cambodians to leave their villages. Researchers suggest that this trend is very rapid, as a comparison between results of the 1996 Demographic Survey and the general census of 1998 shows:

Table 5.3 Migrants from Rural Areas, 1996 and 1998[31]

	1996 Demographic Survey	1998 Population Census	Two-year Increase (%)
"Recent" rural migrants (5 years)	634,786	881,439	38.9
"Very recent" rural migrants (12 months)	172,305	273,534	58.7

Cambodia now has formal arrangements to assist people to find paid employment abroad and Cambodians are working legally in various, usually low-paid occupations, in regional and other Asian countries from South Korea to Singapore. Thailand, however, is the main destination for legal and illegal job-seekers alike. In 2005, it was estimated that 183,000 Cambodians were working illegally in Thailand.[32] The International Organisation for Migration estimated that between 50,000 and 70,000 Cambodian migrants were crossing the border at Poipet each year to work as housemaids, agricultural labourers, construction workers, dock workers and so on, attracted by the promise of considerably higher wages than can be earned in Cambodia.[33] Rapid assessment surveys conducted by the CDRI in 2002 found that some of these migrants commute daily or for just a few weeks at a time to do farm work while longer-term migrants, the majority of whom are men, go deep into Thailand with the assistance of guides.[34]

Human Development

During the 1980s, there was no way of measuring living standards in Cambodia against an international norm. Nevertheless, Cambodians who remained in their country throughout that decade were indeed poor, and universally so. If some merchants or officials accumulated more wealth than others, their wealth was not conspicuous. Throughout the 1990s there was a dramatic change in that situation. The wealth gap was both conspicuous and real. It was also obvious that that gap was widening rather than narrowing as the decade progressed.

The first national poverty survey report, released in October 1997 by the Ministry of Planning and UNDP, found that nearly four out of ten Cambodians, or 36 per cent of them were living below the poverty benchmark of 35,000 riels (or around US$11) per person per month.[35] The vast majority of the poor, roughly 90 per cent, lived in the countryside. Cambodia's HDI score was then 0.421.[36] This was one of the lowest scores among Asian countries but appropriately on par with its level of per capita GDP. Its rating of 42.35 on the Human Poverty Index, however, was high in relation to per capita income, reflecting Cambodia's persistent high levels of mortality, child malnutrition and poor access to public services throughout the country. The Human Development Report of 1998 pointed to the large disparities that existed in relation to HDI indicators. "For instance," it noted, "the HDI score for urban Cambodia is nearly 50 per cent greater than that for rural Cambodia. The richest 20 per cent of Cambodians have an HDI score that is nearly two and one-half times as much as that of the poorest 20 per cent of Cambodians. Women have a nearly 30 per cent higher level of human poverty than do men."

The real growth in the Cambodian economy after 1989 was concentrated in Phnom Penh. The first socio-economic survey undertaken in 1993–94 found that average monthly household expenditure for the whole country was US$116; in Phnom Penh, it was 169 per cent higher, or US$312.[37] There is no doubt that UNTAC personnel spending was concentrated in the city and that this contributed to the huge disparity in spending between the city and the rest of the country that year. The pattern, however, was sustained throughout the decade. The Cambodia Poverty Assessment of 1999 found that the poverty severity index in the city was only about one-sixth that in either other urban or rural areas.[38] While 90.5 per cent of all Cambodians living below the poverty line were in rural areas, and 7.2 per cent were in other urban areas, only 2.3 per cent lived in Phnom Penh. In fact, per capita income in the city continued to rise steadily throughout the decade and reached about US$1,000 in 2002. That figure, of course, is a gross distortion of the reality for most citizens because while inequality is very high generally (as measured by the Gini coefficient, inequality in Cambodia is higher than in most other Asian countries at Cambodia's level of development), it is consistently higher in Phnom Penh than in other parts of the country. Meanwhile, in the provinces, average per capita income actually fell slightly and in 2002, it was less than US$200.[39]

An overview of the living standards of Cambodians, according to their geographical location, is provided by the following figures for monthly household expenditure for the period 1993 to 1999:

Table 5.4 Average Monthly Household Expenditure by Stratum, Cambodia 1993–99[40]

Stratum	In thousand riels[1]				In US dollars			
	1993–94	1996	1997	1999	1993–94	1996	1997	1999
Cambodia (Extrapolated)	290.6	258.9	286.6	361.4	113.1	98.0	103.6	95.0
Phnom Penh	781.2		727.3	1,007	304.0		262.9	264.6
Other urban areas	439.5		403.3	452.8	171.0		145.8	119.0
Rural areas	238.8		220.0	284.2	92.9		79.6	74.7

Note: [1]Exchange rates (riels per US$1) in successive years: 2,570r, 2,640r, 2,766r, 3,805r.
Source: Cambodia Socio-Economic Surveys 1993–94, 1996, 1997, and 1999.

Care must be taken when interpreting these figures. The 1993–94 figures, as already noted, were inflated because of the presence of 20,000 international UNTAC personnel in Cambodia which injected a lot of money into the economy. The figure for 1996, therefore, was probably an adjustment to the post-UNTAC reality. In 1997, Cambodia was hit hard by political turmoil in July and suffered some of the shockwaves of the Asian financial crisis. Since 1999, however, there has been a steady upturn. Household final consumption expenditure in constant prices increased by 1.9 per cent in 2002 according to the National Accounts Bulletin.[41] "Based on the official mid-year population projection of 13.473 million for 2002," it noted, "average annual per capita household final consumption expenditure in constant prices is estimated at 897,000 riels or US$291."

The abiding issue of entrenched rural poverty remains the primary concern for policy-makers. Economic growth has barely touched the countryside. If living standards have risen among some rural families it is most likely due to remittances from daughters who have gone to the city to work in foreign-owned garment factories or from sons who have found paid employment outside the village, even outside the country, and not from agricultural development. Growth in the rural economy, in general, is not keeping pace with population growth. Landlessness and unemployment, or at least severe underemployment, compounded by restricted access to common land and to natural resources including forests and fisheries have all resulted in shrinking opportunities for rural folk and stagnation or worse in their living standards.

Health

After the Paris Peace Agreements were signed, the health sector received almost immediate support. The World Health Organization and all the major international non-government organisations committed to primary health care, maternal and child health, and emergency care for victims of landmines established themselves throughout the country. The NGO sector quickly organised itself and coordinated activities through a central peak body, Medicam, which worked closely with the national health ministry and provincial departments. In other circumstances, a system that could have produced a vastly improved health service for all Cambodians, unfortunately had to confront two major obstacles: the epidemic rapid spread of HIV/AIDS and the dislocation of services caused by the SAP.

Throughout the decade of the PRK, health services were rudimentary but they were free. A certain measure of corruption persisted throughout that regime, but the level was capped both by the capacity of the people to pay and also by a measure of ideologically-governed oversight. Privatisation policies after 1989, however, allowed doctors employed in the public hospitals to establish private clinics, often in their own homes. Thus, patients who attended the hospitals for treatment during morning surgery were commonly referred to the doctor's own clinic for further attention in the afternoon.

Cambodians spend a lot of money on health; household expenditures account for 73 per cent of total health expenditures, one of the highest rates in the world.[42] The cost of medical treatment is a major cause of landlessness. An Oxfam study conducted in 1999–2000 found that among families without land, 56.4 per cent had never owned land to begin with, but among the remainder, almost half of them said they had sold their land in order to pay for the medical treatment of a family member.[43]

The HIV/AIDS epidemic put heavy strains on the medical system. The first case of HIV infection was reported in 1991 and the rate of transmission rose rapidly through the decade. By 1997, up to 210,000 Cambodians were infected. The government, in full cooperation with NGOs and international agencies responded positively to this health crisis that threatened all the gains the country had made since the beginning of the decade. After 1997, the prevalence rate began to fall among the general population. In April 2001, the annual survey by the National Centre for HIV/AIDS estimated that 169,000 adult Cambodians between the ages of 15 and 49 were living with the virus, down from 184,000 in 1999.[44] The reporting rate, however, is low and the decline in the prevalence rate may be attributed as much to AIDS-related deaths as to a decline in new infections.

The HIV prevalence rate of 2.6 per cent among newborns, a result of mother to child transmission during birth is a contributing factor to the continuing high infant and child mortality rates. According to the

2002 National Health Survey, the child mortality rate is increasing; that year it was 95/1,000 compared with 85 in 1998. The survey cited multiple factors including disease and malnutrition combined with poor maternal health, limited availability of basic health services and low standards of household hygiene.[45] The UNICEF Progress on Children report of late 2004 claimed that Cambodia was the only country in the region where child mortality rates had increased since 1990 and pointed again to the urban-rural wealth gap. "Children born to poor rural families in Cambodia have a three times greater chance of dying in early childhood than those born to better-off urban families," it noted.[46] The infant mortality rate in rural areas is generally 33 per cent higher than it is in urban areas, and the child mortality rate is 35 per cent higher.

In 1997, the health ministry introduced user fees to reduce the practice of unofficial payments, to generate revenue for commune clinics and district referral hospitals and to improve the quality of services. The Cambodia Gender Assessment report of April 2004 found that in practice, however, the fee exemptions stipulated in the plan were not uniformly applied to poor people and that unofficial payments had not been eliminated, even in hospitals that were carefully monitored.[47]

Education

The Constitution of 1993 committed the state to providing free primary and secondary education to all on the basis of nine years of schooling. This provision was in line with the decisions taken at the seminal Education for All conference of 1991.

At the time of that conference, the education sector was seriously stressed. Throughout the PRK/SoC years, primary enrolment had expanded from 0.94 million to 1.62 million, an overall increase of around 70 per cent due only in part to the shift from four years to five years of primary schooling in the mid-1980s.[48] The "baby boomers" entered the school system just as funding support from the Soviet bloc stopped and the ADB education sector study of 1994 noted that real per capita spending had declined by 35 per cent in the intervening five years.[49] The funding gap was exacerbated by inefficiencies: for example, one-quarter of primary school students were repeating grades, many schools and teachers operated for only four hours per day, and more than 90 per cent of school spending went to teacher salaries. In addition, the system was burdened with a high rate of unqualified teachers, the absence of a national curriculum framework, inadequate textbook supplies and crumbling infrastructure.

Education expenditure was in urgent need of review. In 1993, the sector received only 7.6 per cent of recurrent budget and less than one per cent of GDP, funding that was poor even by low-income country norms. At the same time, more than half the public service was employed by the Ministry of Education. The ratio of administrators to teaching staff was low (1:3.5) but the teacher-pupil ratio was very high. Parents' contributions to education were roughly six times that of the government, due to unofficial enrolment charges, private tuition fees, and bribes paid for examination passes and entry into higher levels of education.

The policy advice given by the ADB sector study helped to prioritise the government's goals for education for the rest of the decade, namely to universalise nine years of basic general education, to modernise and improve the quality of the system itself, and to link training to the needs of the workplace. The Bank proposed a medium-term investment programme of US$152 million for the period 1994 to 2000. The Ministry of Education's plan stemming from the study was adopted by the government at the end of 1994. International donors pledged support and the government committed itself to increasing budget share to 15 per cent by the year 2000.

Perhaps more than any other service sector, national education was hostage to every political crisis that assailed Cambodia throughout the 1990s. According to David Ayres:

> [E]ducational policies in post-UNTAC Cambodia were subjected to the whims of the nation's political leaders. Education policies developed by the Ministry of Education in consultation with international advisers and in congruence with international practice, were implemented only where they did not conflict with the immediate political imperatives of those in control of the apparatuses of the state.[50]

By way of example, he cited the salary supplement of around US$8 per month for the lamentably low-paid teachers that the government introduced in March 1994. The ADB review called this "a chance missed" to influence policy as an incentive to improve staff performance; Ayres called it "a blatant attempt by Funcinpec to secure legitimacy among the staff of a Funcinpec-headed ministry."[51]

Perhaps the worst blow to education reform came in the aftermath of the July coup against Funcinpec in 1997. Many international donors suspended funding at that time. In the cruelest blow, the U.S. government terminated its support to the Cambodian Assistance to Primary Education (CAPE) project, a US$26 million, five-year programme that was in its first year of operation to establish resource centres in cluster schools across the country and to train up to 40,000 primary school teachers. Unlike other donors, the U.S. did not resume direct bilateral support to the Cambodian government for at least another decade.

By the end of the 1990s, total enrolment in the formal education system was 2.4 million, or around one-fifth of the total population.[52] The cost of supporting that system was very high for a country where annual per capita GDP in 1998 was still less than US$300. A decade after committing itself to the World Declaration on Education for All, the government held another national conference in April 2000. It recommended that the share of the education budget from the national budget be increased from 9 per cent in 1999 to 15 per cent in 2000 and 20 per cent for the following years, and that the adult literacy rate be increased to at least 80 per cent by the year 2015.[53]

Government spending on education did not reach the target of 15 per cent budget share set for 2000. After the final collapse of the Khmer Rouge, however, levels of spending for the social services sector increased, as military expenditure declined. In 2000, the budget allotted the most money ever to the sector, including US$58.8 million for education.[54] In 2001, education received 11 per cent of budget spending, a further rise. Teachers' salaries received a boost in 2005, but still averaged only about US$33 per month.

Some of the reforms proposed by the ADB study of 1994 have been implemented. In 2004, for instance, schools were instructed that between 70 and 90 per cent of pupils should graduate from primary school to avoid the cost of repetition. The results of reforms, however, have been mixed. A UNICEF representative was quoted as saying in 2006 that the biggest achievement of the last decade had been "beating the bushes" to find children and enrol them in first grade.[55] In 2005, 91 per cent of six-year-olds had been enrolled to start primary school.

Economic Activity

Land Tenure

It was not politics and democracy, or rehabilitation and reconstruction that absorbed the people's interest during the 1990s, but rather land and property rights. Land is Cambodia's most important productive asset and the main economic resource for more than 80 per cent of the population whose income derives from agricultural activities, including fishing and forestry. Important legislation relating to land ownership, occupancy and use since 1989 has changed traditional ways of defining proprietorship throughout the country.

Legislation in 1989 gave private ownership of agricultural land to farmers who had continuously tilled their land for five years, and residential land and dwellings to individuals who occupied that property at the date the legislation was passed, thereby invalidating pre-1975 ownership claims. In fact, the terms and conditions of that legislation were confusing and the subsequent Land Law of 1992 specifying the procedure for converting possession rights to full ownership only compounded the confusion. Land encroachment and land grabbing, speculation, disputes, corruption and even violence thrived on the lack of clarity in the law.

By the end of the 1990s, the situation had reached crisis point. The privatisation issue was exacerbated by increasing pressure on land arising from the demographic bulge dating from the early to mid-1980s with young people coming of age and seeking land, as well as by the concession system which was revived in a major way after 1990 and which worked to remove access to common land, forests and fisheries that rural dwellers had always regarded as theirs by customary right. The sticking point, however, was that the majority of people occupied their land without holding formal documents.

After 1989, many applications were made for ownership deeds but over the course of the decade very few titles were actually issued. The Cadastral Department admitted to CDRI researchers in 2000 that only 14 per cent out of a total of 4.5 million applicants had received full certificates, leaving more than 70 per cent of households with nothing to prove their possession rights for either residential or agricultural land.[56] The majority of people believed that if they were occupying land without conflict or controversy it was legally theirs, irrespective of whether they formally possessed deeds, another CDRI study noted.[57] "Historically this has been the traditional position," it explained.

Land not distributed for private ownership under the 1989 legislation was retained as state or common land for future development. In the legislation, however, there was a lack of distinction between state property and common property, and specifically a failure to define common property. This legal loophole allowed millions of hectares of forests and agricultural land to be transferred to private companies for long-term investment and for exploitation as concessions, very much in the way that the French Protectorate had awarded vast tracts of lands to private investment companies in the 1920s. In addition to these concessions approved by the Ministry of Agriculture, Forestry and Fisheries (MAFF), the military also retained the right it was granted by the government in 1994 to control parts of forest and other lands for security reasons. Military officials sold concessions on some of this land, frequently bypassing the MAFF and normal regulations. The scale of expropriation of land, even excluding military-held territory, was vast for a country whose total surface area is just over 181,000 square kilometres. A survey data review of 2000 noted:

> According to the Department of Planning and Statistics of the MAFF, 4,739,153 hectares of forest have officially been granted to private companies for long-term investment (up to 20–30 years). This includes 264,924 hectares for three forest concessions which were recently cancelled. Likewise, 662,496 hectares of agricultural land have been granted to private companies for long-term investment (up to 70 years). This includes 46,600 hectares for five agricultural concessions which were recently cancelled. In addition, one million hectares of fishing lots have been allocated for commercial use.[58]

The author of that research, Sik Boreak, believed that the transfer of common property resources to private owners was actually much higher than those figures suggest because of the frequency of land grabbing and land encroachment. As a result of the development of plantations, logging concessions and commercial fishing lots, commonly held property on which rural Cambodians had always relied for gathering food, medicine, firewood and building materials, as well as for grazing their stock became more and more inaccessible. The lack of access to common property and common resources had a severe impact on rural livelihoods.

Rural landlessness has always been relatively uncommon in Cambodia. Compared with its neighbours, it is sparsely settled and the settlement pattern has remained constant with approximately 70 per cent of the population inhabiting only 30 per cent of the land, since much of the total land area is unsuitable for close settlement and intensive cultivation. In recent years, however, both the frequency of disputes over land and the rate at which agricultural land is being transferred bear out the fact that there is growing pressure on this key resource from the rapidly increasing population on the one hand and from competing capitalist interests on the other.

An Oxfam study conducted in 1999–2000 found from its sample that the rate of landlessness was 13 per cent, or that "more than one in eight families had no agricultural land and did not have the means to purchase it."[59] Among these landless families, a little over half of them, including newly married couples and returnees from the border camps, had never owned land; the remaining 43.6 per cent had lost their land, chiefly to pay for healthcare and debts but also because of disputes and land-grabbing. The same study suggested that landlessness was a growing trend, noting that in 1969 it was only 4.01 per cent but had reached 11.97 per cent by 1999.

During roughly the same period, the total supply of agricultural land increased; Cambodian researcher, Sik Boreak, measured the additional supply as 14 per cent between 1993 and 1998.[60] Nevertheless, he argued, many farmers complained with justification about not having enough land for self-sufficient farming. He blamed this on land concentration, noting that the rich minority hold very large areas of agricultural land, leaving the poor majority little on which to live and work.[61] The 1999 CSES found that a rural household had, on average, only 1.03 hectares of paddy land or 0.19 hectares per person.[62] The same household was likely to own 1.37 parcels of land, the average size of a parcel being 0.90 hectares. This brought the total area cultivated per average household to 1.23 hectares.[63] Within this generalisation, however, there were important differences based on geographical region and gender; households run by single women, for example, owned considerably less land than others.

The current, long-awaited Land Law was adopted by the National Assembly on 20 July 2001, and after passing through the Senate, it was promulgated by the king on 30 August that year. Two years previously, the Ministry of Land Management, Urban Planning and Construction had been established to prepare for the law's implementation. Surveying for an estimated eight million applications for land titles alone was expected to take around 15 years. The backlog of unresolved disputed claims, including large class action suits, however, delayed the law's effectiveness and many Cambodians have been disappointed by its outcomes, some arguing that the law has worsened the plight of the poor by allowing the rich to lay prior claims to contested land. An important provision of the law that is supposed to guard against consequences such as this is the social concession, or specified areas of state land that may be granted to poor families for residential or farming purposes on a case-by-case basis. A sub-decree establishing the procedures for social land concessions was promulgated in 2003.

Agriculture

The major contribution of roughly 50 per cent made by agriculture, including forestry and fisheries, to Gross National Product during the final years of the PRK and the SoC up to and including the year of the UNTAC operation is illustrated in the following table:

Table 5.5 GDP by Industrial Origin, 1989–93 (at 1989 constant prices, US$)[64]

Year	Agriculture	Industry	Services	GDP
1988	117.5	36.5	78.8	232.8
1989	125.9	37.1	77.9	240.9
1990	127.4	36.3	80.0	243.7
1991	135.9	39.5	86.8	262.2
1992	138.5	45.7	96.4	280.6
1993 (est.)	143.0	50.3	103.3	296.6

Source: World Bank (1994).

Agriculture always was and remains the dominant form of economic activity. The CSES 1999 commented on the "sheer size of the major group of skilled agricultural and fishery workers" that accounted for almost three-quarters or 74 per cent of the total Cambodian labour force. In the rural sector, 82 per cent of the workforce was engaged in agriculture and fishery.[65] Crop production, and rice-growing in particular, is still the chief occupation of the vast majority of Cambodians.

Given the central importance of rice to both the national diet and GDP, the chart below which traces both paddy cultivated area and the volume of the harvest for the two decades after the fall of Democratic Kampuchea is worth careful study.

Paddy cultivation is impervious to almost everything but pests and the weather. As the graph suggests, political changes produced very little

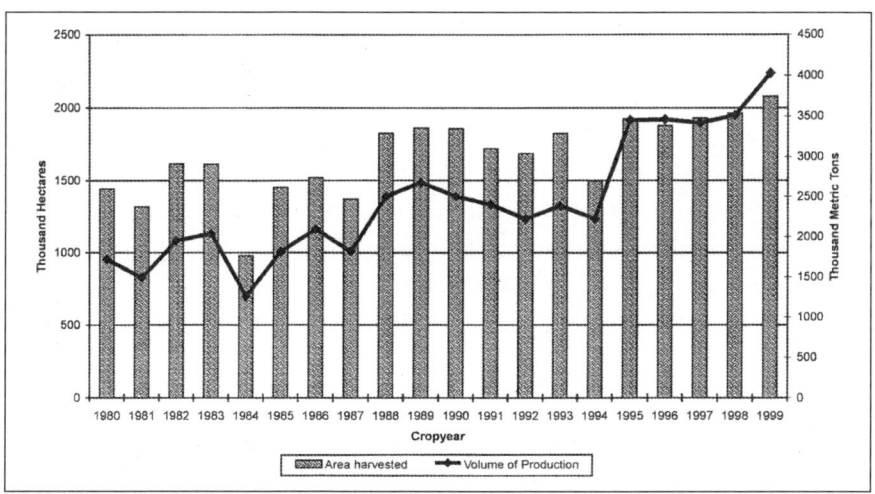

Figure 5.1 Paddy Production and Area Harvested, 1980–99[66]

effect on this industry between 1980 and 2000. The 1984 slump, for instance, had nothing to do with politics or war; that crop suffered from protracted drought through the growing months and then torrential rains just as harvest commenced. The wet season crop is still overwhelmingly rain-fed (less than ten per cent of ricefields were irrigated in 2000) and the graph indicates clearly the years when the crop suffered from bad weather.

The total area harvested grew from 1,861,000 hectares in 1989 to 2,079,4400 hectares in 1999, a small increase relative to the general population growth of almost 3.3 million in that decade. On the other hand, production improved significantly and quite suddenly after 1994 with the introduction of new, high-yielding seed varieties. From 2.22 million tonnes in 1994, production rose to 3.45 million tonnes the following year, and average yields which had hovered between 1.3 and 1.4 tonnes per hectare between 1989 and 1993 rose strongly to 1.94 tonnes per hectare in 1999.[67]

Before 2001, paddy could not be legally exported without a government issued licence. Nevertheless, a vigorous informal trade across the borders had already existed for many years because farmers experienced difficulties finding domestic buyers for their paddy. Furthermore, because of high transportation costs and poor marketing and distribution networks, it is easier and cheaper for Cambodian traders to sell paddy to Thailand or Vietnam than it is to take it to a central distribution point. Local millers, meanwhile, lack the capacity to process the growing rice surplus. In both 2005 and 2006, Cambodian farmers produced around one million tonne surpluses and the surplus from the 2007 harvest was expected to be even bigger. Estimates suggested that 800,000 tonnes of the 2007 surplus would be exported.[68]

Paddy production will continue to be weather-affected for many years to come as irrigation plans are still hampered by institutional immaturity. Nevertheless, as the figures above show, small-scale family producers have managed to boost productivity since 1994. The problem for the government is that agriculture, which accounts for such a large proportion of both employment and GDP, contributes little to public revenue and accounts for only three per cent of the nation's official exports.

In 1999, major crops apart from rice included maize grown on almost 60,000 hectares and rubber from the state's plantations of around 37,000 hectares. Lentils (soy and mung beans), sesame and cassava remained significant food and short-term industrial crops, but by the end of twentieth century, generally speaking, there was little diversification either in the crops produced or in the way that they were cultivated. Jute, pepper, cotton and tobacco, those other traditional cash crops, were all showing a tendency to decline.

International development programmers such as those from the Asian Development Bank, in 2007, were encouraging farmers to move away from rice production, or rather from concentrating mainly on rice production, to value-added and processing activities, namely agro-industry. The Cambodian government strongly supported private sector investment in plantations producing crops such as palm oil, cassava, coconuts, coffee, sugar cane and horticultural crops. It declared its preparedness to open up some 1.2 million hectares of "unused" land to such activities.[69] In 1998, for example, a Chinese company was granted a 70-year contract for a plantation of 20,000 hectares in Kompong Speu province for dairying, palm oil and sugar cane production.[70] A handful of around 20 local entrepreneurs who have formed a working group on agriculture were also very active in the production of similar cash crops for export. Agro-industry, however, is an important part of the general debate over land concessions. Donors, NGOs and local community groups have all condemned large concessions awarded on indigenous land and in environmentally sensitive areas for pulp-tree, rubber and cashew plantations.

The agriculture sector has yet to deal with many long-standing issues such as the lack of irrigation infrastructure, poor marketing, transportation, and distribution networks, administrative issues including graft and political interference, and an overwhelming need for public and private investment. Some agricultural industries which survived even the regime of Democratic Kampuchea have collapsed. The Battambang jute factory, for instance, which Hou Yuon helped to establish in the 1960s closed in 2000.[71] The once thriving Kampot pepper industry has all but disappeared. Cambodian rubber which once held the reputation for the finest quality product in the world suffers from lack of capital investment, particularly for latex processing, and also from issues of transparent management and political interference.

Tobacco, however, represents an agricultural success story. After showing a tendency to decline, cigarette production increased strongly after 1999 and by 2003 it was a US$50 million business due to a successful joint venture between an international firm and a Cambodian partner. The plant which is managed and operated entirely by Cambodians is tied to domestic primary production. Tobacco companies distribute high quality seed and advise farmers on best practice so that the returns for a tobacco farm of three hectares are well above those of a typical rice farm.[72]

Fisheries

Only 1.9 per cent of the employed population of Cambodia worked in the fishery sector in 1999 but this figure is hardly a reflection of the importance of small-scale, family fishing to rural diets and livelihoods.[73] Cambodia's freshwater fisheries are still among the most productive in the world and marine fishing is also important, although more of its product is exported than consumed domestically.

Throughout the 1990s, Cambodia's fisheries were the scene of much controversy. Studies found that the environmental health of the Great Lake remained basically sound, despite some concerns about silting and the run-off of pesticides and herbicides from surrounding farmland. The main problems of the industry stemmed from the fishing lot system, the abuses of the system and the impact on local fishermen, the loss of public revenue and the impact on fish stock and species.

The lot system, like the agricultural land concession system, was introduced by the French Protectorate in the 1920s and reintroduced by the PRK government in 1988. By 2000, the most productive fisheries in the country were included in its sweep. That year, there were 279 lots spread over 8,529 square kilometres of the Great Lake and Cambodia's river systems.[74] Those lots were won by bidding and the successful bidder had exclusive rights over a specific area for two years. Most lots, as required by law, set aside areas for use by local people. In theory, more than 24 square kilometres of rivers, ponds, lakes and wetlands remained available for public use. In practice, however, armed guards, including police and military personnel who cooperated with lot owners, routinely intimidated villagers attempting to use areas to which they had right of access. Villagers and environmental lobby groups further accused lot owners of destructive fishing practices including electrocution, small mesh nets and pumping lakes dry to maximise the catch. The protestors' arguments were supported by the report of a Cambodian ADB consultant for critical wetlands management who demonstrated that there had indeed been a decrease in freshwater fish stocks since the lot system was reintroduced, especially for the more valuable commercial species. His report referred to a corrupt fishing lot bidding and payment system that enriched officials but robbed the national treasury of funds and claimed that the amount of fish smuggled to Thailand was perhaps ten times the official figure.[75] Estimates varied but in 2000, the value of the catch may have been as high as US$200 million even though the Department of Fisheries officially collected only about one per cent of that figure, or about US$2 million in revenue.[76]

Late in 2000, the Prime Minister apologised to the country for abuses by fisheries officers and fishing lot owners. Half of all the fishing lots, or 495,000 hectares in twelve provinces, were returned to communal fishing grounds.[77] More than two hundred community fisheries were established to manage the grounds. Subsequently, the number of disputes declined and local fishermen admitted that their livelihoods had improved. In February 2001, Cambodia's freshwater fisheries were given further protection when a decree was adopted by the government granting the Great Lake status of a biosphere reserve.[78] The decree placed three core areas measuring 36,287 hectares off-limits to development and put fishing under tight regulations with increased patrols. The whole lake is now surrounded by transitional and buffer zone areas where commercial development is permitted as long as it does not affect the core area, and development in the transitional zone is tightly controlled.

Forestry

The democratic principles of the Royal Government of Cambodia were severely tested in the arena of environmental politics. As noted, lobbying and debate was conducted with considerable success within the fisheries sector. In the forestry sector, that sort of political activity assumed dimensions rarely if ever seen in Cambodia's history. Philippe Le Billon put timber at the heart of the debate about political transition during the 1990s, arguing, "Timber represented a key stake in the rapacious transition from the (benign) socialism of the post-Khmer Rouge period to (exclusionary) capitalism, thereby becoming the most politicised resource of a reconstruction process that has failed to be either as green or as democratic as the international community had hoped."[79]

The stripping of Cambodia's rich tropical forests began in the final years of the PRK. Logging bans in neighbouring Thailand and increasing world demand for timber made it a lucrative resource for the warring factions that were forced to look elsewhere to fund their military efforts as the end of the Cold War dried up their usual sources. The Khmer Rouge were thought to be earning up to US$20 million every month in the lead-up to the 1993 elections from logging and gem mining in the area under their control in the northwest.[80] The environmental damage was alarming. When the SNC placed a ban on the export of logs, they evaded the restrictions by setting up sawmills just inside the border and exported roughly sawn timber instead. The Khmer Rouge were by no means alone in this quasi-legal activity.

The felling and export of timber reached a peak around 1995, when, as Le Billon estimates, forest exploitation represented about 43 per cent of Cambodian export earnings although virtually none of those earnings reached the public coffers. The total public revenue collected between 1991 and 1998, he notes, represented only US$97 million or about 12 per cent of what the government should have received under a proper system of taxation.[81] He offers the following table, with figures derived from various sources, to illustrate the extent of logging and the loss to public revenue:

Table 5.6 Value of Timber Exports and Revenue of the Government[82]

	1990	1991	1992	1993	1994	1995	1996	1997	1998
Volume of timber exports ('000 m³)	515	848	1,393	1,360	1,495	1,691	992	1,045	1,090
Estimated value (US$ million)	77	170	348	340	374	423	248	188	218
Forestry government revenue (US$m)	n.a.	n.a.	1.5	3.3	39	27	11	12	5

Note: The volume of timber exported — much of which is smuggled — is only an estimate.
Source: Reports from the RGC, Thai Forestry Department and Global Witness.

After 1995, the figures suggest, there was a measure of restraint. This was because, according to Le Billon, the international community began to see illegal logging as a symbol of what was "wrong" with the new government in Cambodia and "to attach critical importance to forestry legalization as a key means for improving the transition of Cambodia from war to peace and from poverty to prosperity."[83] In 1996, the IMF suspended the first *tranche* of a US$60 million loan and resumed payment only after the government promised to reform the industry and put an independent monitor in place to oversee logging practices. On 31 December 1996, a ban on the export of round logs went into force and the following April, a government decision was issued, setting out what comprised legal and illegal exports. In effect, this meant that logging could be conducted only by legal concessionaires in cutting areas licensed by the government's Department of Forestry.

The logging concession scheme set up in 1995 was widely seen as corrupt and abusive. Concessionaires without proper management plans were issued licences to cut virtually wherever they liked, while villagers were denied access to their resin trees and other forest resources that

Logs felled by foreign companies in Sandan district, Kompong Thom province, c. 2003

Logs line the road beside land newly planted with rubber in Tumring, Kompong Thom province, c. 2003

A women's micro-credit meeting in Siem Reap province, c. 2007

supplemented their diet and family income. The concessions were so vast that by the end of 1997 they covered almost seven million hectares, virtually the whole of the country's forests except for national parks and other protected areas, and even then because the protected areas were adjacent to the concessions, access roads frequently ran through them so that all forested lands were at risk. It was feared that the concession system as it operated at the end of 1997 would completely destroy Cambodia's forests within 10 to 15 years with little or no benefit to the state.

In January 1999, the Prime Minister ordered a crackdown on illegal logging and some months later, forest crimes monitoring units were established by relevant ministries. The international organisation, Global Witness, was appointed as independent forestry monitor that year. Illegal activity dropped dramatically but climbed again during the 2000 and 2001 logging seasons. Global Witness accused the military of carrying out illegal logging inside and around the legal concessions and claimed that government officials were often involved or received bribes to turn a blind eye.

In 2000, the ADB commissioned a major study of Cambodia's logging industry. It found the forests were so depleted and the cutting rates so rapid that most concessions were almost logged out. It blamed "greed, corruption, incompetence and illegal acts" and warned that the economic system based around the logging industry could be destroyed.[84] In fact, of the 32 companies awarded concessions in 1995, only 14 remained by then, controlling 3.87 million hectares. The study noted that in some of the original concessions, logging had proved to be uneconomical, others had been logged out and abandoned, and in a few cases the government had cancelled concessions. It recommended that all logging be halted until new management plans were approved. In response to the ADB's recommendations and also to the public anger over extensive flood damage that year caused, many people believed, by deforestation, the government ordered the suspension of logging from 1 January 2002.

Frustration over limited public access to and scrutiny of the new 25-year management plans for concessions boiled over into a violent confrontation between villagers and police in front of the Department of Forestry office in Phnom Penh in December 2002. One villager died not long after the altercation with police. Less than a month after that event, the government announced that it would no longer work with Global Witness. Another organisation, a Swiss accounting firm, was appointed to be the new forestry monitor in July 2003 with a mandate to review efforts to fight illegal logging rather than to conduct investigations as before. Meanwhile, the World Bank admitted that the use of commercial concessions to manage Cambodia's forests had been a failure. "The basic institutional skills required to assess assets, screen investors, manage transparent bidding processes, and enforce contract conditions are weak or non-existent," its report judged.[85] It added, "Clearly concessionaire and government performance has been largely a continuation of the 'system of failure' described in the ADB-supported assessment conducted in 2000." It concluded that the concession system should be abandoned, possibly over a transitional period of ten years.

Industry and Services

Statistically, the industrial sector demonstrated rapid growth throughout the 1990s. The National Institute of Statistics (NIS) conducted regular surveys of industrial establishments (SIEC) between 1993 and 2000 and measured the compound growth rate as close to 12 per cent annually during that time. This compared very favourably with agriculture which grew by only 2.2 per cent in the period 1990–98 and with average GDP growth rate of 5.5 per cent over the same period.[86] In real terms, the NIS declared, "[T]he total number of industrial establishments in Cambodia [in 2000] was 8,089 out of which over 97 per cent belonged to the manufacturing sector and the rest were distributed among the other two sub-sectors, viz. mining and quarrying, and electricity, gas and water supply."[87]

The industrial sector, which had contributed little to the PRK economy, grew strongly and assumed an ever larger share of GDP following the resumption of private ownership in 1989. According to the NIS survey, by 2000, there were 63 state-owned corporations engaged in manufacturing, but they represented only 0.8 per cent of all manufacturing establishments. State involvement in another major sub-sector, electricity, gas and water supply rated higher, at a little over 13 per cent (16 establishments). The SIEC 2000 summed up the situation thus: "The majority of institutions in each of the three major groups were single proprietorship establishments (93.6 per cent, 90.3 per cent and 80.3 per cent respectively)."[88] As in agriculture, the Cambodian industrial economy at the turn of the century remained almost exclusively the preserve of private entrepreneurs operating small businesses, typically on a household basis.

Despite this fact, it is the garment factory that symbolises modern industry in Cambodia today. The garment and textile factories were to the Cambodian economy of the 1990s what the rubber plantations had been in the 1920s and 1930s, their primary function being to generate foreign exchange through export earnings. Cambodia offered generous incentives to attract this type of labour-intensive, export-oriented investment and was rewarded for its compliance with the SAP conditions by the granting of preferential trade agreements with the U.S. including Most Favoured Nation (MFN) in 1996 and subsequently the Generalized System of Preferences (GSP) in 1997. Both MFN and GSP were strong incentives for international companies to relocate their manufacturing activities to Cambodia from neighbouring countries, especially Thailand and Malaysia, which had lost these privileges as their economies developed.

As a result of market-oriented reforms, the garment manufacturing industry mushroomed. The statistics speak for themselves. In 1995, there were 20 factories employing 19,000 workers, mainly young women; almost ten years later, there were ten times that number of factories employing around 200,000 workers. The following incomplete table illustrates that growth; the figures have been derived from a variety of sources that do not always correlate, although the disparities are not significant:

Table 5.7 Garment and Textile Manufacturing Industries, 1995–2004

Year	Factories	Workers	Export Earnings
1995	20	19,000–20,000	$26.2 million (8% of exports)
1996	32		30% of exports
1998			$360 million
1999		80,000	$653 million
2000			$900 million
2001		150,000	$1.1 billion
2002			$1.33 billion
2003	197	240,000	$1.58 billion (40% of economic activity/ 80% of total merchandise exports)
2004	200+	180,000	$1.54 billion

In January 1997, the National Assembly ratified the current Labour Law, replacing the labour code of 1992.[89] In specific detail, it differed little from the original French code, but it did spell out quite clearly that Cambodia was committed to a free market economy. Two years later, U.S.A. and Cambodia signed the Bilateral Textile Agreement, the first of its kind in the world, which linked increased market access to labour law compliance. The International Labour Organization (ILO) started monitoring factories that produced garments for export to the U.S. in 2001. Their positive reports paid enormous dividends for the industry as the table above suggests. This agreement, along with preferential quotas, was set to expire at the end of 2004, just as Cambodia was admitted to the World Trade Organization.

Another feature typical of countries that accepted a SAP in compliance with IMF conditions for its loans was the development of specialist economic parks or export-processing zones specifically for the requirements of investors in global trade markets. By 2002, four of these zones existed near the Thai border and they were designed to attract manufacturers eager to benefit from the preferential tariffs Cambodia enjoyed under the GSP for which Thailand no longer qualified. The zones were planned as "co-production areas" and they were expected to attract investment of US$320 million and provide 84,000 jobs in 420 factories.[90] Another industrial zone at Bavet on the Vietnam border was inaugurated by the Prime Minister in August 2005.[91] By late that year, the Ministry of Economy and Finance had begun reviewing the draft of a subdecree on special economic zones in Cambodia granting nine-year tax breaks for zone developers and tax-free entry for imports of raw materials for companies that bought into the zones.[92] The main target area for large-scale development of commercial zones was around the deepwater port at Sihanoukville.

Within the services sector, tourism was expected to make an important contribution to GDP after the formation of the new government in 1993. Ongoing conflict, however, as well as health scares such as the SARS (Sudden and Acute Respiratory Syndrome) epidemic and the failure of Cambodia's national airline, Royal Air Cambodge, all resulted in lower than anticipated numbers of tourists to the kingdom by the end of the decade. Since 1999 and especially since the implementation of the "open skies" policy, tourist arrivals have grown dramatically. From just under 200,000 tourists in 1999, the number more than doubled in the space of three years to 441,411 in 2002.[93] Apart from the main attraction of the Angkor-era temples in Siem Reap province, casinos at border crossing points as well as in Phnom Penh have acted as major attractions, especially for fellow-ASEAN visitors. International tourists and gamblers have also contributed to growth in the hotel and restaurant industry, the transport and communications industry, and other services.

The services sector is expected to make a major contribution to the economy in the twenty-first century, but as the following table shows, by 2002 its growth rate as a percentage of GDP remained considerably slower than that of industry. The official figures in the table are based on constant 2000 prices.

Table 5.8 GDP Growth Rates by Sector and Total[94]

	GDP Growth Rates in Constant 2000 Prices (%)								
Sector	1994	1995	1996	1997	1998	1999	2000	2001	2002
Agriculture	11.2	3.3	1.0	6.4	5.8	3.4	−1.5	2.2	−2.7
Industry	17.2	23.2	5.2	19.6	−2.5	19.3	30.7	12.9	17.7
Services	−2.0	8.4	7.8	3.4	4.8	10.9	5.7	4.2	4.5
Total	9.0	6.9	5.0	6.8	3.7	10.8	7.0	5.7	5.5

Source: NIS, National Accounts of Cambodia, 1993–2002.

Labour

Cambodia has a very high economic participation rate. In 1999, according to the CSES, it was 66.1 per cent, shared almost equally between men and women, and more than 83 per cent of the total work force was rural. The 1999 survey noted an employment rate of 99.4 per cent, although it conceded that underemployment was much higher than figures suggested. Furthermore, almost half (46 per cent) of the total employed population still worked without pay in family owned and operated businesses or farms. As might be expected, the number of unpaid workers was much higher in the countryside than in Phnom Penh where more than one out of two employees were paid in 1999.

In 2000, more than 80 per cent of all paid workers were employed in the manufacture of textiles, wearing apparel and the tanning and dressing of leather.[95] Textile manufacturing employed almost 44 per cent of total paid workers and within that sub-sector, there were three times as many women as men on the payroll; in wearing apparel there were eight times as many women as men, and in tanning and dressing leather, the ratio was 15.7 women workers for every male worker.

Wages remained low throughout the 1990s. The table below, prepared by the NIS, suggests that public sector salaries declined in the four and a half years between December 1994 and June 1999. The strongest growth in wages occurred in the textile factories where labour was organised in unions even before the Labour Law took effect in 1997. As mentioned previously, the tobacco industry has proved to be something of a model of industrial management in Cambodia and conditions for the workforce there are good; whether it is typical of the private sector in general, however, seems unlikely. The table omits salaries of staff employed by non-government or other donor-funded organisations that are typically several times higher than those represented in the table. The average wage was equal to approximately US$883 per year or $73.6 per month in 2000, when the riel was valued at 3,859 to one U.S. dollar.

Table 5.9 Monthly Wages by Sector, 1994–99 (by end of quarter)

Average Rates	December 1994	June 1999
Public Sector		
Wage in '000 riels	41.7	51
Wage in US$	16.1	13.3
Private Sector (Cigarette Factory)		
Wage in '000 riels	164.6	318.2
Wage in US$	58.5	75.6
Textile Factory		
Wage in '000 riels	142.6	332.7
Wage in US$	55	87
Hotel		
Wage in '000 riels	129.6	248.6
Wage in US$	50	65
Construction		
Wage in '000 riels	168.5	267.7
Wage in US$	65	70

Source: NIS, *Cambodia Year Book 2000*, 41.

The most dramatic change in the Cambodian labour force since 1990 has been the growth of paid employment among women. The female participation rate has always been high, but traditionally most women workers were own account workers in market stalls and other microenterprises, typically in the informal sector, or unpaid workers on family farms, or in artisanal industries such as weaving, tanning and dyeing. The relatively large and growing female paid workforce engaged by the garment and textile industry, therefore, is a marked change in the structure of social relations within production. Whether this factor is significant enough to produce important social and political effects, however, remains to be seen.

Apart from this, at the beginning of the twenty-first century, the vast majority of the population remained engaged in subsistence agriculture, industry was family owned and operated, unpaid family workers still made up the largest category of all employees, wage rates, particularly within the public sector, were low, as were education and skill levels among the workforce in general. Small changes occurred in relation to all these points throughout the 1990s, but the process of change was very slow.

Foreign Trade, Aid, Investment and Debt

Trade

After the Cold War, Cambodia shifted its major trade relations back to the Southeast Asian region. Cambodia's entry to ASEAN on 1 January 2000 secured its place in that regional trading bloc. Throughout the 1990s and the early years of the twenty-first century, there were changes in both the volume and the composition of trade compared with the preceding decade. In order to protect its growing trade in wearing apparel and textiles, in September 2004, Cambodia secured its membership in the World Trade Organization (WTO). These are the outstanding features of developments in external trade for this period.

A developing country with limited natural resources, Cambodia imports more than it exports. As illustrated in the preceding chapter, imports rose sharply after the return to free market economy in 1990. Apart from high demand for consumer goods and construction materials, raw materials and capital equipment were needed for the new export-oriented industries. After 1996, however, the trade deficit started to shrink, due largely to strong growth of garment, footwear and textile exports along with tourism and gambling related services exports. The following table from the National Accounts Bulletin of July 2002 shows that ratios of exports and imports to GDP improved steadily after 1993.

Table 5.10 International Trade in Goods and Services[96]

Ratios (2000 Prices)	Export and Import Ratios in Constant Prices									
	1993	1994	1995	1996	1997	1998	1999	2000	2001	2002
Exports as % of GDP	16.8	26.7	33.7	25.9	33.8	31.4	39.1	50.9	58.2	65.7
Imports as % of GDP	33.8	40.6	50.5	46.0	46.4	44.6	51.6	63.0	67.3	74.6
External balance as % of GDP	17.0	13.9	16.8	20.1	12.6	13.1	12.5	12.1	9.2	8.9
Terms of Trade	100.8	101.4	98.7	102.6	101.2	100.6	98.1	100.0	99.3	99.7

Entry to ASEAN was one of the new government's main goals. The decision to admit Cambodia was made at the end of May 1997, about six weeks before the coup. In a rare departure from its usual neutral stand, ASEAN voted to postpone Cambodia's entry until 1 January 2000. When Cambodia eventually became the tenth ASEAN member, it also committed itself to the AFTA (Asian Free Trade Area) guidelines which included deregulation schedules and reciprocity of tariff exemption privileges.

Under the AFTA provisions, members are allowed ten years to bring tariffs under five per cent and five more years to bring them down to zero.[97] Flexibility provisions, however, would allow a further two years' grace by which time, commerce ministry officials believed, Cambodia's agricultural production would be able to compete with its neighbours.

Most analysts feared that government revenue would suffer heavy losses as a result of meeting the tariff deregulation schedule. In 1996, when Cambodia sought entry to ASEAN, customs duties accounted for almost 65 per cent of government revenue.[98] Overall trade would have to expand in order to sustain that level of customs revenues. In addition, Cambodia needed to improve its balance of trade with ASEAN members in order to really benefit from AFTA. By 2001, however, only 4.2 per cent of Cambodia's total exports went to ASEAN countries, while 44.4 per cent of its imports came from within ASEAN.[99]

The composition of Cambodia's exports has changed markedly since the mid-1990s. The following table compiled by the National Bank of Cambodia for the years 1993 to 1999 inclusive shows a dramatic shift away from reliance on traditional export products, namely rubber, timber and fish, to GSP (Generalized System of Preferences) products. The ban on paddy exports remained in force throughout the decade, so rice exports are not included in this table.

Table 5.11 Export by Commodity, 1993–99[100]

In Million US$	1993	1994	1995	1996	1997	1998	1999
Logs (Wood)	36.3	142.3	111.6	52.5	128.1	88.0	37.2
Customs$	3.2	100.0	51.6	0.0	0.0	0.0	3.6
Unrecorded$	33.1	42.3	60.0	52.5	128.1	88.0	33.6
Sawn Timber	44.5	81.3	73.1	95.9	95.6	90.1	73.5
Customs$	19.0	63.0	15.5	20.9	11.2	6.1	29.5
Unrecorded$	25.5	18.3	57.6	75.0	84.4	84.0	44.0
Fish products	1.3	2.4	1.9	3.1	2.9	2.5	3.4
Customs$	0.1	2.4	1.9	3.1	2.9	2.5	3.4
Unrecorded$	1.3	0.0	0.0	0.0	0.0	0.0	0.0
Rubber	27.5	25.6	41.2	31.9	22.8	26.9	28.1
Customs$	12.6	25.6	37.2	27.7	19.1	25.3	27.4
Unrecorded$	14.9	0.0	4.0	4.2	3.7	1.5	0.7
GSP exports	4.3	3.4	27.5	101.8	278.5	392.4	536.4
Other domestic exports	11.7	8.5	12.9	9.9	6.4	4.0	5.5
Total domestic	125.6	262.0	268.2	295.2	534.3	604.0	684.1
Re-exports	227.7	227.7	585.7	348.4	327.3	308.9	289.1
Total	353.3	489.8	853.9	643.6	861.8	912.9	973.2

The figures for unrecorded exports, or cross-border smuggling, are underestimates. According to the NIS, unrecorded exports of fish products were worth US$35.1 million and US$38.6 million in 1998 and 1999 respectively, or more than ten times the value recorded by customs, while unrecorded rubber exports in 1999 were worth more than US$21 million, not US$700,000 as the National Bank figures suggest. The value of Cambodian paddy sold illegally was worth more than US$50 million in 1999.[101]

It was issues such as these that had to be resolved before Cambodia could fulfil conditions for accreditation to join the World Trade Organization. When Cambodia gained formal entry in September 2004, it became only the second country in the world with LDC (least developed country) status to do so. Given the strict compliance conditions for inclusion in the world trade body, many analysts doubted that Cambodia could benefit from membership. The government, however, argued that membership provided protection from exclusionary practices of the trading giants, such as the 1999 U.S. garment quota that restricted the export of dozens of textile items to American markets. Given Cambodia's almost total reliance on the export of garments and textiles, and the problems associated with export of agricultural products, the commerce minister argued that Cambodia would be more vulnerable to shifts in the world markets by not belonging to the WTO. Moreover, as an LDC member, Cambodian-made exports to the U.S., European Union, Canada, Korea and Japan are permitted lower tariffs and this is an incentive for foreign firms to establish factories in Cambodia.

Aid

The international donor community was very generous towards the Kingdom of Cambodia. After decades of destruction, civil war and isolation, Cambodia needed comprehensive assistance for rehabilitation and reconstruction before it could initiate plans for economic development. That assistance was readily forthcoming and it was delivered on particularly liberal terms. At the same time, donors and credit agencies increasingly applied conditionality to the grants and loans they provided, which made for robust exchanges at annual ICORC and Consultative Group (CG) meetings where pledges for assistance were made. An important adjunct to the provision of vital external assistance, which was the equivalent of 14 per cent of GDP in 2001, was the rapid development of aid-dependent civil society groups, local non-government organisations, that took an active part in monitoring aid disbursements and the RGC's implementation of policies for poverty reduction and equitable and sustainable development.[102]

The Declaration on the Rehabilitation and Reconstruction of Cambodia called on the United Nations to support ICORC, "notably in ensuring a smooth transition from the rehabilitation to reconstruction phases." In practice, as Grant Curtis pointed out, the UNTAC Rehabilitation Component was ineffectual in coordinating donor activities and the major donors "rapidly chose their own sectoral priorities, projects and programmes, as well as their own implementation mechanisms and structures."[103] At the same time, he notes, until the end of 1996 at least, the donor community demanded very little from the RGC in terms of its performance. Between 1992 and 1995, inclusive, external assistance disbursements totalled approximately US$1.4 billion, overwhelmingly in the form of bilateral assistance where Japan, France and the U.S. were the main donors, and they were allocated largely as "investment project assistance" (28.08 per cent) and "free-standing technical cooperation" (24.8 per cent). Budgetary aid and balance of payments support accounted for 15.9 per cent of total disbursements during that period.[104]

Soon after the formation of the RGC, in October 1993, bilateral donors paid Cambodia's arrears to the International Monetary Fund and a new loan was issued a few days later. As already noted, loans from the World Bank and the Asian Development Bank were tied to structural reforms and policy directions for the government. On the other hand, they were on very easy 40-year terms with 10-year grace periods and an annual service charge of only 0.5 per cent. The government set up the Council for the Development of Cambodia (CDC) in 1994 to keep track of all forms of foreign assistance to the country. This body was chaired by the Prime Minister with the minister for finance acting as the deputy head. Before each annual CG donors' meeting, the CDC produced a development cooperation report.

In March 1995, the Cambodian government and international donors met for the third annual ICORC review and CG meeting in Paris. Although the government's request for assistance was exceeded, the World Bank report on Cambodia's progress expressed the growing concern and frustration of major donors about excessive spending on the military, the slow pace of tax reform and the failure to collect logging revenues. The IMF agreed to a $120 million loan over three years, but in November the following year, it cancelled payment of a $20 million instalment of the loan in an acrimonious debate with the government over the logging issue. By 1996, the ADB had also approved loans worth more than

US$240 million and more than 50 technical assistance projects valued at $41 million.[105]

The July 1997 fighting provoked a sudden and concerted suspension of assistance by several major donors. Japan, the most important donor country, halted its aid programme. The U.S. cancelled its bilateral support and military assistance, although the humanitarian aid programme remained unaffected.[106] Germany also announced that it would freeze aid to Cambodia. Given the extent of the government's dependency on foreign assistance, the CPP coup against its coalition partner was a dangerous wager. According to the development cooperation report of 1996, Cambodia had received a total of approximately US$518 million in 1996.[107] Japanese aid alone was worth $111 million and the U.S. and Germany, the other donors who suspended assistance, had provided $28.7 million and $9.6 million respectively.[108]

The credibility of the outcome of the 1998 elections, the first elections organised by the Cambodians themselves after the UNTAC operation, was the crucial test for the resumption of aid. Those elections were orderly and international observers judged them sufficiently free and fair to confirm the CPP victory even though the party did not succeed in gaining the two-thirds majority of the primary vote it needed in order to rule in its own right. The president of the ADB announced that assistance would resume "soon"; it had not approved new loans since the coup but it had released three grants for technical assistance programmes worth close to two million dollars. The World Bank, for its part, had not approved any new loans since the July fighting. Total external assistance in 1998 was worth US$418 million of which technical assistance accounted for a little more than half, or $239 million.[109]

Cambodian leaders learnt from the 1997 experiment that suspension of aid was used as only a temporary punishment by donors who rarely agreed among themselves. Regardless of a poor report card and strict conditions laid down at annual CG meetings, aid was always resumed, usually at levels higher than anticipated. At the 2000 meeting, the practice of linking aid to reform through a system of benchmarks was introduced. Nevertheless, in June 2001, at the Tokyo meeting, donors pledged $615 million or more than the $500 million sought, even though some donors criticised the RGC for the slow pace of judicial and administrative reforms and for the failure of anti-corruption measures. The benchmarks were rarely met or met only in part, without consequence. In 2002, the donors pledged $635 million which again was more than requested. In April 2004, the finance minister announced that his government would seek US$1.5 billion over three years, in line with requests for the preceding years.[110] The benchmarks continued to relate to legal and judicial reform, natural resources management, strong fiscal management, public administration reform, and increased budget spending on social services.

The role of watchdog, of keeping the government true to its promises and policies, passed increasingly to the local non-government organisations. International humanitarian aid organisations had operated in Cambodia during the Khmer Republic and they returned after 1979; they had also been very active in the border camps among the refugees. The local civil society group, however, was never a feature of traditional Khmer society. During the years of socialist experimentation, associations had been formed among youth, women and trade unions but these revolutionary associations were designed to mobilise support for the government, not to challenge state institutions. The first Cambodian NGO was established in 1991 and others emerged in quick succession supported entirely by external donor funding. According to a 1998 government report, 296 NGOs were registered, among which 133 were local organisations and there were also four NGO peak bodies.[111] By 2003, there were 1,173 registered NGOs, the majority of them local ones.[112] There may, in fact, be many more small organisations that operate without formal registration.

Cambodian NGOs conduct programmes that range in activities from rural development at village level to human rights and political advocacy on a national basis. It is in this latter capacity and also in environmental protection that they have proved most effective.

Investment

In August 1994, the National Assembly adopted the Cambodian Investment Law that listed the government's preferred fields of investment as pioneer or high technology industries, labour-intensive and export-oriented industries, and tourism, followed by agro-industry, physical infrastructure and energy, rural development, environmental protection, and finally investments in "Special Promotion Zones."[113] The law offered generous incentives including corporate tax exemptions of up to eight years as well as tax-free distribution of dividends, and total exemption from import duties for start-up construction of projects oriented towards those preferred fields of investment. Export tax was waived and firms were free to hire foreign management and technical personnel. Investors were promised long-term leases of up to 70 years, renewable on request.

To facilitate the investment process, the Council for the Development of Cambodia (CDC) was established, with two operational boards, as a "one-stop service organisation" to oversee investment activities and to evaluate and decide on all investment project activities. Given the optimism that accompanied the successful 1993 elections, foreign investors were only too happy to take advantage of such liberal terms. Six months after the law was passed, Grant Curtis noted, the CDC claimed that more than US$625.4 million had been invested and it had approved projects worth US$1.55 billion proposed by 17 Malaysian companies.[114] In the first five months of 1995, 30 more projects worth US$374 million were approved. Altogether, less than a year after the bill was adopted, according to the government, foreign investment had created more than 40,000 local jobs.

Much of that early investment was skewed heavily towards the tourism and hospitality sector. Investment for hotel construction was sometimes merely an excuse for land speculation, and at other times contracts were awarded without sufficient inquiry into the applicants' capital resources so that companies folded and opportunities were wasted. The CDC approved a total of 971 companies or projects in the eight years between 1995 and 2002, but only 438 (45 per cent) of them were still operational and actively monitored and a further 82 companies were assumed to be operating but were not monitored at the end of that period.[115]

Nevertheless, after the initial speculative boom, Cambodia did attract the preferred type of export-oriented investment that would create jobs and ensure long-term economic growth. Most of this investment was in the industrial sector, mainly in garment, textile and footwear manufacturing. Investment in agriculture was patchy and generally disappointing, while tourism and the service sectors showed strong growth towards the end of the decade. The following table, showing fixed assets investment during the seven years after the investment law was adopted, illustrates the areas of interest as well as trends:

Table 5.12 Distribution of Capital Investment by Sector, 1995–2001 (%)[116]

	Fixed Assets Investment (%)						
Sector	1995	1996	1997	1998	1999	2000	2001
Agriculture	0.3	15.6	8.8	6.1	14.3	4.4	0.2
Industry	13.4	54.0	68.8	76.2	36.0	27.9	42.0
Service	18.9	14.8	16.8	4.6	11.3	31.4	21.8
Tourism	67.4	15.6	5.6	13.2	38.4	36.3	36.0
Total	100.0	100.0	100.0	100.1	100.0	100.0	100.0

The growth of foreign direct investment was not as straightforward as those figures might suggest. The July 1997 fighting shook investor confidence and the regionwide monetary crisis that occurred soon after those events threatened to destabilise the economy. Around 60 per cent of total capital investment came from the region, especially South Korea, Hong Kong and Malaysia, and there were fears that projects would be delayed or cancelled. In fact, there was a slowdown in investment activity in 1998 and political uncertainty about the outcome of the general elections was a further contributing factor, but the effects of the Asian financial crisis were less serious than feared in Cambodia where the economy was still small and remained highly dollarised. The business community was reassured by the CPP victory at the elections and investor confidence quickly returned. In 1998, several multinational companies commenced operations in Cambodia, including the milk company, Nestlé, and the electronics giant, Siemens.[117]

In 1999, the government issued a sub-decree amending the 1994 Investment Law. In an effort to tighten supervision of investment projects, the CDC was given the power to cancel investment licences if a company did not invest in the first six months after the licence was granted and to withdraw tax concessions from investors who failed to present quarterly reports.[118] The level of capital investment required for firms to qualify for the generous profits tax rate of nine per cent was raised from US$500,000 to US$1 million. The World Bank made further review of the investment law one of the benchmark conditions for the granting of the second loan *tranche* of its structural adjustment credit at the 2001 CG meeting. Political opposition leader, Sam Rainsy, who had drafted the original investment law during his brief tenure as finance minister, in advance of that meeting reportedly said, "The trouble is, we treat all sorts of investments the same way. Those who come here to exploit the country's natural resources and add no value to their exports, create few jobs and do not bring in any technology are undeserving candidates."[119] This criticism reflected that of long-time Cambodia watcher, Grant Curtis who noted, "In the post-UNTAC period, the RGC welcomed any investment in the country's further development. The government thus adopted the same *laissez-faire* stance toward direct foreign investment as it took on external assistance."[120] He thought it was "disappointing" that the Cambodian authorities had made little attempt to secure the sort of investment that built on the country's comparative advantages or that promoted value-added manufacturing and employment creation.

By the end of 2005, however, there was little change in the nature of foreign direct investment in Cambodia. As long as the government perceived the country's most pressing needs as employment for a rapidly growing population of school leavers and adequate foreign currency reserves to pay for foreign loans and the balance of payments, labour-intensive, export-oriented industries would remain welcome. While there was little change in the nature of FDI, however, there was an important change in the source of much of that investment. Of the US$546 million in projects approved by the CDC during the first half of 2005, US$402 million came from firms registered in the People's Republic of China.[121]

Debt

The Second Kingdom of Cambodia inherited debt from all former regimes but the legitimacy of those regimes, and consequently the foreign debts that they incurred, was not acknowledged by all members of the new government. The country's total debt remained unclear at that point. As noted previously, in October 1993 bilateral donors paid the arrears on the outstanding debt to the International Monetary Fund so that a new loan could be issued. There was a further loan dating from the 1960s of US$30 million owed to France, but that was the only debt incurred before 1992 that the RGC was prepared to recognise. The contested debts were owed to the former Soviet Union and to the United States of America. Assistance given to the People's Republic of Kampuchea by the USSR and its allies for the rebuilding of Cambodia after the fall of Democratic Kampuchea is estimated to have been worth US$1.1 billion, Russia alone being owed US$800 million of that amount.[122] The U.S.A. claims it is still owed $500 million, from loans taken out by the Khmer Republic in the early 1970s. These debts to France, Russia and the U.S.A. are in the process of being renegotiated through the Paris Club, a group of creditor nations that helps debtor nations to find solutions to overdue loans. The RGC was optimistic that 70 per cent of its debt to Russia, for instance, would be written off with help from the Paris Club.[123]

At the end of 1992, the Asian Development Bank (ADB) made the first loan by an international finance institution to Cambodia in more than 20 years. This was US$67.7 million for infrastructure, repayable over 40 years with a ten-year grace period on interest payments. The first payment on that loan, US$1 million, was paid in June 2003 and similar payments were scheduled every six months for another 30 years. Between that first loan and the end of 2003, Cambodia took out further loans from IFIs worth US$700 million. As of March 2003, Cambodia owed

US$762 million to the ADB and the World Bank/IMF, with a further US$286 million pending up to 2005.[124]

The RGC also secured several bilateral loans. For instance, it borrowed US$40 million from Japan to refurbish the port at Sihanoukville, and US$20 million from South Korea. The collapse of the national airline, Royal Air Cambodge, left Cambodia with a US$30 million debt for which it was sued by creditors in the United Kingdom. The debt owed to China is less well-known. In February 1999, however, the RGC signed the agreement for a $200 million interest-free loan in Beijing and in December 2001, another five-year $10 million loan for economic and technical cooperation was floated.[125]

Apart from the debt owed on the failed national airline, the RGC proved itself to be a reliable borrower and loans offered to the new government since 1993 have been very generous. Government planners realize, however, that the terms of future loans might not be as generous as they were in the past.

Public Finance, Banking and Credit

In 1989, the Cambodian economy entered a period of rapid and virtually unregulated privatisation. The withdrawal of Vietnamese troops, spiralling inflation and the cessation of Soviet aid left Cambodia's finances in a very fragile condition. The riel had remained relatively stable throughout the preceding decade but between 1988 and 1993 the average inflation rate was around 90 per cent.[126]

During those six difficult years, budget deficits grew and were financed, as the inflation rate suggests, by increases in money supply. According to the ADB report, "Government spending was met by tax revenues by about 30 per cent, by non-tax revenues by 30 per cent, and the remaining 40 per cent by increase in money supply."[127] The quality of government services dipped further as limited government resources were diverted to the military and security sectors. Half of the recurrent budget was spent on defence throughout the 1990s and salaries for government employees consumed the rest.

The annual GDP growth rate was only 1.2 per cent in 1989–90 but from 1991 to 1994 it recovered to a rate of between seven and eight per cent, thanks to the artificial economic boom created by the demands of the UNTAC operation for services and housing.[128] Per capita income during that heady period was between US$150 and $240 annually.[129] Ominously, however, almost half of the national budget was donor-financed in 1993 and that situation did not change for at least another decade.

Given the extent of the country's dependence on foreign aid, policies and programmes designed to reinvigorate the economy after the formation of the new government in September 1993 were largely donor-driven. When the IMF loan was granted in October, the World Bank set four main goals for Cambodia's medium-term recovery: to maintain real annual growth rates of between seven and eight per cent, to reduce inflation to five per cent by 1995, to reduce the current account deficit to nine per cent of GDP by 1996, and to raise international reserves.[130]

Public finance reform commenced with the first national budget that was designed to fight inflation and to establish macroeconomic stability. Under new laws, the national treasury attempted to regain centralised control over tax revenues that had been in the hands of the provinces and ministries; in 1992, tax revenues had formed only 2.4 per cent of GDP, an extremely low ratio.[131] These efforts, however, met with such strong opposition from local business interests and entrenched patronage networks that the new minister for economy and finance himself was forced to leave office.

During most of the government's first term, from 1993 to mid-1997, the Cambodian economy did maintain an average annual growth rate of around seven per cent, thanks largely to expansion in the industrial sector and despite sluggish agricultural development. Total public revenues grew to between eight and ten per cent of GDP, still far too low to satisfy the World Bank that blamed the government failure to collect adequate revenue on a multitude of causes including inadequate implementation of the Law on Taxation, *ad hoc* tax and customs duty exemptions, weak capture of forestry revenues, and poor capacity in tax and customs administration. Public revenues were still heavily dependent on customs duties which provided between three and five per cent of GDP.[132]

The "two-headed" government that had somehow survived more than three and a half years of shared power collapsed completely in July 1997. The armed conflict combined with the effects of the Asian financial crisis to reduce GDP growth to between zero and one per cent for the following year. The riel, which was worth 2,769 to the U.S. dollar before the fighting, depreciated rapidly and was close to the 4,000 mark by June 1998. Aid freezes cost the government at least US$100 million and the tourist industry which had earned US$100 million in 1996 stood to lose at least one-quarter of that amount.[133] The budget faced a shortfall of almost US$60 million and the government cut its expenditures by one-fifth.[134]

One of the most serious consequences of the July coup was the termination of an IMF loan package worth US$120 million that was designed to support the central bank's monetary reserves. It was not the failure of the coalition government and the return to violence that led to this decision, however, but rather the Cambodian government's failure to increase the revenue ratio above the extremely low 9 per cent figure. The government was told to improve forestry management, restrain corruption, and adopt fiscal measures that would put the budget on a sound footing. Full implementation of the Law on Taxation and approval of strict regulations for the implementation of the Law on Investment, the government was told, would be essential conditions for further Fund programmes.[135]

Following elections in 1998, a new coalition government was formed and the economy started to recover. The IMF returned the following year and offered to resume payment on the loan in US$10 million increments, depending on Cambodia's compliance with the new poverty reduction strategy. An important reform measure adopted in 1999 was the 10 per cent value added tax (VAT) imposed initially on one thousand of the largest businesses operating in the country. During its first year, the VAT generated significant income for the government and revenues grew to 11.5 per cent. Other efforts in compliance with the IMF demands contributed to that growth while tight monetary discipline helped to control inflation and to keep the exchange rate stable. In 1999, Cambodia's total GDP was worth US$3 billion (up five per cent) and per capita GDP was measured at US$256.30.[136]

Inadequate banking institutions had long been a brake on both foreign investment and domestic savings. In November 1999, the National Assembly adopted the Law on Banking and Financial Institutions, accompanied by a number of *prakas* or regulatory orders concerning specialised rural credit banks, and licensing of commercial banks and microfinance institutions. In essence, the new law gave the National Bank of Cambodia (NBC) greater authority to supervise and control commercial banking in order to build confidence in the financial sector.

The plan dating back to the 1960s of establishing a rural credit scheme finally came to fruition with the creation of the Acleda Bank in 1993. It was granted a full commercial banking licence by the NBC at the end of 2003 by which time it had branches in 18 of the country's provinces and had lent more than US$245 million in loans that were considered too small and therefore unprofitable for the larger commercial banks to administer.[137] In addition to Acleda, many non-government organisations were operating rural credit programmes either as microfinance institutions (there were six licensed MFIs in 2004) or through self-help groups of villagers who operated their own savings and credit schemes. In March 2001, the Asian Development Bank finalised a US$20 million loan for microfinance purposes.

Conclusions

Throughout the 1990s, essential institutions were created and laws and regulations drafted and promulgated with a view to macroeconomic stabilisation. The UN-supervised elections, however, created a highly unstable political structure and it is inconceivable that any country could have developed under the kind of power-sharing arrangement that ruled Cambodia between 1993 and 1997. In the decade after the brief but violent clash between factional forces in July 1997, there was a return to traditional absolutism under the guise of electoral democracy. The government continued to work within the framework of institutional reform and the commitment to market liberalisation.

Economic reorganisation, however, had to deliver genuine reform. Whatever the political nature of the state, the Cambodian economy had to grow in order to provide jobs and acceptable living standards for the population that was growing at roughly 2.5 per cent each year. The starting point for that growth was very low and Cambodia had just emerged from two decades of war and relative isolation into a very changed world order where national economies served global markets and local industries could no longer expect protection from their own governments.

The recipe for growth, one drawn up and driven by major donors and the IFIs, was foreign investment, for the most part in labour intensive and export-oriented industries. While this form of capital investment promised few returns for government revenue in terms of corporate taxes and almost nothing for domestic profits and savings, it did create jobs and it earned needed foreign exchange through the sale of quotas, licences and so on. Income earned from foreign investment plus gradual reform in the public finance sector gradually allowed the government share of GDP to grow from only 2.4 per cent in 1992 to nine per cent by 1998, with targets set to raise it further to 13 per cent by the year 2000.[138]

As a result of institutional reforms, generous external aid, and foreign investment attracted with very liberal terms, the Cambodian economy grew at an average rate of 6.3 per cent before 1997. The July coup, however, and the Asian financial crisis combined with uncertainty about the 1998 general elections kept investor confidence weak and economic growth struggled below the six per cent mark until the resolution of the post-2003 election crisis. In the few years since then, the Cambodian economy has continued to grow strongly. In 2006, the World Bank measured that growth as 8.9 per cent, noting that it was one of the best performing economies in Asia, behind only China.[139] Consequently, the 2007 national budget, with US$1.155 billion to spend, allocated the health and education sectors more funds than any other government ministries, thus achieving the targets set for them in the early 1990s.[140]

Despite these very positive indicators, the Cambodian economy has become severely imbalanced. There is one economy for the capital, Phnom Penh, and the maritime port at Sihanoukville which is worked by paid labour, regulated by laws, codes and standards and integrated into a regional, even global system, and another for the rest of the country that still functions along traditional lines. As a direct consequence, the urban-rural wealth gap is widening. The government regularly claims a one per cent per year fall in poverty levels but other observers remain sceptical about these claims because they are not borne out by real growth in the agricultural sector on which poor villagers' livelihoods depend.[141]

Very little of the capital invested in Cambodia since 1992 has gone to agriculture and the aid money spent on rural projects has not reached all provinces, let alone all provinces equitably. The main socio-economic indicators, particularly those for life expectancy and infant mortality, suggest that little has changed in the countryside in the decade or so since the UNTAC operation arrived to democratise the country. Promises of benefits deriving from decentralisation through local governance institutions such as the commune council have not eventuated. Meanwhile, the rural environment has been severely affected by the encroachments of *laissez-faire* capitalism, especially in the form of forest logging concessions and fishing lots.

The rural economy is divorced from the urban economy except for the export of its surplus labour. In the city and the special economic zones around the port, factories produce goods destined for foreign markets with materials imported from other foreign markets. Their presence in the country depends on the supply of cheap, unskilled labour and preferential trade agreements stemming from Cambodia's status as a least developed country. Paradoxically, in order to develop, Cambodia has to remain poor. Furthermore, apart from the under-resourced rubber industry, the under-capitalised rice milling industry, the small tobacco industry, and some locally-owned factories involved in food and beverage processing, there is very little linkage between domestic primary production and secondary output.

The Cambodian economy at the end of a century of dramatic technological change and political upheavals, of radical attempts to reorganise it and alternately to isolate it from and then reintegrate it into wider marketing systems, has exhibited an admirable resilience to recover and to provide for the people's basic needs. In light of this well-practised habit, the final decade of the twentieth century, that of imposed "rehabilitation and reconstruction" and total immersion in the global liberal marketplace, far from representing the end of Cambodia's economic history, was only another attempt, a further conscious human effort, to create a modern economy.

CONCLUSION

Economic Outlook for the Twenty-first Century

The research for this economic history of Cambodia was completed, for the most part, by mid-2004. This was a convenient cut-off point as it marked one hundred years since the death of King Norodom I, the event which had signalled French determination to implement and enforce the terms and conditions of the two conventions already signed with the monarch rendering Cambodia a protectorate of the French colonial empire. More significantly, by 2004, Cambodia seemed to have effectively "turned the corner" from its status as a post-conflict society to one where some observers were beginning to speak in terms of its genuine transformation, both political and economic, into a stable, modern democratic state firmly aligned with other globalised neoliberal market-oriented economies. In fact, the Cambodian economy boomed after what was widely regarded as the final step in Prime Minister Hun Sen's consolidation of power over the ruling Cambodian People's Party and thus the state apparatus when, at the end of 2003, he aggressively and definitively asserted his authority over the conservative left faction within the party.[1]

The boom years from the beginning of 2004 to the final quarter of 2008 appeared to justify the efficacy of neoclassical/neoliberal economic theory and strategies as applied via the intervention of international financial institutions (IFIs) to developing countries like Cambodia whose economies had been seriously affected by decades of internal strife. Between 2005 and 2007 inclusive, Cambodia's real GDP growth averaged around 11 per cent; in 2005, it achieved 13.3 per cent, a growth rate second only to that of China.[2] Despite warnings by non-government commentators that the growth was narrowly based on the textiles and clothing industry, tourism, and the construction sector, all of which were particularly vulnerable to exogenous shocks, and that the profits of development had been unevenly distributed so that rural poverty had hardly eased over the preceding decade, all the key economic indicators pointed to further robust growth.

With the wisdom of hindsight, regular citizens and economic policy makers and planners alike may discern the early tremors and warning signs of the sudden bust of global financial markets that occurred in the final quarter of 2008. While in developed western countries there had been some concern over the ever-escalating level of personal debt, spurred on by easy access to cheap loans, and the concurrent boom in real estate property prices, in Cambodia, too, the rush to speculate in land, fluctuations in the price of gold which reached an absolute high of one thousand dollars an ounce in May, along with rising food prices and unusually high inflation that peaked at 26 per cent around mid-year had further exacerbated the widening gulf between the few very rich and the many poor.[3] By the end of the first quarter of 2009, the ramifications of the credit crisis for the so-called "real" economy were being felt around the world. Leading economic specialists were unwilling to predict how deep or how long the recession would persist, or how well, or even if, the institutions so familiar to the neoliberal marketplace would weather the storm.

While the Cambodian economy experienced several shocks after rehabilitation commenced in 1993, it had yet to experience a recession serious enough to assess the ideological foundations on which that rehabilitation was built. Throughout the 1990s, Cambodia had been a political and economic laboratory for testing ideas about political transition and economic development: from a command to *laissez-faire* capitalist economy, from large to small bureaucracy, from domestic to export-oriented production, and so on. Cambodia's compliance with the demands of the IFIs to adjust the structures of its national administration in accordance with small but "good" governance stipulations so that market forces could operate with maximum freedom had to be supported and guaranteed by generous grants and soft loans from those same IFIs. Thanks to these buffers, the Cambodian economy was largely sheltered from the Asian financial crisis of 1997–98; the sharp downturn in the economy that year had more to do with repercussions from the July 1997 coup than with the regional financial collapse. The high degree of dollarisation also protected the national currency from the worst effects of that crisis as it played out in other regional countries, while preferential treatment awarded to its garment exports was an incentive for foreign investors to maintain their enterprises in Cambodia. In 2008, however, the situation was markedly different. The 2008 financial crisis originated in the U.S.A., the chief market for the garments and footwear manufactured in the foreign-owned factories located in and around Phnom Penh that are worked by Cambodian labour. Consequently, as the economic situation in America worsened, so did the economic outlook for Cambodia and its dollar dependent riel, causing many observers to question the soundness of the structural changes that the economy had undergone over the previous 15 years.

The Global Financial Stability Report that was released by the International Monetary Fund (IMF) in April 2009 stated baldly that "the withdrawal of foreign investors and banks together with the collapse in export markets create funding pressures in emerging market economies that require urgent attention."[4] The report warned that as recessions tend to be deeper and longer lasting when associated with a financial crisis not only would net private capital flows to emerging markets be negative in 2009 but also that "inflows are not likely to return to their pre-crisis levels in the future." The general advice from the IMF was for governments to initiate fiscal stimulus packages and to improve financial regulation and supervision.

Just one month prior to the release of that major report, an IMF mission visited Phnom Penh to review what it termed "recent economic and financial developments."[5] It noted that construction activity and foreign investment were slowing rapidly, that garment exports were under serious pressure, and that the tourist arrival growth rate had reversed. Ominously, while agriculture had performed better than anticipated the previous year, the mission predicted that the fall in global agricultural prices would have an impact on farmer incomes in 2009. The only positive note in the mission's statement was that inflation would probably fall back to single digits, in line with lower oil and food prices and weakening consumer demand. The mission estimated that real GDP would fall by 0.5 per cent, although it admitted that the drop might, in fact, be worse and that the outlook for the years 2010 and 2011 was "uncertain." Its recommendation to the Cambodian government was to allow the deficit to rise to 4.75 per cent of GDP with spending focused on "pro-poor social outlays and safety nets and high-quality infrastructure projects that would strengthen competitiveness." It further urged the government to continue strengthening its tax administration efforts in order not to erode its already low revenue base.

Although estimates vary according to sources, real GDP growth for Cambodia is projected to be 6.5 per cent in 2008 and 4.75 per cent in 2009, which is certainly disappointing compared with average growth of 11 per cent over the previous five years, but still better than that of some other countries at a comparable level of development.[6] Nevertheless, Cambodians, particularly young people aged between 15 and 24 who make up almost one-quarter of the total population, can expect to experience unemployment, dislocation and increasing anxiety as the economic catastrophe unfolds. As mentioned previously, Cambodia needs to maintain a minimum of 6 per cent growth in order to provide opportunities for job seekers leaving school. Given the economy's job dependence on garment exports and foreign direct investment for sustained growth in the construction sector, and the major contraction in both those sectors, it is obvious that jobs will be very difficult to find and that young job-seekers will be faced with difficult choices.

The garment and textile industry in Cambodia is particularly vulnerable. Almost all of the capital involved in the industry is foreign-owned; Taiwan owns one-quarter of all the factories and Hong Kong, China and South Korea, together, account for around one-half.[7] As jobs are lost in home countries, the allocation for jobs elsewhere will inevitably shrink. In an effort to sustain production, the Cambodian government has responded by suspending its tax on factory expenditures, but this is surely a self-defeating measure that will ultimately affect general revenue.

As well as the garment factories, the construction industry has generated jobs for thousands of young rural workers, thereby supplementing the incomes of their families and easing the burden of rural poverty. As an almost immediate response to the financial crisis, however, more than 30 per cent of construction jobs either evaporated or were scaled back.[8] To date, about three-quarters of the construction sector has been funded by foreign investors; for the rest, the Cambodia Institute of Development Study notes, a regulation of the National Bank of Cambodia limiting bank lending to the property sector to 15 per cent of the bank's total loan portfolio has made it difficult for local developers to access finance to complete projects. As a combined result, property prices plummeted by around 25 per cent in the last half of 2008 and more construction projects were cancelled or scaled back.

The tourist industry is notoriously susceptible to sudden global economic downturns, to rumours of health epidemics and even to the whims of fashion. Tourism, however, was one of the pillars on which Cambodia built its post-1993 economy. In 2008, 2.1 million international tourists visited Cambodia, earning the sector around US$1.62 billion.[9] The unprecedented growth in tourism drove the rapid rise in property prices and the construction boom in and around the main sites and venues located in Siem Reap, Phnom Penh, and Sihanoukville. The small and medium enterprises that cater to the construction and tourist industries, such as building materials outlets, transport companies, tourist agencies, *tuk tuk* drivers and *motodaps*, will be adversely affected by the turn-around in economic activity, although they will undoubtedly prove to be more resilient than the big investors. Family-owned and operated small businesses still typify the national economy; traditionally, they rely on their own capital or have only minimal borrowings from banks or other money-lenders.

Similarly, while the agriculture sector generally may suffer from a drop in commodity prices as a result of global recession, it seems likely that food crop producers will be the last and least affected by the crisis. Like the small and medium retail, processing and industrial enterprises, the crops sector has benefited very little from foreign investment. In fact, from some perspectives, Cambodia's quest for foreign direct investment has had chiefly deleterious effects on the farming economy. The most disturbing impact of the recent boom in property prices has been on family-scale agriculture. Throughout the country, but most particularly in those areas close to the city and to major tourist venues, farmers have been squeezed out by property development. In some cases, agricultural land has been confiscated by powerful political parties backed by military force. During the timber boom, farmers lost access to forests and other natural resources, while common land was increasingly incorporated into private holdings. All of this, along with population pressure on land and the division of family property into ever-smaller plots, has kept rural poverty levels virtually unchanged even through those periods when GDP growth rates were registered in double-digit figures.

There is no social security net for unemployed, dispossessed Cambodians. Moreover, there are few charitable institutions or other mass organisations that can provide relief for them. Therefore, when the full force of the global recession hits the Cambodian economy, those most affected by it, namely the retrenched garment workers and the short-hire, minimally skilled construction workers, along with job-seeking school leavers, and the underemployed in the shrinking tourist industry will turn either to the informal sector in the towns to sustain their livelihood or they will return to the village and the family farm, if it still exists or if its capacity will still support them. Others will seek paid employment abroad, if possible, as emigrant workers and more may follow them as they find it too difficult to readjust to life in the countryside.

These, then, are the most urgent challenges for the immediate future: to create job opportunities, especially for youth; to maintain current standards of health and education services; and to ensure political stability and security. It is inconceivable that the Cambodian economy will revert either to the command type of the period 1975 to 1989 or to a pre-capitalist, semi-subsistence type that persisted before the revolution. At the same time, however, the gains made since 1993 must be maintained. As every other crisis in Cambodia's modern history has demonstrated, it has been the resilience of the traditional rice farmer that has brought the economy back from the brink of total collapse. Undoubtedly, this will again be the case, but the Cambodian rice farmer who dominates at least 90 per cent of the agriculture sector, deserves some assistance to fulfil this task.

At the 2008 international donors' meeting held in Phnom Penh in December, almost twice the regular annual sum of assistance was pledged, or US$951 million. It is expected that this added bonus will be used as a stimulus package and invested in national infrastructure projects. Should a large percentage of this package be spent on irrigation infrastructure, improved distribution and marketing facilities, and credit facilitation for local rice milling operations, Cambodian agriculture might finally achieve its long-term goal of modernisation.

Cambodia will survive the current global financial crisis. In the longer term, however, the national economy will have to respond and adapt to greater and more intractable challenges. Climate change will necessitate genuine commitment to fulfilling national policies on natural resources management. During the 1990s, Cambodia squandered its precious forests with little benefit to the treasury and with serious consequences for the environment and the economy. When climate change affects the delicate balance of ice and melt that regulates the tides of the Mekong, and when population pressure and resultant consumer demand for power and irrigation upstream interfere with natural flow through water capture and harvest, how will Cambodia, with its economy still largely based on agriculture and agro-processing, fare?

To a large extent, the answer depends on the sort of relations that Cambodia can forge with the other countries in the sub-Mekong basin and especially with China. Incorporation into the family of Southeast Asian nations was heralded with joy and relief when Cambodia became the tenth member of ASEAN, and despite occasional rifts with Thailand ostensibly over ownership of Preah Vihear temple and the ever-present suspicion of Vietnam's intentions along the border, ASEAN membership will continue to be an important plank in Cambodia's ongoing economic development. The economic effects of the growing influence of China in the region, however, will be of greater concern throughout the century. Since

2005, China and South Korea have emerged as the dominant investors in the Cambodian economy. In that year, together, they accounted for 74.2 per cent of all foreign direct investment, with South Korea as the main investor; in 2008, by the time of the crash in November, China had surpassed all others, providing 61.7 per cent of FDI to Cambodia, with South Korea in second place with 34.7 per cent. Thus, together, they accounted for 96.4 per cent of all foreign investment; none of the other investors reached even one per cent.[10] This is hardly an ideal situation for a small, aid-dependent nation with low levels of domestic savings and capital. As further proof of South Korea's increasingly dominant role in Cambodia's economic development, an agreement with the Korea Exchange was announced in September 2007 to open a Cambodian stock market by the end of 2010. The Securities and Exchange Commission of Cambodia was launched in April 2009 to establish disclosure and capitalisation guidelines for companies planning to list on the proposed stock exchange.[11]

Protecting national security and ensuring Cambodia's political stability will, naturally, be essential for further economic growth. Given the political turbulence of the twentieth century, and the critical challenges of this century, no one can be sure what will happen when the present generation of leaders exits the scene, or when the CPP loses its ascendancy, but it is certain that both the likelihood and the degree of political turmoil resulting from such changes will be determined by the nature and the state of the economy. Economics, as Francis Fukuyama reminds us, "is grounded in social life and cannot be understood separately from the larger question of how modern societies organize themselves. It is the arena in which modern recognition struggles play themselves out."[12]

Few would argue with Cambodian economist, Ear Sophal's assertion that politics in Cambodia is predicated on power and money: the more wealth a leader possesses, the more status is accorded him and, by corollary, the more power one has, the greater are the opportunities for accruing wealth.[13] He also underscores the paradox that Cambodia has grown rapidly in recent years despite lacklustre governance, noting that the country appears to be slipping even further down the Corruption Perception Index, ranking 162 out of 179 countries in 2007, and that tax revenues remain at abysmal levels, "on par with Niger, Tanzania, and Togo." For him, the tax collection system, characterised as it is by informal payments or "bribe taxes" that are off budget, serves only to weaken state capacity and to strengthen the culture of patronage. It demonstrates, he says, that "authorities do not need a modern rational bureaucracy, just loyalty in the chain of hierarchy."

The persistent and all-pervasive patronage system is indeed irrational. How is it possible, then, to argue that economic transformation, engineered according to ultra-rationalist neoclassical economic theory, has taken place? Caroline Hughes and Un Kheang point to several positive outcomes of Prime Minister Hun Sen's consolidation of power in 2003, adding that Cambodia's political institutions are now significantly better developed and more predictable than they were ten years ago.[14] They use the term "economic transformation" guardedly, to describe the current context only, noting that it represents "a visible change in the level and nature of economic activities from the 1990s to the 2000s." Nevertheless, they are confident that the global financial crisis will cause only a slowdown in the transformation process, not a reversal of the transformations wrought over the past five years:

> … [P]eace and stability seem better assured and the government is pursuing an altered course, which is focused less on exploiting the illegality made possible by state weakness and more on guaranteeing market returns, not only to military and political elites, but also to investors from across the region and the world.

It must be reiterated that no one argues that a return to past practices is likely; on the other hand, not all analysts are comfortable with the generous sweep of the term "transformation." At the peak of Cambodia's boom, in late 2005 when GDP growth rates were at an all-time high, respected economist Sok Hach lamented that "[t]he structure and embedded political tradition has limited economic growth coupled with high economic aid stalling necessary internal economic competition."[15] Furthermore, he doubted the authenticity of the political reforms, noting that the country was democratising "not from a desire for genuine reform, but in response to the imperatives of aid dependency." The civil administration reform, he argued, had only created a more complex system with more over-lapping committees but "the fundamental and systemic cause of administrative dysfunctions relates to the maintained patronage system that Cambodia does not seem to be able to relinquish." He proposed that the patronage system stifled competition in the private sector, because smaller businesses were at an unfair disadvantage due to the concentration of enterprises owned and controlled by just a few people with close ties to the leadership. Consequently, the owners of small and medium enterprises have no influence on economic policymaking, and instead, face ongoing problems that can hardly be resolved by weak legal institutions.

While, for the most part, Sok Hach's arguments are convincing, his assumption that the Cambodian private sector has "a massive potential" to contribute to sustainable growth and poverty reduction provided that the patronage system releases its grip on economic policy-making may be over-stated. The garment industry, for instance, foreign-owned and largely unaffected by the patronage system, has not proved to be a catalyst for further light manufacturing or any other economic activity beyond an increase in the number of small retail outlets for seconds and discards from the factory floor. Given the basic preconditions of peace, political stability and an encouraging global economic environment, the private sector, in general, will no doubt continue to grow and to contribute further to economic development, but the scale of enterprises within the sector will remain as small or as large as individual families can manage. This is the traditional habit of small and medium enterprise in Cambodia. The same holds true for agricultural activity. There is little scope for the development of modern, large-scale corporations on the scale of, say, Sony or Hyundai, on which national economic growth could be based.

For an historian, it is intriguing to illustrate the parallels of the current situation with Cambodia's other short-lived "Golden Age" of stability and prosperity that existed between 1956 and 1961. In her seminal paper on the economy of the *Sangkum Reastr Niyum* (SRN), Laura Summers posited that "in matters of economy, ... status considerations rather than market conditions or impersonal economic needs, were paramount in government policy making and economic practices."[16] In other words, throughout that period when Sihanouk believed he was engineering economic transformation, in fact, in the view of the ruling elite, "the flow of goods, services and money inside the country was most properly subordinated to and submerged within the patterns of deference, consumption and largess in Khmer society."[17] As in the boom years of 2004–8, the prosperity of the early years of the SRN was aid dependent. When Sihanouk terminated the flow of American aid in 1963, it was not the rich but rather the poor peasants who suffered the consequences. Their gradual exclusion from the rural status order, Laura Summers suggests, contributed to the emergence of a "class situation" by the late 1960s, while "exclusiveness in industrial employment practices and slow expansion in industry promoted a deep sense of grievance among the young." No one would suggest that Cambodia is likely to undergo another abortive attempt at social revolution, but the similarities with the not-so-distant past are a cause for reflection on the peculiarities of Cambodian culture that give rise to crises of this sort.

Therefore, in general, I accept the assessment that during the five years from 2004 to 2008, the Cambodian economy grew in a way that suggested the changes deliberately made to institutions and infrastructure in the preceding decade were positive and long-lasting, and that these changes represented "transformation" insofar as the situation was more stable and more predictable than it had been throughout the 1990s. It is undeniable, however, that this development came about despite lacklustre governance and actually increasing levels of official corruption. Official corruption is symptomatic of the persistent and all-pervasive patronage system that not only hinders the establishment of a rational bureaucracy but also acts as a brake on genuine economic competitiveness and therefore on the potential for growth of the private sector. Furthermore, as modern Cambodian history shows, an economic crisis, such as the one precipitated by the termination of U.S. aid in November 1963 or the current one, is insufficient motivation to change old habits of governance, however irrational they are or how disastrous the consequences of intransigence might be.

The persistence of the patronage system is, of course, intricately tied to the web of social relations, habits and mores that constitute Cambodian culture, and since economic life is embedded in social life, it cannot be divorced from culture. Francis Fukuyama advises that one of the most important lessons we can learn from an examination of economic life is that a nation's well-being, as well as its ability to compete, is conditioned by a single, pervasive cultural characteristic: the level of trust inherent in the society.[18] He warns that modern institutions are a necessary but insufficient condition for national prosperity; they must be combined with certain social and ethical habits if they are to work properly:

> Societies that have very strong families but relatively weak bonds of trust among people unrelated to one another will tend to be dominated by small, family-owned and managed businesses. On the other hand, countries that have vigorous private nonprofit organizations ... are also likely to develop strong private economic institutions that go beyond the family.[19]

This description, as Fukuyama intended, most readily applies to overseas Chinese societies and, as elsewhere in the Southeast Asian region, Chinese families also dominate the small and medium enterprise sector in Cambodian economic life. These Chinese family businesses sometimes have extended networks throughout the region, with trust forged by family or clan bonds. Although Khmer participation in commercial activity has increased markedly since 1990, Khmer entrepreneurs typically owe their success not to family ties, which tend to be weak beyond the nuclear unit, but rather to political patronage. The patronage system, in effect, forges trust in a low-trust society, a cultural characteristic of Cambodia that surely pre-dated the Pol Pot regime. It effectively marries power and wealth and distributes the benefits of both in ever-diminishing returns down the hierarchy, the *khsae* or strings that tie the beneficiaries to their individual patron. The demands of reciprocity are real and understood. It goes without saying, therefore, that the rise and fall of entrepreneurs has less to do with commercial skill and diligence than with political favours. In such conditions, it is difficult to accept that genuine transformation has occurred in the Cambodian economy.

The antidote to all this, as Fukuyama and the long line of specialists in moral economy back to Adam Smith prescribe, is a rich and complex civil society. It is still far too early to predict whether the multitude of non-government organisations that emerged in Cambodia throughout the 1990s will fulfil this Herculean task, but a beginning has been made.

Notes

Preface

1. Charles Robequain, *The Economic Development of French Indo-China* (London: Oxford University Press, 1944).
2. Jean Delvert, *Le Paysan Cambodgien* (Paris: L'Harmattan, 1994).
3. Rémy Prud'homme, *L'Économie du Cambodge* (Paris: Presses Universitaires de France, 1969).
4. Delvert, *Le Paysan* ..., p. 9.
5. Prud'homme, *L'Économie* ..., p. 11.
6. Extracts from Hou Yuon's dissertation, "*La paysannerie du Cambodge et ses projets de modernisation*," University of Paris, 1955 and Hu Nim's, "Land Tenure and Social Structure in Kampuchea," University of Phnom Penh, 1965, in *Peasants and Politics in Kampuchea, 1942–1981*, ed. Ben Kiernan and Boua Chanthou (London: Zed Press, 1982).
7. *Bulletin Bi-Hebdomadaire, Chambre Mixte de Commerce et d'Agriculture du Cambodge*. Copies held in the State Archives of Cambodia (ANC), Boxes 144–73.

Introduction

1. Asian Development Bank, Technical Assistance Report, "Preparing the Tonle Sap Lowland Stabilization Project," December 2005. ADB website <http://www.adb.org/Documents/TARs/CAM/37287-CAM-TAR.pdf> [accessed 16 May 2006].
2. Delvert, *Le Paysan* ..., p. 387.
3. Ibid., p. 357.
4. These figures applied in 2000, before the national commune elections of 2002.
5. National Institute of Statistics (NIS), *General Population Census of Cambodia 1998: Final Census Results*, Ministry of Planning, Phnom Penh, July 1999.
6. Article 1, Chapter 1, *The Constitution of the Kingdom of Cambodia* (as amended on 4 March 1999).
7. Ibid., p. 10.
8. NIS, Cambodia: *Statistical Yearbook 2000* (Phnom Penh: Ministry of Planning, February 2001), p. 1.
9. Delvert, *Le Paysan* ..., p. 24.

10 Centre for Advanced Study, "Interdisciplinary Research on Ethnic Groups in Cambodia: final draft reports," Phnom Penh, July 1996, p. 109.
11 ADB, "Indigenous Peoples, Ethnic Minorities and Poverty Reduction," Manila, June 2002, pp. 5–6. The figures are supported by a table entitled "Indigenous Peoples Identified by Language Spoken" sourced from the National Population Census of 1998 and based on 17 language groups. The data in the table include indigenous groups in the five northeastern provinces only.
12 United Nations Development Program, *Human Development Report 2000* (Oxford: Oxford University Press, 2000).
13 NIS, *Report on the Cambodia Socio-Economic Survey 1999*, Ministry of Planning, Phnom Penh. The "poverty line" refers to the commonly used World Bank income/consumption measure that defines as extremely poor those adults who cannot afford to consume the benchmark per capita calorie requirement of 2,100 calories per day plus a small measure for essentials such as shelter and clothing. Commonly, this is understood to refer to those who survive on less than US$1 per day. In Cambodia's case, however, the benchmark is set at around 50 U.S. cents. Separate calculations for Phnom Penh, Other Urban Areas and Rural Areas of Cambodia give benchmark figures of 1,629 riels, 1,214 riels and 1,036 riels respectively. These calculations were made in 1998 when the official exchange rate was 3,807.8 riels per U.S. dollar.
14 *Cambodia Poverty Assessment*, Ministry of Planning, Phnom Penh, December 1999, p. 1.
15 NIS, *Report on the Cambodia Socio-Economic Survey 1999*, Ministry of Planning, Phnom Penh, p. 49.
16 *Cambodia Human Development Report 1998: Women's Contribution to Development*, Ministry of Planning, Phnom Penh, p. iv.
17 *Poverty and Vulnerability Analysis Mapping in Cambodia: summary report*, Ministry of Planning and United Nations World Food Programme, Phnom Penh, March 2003, p. 6.
18 Chan Sophal, Martin Godfrey, *et al.*, *Cambodia: The Challenge of Productive Employment Creation*, Working Paper 8, CDRI, Phnom Penh, January 1999, p. 39.
19 Kay Kimsong, "UN Report Says Wealth Disparity is Growing," *The Cambodia Daily*, 29–30 May 2004.
20 Figures are extrapolated from those presented by the "NGO Parallel Report on Implementation of the International Covenant on Economic, Social and Cultural Rights," August 2002, and from *Cambodia Economic Watch*, p. 40.
21 *Report on the Assessment of the Functional Literacy Levels of the Adult Population in Cambodia*, Ministry of Education, Youth and Sports, Phnom Penh, May 2000.
22 Ibid., p. viii.
23 Kang Chandararot and Chan Sophal, *Cambodia's Annual Economic Review*, CDRI, Phnom Penh, September 2003, pp. 82–3.

24 Sok Hach et al., "Prospects for the Cambodian Economy in 2000," CDRI, Phnom Penh, 16 February 2000, p. 12.
25 Ibid.
26 As a sharp reminder of the vagaries of the Cambodian climate, extremely favourable conditions allowed the agricultural sector to recover markedly in 2003 with 8.2 per cent growth; paddy production alone increased by 26.9 per cent. Oum Sothea and Sok Hach, *Cambodia Economic Watch*, EIC, pp. 6–7.
27 NIS, *Statistical Yearbook 2000*, p. 80. Data from *Agricultural Statistics Bulletin*, MAFF.
28 Patrick Falby, "Agro-industry: promise versus delivery," *Phnom Penh Post*, 5–18 July 2002, p. 7.
29 Carsten Stormer and Chea Sotheacheath, "Jute factory closes, at a cost of five hundred jobs," *Phnom Penh Post*, 31 March–13 April 2000.
30 In 1995, the four nations of the Lower Mekong Basin: Cambodia, Laos, Thailand and Vietnam signed the landmark "Agreement on Cooperation for the Sustainable Development of the Mekong River Basin" that has the status of an international treaty. The signatories agreed to cooperate in development and management of the river basin and its resources, including navigation, flood control, fisheries, agriculture, power production, and environmental protection. See Joern Kristensen, "Cooperation Key to Fair Mekong Development," *The Cambodia Daily*, 11 July 2001.
31 Joern Kristensen, "Poor Depend on Sound Management of Mekong Fisheries," *The Cambodia Daily*, 8 April 2003.
32 Matt McKinney, "Logging a Major Issue as Donor Meeting Begins," *The Cambodia Daily*, 19 June 2002.
33 NIS, *Statistical Yearbook 2000*, p. 186.
34 Wency Leung, "Cambodia's Economic Growth Lags," *The Cambodia Daily*, 21 April 2004.
35 Sok Hach et al., "Prospects …," p. 8.
36 Timothy Wheeler, "Scrappy garment industry making gains in post-quota environment," *Phnom Penh Post*, 15–28 July 2005, p. 8.
37 NIS, *Statistical Yearbook 2000*, p. 172. Data from Ministry of Interior and EIC, p. 12.
38 Chan Sophal et al., *Land Tenure in Cambodia: a data update*, Working Paper 19, CDRI, Phnom Penh, October 2001, p. 5.
39 Ibid., p. 26. The Mekong River Commission study of 1995–96 showed 24 per cent, both NIS and CASD/WFP studies of 1997 reported 10 per cent, and the 1998 WFP target survey calculated 17 per cent. Studies in 1999 by WFP and FAO reported a landlessness rate in rural Cambodia of over 20 per cent. Chan Sophal et al. (CDRI Working Paper 19) warn there is a huge inconsistency in the parameters generated from the different data sets on variables relating to land.

40 Robin Biddulph, "Interim Report on findings of Landlessness and Development Information Tool (LADIT) research, September 1999–April 2000," Oxfam, Phnom Penh, 15 June 2000, p. 6.
41 In September 1999, the Prime Minister issued an eleven-point order to halt "anarchical" land grabbing. Civil society groups that provide legal aid reported that half of all their civil cases involved land disputes. See Toshiyasu Kato et al., *Cambodia: Enhancing Governance* …, fn. 12.
42 Sik Boreak, *Land Ownership, Sales and Concentration in Cambodia: a preliminary review of secondary data and primary data from four recent surveys*, Working Paper 16, CDRI, Phnom Penh, September 2000, p. 13.
43 Ibid., p. 21.
44 Lor Chandara, "Protection Decree for Tonle Sap Lake Signed," *The Cambodia Daily*, 13 March 2001.
45 NIS, *Statistical Yearbook 2000*, p. 181. Data from Ministry of Economy and Finance.
46 Sok Hach et al., "Prospects …," p. 13.
47 William Shaw, "PM Paints Positive Picture at UN Summit," *The Cambodia Daily*, 17–18 September 2005.
48 Martin Godfrey, "How Important is External Assistance to Cambodia?" *Phnom Penh Post*, 31 March–13 April 2000.
49 Sok Hach et al., "Prospects …," p. 4.
50 Erik Wasson, "Chinese Chamber Leader says investment is just profit-driven," *The Cambodia Daily*, 12 August 2005.
51 Sok Hach et al., "Prospects …," p. 13.
52 Oum Sothea and Sok Hach, *Cambodia Economic Watch*, EIC, p. 36.
53 Patrick Falby, "Questions over repaying Cambodia's debt," *Phnom Penh Post*, 29 August–11 September 2003.
54 Oum Sothea and Sok Hach, *Cambodia Economic Watch*, EIC, p. 36.
55 NIS, *Statistical Yearbook 2000*, pp. 180–1. Data from Ministry of Economy and Finance.
56 Sok Hach et al., "Prospects …," p. 11. In 2002, revenue from the consumption tax exceeded that from customs duties and accounted for 40 per cent of total tax revenue. See, CDRI *Cambodia's Annual Economic Review* (2002), p. 18.
57 Ibid., p. 12.
58 World Bank, "Cambodia Country Assistance Strategy," p. 7.
59 Sok Hach et al., "Prospects …," p. 9.
60 World Bank, "Cambodia Country Assistance Strategy," p. 52.
61 Sok Hach et al., "Prospects …," p. 10.
62 World Bank, "Cambodia Country Assistance Strategy," p. 52.
63 David Kihara, "Bank Official: Cambodian Microfinancing Rates Too High," *The Cambodia Daily*, 18 July 2001. This account explains that the ADB offers the loan to the Ministry of Finance at one per cent per annum (1.5 per cent after eight years) which lends the money to the Rural Development Bank at approximately seven per cent. The RDB distributes it among microfinancing

institutions at 11 per cent and they disburse to farmers at rates between 24–60 per cent per annum.

64   Oum Sothea and Sok Hach, *Cambodia Economic Watch*, EIC, p. 29.

Chapter 1

1. *The French in Indo-China: with a narrative of Garnier's exploration in Cochin-china, Annam and Tonkin* (Bangkok: White Lotus, 2000), p. 90.
2. Zhou Daguan, *The Customs of Cambodia*, third edition (Bangkok: The Siam Society, 1993), p. 69.
3. Ibid., p. 21.
4. Ibid., p. 43.
5. Ibid.
6. Ibid., p. 45.
7. Gabriel Quiroga da San Antonio, *A Brief and Truthful Relation of Events in the Kingdom of Cambodia* (Bangkok: White Lotus, 1998).
8. Ibid., p. 8.
9. Ibid., p. 6.
10. Ibid., p. 101.
11. In his doctoral dissertation, David Chandler suggests that Thailand already exercised *de facto* jurisdiction over these *srok* "simply because they were able to do so, once the Cambodian administration had become so far off, so fragmented and so weak." See "Cambodia Before the French: politics in a tributary kingdom 1794–1848," Doctoral Thesis, University of Michigan, 1973, p. 79.
12. Ibid., p. 132.
13. Ibid., p. 144.
14. Ibid., p. 185.
15. Ibid., p. 103, fn. 10.
16. Ibid., p. 33.
17. Henri Mouhot, *Travels in Siam, Cambodia and Laos 1858–1860* (Singapore: Oxford University Press, 1992), pp. 20–1.
18. Ibid., p. 226.
19. Ibid., p. 236.
20. Ibid., p. 275.
21. Ibid., p. 277.
22. Ibid.
23. Ibid., p. 83.
24. Louis de Carné, *Travels on the Mekong: Cambodia, Laos and Yunnan* (Bangkok: White Lotus, 2000), p. 7.
25. Ibid., p. 38.
26. Ibid., p. 47.
27. Ibid., p. 99.
28. *The French in Indo-China* ...

29 Ibid., p. 124.
30 Edward Said, *Culture and Imperialism* (London: Vintage, 1994), p. 269.
31 Ibid., p. 204.
32 E.J. Hobsbawn, *The Age of Empire 1875–1914* (London: Weidenfeld and Nicolson, 1987), p. 71.
33 Theodore Zeldin, *France 1848–1945, Vol. 1, ambition, love and politics*. Alan Bullock and F.W.D. Deakin, general editors, *The Oxford History of Modern Europe* (Oxford: Clarendon Press, 1973), p. 940.
34 Virginia Thompson, *French Indo-China* (New York: Macmillan, 1937), p. 393.
35 An interpretation of the differing polities of Cambodia and Vietnam in historical perspective is given by Martin Stuart-Fox, *Buddhist Kingdom Marxist State: the Making of Modern Laos* (Bangkok: White Lotus, 1996), chapter 1.
36 Robequain, *The Economic Development of French Indo-China*, p. 48.
37 Ibid.
38 Milton E. Osborne, *The French Presence in Cochinchina and Cambodia* (Bangkok: White Lotus, 1997), p. 54.
39 For a discussion of these changes, see Osborne, *The French Presence…*, chapter 9.
40 The eleven articles of the Convention of 17 June 1884 are reproduced in Paul Collard, *Cambodge et Cambodgiens: métamorphose du royaume khmer par une méthode française de protectorat* (Phnom Penh: Cedoreck, 2001), pp. 110–1.
41 Osborne, *The French Presence…*, p. 238.
42 Collard, *Cambodge et Cambodgiens*, p. 136.
43 Henri Locard, "A Brief Overview of the History of Commune Elections," *Phnom Penh Post*, 1–14 February 2002.
44 Thompson, *French Indo-China*, p. 425.
45 Ibid., p. 394.
46 Ibid.
47 Ibid., p. 250.
48 ANC RSC File 5905, *Minute du Livre Vert, Cambodge*, "*Rapport sur l'Exercice du Protectorat*," 1931–32.
49 For details, see David Chandler, "The Assassination of Résident Bardez (1925): a premonition of revolt in colonial Cambodia," in *Facing the Cambodian Past* (Chiang Mai: Silkworm Books, 1996), pp. 139–58.
50 ANC RSC File 230569, *Indigenous Politics*, "Circular of the Governor-General of Indochina to chiefs of local administration," 12 September 1931.
51 Ibid., Confidential letter from Résident Supérieur Cambodge to Gouverneur-Général, Saigon, No. 771/F.X., 30 September 1931.
52 Prud'homme, *L'Économie du Cambodge*, p. 250.
53 Louis Cros, *L'Indochine Française Pour Tous* (Paris: Albin Michel, undated), p. 16.
54 ANC RSC File 2799, "*Rapport sur la situation de Cambodge, 1927–1928*."

55   Jacqueline Desbarats, *Prolific Survivors: Population Change in Cambodia 1975–1993* (Arizona State University, Program for Southeast Asian Studies, 1995), p. 31.
56   Robequain, *The Economic Development of French Indo-China*, p. 24.
57   Figures in this paragraph are taken from Robequain, *The Economic Development of French Indo-China*, chapter 1.
58   Official statistics for 1948, quoted by Jacqueline Desbarats, *Prolific Survivors*, p. 31.
59   Collard, *Cambodge et Cambodgiens*, p. 62.
60   Ibid., p. 249.
61   Ibid., p. 195.
62   Ibid., p. 47.
63   Ibid., p. 193.
64   ANC RSC File 8218, "A confidential report on the material and spiritual situation of the Tonkinese émigrés employed on the plantations of the *Compagnie du Cambodge* and the *Syndicat de Mimot*," by Delamarre, *Inspection des Affaires Politiques et Administratives*, 28 April 1927.
65   David Ayres, *Anatomy of a Crisis: Education, Development and the State in Cambodia, 1953–1998* (Honolulu: University of Hawai'i Press, 2000), p. 24.
66   Collard, *Cambodge et Cambodgiens*, p. 187.
67   Prud'homme, *L'Économie du Cambodge*, p. 277.
68   Ayres, *Anatomy of a Crisis*, p. 25.
69   Nicholas Tarling, *Nations and States in Southeast Asia* (Cambridge: Cambridge University Press, 1998), p. 75.
70   Collard, *Cambodge et Cambodgiens*, p. 77.
71   James C. Scott, *Moral Economy of the Peasant: Rebellion and Subsistence in Southeast Asia* (New Haven: Yale University Press, 1976).
72   Ibid., p. 77.
73   Ibid., p. 261.
74   Ibid., p. 243.
75   ANC RSC File 12240, *Arrêté No. 1314 fixant les conditions de concession aux français des terrains domaniaux du Cambodge*, 26 August 1899.
76   ANC RSC File 13948, *ORs et arrêtés de la RSC*.
77   *Gouvernement général, Journal Officiel de l'Indochine Française*, 39th year, No. 57, Saturday 16 July 1927.
78   ANC RSC File 2799, 1928, "*Rapport sur la situation du Cambodge, 1927–1928*."
79   Ibid., Preparation of *Livre Vert*, Section II, "*Concessions Domaniales*."
80   Hou Yuon, "*La paysannerie du Cambodge et ses projets de modernisation*," Doctoral Thesis, University of Paris, 1955, in *Peasants and Politics ...*, pp. 34–68.
81   Ibid., p. 36.
82   Ibid., p. 37.
83   Ibid.

84 ANC RSC File 8982, "Preparation of *Livre Vert*, 1938–39."
85 Ibid.
86 Ibid.
87 ANC RSC File 15688, Protectorate of Cambodia, "Regulations relative to the distribution of incentives and bonuses for agriculture and raising domestic animals and horses," 26 September 1905.
88 Collard, *Cambodge et Cambodgiens*, p. 262.
89 Prud'homme, *L'Économie du Cambodge*, p. 254. These are tentative figures, based on a 1930 figure given by Yves Henry and for the years before that given by Morizon.
90 Thompson, *French Indo-China*, p. 125.
91 *Bulletin Bi-Hebdomadaire, Chambre Mixte de Commerce et d'Agriculture du Cambodge* (BCMCAC), June 1955.
92 Collard, *Cambodge et Cambodgiens*, p. 262.
93 Gouvernement général, *Journal Officiel de l'Indochine Française*, 1927, pp. 3033–42. *Arrêté*, 25 October 1927, Hanoi. Signed: Alexandre Varenne. The local *arrêté* for Cambodia was promulgated at the end of May 1929.
94 Thompson, *French Indo-China*, p. 203.
95 Ibid., p. 176.
96 Robequain, *The Economic Development of French Indo-China*, p. 316.
97 ANC RSC File 8982, "Preparation of *Livre Vert*, 1938–39."
98 Thompson, *French Indo-China*, p. 174.
99 Hou Yuon quoting A. Chevalier, *Le Riz* (Paris: Presses Universitaire de France, *Que-sais-je?* series 1948), pp. 71–2. See Ben Kiernan and Boua Chantou, eds., *Peasants and Politics ...*, p. 50.
100 Ibid.
101 *Bulletin Economique Hebdomadaire*, 18 January 1954, reproduced in BCMCAC, January 1954.
102 Hou Yuon, *La paysannerie du Cambodge*, p. 51.
103 Collard, *Cambodge et Cambodgiens*, p. 144.
104 Ibid., p. 102.
105 Ibid., p. 266.
106 Thompson, *French Indo-China*, p. 220.
107 Hou Yuon, *La paysannerie du Cambodge*, p. 65.
108 Ibid.

Chapter 2

1 From the article, "*Notre Sangkum*," *Le Monde*, October 1963, reproduced in *Le Sangkum, Revue Politique Illustrée*, No. 1, August 1965. Copy held in National Library, Phnom Penh.
2 Delvert, *Le Paysan ...*, p. 210.
3 Michael E. Latham, *Modernisation as Ideology: American Social Science and "Nation Building" in the Kennedy Era* (Chapel Hill: University of North

4 ANC Box 339, "*La Conquête de l'Indépendance Économique du Cambodge*," by Phlek Chhat, Directeur Général du Plan, Ministry of Information, Phnom Penh, 1964. This report was presented at the Peking Symposium in August 1964.
5 Ibid.
6 Ibid.
7 BCMCAC, 14 March 1961, *Economic Policy of the SRN* (official communiqué of the executive committee of the SRN and the Royal Government), from AKP, 13 March 1961.
8 ANC Box 592, "*Considérations sur le socialisme Khmer*," Ministry of Information, Phnom Penh, 1961.
9 Ibid.
10 There was also a two-year plan for November 1956 to June 1958, but Prud'homme says that it was mainly a catalogue of public expenses, "a sort of biennial budget." See Prud'homme, p. 170.
11 Prud'homme, *L'Économie ...*, p. 169.
12 Ibid.
13 Ibid., pp. 170–1.
14 Collard, *Cambodge et Cambodgiens ...*, p. 153.
15 Delvert, *Le Paysan ...*, p. 199.
16 Ibid., p. 201.
17 For full details of the constitutions of Cambodia since 1947, see *The Cambodian Constitutions (1953–1993)*, collected and introduced by Raoul M. Jennar (Bangkok: White Lotus, 1995).
18 Milton Osborne, *Sihanouk: Prince of Light, Prince of Darkness* (Chiang Mai: Silkworm Books, 1994), p. 91.
19 Ibid.
20 Ibid., p. 159.
21 *BCG du SRN* (BCG), "*Libre Opinion: Corruption et Déclaration de Biens*," No. 124, 17 March 1967, p. 7.
22 BCG, "*Quelques Idées de Mao Tse-Toung sur La Guerre Révolutionnaire, et Quelques Réflexions sur La Rébellion Des Khmers Rouges*," No. 404, 19 February 1968, p. 1.
23 Delvert, *Le Paysan ...*, Notes.
24 Ibid., p. 14.
25 Ibid., p. 21.
26 Ibid., p. 31.
27 Direction du Recensement Général de la Population, *Résultats Préliminaires du Recensement Général de la Population 1962*, Royaume du Cambodge, Ministère du Plan.
28 Prud'homme, *L'Économie ...*, p. 38.
29 Ibid., p. 46.

30 Ibid., pp. 46, 48.
31 Asian Development Bank, "Economic Report on Cambodia," March 1970.
32 Delvert, *Le Paysan* ..., p. 524.
33 BCMCAC, 7–17 July 1970.
34 Prud'homme, *L'Économie* ..., p. 107.
35 Ibid.
36 Ibid.
37 Ibid., p. 108.
38 Norodom Sihanouk, "*Le Comportement du Parti Communiste Khmer face au SRN*," *Le Sangkum*, No.13, August 1966, p. 5.
39 Delvert, *Le Paysan* ..., p. 321.
40 Prud'homme, *L'Économie* ..., p. 31.
41 Ibid., p. 33.
42 Osborne, *Prince of Light* ..., p. 268. The table has been created from figures provided by Osborne.
43 Ibid.
44 Prud'homme, *L'Économie* ..., p. 55.
45 Ibid., p. 300.
46 ADB, "Economic Report ...," p. 6.
47 Prud'homme, *L'Économie* ..., p. 70.
48 Delvert, *Le Paysan* ..., p. 490.
49 The Cadastral Service made a distinction between "owners" and "occupiers." Strictly speaking, only those households whose names appeared on the register were officially owners, and many communes still had not been surveyed and registered. Delvert considered this legal point had no practical importance since "occupiers" had the same rights and responsibilities as "owners." Possession was obtained by purchase, inheritance or by the traditional method of occupation and development over five years on land belonging originally to the Domain (State Domain or Local Domain) and on which the peasant had obtained a "permit to cultivate." The old Khmer principle of "acquisition by the plough" was still important in under-populated regions but was approved by the state, Delvert noted.
50 Delvert, *Le Paysan* ..., pp. 496, 500.
51 ADB, "Economic Report ...," p. 10.
52 Prud'homme, *L'Économie* ..., p. 72.
53 Ibid., p. 73.
54 Delvert, *Le Paysan* ..., p. 358.
55 Ibid., p. 322 for paddy, p. 372 for sesame and groundnuts.
56 ANC Box 469, Royaume du Cambodge, Direction de L'Agriculture, Division de Statistique Agricole, "*Rapport Annuel: L'Agriculture Cambodgienne en 1968–9*," p. 1.
57 Ministry of Planning, *Statistical Year-Book of Cambodia 1968*, p. 41.
58 Delvert, *Le Paysan* ..., p. 417.
59 Ibid., p. 354.

60 *Photos-Souvenirs du Cambodge, Sangkum Reastr Niyum 1955–1969, Agriculture* (Phnom Penh: Rama Printing International Co. Ltd, undated), p. 10.
61 ANC Box 469, "*Rapport Annuel…*"
62 ADB, "Economic Report …," p. 17.
63 Ibid.
64 BCMAC, 17 March 1964, "Study on Tax Exemptions in Favour of Agriculture," from Phan Thul, *Revue Financière* No. 2, October 1963.
65 Ibid., 3 July 1964.
66 Ibid., 17 January 1965, "*Procedure D'Octroi de Permis de Culture*," Circular No. 1, DAF/D, 3 January 1967.
67 ANC Box 331, "Basic Information Concerning the Present Situation in Cambodia," Official visit of HRH Prince Norodom Sihanouk to India, China and Burma, 10 August 1958, and BCMCAC, 10 March 1959, "*La Société Khmère des Plantations d'Hévéas Communiqué.*"
68 Details about the rubber industry are provided in *Photos-Souvenirs…. Agriculture*, pp. 89–107.
69 BCMCAC, 27 October 1964.
70 The defoliation of 173,000 hectares of Kompong Cham by Agent Orange in April and May 1969 remains the best documented case of the toxic herbicide doused on then neutral Cambodia. Refer to Phann Ana and Kevin Doyle, "Agent Orange's Legacy," *The Cambodia Daily*, 20–21 March 2004, and Andrew Wells-Dang, "Agent Orange in Cambodia: The 1969 Defoliation in Kampong Cham," website: <www.ffrd.org/agentorange.htm>.
71 ADB, "Economic Report …," quoting figures from *Banque Nationale du Cambodge*, "*Rapport Annuel*," 1968.
72 Prud'homme, *L'Économie* …, p. 80.
73 ADB, "Economic Report …," quoting *Banque Nationale du Cambodge*, "*Rapport Annuel*, 1968" and *Bulletin Mensuel*, March–April 1968.
74 Ibid., p. 12.
75 Ministry of Planning, *Statistical Year-Book of Cambodia, 1968*, p. 48.
76 Ibid., p. 45.
77 ANC Box 113, Secretariat of State for Agriculture, *Service des Eaux, Forêts et Chasse*, "*Rapport National Sur les Plantations de Teck*," 1960.
78 Khieu Samphan, *Cambodia's Economy and Industrial Development*, translated and with introduction by Laura Summers (Ithaca: Cornell University SEAP Data Paper 111, 1979).
79 Ibid., p. 116.
80 BCMCAC, 18 December 1962.
81 ANC Box 55, *Photos-Souvenirs du Cambodge, Sangkum Reastr Niyum – Industrie*, 9 November 1993.
82 BCMCAC, 7 June 1963, "The New Factories of Cambodia," French translation of an article by P.H.M. Jones, published in the *Far Eastern Economic Review*, 9 May 1963.

83 Ibid., 11 October 1957, Ministry of Labour and Social Action, "*Acte Officiel, Conditions d'emploi des étrangers dans les entreprises privées,*" *Prakas* No. 3614, 5 October 1957.
84 BCG, "*Quelques Aspects du Problème de L'Emploi,*" No. 119, 11 March 1967, pp. 4–5.
85 Prud'homme, *L'Économie* …, p. 90.
86 Ibid. See also following note.
87 BCMCAC, 26 February 1954, quoting *Bulletin Économique et Statistique du Cambodge*, April, May and June 1954.
88 Ibid., 11 April 1958.
89 ANC Box 331, "Basic Information …"
90 Quoted by Khieu Samphan in his dissertation, using figures from the *Retrospective Statistical Yearbook for Cambodia*, June 1958.
91 BCMCAC, 8 September 1959, "The Spirit of Economic Aid," speech to the Rotary Club of Phnom Penh by Charles A. Mann, director of the American Economic Aid Mission to Cambodia.
92 Ibid., 15 March 1957.
93 Rémy Prud'homme considered that an average rate for the whole period up to 1963 was 82 riels to the dollar, compared with the official rate of a little over 35 riels. In December 1957 and again exactly one year later, the French franc was devalued against the U.S. dollar and against gold. Cambodia refused to change the rate of the riel against the franc or the dollar, but there were disparities in the money markets of Phnom Penh where the official rate was maintained at 10 riels to the franc and 35 to the dollar.
94 Prud'homme, *L'Économie* …, pp. 125–8.
95 BCMCAC, 15 November 1963.
96 Ibid., 13 December 1963, "Summary of Sihanouk's Speech at Kep on 6 December," from AKP, 8 December 1963.
97 Ibid.
98 Less than a fortnight before the nationalisation law was passed, the Diem regime in South Vietnam was overthrown in a bloody coup. American complicity was clearly understood by the prince and he no doubt interpreted the event as a warning.
99 BCMCAC, 20 December 1963.
100 Milton Osborne, *Politics and Power in Cambodia* (Camberwell: Longman Australia, 1973), p. 88.
101 ANC Box 314, "*Oeuvre de SRN,*" speech given by H.E. Gen. Lon Nol, Prime Minister, 27 December 1966.
102 Prud'homme, *L'Économie* …, p. 170.
103 In 1958, for example, U.S. economic aid was worth 373 million riels compared with France's contribution of 132 million riels. That year, an agreement on economic and technical cooperation worth 150 million riels was signed with Japan. Refer to BCMCAC, 6 November 1959, quoting AKP, 31 October 1959.

104 BCMCAC, 8 September 1959, "The Spirit of Economic Aid."
105 Ibid., 16 May 1967, "Report on the meeting to discuss economic problems at the Chamber of Commerce," presided over by Chau Seng, Minister of State for National Economy.
106 Ibid., 11 August 1967.
107 Refer to BCMCAC, 1 March 1957, 27 September 1957, and 29 August 1958.
108 Osborne, *Power and Politics*, p. 103.
109 ADB, "Economic Report …," p. 38.
110 Ibid.
111 Ibid., p. 63.
112 Ibid., p. 62.
113 BCMCAC, 13 September 1954.
114 BCG, No. 408, 23 February 1968, p. 1.
115 Prud'homme, *L'Économie …*, p. 221.
116 Ibid., p. 223.
117 Delvert, *Le Paysan …*, pp. 514, 518.
118 Ibid., p. 523.
119 Hou Yuon, "*La Paysannerie du Cambodge …*," in *Peasants and Politics …*, p. 66.
120 Prud'homme, *L'Économie …*, p. 188.
121 Ibid.
122 *Photos-Souvenirs … Agriculture*, p. 245.
123 BCG, "OROC and the Cooperative System," No. 90, 6 February 1967.
124 ADB, "Economic Report …," p. 16.
125 Delvert, *Le Paysan …*, p. 519.
126 BCG, "*Le Credit Agricole*," No. 652, 27 December 1968.
127 ADB, "Economic Report …," p. 16.
128 BCMCAC, 9 December 1969.
129 A friend of the author and her husband were volunteers on a cooperative in Pursat province in the 1960s. They confirmed the low interest rate which they put at 0.7 per cent per month, which was very low compared with unorganised credit. They said that the credit system at their cooperative did not work because the farmers refused to repay loans.
130 Ellen Meiksins Wood, *The Origin of Capitalism: a longer view* (London: Verso, 2002), p. 4.
131 Ibid., p. 2.
132 Ibid., p. 16.

Chapter 3

1 *Le Cambodge Economique* (formerly the BCMCAC), 16 October 1970. The twice-weekly bulletin of the Chamber of Commerce and Agriculture was renamed *Le Cambodge Economique* (LCE) with its first issue on 8 May 1970. On 29 January 1971, it was renamed *Revue Economique* (RE). The *Revue Economique* continued publishing until 29 March 1974. Copies referred to below are held at the State Archives of Cambodia (ANC), starting with Box 165.

2 Justin Corfield, *Khmers Stand Up! A History of the Cambodian Government 1970–1975*, Monash Papers on Southeast Asia No. 32, Centre of Southeast Asian Studies, Monash University, 1994, p. 106.
3 *Revue Economique* (formerly *Le Cambodge Economique*), from AFP, 7 December 1971. On 3 December 1971, *Le Monde* published the text of an interview given to Christian Hovelacque by Sirik Matak. The journalist called it "a war of destruction … by Vietnam" and estimated that the North Vietnamese and their allies controlled "only twenty to twenty-five per cent of the population."
4 *Le Cambodge Economique* (LCE), 26 May 1970. "Act of Government — Message to the Nation by H.E. General Lon Nol, Radio Broadcast 22 May 1970," from AFP, No. 7005, 23 May 1970.
5 David Chandler, *A History of Cambodia*, third edition (Chiang Mai: Silkworm Books, 2003), p. 206.
6 Corfield, *Khmers Stand Up!*, p. 124.
7 Craig Etcheson, *The Rise and Demise of Democratic Kampuchea* (Boulder, Colorado: Westview Press, 1984), p. 99.
8 LCE, 8 May 1970. "*Le Tournant.*"
9 Ibid., "Minutes of Meeting of 9 April 1970."
10 Ibid.
11 According to these laws, the public sector would retain monopoly of the production and distribution of electricity (of more than 500KVA), the production of arms and munitions, rail transport, and the post and telecommunications services. Other areas of economic activity were open to competition from the private sector. In commerce and trade, the state retained monopoly of exports of rice and derivatives, maize, rubber, and precious or semi-precious stones. Some listed imports also remained under state monopoly. Otherwise, the law stated, "All the other operations of export and import can be exercised as well by the private sector as by the public sector and without privilege of any sort for the latter." See BCMCAC, 17 February 1970.
12 *Revue Economique* (RE), 6 May 1971. "Declaration of Lt. General S. Sirik Matak, President of the Council of Ministers on the occasion of the Investiture of the Lon Nol Government."
13 Raoul Jennar, *The Cambodian Constitutions*, p. 58.
14 Han Suyin, who had close personal contact with the leadership of the Chinese Communist Party wrote, "[T]hrough the port of Sihanoukville in Cambodia, war matériel was being transported to the thirteen [North Vietnamese] bases [on Cambodian territory] and on to the Liberation Front of South Vietnam. This matériel was not only Russian but also Chinese. It was the Chinese who paid for the conveying of goods, and the man who was being paid was … Lon Nol, through his wife's transport company. In 1969, during an official visit to Beijing as Premier of Cambodia, Lon Nol had asked for more money. 'He made quite irrational demands,' Zhang Wenjing told me. Then why the coup? Perhaps Lon Nol would get more money from the Americans …". See Han

Suyin, *Eldest Son: Zhou Enlai and the Making of Modern China 1898–1976* (London: Pimlico, 1994), p. 373.
15 LCE, 12 May 1970.
16 George Hildebrand and Gareth Porter, *Cambodia: Starvation and Revolution* (New York: Monthly Review Press, 1976), p. 30.
17 Ibid., p. 31.
18 RE, 7 September 1971.
19 RE, 20 March 1972, from AFP, 14 March 1972.
20 Desbarats, *Prolific Survivors ...*, pp. 85–6.
21 Ibid.
22 Ibid., p. 108.
23 Ibid., p. 109.
24 Ibid., p. 107.
25 Ibid., p. 91.
26 Etcheson, *The Rise and Demise ...*, p. 148.
27 Jonathan S. Grant, "The Regime of Lon Nol," in *Cambodia: The Widening War in Indochina*, ed. J.S. Grant *et al.* (New York: Washington Square Press, 1971), p. 120.
28 Hildebrand and Porter, *Cambodia ...*, p. 42.
29 Penny Edwards, "Ethnic Chinese in Cambodia," in *CAS Interdisciplinary Research on Ethnic Groups in Cambodia*, Phnom Penh, July 1996, p. 139.
30 Desbarats, *Prolific Survivors ...*, p. 130.
31 RE, "Activity of the Bank of Asia," 13 November 1973.
32 RE, 4 August 1972.
33 Hildebrand and Porter, *Cambodia ...*, p. 21.
34 RE, 29 August 1972.
35 Hildebrand and Porter, *Cambodia ...*, p. 23.
36 RE, 20 October 1971.
37 Hildebrand and Porter, *Cambodia ...*, p. 21.
38 RE, 4 January 1974.
39 Ibid., 15 August 1972.
40 Ibid., 18 August 1972.
41 Elizabeth Becker, *When the War was Over: Cambodia and the Khmer Rouge Revolution* (New York: Public Affairs, 1986), p. 152.
42 Desbarats, *Prolific Survivors ...*, p. 153.
43 Ibid., p. 162.
44 Hildebrand and Porter, *Cambodia ...*, p. 29.
45 ANC Box 357, Maréchal Lon Nol, "*Neo-Khmerisme*," Phnom Penh, undated.
46 Ayres, *Anatomy of a Crisis ...*, p. 77.
47 Ibid., p. 80.
48 LCE, 15 January 1971. "Annual Management Report of the National Bank of Cambodia for the 1968–1969 Financial Year."
49 RE, "Annual Report of the National Bank of Cambodia for the 1969–70 Financial Year," 16 November 1971 and following issue.

50   LCE, 26 May 1970.
51   Ibid., 30 June and 3 July 1970.
52   RE, 16 March 1971.
53   Ibid., 12 February 1971.
54   Ibid., 16 March 1971.
55   Hildebrand and Porter, *Cambodia* ..., p. 20.
56   LCE, "The Future of Mixed-Economy Companies," 22 January 1971.
57   Michael Vickery, *Cambodia 1975–1982* (Chiang Mai: Silkworm Books, 1999), pp. 23–4.
58   LCE, 22 January 1971.
59   RE, "State Participation in Mixed-Economy Companies," 26 February 1971.
60   Ibid., 28 October 1972.
61   Ibid., "Radio Broadcast by the President of the Republic," 28 July 1972.
62   Ibid., 12 January 1973.
63   LCE, 26 May 1970.
64   William Rosoff, "Dissension in the Kingdom," in *The Widening War in Indochina*, ed. J.S. Grant *et al.*, p. 91.
65   BCMCAC, 17 February 1970.
66   LCE, 11 September 1970.
67   Ibid., 20 November 1970. Press Release of 11 November 1970, signed by S. Sirik Matak, first vice-president of the Council of Ministers.
68   Hildebrand and Porter, *Cambodia* ..., p. 19.
69   Becker, *When the War Was Over* ..., pp. 128–9.
70   Hildebrand and Porter, *Cambodia* ..., p. 36.
71   Ibid., p. 34.
72   Table compiled from figures in RE, 29 March 1974.
73   Hildebrand and Porter, *Cambodia* ..., p. 33.
74   Etcheson, *The Rise and Demise* ..., p. 94, citing Sak Sutsakhan, *The Khmer Republic at War and the Final Collapse* (Washington, D.C.: U.S. Army Center for Military History, 1980).
75   LCE, 26 May 1970.
76   RE, "Annual Report of the National Bank of Cambodia," 16 November 1971.
77   Ibid., "The Economic Situation of Cambodia," an interview given by Op Kim Ang, third vice-president of the Council of Ministers in charge of finances, planning and the coordination of economic affairs to AFP, 23 June 1970.
78   RE, 3 August 1973.
79   Ibid., 16 November 1971.
80   Ibid., 9 November 1971.
81   Ibid.
82   RE, "The Economic Problems of the Khmer Republic," the summarised speech of Sok Chhong, second vice-president of the Council of Ministers in charge of finances, economic and financial affairs, posts and telecommunications, 21 October 1971.

83 Ibid.
84 Ibid., "Speech of Sok Chhong at the opening of the Conference on Exchange Support Funds, 14 January 1972," 21 January 1972.
85 Ibid., 8 January 1974.
86 Hildebrand and Porter, *Cambodia...*, p. 21.
87 LCE, "The Budget of 1970," 8 May 1979.
88 RE, "Annual Report of the National Bank of Cambodia," 16 November 1971.
89 Ibid., "Document of the 7th General Assembly of the APU," December 1971.
90 Corfield, *Khmers Stand Up!*, p. 132, citing *New York Times*, 19 March 1972, p. 3.

Chapter 4

1 Khieu Samphan, *Cambodia's Economy and Industrial Development*.
2 Sir John Clapham, "Economic History as a Discipline," in *The Varieties of History: From Voltaire to the Present*, second edition, ed. Fritz Stern (London: Macmillan, 1970), pp. 308–13.
3 "Cambodia" and "Kampuchea" are used interchangeably in this chapter. In Western literature and reporting, the latter usually denotes the revolutionary society, but both names have a long history of use.
4 Hildebrand and Porter quote Deputy Premier Ieng Sary who said in September 1975 that further increases in the city's population were expected as productive facilities were restored and expanded. See *Cambodia: Starvation and Revolution*, p. 46.
5 Many reasons have been cited for the decision to evacuate the city. They vary from practical problems of food stocks, transportation and security to ideological ones. Khieu Samphan argues that there would have been "confusion" among the revolutionary troops if the city had not been evacuated. The battle-hardened fighters, he said, were "very brave in front of bullets but not prepared to confront the *kroab skâr* (sweets or candy)." See In Sopheap, *Khieu Samphan: Aggrandi et Réel* (unpublished), p. 82. Others suggest that the movement had long lost touch with its urban cells, so setting up an administration to run a city the size of Phnom Penh was beyond the capacity of the victors. See Peter Sainsbury and Chea Sotheacheath, "Good intentions paved road to mass murder," an interview with a Phnom Penh-based founder of the CPK and former student colleague in Paris of Pol Pot, Ieng Sary and other leaders, in *Phnom Penh Post*, 14–27 April 2000.
6 Michael Vickery explained, "[Battambang] with the greatest potential social contradictions had, in 1975, the largest number of republican supporters outside Phnom Penh, and also the weakest local Communist organisation." For details of his interviews conducted with refugees in 1980, see *Cambodia 1975–1982* (Chiang Mai: Silkworm Books, 1999).

7   Ith Sarin, *Sronoh Proelung Khmer* [Regrets for the Khmer Soul] (Phnom Penh, 28 July 1973). Ith Sarin's views of life in the *maquis* before 1973 are largely corroborated by those of Khieu Samphan in In Sopheap's biography of him and also by Serge Thion in "Cambodia 1972: Within the Khmer Rouge," *Watching Cambodia* (Bangkok: White Lotus, 1993), pp. 1–17.
8   The *Gouvernement Royal d'Union Nationale du Kampuchéa* (GRUNK) was created by Prince Sihanouk to administer the *Front National Uni du Kampuchéa* (FUNK) after the coup in March 1970.
9   In Sopheap, *Khieu Samphan* ... Khieu Samphan named Doeun as head of Office 870 and claimed that the political matters Doeun dealt with were carried out in complete secrecy.
10 Ibid.
11 Ibid.
12 Ibid.
13 "The Party's Four-Year Plan to Build Socialism in All Fields, 1977–1980, " in *Pol Pot Plans the Future*, ed. David Chandler *et al.*, Monograph Series 33/Yale University Southeast Asia Studies, 1988, pp. 45–9.
14 *Service d'Information du FUNSK, Front D'Union Nationale Pour Le Salut Du Kampuchea*, January 1979, p. 13.
15 FBIS, Phnom Penh Domestic Service, 15 October 1985.
16 Hun Sen, *Dap Chhnam ney Damnaeur Kampuchea: 1979–1989* [The Ten-Year Journey], Phnom Penh, December 1988, p. 480.
17 David Chandler *et al.*, *Pol Pot Plans the Future*, p. 44.
18 Charles H. Twining, "The Economy," in *Cambodia 1975–1978: Rendezvous with Death*, ed. Karl D. Jackson (Princeton: Princeton University Press, 1989), p. 127.
19 Vickery, *Cambodia 1975–1982*, p. 73.
20 Timothy Carney, "The Organisation of Power," in *Cambodia 1975–1978*, p. 91.
21 ANC PRK, "Decision of the centre concerning the setting out of duties and the system of organisation of the work of the party centre, the government and the front," for Central Committee, First Secretary, 1979 (unsigned, undated).
22 Stephen Heder, "Kampuchea: From Pol Pot to Pen Sovan to the Villages," in *Indochina and Problems of Security and Stability in Southeast Asia*, ed. Khien Theeravit and MacAlister Brown (Bangkok: Chulalongkorn University Press, 1983), pp. 16–62.
23 Nayan Chanda, "Cambodia in 1986," *Asian Survey* 27, 1 (January 1987): 115–23 and Hun Sen, *The Ten-Year Journey*, p. 421.
24 Judith Banister and Paige Johnson, "After the Nightmare: The Population of Cambodia," in *Genocide and Democracy in Cambodia: The Khmer Rouge, the United Nations and the International Community*, ed. Ben Kiernan (Monograph Series 41/Yale University Southeast Asia Studies, 1993), p. 90.

25 The most commonly quoted figure in newspapers and journals is 1.7 million "deaths." Vickery notes that given the normal pre-war mortality rate of 18 per thousand, there would have been at least 511,200 normal deaths in the same period. See *Cambodia 1975–1982*, p. 198.

26 Kimmo Kiljunen, ed., *Kampuchea: Decade of the Genocide, Report of a Finnish Inquiry Commission* (London: Zed Books, 1984), p. 33.

27 Desbarats, *Prolific Survivors …*, p. 87.

28 Ibid., p. 88.

29 Michael Vickery's *Cambodia 1975–1982* refutes the journalistic "standard total view" that developed from early reports about the DK regime. From interviews with refugees in Thai camps, he presented the case that conditions in Pursat and other parts of the northwest were generally the worst for most of the regime, and while there were few refugees to represent Kratie, he believed that conditions there had been relatively benign. The present author agrees with this argument on the basis of hundreds of informal conversations with Cambodians who experienced the regime as "new people" in all regions of the country as well as figures from the 1998 census.

30 Desbarats, *Prolific Survivors …*, p. 93.

31 Kimmo Kiljunen, ed., *Report of a Finnish Inquiry Commission*, p. 33.

32 Jerrold W. Huguet, *The Population of Cambodia, 1980–1996, and Projected to 2020*, National Institute of Statistics, Ministry of Planning, Phnom Penh, May 1997, p. 28. Huguet explained his method as follows: "To project back to 1980, the 1985 population, including the camp population, was used. The estimated 200,000 return migrants were subtracted, the population was reverse survived to 1980, the 140,000 persons in camps in Thailand were subtracted, and the 72,000 persons who emigrated after 1980 were added to obtain the estimated population as of mid-1980, or 6,549,687 persons."

33 Ibid., p. vii.

34 Desbarats, *Prolific Survivors …*, p. 107.

35 These figures are quoted by Jacqueline Desbarats, *Prolific Survivors …*, pp. 92–4.

36 Ibid., p. 88.

37 Figure for 1980 from Banister and Johnson, "After the Nightmare …," p. 68 and for 1989 from UNDP *Kampuchea Needs Assessment Survey* [KNAS] *1989*, p. 19.

38 Kimmo Kiljunen ed., *Report of a Finnish Inquiry Commission*, p. 35.

39 Ibid., using various sources, p. 113.

40 The table has been compiled from information provided in Appendix A, 'International Migration Assumptions' by Banister and Johnson, "After the Nightmare," pp. 121–4.

41 UNDP KNAS, p. 184.

42 Ibid., p. 19. The *Finnish Inquiry Commission* reported in 1982, "Today national minorities account for approximately three per cent of the population, the largest being the Chinese minority which formerly made up five to six per

cent of the population. Since 1981 some ethnic Vietnamese have returned," p. 34.
43 Ibid.
44 Banister and Johnson, "After the Nightmare …," p. 97.
45 Penny Edwards, "Ethnic Chinese in Cambodia," CAS Study, 1996, p. 140.
46 Ibid., p. 141.
47 Kimmo Kiljunen, ed., *Report of a Finnish Inquiry Commission*, p. 34.
48 Michael Vickery, "A reader's guide down the garden path of Cambodian statistics and into the treacherous jungle of demography," Penang, October 1990, p. 24.
49 Desbarats, *Prolific Survivors …*, p. 131.
50 Twining, "The Economy," p. 149.
51 Margaret Slocomb, "Chikreng Rebellion: Coup and Its Aftermath in Democratic Kampuchea," *Journal of the Royal Asiatic Society* 16, 1 (April 2006): 59–72. Hildebrand and Porter made mention of the dam on the Chikreng River, noting, "[I]n early 1975 the Chinese journalists' delegation that visited Chikreng saw fifteen thousand people building a 'huge dam,' and since then a 43-kilometre canal has been completed as a part of the district's development plan." See *Cambodia: Starvation and Revolution*, p. 87.
52 Ibid., p. 150.
53 Desbarats, *Prolific Survivors …*, p. 162.
54 Slocomb, "Chikreng Rebellion," p. 66.
55 ANC PRK, "Request to Provincial People's Revolutionary Committees," People's Revolutionary Council of Kampuchea, Heng Samrin, 7 April 1979.
56 Desbarats, *Prolific Survivors …*, p. 163.
57 Ibid.
58 Banister and Johnson, "After the Nightmare …," p. 102, quoting Josiane Volkmar-Andre, "Medical Care Inside Kampuchea," in *Years of Horror, Days of Hope*, ed. Barry S. Levy and Daniel C. Susott (Millwood, New York: Associated Faculty Press, 1987).
59 Twining, "The Economy," p. 134.
60 Kimmo Kiljunen, ed., *Report of a Finnish Inquiry Commission*, p. 39.
61 Hildebrand and Porter, *Cambodia …*, p. 54.
62 Vickery, *Cambodia 1975–82*, p. 102.
63 In Sopheap, *Khieu Samphan …*, p. 109. The anti-malarial campaigns did take place. Karl D. Jackson notes, "In November 1976, in one of its first international trading transactions, the Kampuchean government was forced by dire circumstances to purchase $450,000 worth of DDT for its anti-malarial campaign," *Cambodia 1975–1978: Rendezvous with Death*, p. 48.
64 Desbarats, *Prolific Survivors …*, p. 151.
65 Ibid., p. 96.
66 In Sopheap, *Khieu Samphan …* David Ayres identifies these remarks from a document circulated by the Centre in September 1975. See *Anatomy of a Crisis …*, p. 105.

67 Vickery, *Cambodia 1975–82*, p. 184.
68 Ayres, *Anatomy of a Crisis* ..., p. 109.
69 Ibid., p. 113.
70 ANC PRK, "Decree-Law concerning the system of general education," No. 30 KrJ, for Council of State, President, Heng Samrin (signed and stamped), Phnom Penh, 20 November 1986.
71 ANC PRK, "Report summing up the results of the campaign against illiteracy and for complementary education," National Committee for the Campaign, unsigned and undated.
72 Curtis, "Cambodia: a country profile," p. 134.
73 Ibid.
74 ADB Report, 1970, p. 10.
75 Ibid., p. 10.
76 Ibid., p. 14.
77 Hildebrand and Porter, *Cambodia* ..., p. 88.
78 Twining "The Economy," p. 144 and Vickery, *Cambodia 1975–82*.
79 "Pol Pot's Interview with Yugoslav Journalists," *Journal of Contemporary Asia* 8 (1978): 414.
80 Vickery, *Cambodia 1975–82*, p. 117.
81 Hildebrand and Porter, *Cambodia* ..., p. 92.
82 Ibid. The authors do not say, but this decision to nationalise the plantations was presumably taken by the government of the United Front (GRUNK), not the government of the Khmer Republic.
83 Twining, "The Economy," p. 185.
84 The five per cent figure was quoted by Nayan Chanda, *Far Eastern Economic Review*, 17 August 1979, p. 16. The specific area in hectares is from "Announcement of the People's Revolutionary Committee and the Central Committee of the FUNSK concerning the state of affairs for the first six months of 1979 and duties for the future," President Heng Samrin, Phnom Penh, July 1979 (ANC PRK files).
85 Desbarats, *Prolific Survivors* ..., p. 65.
86 Hildebrand and Porter, *Cambodia* ..., p. 92. May Someth, *Cambodian Witness* (London: Faber and Faber, 1986).
87 Twining "The Economy," p. 135.
88 UNDP KNAS, p. 42. This survey report blamed the drop in production on an acute lack of fishing nets, harm caused by pesticides for the rice crop or perhaps a fish disease.
89 ANC PRK, "Account of the Commission for the Economy and the Budget," draft, unsigned, undated.
90 ANC PRK, "Report concerning the results of implementing the state budget for nine months of 1987, the plan for the fourth quarter and estimates for implementation throughout 1987," No. 08RBK, for Council of Ministers, Chairman, Hun Sen, Phnom Penh, 27 October 1987.
91 UNDP KNAS, p. 42.

92 Ibid., p. 44.
93 Ministry of Environment, *National Environmental Action Plan 1998–2001*, Phnom Penh, January 1998, p. 3.
94 Twining "The Economy," p. 136.
95 ANC PRK, "Concerning measures to ensure the implementation of the exchange of goods in 1988 with effectiveness, management and distribution of imported goods for 1988," No. 1103 SJN, signed vice-minister, Sieng Saron, Phnom Penh, 10 September 1987.
96 UNDP KNAS, p. 47.
97 ANC PRK, "Report on Activities of the Commission for the Economy and Budget to 13th Session of the National Assembly, First Legislature," draft, 7 July 1987.
98 UNDP KNAS, p. 47.
99 Kimmo Kiljunen, ed., *Report of a Finnish Inquiry Commission*, p. 6.
100 In Sopheap, *Khieu Samphan*...
101 Vickery, *Cambodia 1975–82*, p. 86.
102 Pol Pot, "Speech ... on the occasion of the 18th Anniversary of the founding of the Communist Party of Kampuchea," Phnom Penh, 27 September 1978, Department of Press and Information, Ministry of Foreign Affairs, Democratic Kampuchea, pp. 30–3.
103 The UNDP KNAS reported that the industrial workforce was three times the 110,000 figure it had been in 1967, p. 57.
104 Twining, "The Economy," p. 140.
105 UNDP KNAS, p. 73.
106 Nayan Chanda, "Consumers' comeback," *FEER*, 91 June 1981, pp. 24–6.
107 Ibid.
108 ANC PRK, "Report: The financial situation and the proposed state budget for 1984 to the National Assembly, sixth session, first legislature," submitted by Comrade Chan Phin, Minister for Finance.
109 Ibid.
110 Ibid.
111 Desbarats, *Prolific Survivors*..., p. 60.
112 Ibid., p. 197.
113 Ibid., p. 199.
114 Twining "The Economy," p. 146.
115 Ibid. Hildebrand and Porter note the West African interest in importing rice from Democratic Kampuchea, p. 89.
116 Ben Kiernan says contact was made with UNICEF and then with US firms about aid and purchases of drugs and anti-malarial equipment. See "Conflict in the Kampuchean Communist Movement," *Journal of Contemporary Asia* 10, 1–2 (1980): 56.
117 Etcheson, *The Rise and Demise*..., p. 174.
118 Twining is quoting Elizabeth Becker. Ben Kiernan mentions this point also but he says it went to Singapore in late 1976 during the brief period of less

119 than a month when Pol Pot had been deposed and there was a fair degree of trade liberalisation.
119 Edwards, "Ethnic Chinese in Cambodia," p. 142, fn. 6.
120 UNDP KNAS, p. 8.
121 Stephen Heder estimates that the number of Chinese advisers in Cambodia was "a few thousand at any one time." See Phelim Kyne, "The Chinese-KR connection," *Phnom Penh Post*, 14–27 April 2000, p. 6.
122 ANC PRK, "Summary of opinions expressed by Comrade Pen Sovann, Chairman of the Council of Ministers, at the Second Session of the Council of Ministers, 28–29 July 1981."
123 "Vietnam-Kampuchea Summit Meeting in Phnom Penh," *Vietnam Courier* 3 (March 1979): 4–6.
124 ANC PRK, "Agreement on assistance and cooperation in agriculture between the ministry of agriculture of the PRK and the ministry of agriculture of the SRV for 1983," 15 June 1983.
125 ANC PRK, "Agreement between the government of the USSR and the government of the PRK concerning the provision of economic and technical assistance to the PRK in order to redevelop the basis of the national economy and to practise other works," 1982.
126 Desbarats, *Prolific Survivors …*, pp. 71–2.
127 UNDP KNAS, p. 10.
128 Ibid.
129 Robert Muscat, with Jonathan Stromseth, "Cambodia: Post-Settlement Reconstruction and Development." Occasional Paper, East Asian Institute, Columbia University, 1989, p. 20.
130 UNDP KNAS, p. 11.
131 In Sopheap, *Khieu Samphan …*, p. 83.
132 Pol Pot, "Speech … 27 September 1978," p. 31.
133 Twining "The Economy," p. 123.
134 ANC PRK, "Report concerning the work of managing the collection of taxes on imports in Kompong Som and Koh Kong since the issuing of the decree-law No. 15KrJ of 27 November 1982," Minister for Ministry of Finance, Chan Phin (signed and stamped), Phnom Penh, 15 February 1983.
135 ANC PRK, "Concerning the state budget," unsigned, undated.
136 ANC PRK, "Report on the financial situation and the proposed state budget for 1984 to the National Assembly, sixth session, first legislature," submitted by Comrade Chan Phin, Minister, Ministry of Finance.
137 ANC PRK, "Memo to Council of State concerning request to change the tax policy for industry and commerce," Council of Ministers, Chairman, Hun Sen, Phnom Penh, 1 February 1986. The official exchange rate was then 30 riels to the U.S. dollar, but on the black market, the dollar could buy 130 riels.
138 ANC PRK, "Circular concerning collecting debts from the people," No. 04SR, for Council of Ministers, Chairman, Hun Sen, Phnom Penh, 21 March 1988.

139   ANC PRK, "Decree-law concerning foreign investment in the State of Cambodia," No. 58Kr, for Council of State, President Heng Samrin, Phnom Penh, 26 July 1989.

Chapter 5

1. This was the fourth document of the Paris Peace Agreements signed in October 1991.
2. Prince Sihanouk returned to Phnom Penh in November 1991 and assumed the presidency of the SNC when it was formed. Apart from the prince, there were 12 members, 6 appointed by the SoC and 6 representing the other 3 factions in the conflict. The SNC was not the Cambodian government, as the SoC continued to administer the country. The SNC's role was to represent the sovereignty of Cambodia during this transitional period, including its representation at the UN.
3. David Ayres, *Anatomy of a Crisis*, pp. 164–5.
4. Grant Curtis, *Cambodia Reborn?*, p. 61.
5. Robert Carmichael, "The PRSP: Ready or not, an end to poverty?" *Phnom Penh Post*, 27 September–10 October 2002.
6. Molly Ball, "Study offers new plan to ease poverty," *The Cambodia Daily*, 28 March 2003.
7. This clause in Article 100 of the 1993 constitution resulted in a political deadlock following the 2003 general elections. Fearing that he would not receive the vote of confidence from the Assembly, Hun Sen, who led the CPP to victory at those elections, delayed the assembly for almost a full year. During that crisis, the pre-poll government was extended and functioned with a budget that was released in monthly increments.
8. The Constitutional Council Law requires that the eldest or second eldest member convene or preside over a meeting of at least seven of the nine members. The king's appointees were Son Sann, aged 86, Chau Sen Cocsal Chhum, 92, and Pung Peng Cheng, 81. Chau Sen Cocsal Chhum left the country rather than submit to pressure to convene the meeting, Son Sann refused to attend it and Peng Cheng declined attempts by the other six members to preside over it. See Samreth Sopha and Eric Pape, "Council in jeopardy after elders boycott meeting," *Phnom Penh Post*, 5–18 June 1998.
9. Francis Fukuyama, *After the Neocons: America at the Crossroads* (London: Profile Books, 2006), p. 109.
10. Toshiyasu Kato, *et al.*, *Cambodia: Enhancing Governance* …, p. 1.
11. Transcript of speech, "Achievements and Perspectives of the Public Administrative Reform," delivered by Paul Matthews, UN Resident Co-ordinator and UNDP Resident Representative, in Phnom Penh, 22 June 1998.
12. Transcript of speech, "*La politique du GRC sur la réforme administrative*," delivered by Sok An, Co-president of the Interministerial Technical Commission for Administrative Reform, in Phnom Penh, 22 June 1998.

13 The population size of communes ranged from 305 to 44,513 individuals and the average size was around 7,000, according to the draft speech "The New Decentralised Government Structure and the Role of the Commune Councils in Local Development," for Prum Sokha, Secretary of State, Ministry of the Interior, 31 August 2000.
14 Yun Samean, "Ministry: Councils have come a long way," *The Cambodia Daily*, 8 April 2003.
15 William Shawcross, *Cambodia's New Deal*, Contemporary Issues Paper #1, Carnegie Endowment for International Peace, Washington, DC, 1994, p. 72.
16 Ibid.
17 Toshiyasu Kato, et al., *Cambodia: Enhancing Governance* …, p. 10.
18 Michelle Vachon, "Donor Meeting looks at Wide Range of Reforms," *The Cambodia Daily*, 16 January 2002.
19 Christopher St John, "World Bank imposes Sanctions on Four Firms," *The Cambodia Daily*, 25 November 2004.
20 Ayres, *Anatomy of a Crisis*, p. 152.
21 Curtis, *Cambodia Reborn?*, p. 32.
22 David W. Roberts, *Political Transition in Cambodia 1991–99: Power, Elitism and Democracy* (Richmond, Surrey: Curzon Press, 2001), p. 34.
23 Douglas Gillison and Yun Samean, "Cambodia falls near Bottom of Graft Index," *The Cambodia Daily*, 8 November 2006.
24 Richard Woodd, "Bribe tax main barrier to business growth," *Phnom Penh Post*, 7–20 May 2004.
25 Quoting from the draft report, "Toward a Private Sector Led Growth Strategy for Cambodia," Luke Reynolds, "World Bank Draft Report Slams Graft," *The Cambodia Daily*, 11 June 2004.
26 Bill Bainbridge, "How smuggling and graft sap a nation's economy," *Phnom Penh Post*, 15–28 August 2003.
27 Phelim Kyne, "Exploring Cambodia's evolution as the Kingdom of Corruption," *Phnom Penh Post*, 11–24 July 1999.
28 NIS, *Cambodia Statistical Yearbook 2000*, p. 1.
29 Desbarats, *Prolific Survivors* …, p. 137, compiled from multiple sources; figures for 1998 taken from National Census.
30 NIS, *Report on the Cambodia Socio-Economic Survey 1999*, Ministry of Planning, Phnom Penh, May 2000, p. 5.
31 Martin Godfrey et al., *A Study of the Cambodian Labour Market: Reference to Poverty Reduction, Growth and Adjustment to Crisis*, Working Paper 18, CDRI, Phnom Penh, August 2001, p. 21.
32 Lor Chandara, "Firm to register Cambodian workers in Thailand," *The Cambodia Daily*, 13–14 August 2005.
33 Nicholas Revise, "Cambodians flocking to Thailand for work," *The Cambodia Daily*, 25 February 2002.
34 Martin Godfrey et al., *A Study of the Cambodian Labour Market*, p. 23.

35 This figure was an improvement on the estimate of 39 per cent given by the 1993–94 SESC. Nick Lenaghan, "Cambodia, 1997: AIDS and poverty," *Phnom Penh Post*, 24 October–6 November 1997, p. 3.
36 Ministry of Planning, "Cambodia Human Development Report 1998: women's contribution to development," Phnom Penh, October 1998.
37 NIS, *Report on the Socio-Economic Survey of Cambodia 1993/94*, Ministry of Planning, Phnom Penh, September 1995, p. 63.
38 World Bank and Ministry of Planning, *Cambodia Poverty Assessment*, Phnom Penh, December 1999, p. 13.
39 Quoting from an EIC report, Kay Kimsong and Daniel Ten Kate, "Gov't reaffirms commitment to agriculture," *The Cambodia Daily*, 31 October 2003.
40 NIS, *Cambodia Statistical Yearbook 2000*, p. 63.
41 NIS, *National Accounts of Cambodia 1993–2002*, Bulletin No. 7, July 2003, p. 32.
42 Unifem et al., *A Fair Share for Women*, p. 89.
43 Robin Biddulph, *Interim Report on Findings of Landlessness and Development Information Tool (LADIT) Research September 1999 to April 2000*, Oxfam, Phnom Penh, 15 June 2000, p. 11.
44 Matt Reed, "AIDS Threatens Cambodia's Gains, UN Says," *The Cambodia Daily*, 22 June 2001.
45 Kuch Naren, "Child mortality rate still rising, Minister says," *The Cambodia Daily*, 31 January 2003. The *CDHS 2005*, however, shows a rapid upturn in the rate after this low point reached in 2002.
46 Liam Cochrane, "Child mortality increases despite millennium goals," *Phnom Penh Post*, 22 October–4 November 2004, p. 7.
47 Unifem et al., *A Fair Share for Women*, p. 89.
48 ADB, *Cambodia: Education Sector Strategy Study*, January 1996, p. 103.
49 Ibid., p. ix.
50 Ayres, *Anatomy of a Crisis*, p. 182.
51 Ibid., p. 171.
52 Ministry of Education, Youth and Sport, *Report on the Assessment of the Functional Literacy Levels of the Adult Population in Cambodia*, May 2000, p. 6.
53 Ibid., p. 7.
54 Kay Kimsong, "Observers: low salaries eroding education," *The Cambodia Daily*, 30 July 2001.
55 Erik Wasson and Kuch Naren, "UN sees schools as benefactor of oil money," *The Cambodia Daily*, 31 October 2006.
56 Sik Boreak, *Land Ownership, Sales and Concentration in Cambodia: a preliminary review of secondary data and primary data from four recent surveys*, Working Paper 16, CDRI, Phnom Penh, September 2000, p. 2.
57 Chan Sophal, Tep Saravy and Sarthi Acharya, *Land Tenure in Cambodia: a data update*, Working Paper 19, CDRI, Phnom Penh, October 2001, p. i.

58 Sik Boreak, *Land Ownership* ...
59 Robin Biddulph, *Interim Report on Findings* ..., p. 6.
60 Sik Boreak, *Land Ownership* ..., p. 25.
61 Ibid., p. 28.
62 NIS, *CSES 1999*, p. 6.
63 Chan Sophal et al., *Land Tenure* ..., using data from the *CSES 1999*.
64 ADB, *Cambodia: Education Sector Strategy Study*, p. 23. Presumably these figures are in ten million dollars, not simply US$.
65 NIS, *CSES 1999*, p. 33.
66 NIS, *Cambodia Statistical Yearbook 2000*, p. 79.
67 Ibid., p. 80.
68 Vong Sokheng, "Bumper rice crop pleases nearly everyone but millers," *Phnom Penh Post*, 1–14 December 2006, p. 4.
69 Patrick Falby, "Agro-industry: promise versus delivery," *Phnom Penh Post*, 5–18 July 2002, p. 7.
70 Touch Rotha, "$40m deal gives agriculture welcome boost," *The Cambodia Daily*, 30 July 1998, p. 13.
71 Carsten Stormer and Chea Sotheacheath, "Jute Factory closes, at a cost of five hundred jobs," *Phnom Penh Post*, 31 March–13 April 2000.
72 Bill Bainbridge, "How smuggling and graft sap a nation's economy," *Phnom Penh Post*, 15–28 August 2003 and *The Cambodia Daily*, 6 February 2001.
73 NIS, *CSES 1999*, p. 31.
74 Stephen O'Connell and Bou Saroeun, "Finger points at Government for ruin of fishers and their fisheries," *Phnom Penh Post*, 4–17 August 2000, p. 8.
75 Ibid. and Bou Saroeun, "Fisheries reform seems all talk, no action," *Phnom Penh Post*, 8–21 December 2000, p. 12.
76 Stephen O'Connell and Bou Saroeun, "Finger points ..."
77 Van Roeun, "Despite gains, some fishing laws not decided, enforced," *The Cambodia Daily*, 19 June 2002, p. 15.
78 Lor Chandara, "Protection decree for Tonle Sap Lake signed," *The Cambodia Daily*, 13 March 2001.
79 Philippe Le Billon, "The Political Ecology of Transition in Cambodia 1989–1999: war, peace and forest exploitation," *Development and Change* 31, 4 (September 2000): 785–805, Abstract.
80 Shawcross, *Cambodia's New Deal*, p. 17.
81 Le Billon, "The Political Ecology ...," p. 787, fn. 5.
82 Ibid., p. 791.
83 Ibid., p. 797.
84 Stephen O'Connell, "Forestry management 'total failure' — ADB," *Phnom Penh Post*, 14–27 April 2000, p. 5.
85 Liam Cochrane, "World Bank admits concessions failed," *Phnom Penh Post*, 22 October–4 November 2004.
86 Rajah Rasiah, *AFTA and the Cambodian Labor Market*, CICP Policy Paper Issue No. 3, Phnom Penh, July 2000, 5, quoting World Bank figures.

87 NIS, *Survey of Industrial Establishment 2000*, Ministry of Planning, Phnom Penh, August 2003, p. 17.
88 Ibid., p. 23.
89 Sok Siphana, J.D. ed., *Labour Law in the Kingdom of Cambodia*, CLRDC (Phnom Penh: Blossom Lotus Publishing, undated).
90 "Who benefits from EPZs?" (no by-line), *Phnom Penh Post*, 13–26 September 2002, p. 7.
91 Erik Wasson, "PM to inaugurate Bavet commercial zone," *The Cambodia Daily*, 11 August 2005.
92 Kay Kimsong, "Master plan revealed for Special Economic Zone," *The Cambodia Daily*, 17 August 2005, p. 17.
93 NIS, *Statistical Year Book 2003*, p. 294, with data provided by the Ministry of Tourism.
94 NIS, *National Accounts of Cambodia*, p. 27.
95 NIS, *Survey of Industrial Establishment 2000*, p. 28.
96 NIS, *National Accounts* ..., p. 33.
97 Molly Ball, "Cambodia braces itself for Asean free trade," *The Cambodia Daily*, 29 October 2002.
98 Rajah Rasia, *AFTA and the Cambodian Labour Market*, p. 13.
99 Molly Ball, "Cambodia braces itself ..."
100 NIS, *Cambodia Statistical Year Book 2000*, p. 147.
101 NIS, *Kingdom of Cambodia Statistical Year Book 2003*, pp. 423–4.
102 Matt McKinney, "ADB calls economic change 'remarkable'," *The Cambodia Daily*, 8 February 2001.
103 Grant Curtis, *Cambodia Reborn?*, p. 74.
104 Ibid., p. 79.
105 AFP, "Asian bank may resume new loans," *The Cambodia Daily*, 30 July 1998.
106 The U.S. did not resume direct bilateral assistance to Cambodia until 2007, ten years after the freeze on aid commenced.
107 Elizabeth Moorthy, "Foreign aid — a guide for the bemused," *Phnom Penh Post*, 15–28 August 1997, p. 15.
108 Ibid.
109 Martin Godfrey, "How important is external assistance to Cambodia?" *Phnom Penh Post*, 31 March–13 April 2000, p. 10.
110 Daniel Ten Kate, "Ministries discuss requests for aid money," *The Cambodia Daily*, 11 May 2004, p. 13.
111 Kao Kim Hourn, *Grassroots Democracy in Cambodia: opportunities, challenges and prospects*, CICP, Phnom Penh, 1999, p. 29, fn. 25.
112 Un Kheang, "Democratisation Without Consolidation: The case of Cambodia, 1993–2004." Doctoral dissertation, Northern Illinois University, December 2004, p. 290.
113 Cambodian Investment Law, Chapter 5, Article 12. Website <www.mekongexpress.com/cambodia/general/caminvestlaw.htm> [accessed 10 April 2007].

114 Grant Curtis, *Cambodia Reborn?*, p. 105.
115 NIS, *Statistical Year Book 2003*, p. 306. The most controversial failed investment was the Ariston project. In 1995, the Malaysian firm committed itself to a US$1.8 billion investment in infrastructure and tourism projects, mostly in Sihanoukville. Finally, in 2005, the RGC and Ariston agreed to abandon the contract and all state land and properties, with the exception of the casino in Phnom Penh, reverted to the government.
116 Ibid., p. 322.
117 Debra Boyce, "Business community pleased with peaceful polls, results," *The Cambodia Daily*, 30 July 1998, p. 13.
118 The six-month clause was later changed to one year. See Kay Kimsong, "Investment in Cambodia up from last year," *The Cambodia Daily*, 2 December 2003, p. 14.
119 Rajesh Kumar, "Rainsy sharpens knives for Tokyo meeting," *Phnom Penh Post*, 8–21 June 2001, p. 4.
120 Grant Curtis, *Cambodia Reborn?*, p. 107.
121 Erik Wasson, "Chinese Chamber leader says investment is just profit-driven," *The Cambodia Daily*, 12 August 2005. After the July 1997 events, P.M. Hun Sen expelled Taiwanese officials whom he accused of colluding to sell arms to Funcinpec. Since then, diplomatic and trade relations with the People's Republic of China have been very close.
122 Deutsche Presse-Agentur (DPA), "Hun Sen to visit Russia, seek debt reduction," *The Cambodia Daily*, 8 February 2001.
123 Patrick Falby, "National debt burden of $3 billion equals GDP," *Phnom Penh Post*, 13–26 September 2002, p. 4.
124 Patrick Falby, "Questions over repaying Cambodia's debt," *Phnom Penh Post*, 29 August–11 September 2003, p. 7.
125 Ibid.
126 ADB, *Cambodia: Education Sector Strategy Study*, p. 72.
127 Ibid.
128 Ibid.
129 Ibid., p. 22.
130 William Shawcross, *Cambodia's New Deal*, p. 77.
131 ADB, *Cambodia: Education Sector Strategy Study*, p. 72.
132 Toshiyasu Kato *et al.*, *Cambodia: Enhancing Governance …*, p. 13.
133 Hurley Scroggins and Huw Watkin, "Gov't budget woes mount," *Phnom Penh Post*, 12–25 September 1997, p. 12.
134 Nick Lenaghan and Huw Watkin, "Budget blowout looms," *Phnom Penh Post*, 10–23 October 1997, p. 1.
135 Hubert Neiss, "Why the IMF pulled the plug," *Phnom Penh Post*, 24 October–6 November 1997, p. 16. Excerpts from the speech delivered by this IMF senior official to the Consultative Group donors' meeting in Paris, 1 July 1997.

136 Susan Postlewaite, "IMF man maps out strategy for Cambodia," *Phnom Penh Post*, 29 September–12 October 2000, p. 15 and NIS, *Cambodia Year Book 2000*, p. 185.
137 Daniel Ten Kate and Van Roeun, "Cycle of Debt," *The Cambodia Daily*, 21–22 February 2004, p. 5.
138 Susan Postlewaite, "IMF man …"
139 Sam Rith and Charles McDermid, "Economy booming, but still few jobs," *Phnom Penh Post*, 17–30 November 2006, p. 1.
140 James Welsh and Un Samean, "25 Percent Gov't Budget Hike Favours Education and Health," *The Cambodia Daily*, 24 November 2006, p. 16.
141 In 2006, government spokesman, Khieu Kanharith, was quoted as saying, "We've succeeded in reducing poverty at the rate of one per cent each year and also right now we have a lot of traffic jams due to all the cars and motorbikes…. The poor now at least have a bicycle to ride." This is an echo of Prince Sihanouk's claims in the 1960s about velos and wristwatches.

Conclusion

1 This action was precipitated by the deadlock following the general elections that were held earlier in the year. For details, see note 7 in the preceding chapter. The Chairman of the CPP and left factional leader, Chea Sim, was effectively abducted and held to ransom until the Prime Minister was assured that the National Assembly would vote to reinstate him in office.
2 Kang Chandararot *et al.*, "Impact of the Global Financial and Economic Crisis on Cambodia: a rapid assessment," a report prepared for the ILO by the Cambodia Institute of Development Study (CIDS), undated; hereafter cited as CIDS report. Viewed on ILO website <www.ilo.org> [accessed 24 April 2009].
3 Inflation figure cited in IMF Country Report No. 09/47, "Cambodia: 2008 Article IV Consultation — Staff Report," February 2009, p. 4. Viewed on IMF website <www.imf.org> [accessed 24 April 2009].
4 IMF, "Global Financial Stability Report: responding to the financial crisis and reassuring systemic risks," Executive Summary, xii, April 2009. Viewed on IMF website <www.imf.org> [accessed 24 April 2009].
5 "Statement of an IMF Mission at the Conclusion of the Staff Visit to Cambodia," Press Release No. 09/67, 6 March 2009. Viewed on website <www.imf.org/external/np/sec/pr/2009/pre0967.htm> [accessed 24 April 2009].
6 Public Information Notice No. 09/18, "IMF Executive Board Concludes 2008 Article IV Consultation with Cambodia," 10 February 2009. Viewed on IMF website, <www.imf.org> [accessed 24 April 2009].
7 Ministry of Commerce figures as of July 2008. See CIDS report, p. 12.
8 CIDS report, p. 13.
9 Ibid.
10 Figures sourced from the CDC and quoted in the CIDS report, p. 9.

11 Both parties advised that the opening of the Cambodian Stock Exchange could be delayed, depending on the global economic climate. Nguon Sovan, "Regulatory commission for stock exchange opens," *Phnom Penh Post* website, 30 April 2009.
12 Francis Fukuyama, *Trust: The Social Virtues and the Creation of Prosperity* (London: Hamish Hamilton, 1995), p. xiii.
13 Ear Sophal, "The Political Economy of Cambodia's Growth: Rice and Garments," paper presented at conference on Cambodia's Economic Transformation, Phnom Penh, 5–7 January 2009.
14 Caroline Hughes and Un Kheang, "Cambodia's Economic Transformation: Historical and Theoretical Perspectives," paper prepared for conference on Cambodia's Economic Transformation, Phnom Penh, 5–7 January 2009.
15 Sok Hach, "The Political Economy of Development in Cambodia: How to Untie the Gordian Knot of Poverty?", Economic Institute of Cambodia, October–December 2005. Viewed on website <www.eicambodia.org/downloads/files/ER10_politicaldevelopment.pdf > [accessed 24 April 2009].
16 Laura Summers, "The Sources of Economic Grievance in Sihanouk's Cambodia," *Southeast Asian Journal of Social Science* 14, 1 (1986): 16–34.
17 Ibid.
18 Fukuyama, *Trust*…, p. 7.
19 Ibid., p. 49.

Selected Bibliography

Archival Sources (State Archives of Cambodia [ANC])

Files: *Résidence Superieure du Cambodge* (RSC)
People's Republic of Kampuchea (PRK)

Cambodian Government Publications (in chronological order)

Royaume du Cambodge. *Considérations sur le socialisme Khmer.* Phnom Penh: Ministère de l'Information, 1961.

———. *Resultats preliminaires du recensement general de la population 1962.* Phnom Penh: Ministère du Plan, March 1963.

———. *Photos-souvenirs du Cambodge Sangkum Reastr Niyum: agriculture 1955–1969.* Phnom Penh, undated.

———. "La Conquête de l'Indépendance Economique du Cambodge," report by Phlek Chhat, Directeur Général du Plan, delivered at Peking Symposium, August 1964. Phnom Penh: Ministère de l'Information, 1964.

———. *Comptes Economiques 1964.* Ministère du Plan, Institut National de la Statistique et des Recherches Economiques, 1964.

———. *Statistical year-book of Cambodia 1968.* Phnom Penh: National Institute of Statistics and Economic Research, undated.

———. "Rapport Annuel: L'Agriculture Cambodgienne en 1968–69," Direction de l'Agriculture, Division de Statistique Agricole.

Royal Government of Cambodia. *Report on the socio-economic survey of Cambodia 1993/94.* Phnom Penh: National Institute of Statistics, September 1995.

———. *National Environmental Action Plan 1998–2001.* Phnom Penh, January 1998.

———. *Réalisations et perspectives de la réforme administrative.* Phnom Penh, 22 June 1998.

———. *Cambodia human development report 1998: women's contribution to development.* Phnom Penh: Ministry of Planning, October 1998.

———. *The constitution of the Kingdom of Cambodia (as amended on 4 March 1999).*

———. *General population census of Cambodia 1998: final census results.* Phnom Penh: National Institute of Statistics, July 1999.

_____. *Report on the Cambodia Socio-Economic Survey 1999*. Phnom Penh: National Institute of Statistics.

_____. *Cambodia Poverty Assessment*. Phnom Penh: Ministry of Planning, December 1999.

_____. *Report on the assessment of the functional literacy levels of the adult population in Cambodia*. Phnom Penh: Ministry of Education, Youth and Sports, May 2000.

_____. *Cambodia: Statistical year book 2000*. Phnom Penh: National Institute of Statistics, February 2001.

_____. *Cambodia demographic and health survey 2000*. Phnom Penh: National Institute of Statistics and Directorate General for Health, June 2001.

_____. *Chhbap Phumibhal* [Land Law]. Phnom Penh: Ministry for Land Management, May 2002.

_____. *Poverty and Vulnerability Analysis Mapping in Cambodia: summary report*. Phnom Penh: Ministry of Planning and United Nations World Food Programme, March 2003.

_____. *Statistical year book 2003*. Phnom Penh: National Institute of Statistics, 2003.

_____. *National Accounts of Cambodia 1993–2002*, Bulletin No. 7, July 2003.

_____. *Survey of industrial establishment 2000*. Phnom Penh: National Institute of Statistics, August 2003.

_____. *A fair share for women: Cambodia gender assessment and policy briefs*. Phnom Penh: Ministry of Women's Affairs, October 2004.

Newspapers and Periodicals

Bulletin Bi-Hebdomadaire Chambre Mixte de Commerce et d'Agriculture du Cambodge
Bulletin du Contre-Gouvernement
Cambodia Economic Watch
Far Eastern Economic Review
Le Cambodge Economique
Le Sangkum
Phnom Penh Post
Politique Illustrée
Revue Economique
The Cambodia Daily
Vietnam Courier

Speech Transcripts (in chronological order)

H.E. Gen. Lon Nol, Prime Minister. "*Oeuvre de SRN*," 27 December 1966.

Pol Pot. "Let us continue to firmly hold aloft the banner of the victory of the glorious Communist Party of Kampuchea ..." Speech made on occasion of

the 18th anniversary of the founding of the Communist Party of Kampuchea, Phnom Penh, 27 September 1978. Department of Press and Information, Ministry of Foreign Affairs, Democratic Kampuchea.
Paul Matthews, UN Resident Co-ordinator and UNDP Resident Representative. "Achievements and Perspectives of the Public Administrative Reform," Phnom Penh, 22 June 1998.
Sok An, Co-president of the Inter-ministerial Technical Commission for Administrative Reform. "*La politique du GRC sur la réforme administrative*," Phnom Penh, 22 June 1998.
Prum Sokha, Secretary of State, Ministry of the Interior. "The New Decentralised Government Structure and the Role of the Commune Councils in Local Development," 31 August 2000.
Samdech Hun Sen, Prime Minister. "Address on 'Rectangular Strategy' for Growth, Employment, Equity and Efficiency," First Cabinet Meeting of the Third Legislature of the National Assembly, Office of the Council of Ministers, Phnom Penh, 16 July 2004.

Monographs, Reports and Journal Articles

Asian Development Bank. *Economic report on Cambodia*. Manila, 1970.
———. *Cambodia education sector strategy study*. Manila, 1996.
———. *Indigenous peoples/ethnic minorities and poverty reduction Cambodia*. Manila, 2002.
Aymonier, Etienne. *Khmer heritage in the old Siamese provinces of Cambodia*. Bangkok: White Lotus, 1999.
Ayres, David M. *Anatomy of a crisis: education, development and the state in Cambodia, 1953–1998*. Honolulu: University of Hawai'i Press, 2000.
Becker, Elizabeth. *When the war was over: Cambodia and the Khmer Rouge revolution*. New York: Public Affairs, 1998.
Biddulph, Robin. "Interim report on findings of landlessness and development information tool (LADIT) research September 1999 to April 2000." Phnom Penh: Oxfam, 2000.
Bray, Mark. *The private costs of public schooling: household and community financing of primary education in Cambodia*. Phnom Penh: UNICEF/Sida, 1998.
Carné, Louis de. *Travels on the Mekong: Cambodia, Laos and Yunnan: the political and trade report of the Mekong exploration commission (June 1866–June 1868)*. Bangkok: White Lotus, 2000.
Centre for Advanced Study. *Interdisciplinary Research on Ethnic Groups in Cambodia: final draft reports*. Phnom Penh, July 1996.
Chan Sophal *et al*. *Cambodia: the challenge of productive employment creation*. Phnom Penh: Cambodia Development Resource Institute, 1999.
Chan Sophal, Tep Saravy and Sarthi Acharya. *Land tenure in Cambodia: a data update*. Phnom Penh: Cambodia Development Resource Institute, 2001.

Chandler, David. "Cambodia before the French: politics in a tributary kingdom 1794–1848." Ph.D. dissertation, University of Michigan, 1973.
———. *Facing the Cambodian Past: selected essays 1971–1994*. Chiang Mai: Silkworm Books, 1996.
———. *A History of Cambodia*, 3rd ed. Chiang Mai: Silkworm Books, 2003.
Chandler, David P., Ben Kiernan and Boua Chanthou. *Pol Pot Plans the Future: Confidential Leadership Documents from Democratic Kampuchea, 1976–1977*. New Haven, Conn: Yale University (Southeast Asia Studies, Monograph Series No. 33), 1988.
Chea Chanto. *Samettephal Seddhkech-Sangkumekech robas Pracheachon Kampuchea reye pel dop boun chhnam 1979–1993* [Socio-economic achievements of the Kampuchean people for the fourteen years, 1979–1993]. Phnom Penh: Faculty of Economics, 1996.
Chomsky, Noam. "A special supplement: Cambodia." *The New York Review of Books* 14, 11 (1970).
Cock, Andrew. "The interaction between a ruling elite and an externally promoted policy reform agenda: the case of forestry under the second Kingdom of Cambodia 1993–2003." Ph.D. dissertation, La Trobe University, 2007.
Coedès, G. *The making of South East Asia*. London: Routledge & Kegan Paul, 1966.
———. *The Indianized states of Southeast Asia*, 3rd ed. Honolulu: University Press of Hawaii, 1968.
Collard, Paul. *Cambodge et Cambodgiens: métamorphose du royaume khmer par une méthode française de protectorat*. Phnom Penh: Cedoreck, 2001.
Corfield, Justin. "Khmers stand up! A history of the Cambodian government 1970–1975." Centre of Southeast Asian Studies, Monash University, 1994.
Cros, Louis. *L'Indochine Française Pour Tous*. Paris: Albin Michel, 1922.
Curtis, Grant. *Cambodia: a country profile. A report prepared for the Swedish International Development Authority*, Phnom Penh, 1989.
———. *Cambodia Reborn? The transition to democracy and development*. Washington, DC: Brookings Institution, 1998.
Deac, Wilfred P. *Road to the killing fields: the Cambodian war of 1970–75*. Texas: A&M University Press, 1997.
Delvert, Jean. *Le Paysan Cambodgien*. Paris: L'Harmattan, 1994.
———. *Le Cambodge*, 3rd ed. Paris: Presses Universitaires de France, 1998.
Desbarats, Jacqueline. *Prolific survivors: population change in Cambodia 1975–1993*. Tempe: Arizona State University, 1995.
Ear Sophal. "The Political Economy of Cambodia's Growth: Rice and Garments," paper presented at conference on Cambodia's Economic Transformation, Phnom Penh, 5–7 January 2009.
Etcheson, Craig. *The Rise and Demise of Democratic Kampuchea*. Boulder: Westview Press, 1984.
Frey, Marc, Ronald W. Pruessen and Tan Tai Yong, eds. *The transformation of Southeast Asia: international perspectives on decolonization*. Singapore: Singapore University Press, 2003.

Frings, Viviane. "The failure of agricultural collectivization in the People's Republic of Kampuchea (1979–1989)." Centre of Southeast Asian Studies, Monash University, 1993.

―――. "Cambodia after decollectivization." *Journal of Contemporary Asia* 24, 1 (1994).

―――. *Le socialisme et le paysan Cambodgien: la politique agricole de la République Populaire du Kampuchea et de l'Etat du Cambodge*. Paris: L'Harmattan, 1997.

Fukuyama, Francis. "The end of history?" *The National Interest*, Summer 1989.

―――. *Trust: The Social Virtues and the Creation of Prosperity*. London: Hamish Hamilton, 1995.

―――. *After the neocons: America at the crossroads*. London: Profile Books, 2006.

Global Witness. "Going Places ... Cambodia's Future on the Move," a briefing document, March 1998.

Godfrey, Martin et al. *A study of the Cambodian labour market: reference to poverty reduction, growth and adjustment to crisis*. Phnom Penh: Cambodia Development Resource Institute, 2001.

Gorman, Siobhan. "Implications of socio-economic change for women's employment in Cambodia: a case study of garment factory workers." M.Ed. dissertation, Centre for Adult and Higher Education, 1997.

―――. "Gender and development in Cambodia: an overview." Phnom Penh: Cambodia Development Resource Institute, 1999.

Gottesman, Evan. *Cambodia After the Khmer Rouge: Inside the Politics of Nation Building*. New Haven: Yale University Press, 2003.

Grant, Jonathan S. et al., eds. *Cambodia: the widening war in Indochina*. New York: Washington Square Press, 1971.

Higham, Charles. *The civilization of Angkor*. Berkeley: University of California Press, 2001.

Hildebrand, George and Gareth Porter. *Cambodia: starvation and revolution*. New York: Monthly Review Press, 1976.

Hobsbawm, Eric. *The age of capital 1848–1875*. London: Weidenfeld and Nicolson, 1962.

Hughes, Caroline and Un Kheang. "Cambodia's Economic Transformation: Historical and Theoretical Perspectives," paper prepared for conference on Cambodia's Economic Transformation, Phnom Penh, 5–7 January 2009.

Huguet, Jerrold W. *The population of Cambodia, 1980–1996, and projected to 2020*. Phnom Penh: National Institute of Statistics, May 1997.

Hun Sen. *Dap Chhnam ney Damnaeur Kampuchea: 1979–1989* [The Ten-Year Journey]. Phnom Penh, December 1988.

In Sopheap. *Khieu Samphan: Aggrandi et Réel* (unpublished).

International Monetary Fund. Country Report No. 09/47, "Cambodia: 2008 Article IV Consultation — Staff Report," February 2009. IMF website: <www.imf.org>.

_____. "Global Financial Stability Report: responding to the financial crisis and reassuring systemic risks," Executive Summary, XII, April 2009. IMF website: <www.imf.org>.

_____. "Statement of an IMF Mission at the Conclusion of the Staff Visit to Cambodia," Press Release No. 09/67, 6 March 2009. Website: <www.imf.org/external/np/sec/pr/2009/pre0967.htm>.

_____. "IMF Executive Board Concludes 2008 Article IV Consultation with Cambodia," Public Information Notice No. 09/18, 10 February 2009. IMF website: <www.imf.org>.

Ith Sarin. *Sronoh Proelung Khmer* [Regrets for the Khmer Soul]. Phnom Penh, 28 July 1973.

Jackson, Karl D. ed. *Cambodia: rendezvous with death*. New Jersey: Princeton University Press, 1989.

Jennar, Raoul M. *The Cambodian constitutions (1953–1993)*. Bangkok: White Lotus, 1995.

Kang Chandararot and Chan Sophal. "Cambodia's annual economic review." Phnom Penh: Cambodia Development Resource Institute, 2003.

Kang Chandararot *et al.* "Impact of the Global Financial and Economic Crisis on Cambodia: a rapid assessment," a report prepared for the ILO by the Cambodia Institute of Development Study (CIDS). ILO website: <www.ilo.org>, undated.

Kao Kim Hourn. *Grassroots Democracy in Cambodia: opportunities, challenges and prospects*. Phnom Penh: Center for International Cooperation and Peace (CICP), 1999.

Keat Chhon. *45 Months at the Ministry of Economy and Finance: outcomes, diagnostic outlook*. Phnom Penh: Cambodian Institute for Cooperation and Peace, 1998.

Kechprumprieng neu tikrong Paris ompi panhha Kampuchea 23-10-1991 [Paris accords on the Cambodia problem, 23 October 1991].

Kennedy, Paul. *The rise and fall of the great powers: economic change and military conflict from 1500 to 2000*. London: Hyman, 1988.

Kheang Un. "Democratization without consolidation: the case of Cambodia, 1993–2004." Ph.D. dissertation, Northern Illinois University, 2004.

Kheang Un and Judy Ledgerwood. "Cambodia in 2001: toward democratic consolidation?" *Asian Survey* 42, 1 (2002).

Khieu Samphan. *Cambodia's Economy and Industrial Development*, translated and with introduction by Laura Summers. Ithaca: Cornell University SEAP Data Paper 111, 1979.

Kiernan, Ben. *The Pol Pot Regime: race, power, and genocide in Cambodia under the Khmer Rouge, 1975–79*. New Haven: Yale University Press, 1996.

_____. "Conflict in the Kampuchean Communist Movement," *Journal of Contemporary Asia* 10, 1–2 (1980).

_____, ed. *Genocide and democracy in Cambodia: the Khmer Rouge, the United Nations and the international community*. New Haven, Conn.: Yale University Southeast Asia Studies, 1993.

Kiernan, Ben and Boua Chanthou. *Peasants and politics in Kampuchea, 1942–1981*. London: Zed Press, 1982.
Kiljunen, Kimmo, ed. *Kampuchea: decade of the genocide. Report of a Finnish Inquiry Commission*. London: Zed Books, 1984.
Le Billon, P. "Power is consuming the forest: the political ecology of conflict and reconstruction in Cambodia." Ph.D. dissertation, Oxford University, 1999.
———. "The political ecology of transition in Cambodia 1989–1999: war, peace and forest exploitation." *Development and Change* 31, 4 (2000).
May Someth. *Cambodian Witness*. London: Faber and Faber, 1986.
Meiksins Wood, Ellen. *The origin of capitalism: a longer view*. London: Verso, 2002.
Mouhot, Henri. *Travels in Siam, Cambodia and Laos 1858–1860*. Singapore: Oxford University Press, 1992.
Mus, Paul. *L'angle de l'Asie*. Paris: Hermann, 1977.
Muscat, Robert J. and Jonathon Stromseth. *Cambodia: post-settlement reconstruction and development*. New York: East Asian Institute, 1989.
Nayan Chanda. "Cambodia in 1986." *Asian Survey* 27, 1 (1987).
Nguon Sovan. "Regulatory commission for stock exchange opens." *Phnom Penh Post*, 30 April 2009. Website: <www.phnompenhpost.com>.
Osborne, Milton. "Regional disunity in Cambodia." *Australian Outlook* 22, 3 (1968).
———. *Politics and Power in Cambodia*. Camberwell: Longman Australia, 1973.
———. *Sihanouk: prince of light, prince of darkness*. Chiang Mai: Silkworm Books, 1994.
———. *The French presence in Cochinchina and Cambodia*. Bangkok: White Lotus, 1997.
Oum Sothea and Sok Hach. *Cambodia economic watch*. Phnom Penh: Economic Institute of Cambodia, 2004.
Prom Tola and Bruce McKenney. "Trading forest products in Cambodia: challenges, threats, and opportunities for resin." Phnom Penh: Cambodia Development Resource Institute, 2003.
Prud'homme, Rémy. *L'Économie du Cambodge*. Paris: Presses Universitaires de France, 1969.
Quiroga de San Antonio, Gabriel. *A brief and truthful relation of events in the Kingdom of Cambodia*. Bangkok: White Lotus, 1998.
Rajah Rasia. "AFTA and the Cambodian labor market." Phnom Penh: Cambodian Institute for Cooperation and Peace, 2000.
Robequain, Charles. *The economic development of French Indo-China*. London: Oxford University Press, 1944.
Roberts, David W. *Political transition in Cambodia 1991–99: power, elitism and democracy*. Richmond, Surrey: Curzon Press, 2001.
Sagar, D.J. *Major political events in Indo-China 1945–1990*. New York: Facts on File, 1991.
Said, Edward. *Culture and Imperialism*. London: Vintage, 1994.
Scott, James C. *Moral economy of the peasant: rebellion and subsistence in Southeast Asia*. New Haven: Yale University Press, 1976.

Shawcross, William. *Cambodia's new deal: a report*. Washington, D.C.: Carnegie Endowment for International Peace, 1994.

Sik Boreak. *Land Ownership, Sales and Concentration in Cambodia: a preliminary review of secondary data and primary data from four recent surveys*. Phnom Penh: Cambodia Development Resource Institute, 2000.

Slocomb, Margaret. *The People's Republic of Kampuchea 1979–1989: the revolution after Pol Pot*. Chiang Mai: Silkworm Books, 2003.

————. *Colons and Coolies: the development of Cambodia's rubber plantations*. Bangkok: White Lotus, 2007.

————. "Chikreng Rebellion: Coup and Its Aftermath in Democratic Kampuchea," *Journal of the Royal Asiatic Society* 16, 1 (2006).

Sok Hach. "The Political Economy of Development in Cambodia: How to Untie the Gordian Knot of Poverty?", Economic Institute of Cambodia, October–December 2005.Website: <www.eicambodia.org/downloads/files/ER10_politicaldevelopment.pdf>.

Sok Hach *et al*. "Prospects for the Cambodian Economy in 2000," paper prepared for the Workshop on Forecasting the Cambodian Economy, Phnom Penh, Cambodia Development Resource Institute, 2000.

Sok Siphana, ed. *Labour Law in the Kingdom of Cambodia*. Phnom Penh: Cambodian Legal Resources Development Centre, undated.

Stern, Fritz, ed. *The varieties of history: from Voltaire to the present*, 2nd ed. London: Macmillan, 1970.

Summers, Laura. "The Sources of Economic Grievance in Sihanouk's Cambodia," *Southeast Asian Journal of Social Science* 14, 1 (1986).

————. "The CPK: Secret Vanguard of Pol Pot's Revolution: A Comment on Nuon Chea's Statement" and "Statement of the Communist Party of Kampuchea to the Communist Workers' Party of Denmark, July 1978, by Nuon Chea, Deputy Secretary, CPK," *The Journal of Communist Studies* 3, 1 (1987).

Tarling, Nicholas. *Nations and states in Southeast Asia*. Cambridge: Cambridge University Press, 1998.

The French in Indo-China: with a narrative of Garnier's explorations in Cochinchina, Annam and Tonkin. Bangkok: White Lotus, 2000.

The World Bank. "Cambodia country assistance strategy: building the foundations for sustainable development and poverty reduction." Draft Version, 11 January 2000.

Thion, Serge. *Watching Cambodia*. Bangkok: White Lotus, 1993.

Thompson, Virginia. *French Indo-China*. New York: The Macmillan Company, 1937.

Toshiyasu Kato *et al*. "Cambodia: enhancing governance for sustainable development." Phnom Penh: Cambodia Development Resource Institute, 2000.

Tully, John. *France on the Mekong: a history of the Protectorate in Cambodia, 1863–1953*. Lanham: University Press of America, 2002.

United Nations. "Report of the United Nations fact-finding mission on present structures and practices of administration in Cambodia, 24 April–9 May 1990." New York, June 1990.

United Nations Development Programme. *Human Development Report 2000*. New York: Oxford University Press, 2000.

Vickery, Michael. *Cambodia 1975–1982*. Chiang Mai: Silkworm Books, 1984.

———. *Kampuchea: Politics, Economics and Society*. Sydney: Allen & Unwin, 1986.

———. "A reader's guide down the garden path of Cambodian statistics and into the treacherous jungle of demography," Penang, October 1990.

Watts, Kenneth *et al.* "Report of the Kampuchea needs assessment study (for UNDP)." August 1989.

Weiner, Andy. "The Forest and the trees: sustainable development and human rights in the context of Cambodia." *University of Pennsylvania Law Review* 151, 4 (2003).

Zeldin, Theodore. *France 1848–1945, Vol. 1, ambition, love and politics. The Oxford history of modern Europe*. Oxford: Clarendon Press, 1973.

Zhou Daguan. *The Customs of Cambodia*, 3rd ed. Bangkok: The Siam Society, 1993.

Index

Acleda Bank, 28, 284
Acquired Immune Deficiency Syndrome (AIDS), 232, 252, *see also* HIV/AIDS
administration, 8–9, 25–6, 33, 38–45, 48, 54, 65, 69–70, 72, 77, 80–4, 92, 111, 132, 137–40, 162–3, 178, 180, 183–8, 196, 208, 224–5, 231–2, 238–45, 278, 283, 286, 289, 294–5, 297, *see also* governance
agriculture, 12, 15–6, 20, 26, 29, 33, 35–6, 51, 53–4, 57–60, 63, 65, 72, 78–80, 82–3, 99–100, 102, 105–6, 112, 114, 118, 121–3, 132, 147–8, 179–81, 185, 204–6, 109–10, 213, 216, 218, 221, 225, 256, 258–61, 268, 271–2, 279, 286, 290, 292–3
agro-industry, 17, 261, 278
aid, 24–7, 65, 77, 82–3, 99, 106–15, 117, 124–5, 132, 136, 138–9, 145, 152–8, 160–3, 178, 181, 200, 202, 215–7, 219–20, 223–4, 241, 245, 273, 275–8, 282–3, 285–6, 294–7, *see also* foreign assistance, military assistance
army, *see* military
ASEAN Free Trade Agreement (AFTA), 24, 273, 274
Asian Development Bank (ADB), xv, 14, 24, 26, 88, 98, 100, 103, 109, 116, 121, 152–3, 246, 253–5, 261–2, 267–8, 276–7, 281–2, 285

Asian financial/monetary crisis, xvi, 14, 25, 234, 251, 280, 283, 285, 289
Association of Southeast Asian Nations (ASEAN), xvi, 1, 24, 231, 234, 244, 270, 273, 274, 293

Bank of Indochina, 70, 116
banking/banks, 1, 12, 26–8, 68, 70, 77, 83, 108–9, 112, 116, 119–20, 122, 125, 132, 135, 159, 220–1, 238, 241, 282, 284, 290, 292, 338
Banque Agricole Paysanne, 123
Banque Khmère pour le Commerce, 119

Cambodian People's Party (CPP), 232, 234, 239, 243, 246, 277, 280, 294
capitalism, 45, 72, 78–9, 112, 121, 126, 263, 286
cattle, 4, 33, 37, 53, 66, 148, 221
census, xiv–xv, 8–9, 11, 35, 45, 47, 81, 86, 91, 140–1, 143, 190, 192, 195, 246–9
Chamber of Commerce, xiv–xv, 79, 106, 134–6, 150, 154, 156, 162
chamcar des berges, 4, 33, 69, 93, 98, 99, 120, *see also* riparian market gardens, market gardens
Cham(s), 9, 10, 33, 84, 199
Chea Sim, 177, 185

China (*including* People's Republic of China), 26, 68, 115, 138, 198, 220, 282, 293
  aid, 106–7, 114, 178, 197, 201–2, 217, 224
  investment, 26, 261, 281, 291, 294
  trade, 66, 109, 216–7, 219
Chinese, 4, 9, 10–1, 26, 30–1, 33, 35, 44, 46–7, 51–2, 65–6, 78, 84, 86, 88, 105–7, 111, 113–4, 120, 123–4, 139, 142–3, 176, 196–9, 201–2, 214, 216–7, 220, 225, 248, 261, 297, *see also* Sino-Khmer
civil service/servants, 8–9, 81, 84, 136, 139, 151, 156, 197, 216, 236, 241–2, 245, 254, *see also* public service/servants
civil society, 19, 24, 241, 275, 278, 298, *see also* NGOs
clientelism/clientism, *see* patronage
collectives, *see* cooperatives
Commercial Imports Programme (CIP), 110–1, 153–6, 158, 160
commune, xiii, 8, 12, 25, 41, 69, 81, 84, 117, 145, 183, 187, 192, 223, 234, 243, 253
commune councils, 8, 41, 69, 81, 101, 187, 243, 286
communism, 76, 78, 124, 154
concessions (*also* concession system, concessionaires), 11, 16, 51, 53–7, 69, 71–2, 92, 101–2, 112, 115, 256, 261
  agricultural/economic, 23, 257, 262
  forestry/logging, 11, 19, 23, 212, 257, 264, 267–8, 286
  social, 23, 258, *see also* fishing lots
constitution, 1, 8, 81–2, 134, 136–9, 163, 182, 184–5, 225, 232, 234, 238–9, 253
Consultative Group, 24, 275, *see also* aid

Convention of 1884, 40, 52
cooperatives, 21, 57, 78, 123–4, 176–7, 181–4, 187, 195, 206, 208–11, 215, 223, *see also* collectives, *krom samaki*, solidarity groups
corruption, 2, 9, 51, 71, 83–4, 117, 121, 124, 133, 137–40, 156, 158, 163, 188, 232, 239, 244–5, 252, 256, 267, 277, 284, 294, 297
corvée, 33, 42, 51, 69, 71
cotton, 4, 32, 35–7, 57–8, 60–1, 63, 99, 101, 105, 107, 111, 155, 201, 261
coup d'état of 1970, 80, 88, 123, 131–2, 134, 137–8, 142–4, 158, 161–2
coup de force of 1997, 14, 234, 254, 273, 277, 283, 285, 289, *see also* July events
credit
  international, *see* loans
  rural, public, 12, 26–9, 68–70, 78, 117–23, 125, 153, 160, 180–1, 220–4, 282–4, 293, *see also* microfinance, moneylending
Credit Populaire Agricole, 70

debt
  external, foreign, public, 24, 26, 65, 68, 108, 115–6, 124, 153, 161, 216–7, 220, 223–4, 238, 281–2
  other, personal, 21, 36, 122
decentralisation, 160, 185, 241, 243, 286
defence, *see* military
demobilisation, 8, 25, 231, 244
democracy, 8, 25, 231, 244

economic activity, xvi, 14–20, 51–65, 92–108, 147–52, 205–16, 255–72, 292, 296

education, 2, 8, 14, 27, 44, 49–50, 70–2, 77, 86, 90–2, 107, 114, 117–8, 122, 124, 138, 146–7, 197, 203–5, 216, 218, 235–6, 243, 253–5, 272, 286, 293
elections, 1, 8, 25, 41, 82, 134, 140, 178, 184–5, 187, 195, 230–2, 234, 238–9, 242–3, 246, 263, 277, 279–80, 284–5
employment, *see* labour
environment, 2, 20–4, 79, 261–3, 278, 286, 293
ethnicity, 9–11, 46, 84, 137, 143, 197–8, 205, 248
Exchange Support Fund (ESF), 155, 160, 163

First Indochina War, 20, 61, 67, 76, 84
fisheries (*also* fish, fishing), 16, 38, 61, 64, 92, 103–4, 209, 262, 274
fishing lots, 23, 61, 69, 257, 262–3, 286, *see also* concessions
flooded forest, 4, 62
Food and Agriculture Organisation (FAO), 210
foreign assistance, *see* aid
Foreign Direct Investment (FDI), 25, 280–1, 291–2, 294, *see also* investment
foreign trade, *see* trade
forestry, 16, 19, 25, 62–3, 79, 89, 92, 103–4, 149, 163, 210–2, 216, 223, 255, 258, 263–4, 267, 283–4, *see also* concessions, logging
Funcinpec, 231, 232, 243, 246, 254

garment industry (*including* garment exports, garment factories, garment manufacturing), 2, 12, 15–6, 19–20, 24–5, 27, 248, 251, 268–9, 272–3, 275, 279, 289–92, 296, *see also* textiles
geography, xiv, 2–4
governance, *see* administration
gross domestic product (GDP), 1, 12, 15–6, 19–20, 24, 26–7, 79, 88, 92–3, 103–4, 108, 126, 215, 234, 236, 245, 250, 254–5, 259–60, 268, 270–2, 275, 282–5, 288, 290, 292, 295

health, 2, 12, 14, 27, 48–9, 70, 79, 90, 114, 118, 122, 146, 197, 201–3, 218–9, 235–6, 243, 245, 251–3, 270, 286, 291, 293
Heng Samrin, 177, 185, 200, 210
Hou Yuon, xiv, 54–5, 67–8, 70, 82, 106, 120, 123, 178–9, 180, 207, 261
Hu Nim, xiv, 82, 93, 178–9
human development, 11–4, 47–50, 88–90, 144–6, 199–201, 249–51
Human Development Index (HDI), 11–2, 250
Human Immunodeficiency Virus/AIDS (HIV/AIDS), *see* AIDS
human rights, 24, 33, 163, 213, 238, 278
Hun Sen, 177, 182, 223, 231–2, 288, 295

Inadana Jati, 119
indigenous groups, 125, *see also* Khmer Leu
Indochinese Union, 41, 65, 116
industry, 2, 4, 12, 19–20, 63–6, 72, 83, 105–8, 118, 149–52, 179, 212–6, 259, 268–71, 278–9
inflation, 15, 27–8, 89, 108, 116–7, 144, 151–2, 158–60, 163, 232, 238, 282–3, 289–90

International Committee on the Reconstruction of Cambodia (ICORC), 235, 275–6
International Labour Organisation (ILO), 20, 269
International Monetary Fund (IMF), 14, 109, 152, 160, 236, 238, 242, 264, 270, 276, 281–4, 290, *see also* World Bank/IMF
investment, xv, 1, 9, 14–5, 17, 24–6, 28–9, 33, 52, 65–8, 70, 72, 79, 99, 101–2, 108–15, 120–2, 124–5, 216–20, 223, 236, 254, 256–7, 261, 269–70, 273, 278–81, 284–5, 290–2, 294
irrigation, 1, 12, 29, 33, 58, 77, 99–100, 122, 205–6, 260–1, 293

Japan, xiv, 25, 33, 68, 101, 110, 153–4, 160, 216, 219, 275–7, 282
July events, *see coup de force* of 1997
jute, 17, 99, 105–6, 148, 207, 261

Khieu Samphan, xiv, 50, 105, 123, 126, 142, 178–80, 185, 102–3, 213, 217, 221
Khmer Leu, 84, 88, 197, *see also* indigenous groups
krom samaki, *see* cooperatives

labour, 12, 15–6, 20, 35, 38, 42–3, 57, 65, 69, 72, 88, 98, 105–8, 118, 126, 148, 151–2, 178, 199, 201, 204, 206, 212–6, 221, 224, 249, 259, 269, 271–2, 286, 290
land (*including* area, distribution, tenure, use), xiv, 2, 15–7, 20–4, 29, 32–3, 40, 51–61, 71–2, 79, 92–103, 125–6, 149, 178, 189, 205–9, 232, 248, 251, 255–8, 261, 279, 289, 292

Land Law of 2001, 23, 258
landlessness, 21–3, 93, 248, 251–2, 257
landmines, 203, 252
least developed country (LDC), 275, 286
life expectancy, 11, 14, 141, 161, 192, 194, 203, 286
literacy (*also* illiteracy), 11, 14, 81, 91–2, 114, 197, 203–5, 255
loans (*also* international credit, creditors), 24–8, 68, 70, 82, 107, 111, 115–6, 153, 157, 160–1, 217–8, 223, 236, 238, 241, 245, 270, 275–7, 280–2, 289
logging, 11, 16, 19, 24, 212, 245, 257, 263–4, 267, 276, 286, *see also* forestry
Lon Nol (*including* regime, era, years), 113, 132–5, 137–8, 140, 142–3, 145–7, 151, 154–5

maize, 4, 36, 57–60, 66, 99, 101, 109, 111, 135, 147–8, 153, 180, 219, 260
Malaya/Malaysia, 25, 35, 110, 158, 160, 269, 279–80
manufacturing, 19–20, 62–4, 88, 92–3, 105–6, 114, 123–4, 135, 179, 214, 268–9, 270, 296
 cigarette, 215
 garment/textile/footwear, 2, 12, 16, 24, 269, 271, 279–80, 290
market economy, *see* markets
market gardens, *see chamcar des berges*
market society, *see* markets
markets (*including* marketing, marketeering), xv, 12, 20, 28–9, 31, 57, 61, 66–8, 71, 99, 106–7, 111, 119–20, 124, 126, 135, 139, 144, 152, 158–9, 177–8, 181–2, 207–8, 212, 214–6, 218,

220–2, 225, 235–6, 238, 241, 245, 260–1, 269–70, 272–3, 275, 285–7, 288–90, 293–6
microfinance, 28, 30, 284–5, *see also* credit
micro-enterprise, 272
migration, 15, 20, 39, 43, 45, 57, 102, 142–3, 176, 189, 193, 195–8, 204, 206, 248–9, 292
military, 8–9, 32, 51, 68, 76, 103, 111, 133, 135, 138–9, 140, 143, 146, 148, 155, 157, 162–3, 177–8, 180, 184, 187, 189, 196, 203, 211, 221–2, 224, 230–1, 243, 245, 256–7, 262, 267, 292, 295
    aid/assistance, 26, 109–10, 114, 133, 139, 152–7, 159, 162–3, 217, 244, 277
    budget/spending, 26–7, 68, 92, 117, 127–8, 151, 157, 160, 163, 220, 223, 243, 255, 276, 282, *see also* army, defence
Mixed Economic Commission, 144
mixed-economy enterprise, 78, 106–7, 109, 112, 119, 124–5, 150–1, 162
modernisation, 50, 72, 75, 77, 105, 123–4, 162, 181, 235, 242, 293
moneylending, 47, 71, 120–2, 126, 223, 292, 359, *see also* credit
mortality, 48, 91, 140–1, 188–9, 192, 201, 250
    child, 12, 141, 252–3
    maternal and infant, 12, 48–9, 71, 90–1, 141, 192, 194, 203, 252–3

National Bank of Cambodia (NBC), 27, 79, 103, 111, 116, 119, 158–9, 218, 221, 274, 284, 291
nationalisation, 83, 108–9, 112–4, 119, 124, 132, 135, 150, 207

natural resources, 2, 16, 37, 45, 224, 251, 273, 278, 280, 292–3
non-government organisations (NGOs), xv, 1, 27–8, 202, 215, 252, 271, 275, 278, 284, 288, 298, *see also* civil society
Norodom Sihanouk, xiv, xvi, 75–6, 79, 82–3, 99, 101, 112, 114, 131–4, 137, 142–3, 146, 150, 162, 224, 231–2, 238, 296

Office of Popular Credit, 70
okhnya, 51, 69
open dollar credits, 110–1, *see also* triangulation
Office Royal de Coopération (OROC), 78, 120–2, 124, 148

paddy
    exports, sales (*including* movements, smuggling), 58, 66–7, 113, 148, 260, 274, 275
    production, cultivation, area, 4, 11, 17, 28, 54, 57–60, 71, 93, 98–100, 149, 162, 179, 205, 208–9, 258–9, 260
    yield, 16–7, 59, 125, 209, *see also* rice
Paris Club, 281
Paris Peace Agreements, 1, 134, 178, 231, 234, 244, 251
patrimonialism, *see* patronage
patron-client relationship, *see* patronage
patronage, 65, 72, 132, 234, 242, 244, 283, 294–8, *see also* clientelism/clientism, patrimonialism, patron-client relationship
Pen Sovann, 185, 209, 217
pepper, 17, 31, 33, 35, 59, 61, 109, 216, 261

plantations, 17, 19, 23, 38, 54, 71–2, 92, 101, 112, 122, 257, 261
  rubber, 4, 10, 17, 43, 45, 49, 57, 62, 65, 71–2, 77, 84, 90, 93, 101–5, 125–6, 133, 148, 157–8, 163, 185, 207, 209, 217, 260, 268
  teak, 105
pogroms, 10
Pol Pot (*including* regime, era, years), 26, 50, 177, 179, 182, 184–5, 189–90, 201–2, 206–7, 213, 216, 220–1, 298
population, xiv–xv, 2, 4, 8, 9–11, 45–7, 84–8, 140–4, 188–95, 246–9
poverty, 1, 12, 14, 28, 175, 198, 222, 236, 238, 243, 245, 248, 249–51, 264, 276, 284, 286, 289, 291–2, 296
Poverty Reduction Strategy Paper, 236, 238
privatisation, 17, 23, 241, 252, 256, 282
Protectorate Treaty, 36, 39–40, 45
public finance (*including* reforms), 26–8, 68–70, 116–9, 158–61, 220–3, 282–5
public service/servants, *see* civil service/servants

refugees, 33, 86, 134, 138–9, 144–7, 154–5, 163, 175–7, 189–90, 193, 195–7, 200–1, 207, 213, 231, 246–7, 278
rice
  exports, 32, 66–8, 70–1, 101, 109–10, 113, 149, 153, 157, 163, 206–7, 216, 218, 274
  production, cultivation, area, 1, 11, 16, 20, 28–9, 31, 37, 51, 54, 59–60, 71, 88, 93, 98, 100, 123, 126, 147–8, 162, 176, 189, 205–6, 209, 259, 260, 261, 293, *see also* paddy
riparian market gardens, *see chamcar des berges*
rubber, 17, 261, 268
  exports, 57, 59, 66, 68, 77, 101, 103, 109–10, 125, 135, 149, 154, 157–8, 207, 209, 216, 219, 274–5
  production, cultivation, area, 4, 36, 57, 71, 103, 133, 147–8, 161, 163, 207, 209, 260
  yield, 148, *see also* plantations
Rural Development Bank, 28

Sangkum Reastr Niyum (*also* Sangkum), xiv, 76, 78–80, 82–3, 90–3, 98–9, 101–9, 113, 117–8, 122–5, 132, 135, 138, 146–7, 149–53, 178–9, 181, 192, 199, 207–9, 211, 224, 245, 296
savings, 15, 78, 120, 122, 123, 125, 162, 180, 284–5, 294
Second Indochina War, 103, 123, 132, 140
Sino-Khmer, *see* Chinese
Sisowath Sirik Matak, 132, 134–9, 156
smuggling, 120, 124, 161, 214–6, 222, 225, 245, 262, 264, 275
soils, xiii, 4, 32, 35, 51, 99, 131, 185
solidarity groups, *see* cooperatives
Sonexim, 109, 119, 148, 158, 162
structural adjustment (*including* SAP, ESAF), 17, 235–6, 242, 252, 269–70, 280

teak, 105, *see also* plantations
tenancy, 21, 98
textiles, 19, 66, 107, 110, 213, 215, 268, 271–2, 273, 275, 279, 288, 291, *see also* garment industry

Thailand (*also* Siam), 2, 12, 15, 27, 30–2, 36, 39, 45, 61–2, 80, 103, 177, 190, 196–7, 207, 210, 213–4, 216, 219, 246–7, 249, 262–3, 270, 293
timber, 2, 62, 263, 292
   production, 63, 104, 211–2
   exports, 105, 109, 209, 212, 218–9, 263–4, 272
tobacco, 4, 35, 37, 58, 61, 99, 105–6, 147, 155, 207, 218, 261, 271, 286
tourism (*also* tourist industry), 2, 11–2, 14–6, 20, 116, 118, 133, 270, 273, 278–9, 283, 288, 290–2
trade, 30–3, 77, 214–5, 225, 236
   balance, 15, 110, 124
   foreign, 24–6, 33, 40, 65–8, 105, 108–15, 119, 125, 132–3, 135, 157–60, 175, 178, 181, 196, 210, 216–20, 260, 269–70, 273–5, 286
triangulation, 110–1, *see also* open dollar credits

United Nations (UN), xiii–xiv, 1, 12, 25, 90, 141, 178, 192, 196, 201, 210, 231–2, 235, 238, 276, 285
United Nations Advance Mission in Cambodia (UNAMIC), 231
United Nations Border Relief Operation (UNBRO), 196
United Nations Children's Fund (UNICEF), 194, 197, 202, 253, 255
United Nations Development Programme (UNDP), 11, 210, 214, 217, 220, 235, 238, 242, 246, 249

United Nations High Commission for Refugees (UNHCR), 195, 246
United Nations Population Fund (UNFPA), 193
United Nations Transitional Authority in Cambodia (UNTAC), 8, 231–2, 234–5, 238, 241–3, 245, 250–1, 254, 258, 276, 277, 280, 282, 286
United States of America (U.S., U.S.A.), 115, 131–4, 142–3, 147, 152–4, 157, 176–7, 221, 241, 195, 212
   aid, 82–3, 88, 108–14, 125, 132–3, 138–9, 146, 153–7, 160–3, 178, 197, 224, 254–5, 276–7, 296–7
   debt, 26, 161, 220, 281
   trade, 20, 109–11, 160, 178, 269, 275
urbanisation, 86, 195, 248

Viet-Khmer, 9–10, 44, 46–7, 84, 86, 88, 132, 137, 142–3, 196–8, 248
Vietnam, xvi, 2, 4, 26, 32–3, 36, 39, 43, 45, 48, 67, 76–7, 83, 99, 109–10, 117, 131–4, 136, 139, 142, 145, 152–3, 157, 177–8, 182, 187–9, 195, 197–8, 200, 202, 207–9, 211, 212, 216, 217–9, 223–4, 260, 270, 293

World Food Programme (WFP), 21–2
World Trade Organization (WTO), 1, 24, 234, 270, 273, 275
World Bank/IMF, xiv–xvi, 14, 17, 19, 24, 26–7, 63, 109, 144, 152, 236, 244–5, 259, 268, 276–7, 280, 282–3, 285